DISCOVERING THE WESTERN PAST

A LOOK AT THE EVIDENCE

VOLUME I: TO 1789

FOURTH EDITION

Merry E. Wiesner
University of Wisconsin—Milwaukee

Julius R. Ruff
Marquette University

William Bruce Wheeler
University of Tennessee, Knoxville

HOUGHTON MIFFLIN COMPANY   Boston   New York

Sponsoring Editor: Nancy Blaine
Editorial Assistant: Shoma Aditya
Senior Project Editor: Christina Horn
Senior Production/Design Coordinator: Carol Merrigan
Manufacturing Manager: Florence Cadran
Senior Marketing Manager: Sandra McGuire

Cover Image: Antonio Canaletto (1697–1798). View of Cordonata and Palazzo Senatorio. Left: the Palazzo Nuovo; right: the Palazzo dei Conservatori. Photo: AKG London.

Cover Design: Diana Coe / ko Design Studio

Printed in the U.S.A.

Library of Congress Catalog Card Number: 99–71905

ISBN: 0–395–97613–8

123456789-CRS-03 02 01 00 99

CONTENTS

CHAPTER FOUR
Philosophy and Faith: The Problem of Ancient Suicide   66

CHAPTER FIVE
Slave Law in Roman and Germanic Society   98

CHAPTER SIX
The Development of the Medieval State   125

CHAPTER SEVEN
Life at a Medieval University   150

CHAPTER EIGHT
Capitalism and Conflict in the Medieval Cloth Trade   176

CHAPTER TWELVE
The Spread of the Reformation   285

CHAPTER THIRTEEN
Peasant Violence: Rebellion and Riot in Early Modern Europe, 1500–1789   309

CHAPTER FOURTEEN
Staging Absolutism   346

PREFACE

The first three editions of *Discovering the Western Past: A Look at the Evidence* elicited a very positive response from instructors and students alike, and that response encouraged us to proceed with this Fourth Edition. As authors, we were particularly gratified by the widespread acceptance of the central goal of *Discovering the Western Past*, that of making students active analysts of the past and not merely passive recipients of its factual record.

The title of this book begins with a verb, a choice that reflects our basic philosophy about history. History is not simply something one learns about; it is something one does. One discovers the past, and what makes this pursuit exciting is not only the past that is discovered but also the process of discovery itself. This process can be simultaneously exhilarating and frustrating, enlightening and confusing, but it is always challenging enough to convince those of us who are professional historians to spend our lives at it. And our own students, as well as many other students, have caught this infectious excitement.

The recognition that history involves discovery as much as physics or astronomy does is often not shared by students, whose classroom experience of history frequently does not extend beyond listening to lectures and reading textbooks. The primary goal of *Discovering the Western Past: A Look at the Evidence* is to allow students enrolled in the Western Civilization course to *do* history in the same way we as historians do—to examine a group of original sources in order to answer questions about the past. We feel that contact with original sources is an excellent means of communicating the excitement of doing history, but incorporating complete works or a collection of documents into a Western Civilization course can be problematic for many instructors.

The evidence in this book thus differs from that in most source collections in its variety. We have included visual evidence such as coins, paintings, aerial photographs, cartoons, buildings, architectural plans, maps, and political posters. In choosing written evidence we again have tried to offer a broad sample—songs, plays, poems, novels, court records, notarial contracts, statistical data, and work regulations all supplement letters, newspapers, speeches, autobiographies, and other more traditional sources.

For students to learn history the way we as historians do, they must not only be confronted with the evidence; they must also learn how to use that evidence to arrive at a conclusion. In other words, they must learn historical methodology. Too often methodology (or even the notion that historians *have* a methodology) is reserved for upper-level majors or graduate students; beginning students are simply presented with historical facts and interpretations without being shown how these were unearthed or formulated. Students may learn that historians hold different interpretations of the significance of an event or individual or different ideas about causation, but they are not informed of how historians come to such conclusions.

Thus, along with evidence, we have provided explicit suggestions about how one might analyze that evidence, guiding students as they reach their own conclusions. As they work through the various chapters, students will discover not only that the sources of historical information are wide-ranging but also that the methodologies appropriate to understanding and using them are equally diverse. By doing history themselves, students will learn how intellectual historians handle philosophical treatises, economic historians quantitative data, social historians court records, and political and diplomatic historians theoretical treatises and memoirs. They will also be asked to consider the limitations of their evidence, to explore what historical questions it cannot answer as well as those it can. Instead of passive observers, students become active participants.

Following an approach that we have found successful in many different classroom situations, we have divided each chapter into five parts: The Problem, Sources and Method, The Evidence, Questions to Consider, and Epilogue. The section called "The Problem" presents the general historical background and context for the evidence offered and concludes with the central question or questions explored in the chapter. The section titled "Sources and Method" provides specific information about the sources and suggests ways in which students might best study and analyze this primary evidence. It also discusses how previous historians have evaluated such sources and mentions any major disputes about methodology or interpretation. "The Evidence" forms the core of each chapter, presenting a variety of original sources for students to use in completing the central task. In "Questions to Consider," suggestions are offered about connections among the sources, and students are guided to draw deductions from the evidence. The final section, "Epilogue," traces both the immediate effects of the issue under discussion and its impact on later developments.

Within this framework, we have tried to present a series of historical issues and events of significance to the instructor as well as of interest to the student. We have also aimed to provide a balance among political, social, diplomatic, intellectual, and cultural history. In other words, we have attempted to create a kind of historical sampler that we believe will help students learn the methods and skills used by historians. These skills—analyzing arguments, developing hypotheses, comparing evidence, testing conclusions, and reevaluating material—will not only enable students to master historical content; they will also provide the necessary foundation for critical thinking in other college courses and after college as well.

Discovering the Western Past is designed to accommodate any format of the Western Civilization course, from the small lecture/discussion class of a liberal arts or community college to the large lecture with discussions led by teaching assistants at a sizable university. The chapters may be used for individual assignments, team projects, class discussions, papers, and exams. Each is self-contained, so that any combination may be assigned. The book is not intended to replace a standard textbook, and it was written to accompany any Western Civilization text the instructor chooses. The *Instructor's Resource Manual*, written by the authors of the text, offers suggestions for class discussions, suggestions for ways in which students' learning may be evaluated, and annotated lists of suggestions for further reading.

New to the Fourth Edition

The Fourth Edition of *Discovering the Western Past* incorporates the responses to the book that we have received from our own students, as well as from student and faculty users of the book around the country. Every chapter in the two volumes has received some reworking, and new chapters are included in each volume.

Volume I includes new chapters on ancient suicide, slave law in Roman and Germanic society, and peasant violence in the period 1500–1789. Volume II offers readers new chapters on the French Revolution (reinstated from the Second Edition), "New Women" of the 1920s, and immigration in Europe.

Acknowledgments

In the completion of this book, the authors received assistance from a number of people. Our colleagues and students at the University of Wisconsin—Milwaukee, Marquette University, and the University of Tennessee, Knoxville, have been generous with their ideas and time. Merry E. Wiesner (-Hanks) wishes especially to thank Judith Bennett, Judith Beall, Martha Carlin, Abbas Hamdani, and Marci Sortor for their critiques and suggestions, and Neil Wiesner-Hanks and Kai and Tyr Wiesner-Hanks for their help in maintaining the author's perspective. Julius Ruff acknowledges the assistance of two valued colleagues who aided in preparing all four editions of this work: the Reverend John Patrick Donnelly, S.J., of Marquette University and Michael D. Sibalis of Wilfrid Laurier University. He also wishes to thank Laura, Julia, and Charles Ruff for their continued support. William Bruce Wheeler wishes to thank Owen Bradley and John Bohstedt for their valuable assistance.

We wish to acknowledge particularly the following historians who read and commented on the manuscript of this Fourth Edition as it developed:

Marjorie K. Berman, *Red Rocks Community College*
Melissa Bokovoy, *University of New Mexico*
Richard Camp, *California State University, Northridge*

Phillip A. Cantrell II, *West Virginia University*
Victoria Chandler, *Georgia College & State University*
Rhonda L. Clark, *Mercyhurst College*
Christopher R. Corley, *Bloomsburg University*
Greg A. Eghigian, *University of Texas at Arlington*
Luci Fortunato-DeLisle, *Bridgewater State College*
Meredith A. Medler, *St. Cloud State University*
Catherine Patterson, *University of Houston*
Charles M. Radding, *Michigan State University*
Bernard Schlager, *University of New Hampshire*
Linda J. Simmons, *Northern Virginia Community College*
Phillip Thurmond Smith, *Saint Joseph's University, Philadelphia*

Finally, the authors extend their thanks to the staff of Houghton Mifflin Company for their enthusiastic support.

M.E.W.
J.R.R.
W.B.W.

CHAPTER ONE

THE NEED FOR WATER

IN ANCIENT SOCIETIES

THE PROBLEM

The title of the course for which you are using this book is probably a variant of "Western Civilization." Why do we use the term *civilization*? What distinguishes human cultures that are labeled civilizations from those that are not? Though great differences separate them, all civilizations share some basic characteristics. The most important of these similarities is the presence of cities; indeed, the word *civilization* comes from the Latin word *civilis* (meaning "civic"), which is also the root of *citizen* and *civil*. Historians and archaeologists generally define a city as a place inhabited by more than 5,000 people, and they have discovered the remains of the earliest communities of this size in ancient Mesopotamia, which is present-day Iraq.

Why should the presence of cities be the distinguishing mark of cultural development? It is not the cities themselves but what they imply about a culture that makes them so important. Any society in which thousands of people live in close proximity to one another must have some sort of laws or rules governing human behavior. These may be either part of an oral tradition or, as in ancient Mesopotamia, written down. A city must provide its residents with a constant supply of food, which means developing ways to transport food into the city from the surrounding farmland, to store food throughout the year, and to save it for years marked by poor harvests. Not only does the presence of cities indicate that people could transport and store food effectively, but it also reveals that they were producing enough surplus food to allow for specialization of labor. If all work time had been devoted to farming, it would not have been possible to build roads, produce storage bins, or enforce laws on which the city depended. This specialization of labor, then, allowed some members of society the opportunity and time to create and produce goods and artifacts that were not directly essential to daily survival. Urban residents in Mesopotamia began to construct large buildings and decorate them with sculptures, paintings, and mosaics; write poetry and history; and develop religious and philosophical ideas, all of which are pursuits we consider essential to a civilization. As the cities themselves grew, they required greater and greater amounts of food to feed their inhabitants, which led to further technological development.

Mesopotamia was in many ways an odd location for the beginning of a civilization. True, the soil is so rich that the region is called the Fertile Crescent, but it does not receive enough natural rainfall to grow crops steadily year after year. In fact, this region is not where agriculture began in the West; that happened closer to the Mediterranean, where the rainfall was more regular. Apparently, as techniques of planting and harvesting crops spread into Mesopotamia, the inhabitants realized that they would be able to use these techniques effectively only through irrigation. They needed to tap the waters flowing in the Tigris and Euphrates Rivers, a project requiring the cooperation of a great many people. Thus, rather than proving a block to further development, the need for irrigation in ancient Mesopotamia may have been one of the reasons that cities first arose there. We may never be able to know this with certainty, because irrigation systems were already in place when written records began and because cities and irrigation expanded at the same time. We do know, however, that in Mesopotamia, neither could have existed without the other; cities could survive only where irrigation had created a food surplus,

and irrigation could survive only where enough people were available to create and maintain ditches and other parts of the system.

Building irrigation systems presented both technical and organizational problems. The Tigris and Euphrates were fast-flowing rivers that carried soil as well as water down from the highlands. This rich soil created new farmland where the rivers emptied into the Persian Gulf. (The ancient Persian Gulf ended more than 100 miles north of its present boundary; all that land was created as the rivers filled in the delta.) The soil also rapidly clogged up the irrigation ditches, which consequently required constant cleaning. Every year these deposits were excavated and piled on the banks until the sides of the ditches grew so tall that cleaning could no longer be easily accomplished. At this point the old ditch was abandoned and a new ditch was cut, tasks that required a great deal of work and the cooperation of everyone whose land was watered by that ditch.

Mesopotamian farmers used several types of irrigation. One technique, known as *basin irrigation,* was to level large plots of land fronting the rivers and main canals and build up dikes around them. In the spring and other times during the year when the water was high, farmers knocked holes in the dikes to admit water and fresh soil. Once the sediment had settled, they let the water flow back into the channel. They also built small waterways between their fields to provide water throughout the year, thereby developing a system of *perennial irri-*

gation. In the hillier country of northern Mesopotamia, farmers built *terraces* with water channels running alongside them. The hillside terraces provided narrow strips of flat land to farm, and the waterways were dug to connect with brooks and streams.

Farmers could depend on gravity to bring water to their fields during spring and flood seasons, but at other times they needed water-raising machines. They devised numerous types of machines, some of which are still in use today in many parts of the world. These solved some problems but created others, as farmers with machines could drain an irrigation ditch during times of low water, leaving their neighbors with nothing. How were rights to water to be decided? Solving this problem was crucial to human social organization, and the first recorded laws regarding property rights in fact concern not rights to land but rights to water. In Mesopotamia, land was useless unless it was irrigated.

Many of the irrigation techniques developed in Mesopotamia either spread to Egypt or were developed independently there. Because it received even less rainfall than Mesopotamia, Egypt was totally dependent on the Nile for watering crops. Fortunately, the Nile was a much better source of water than the Tigris and Euphrates because it flooded regularly, allowing easy basin irrigation. The rise and fall of the Nile was so regular, in fact, that the Egyptians based their 365-day calendar on its annual flooding. The Egyptians also constructed waterways and water-lifting machines to allow

for perennial irrigation. As in Mesopotamia, irrigation in Egypt both caused and resulted from the growth of cities. It contributed as well to the power of the kings, whom the Egyptian people regarded as responsible for the flood of the Nile.

Irrigation was more difficult in places that did not have flood-prone rivers, including many parts of North Africa and the Near East. Here people adapted techniques to conserve water from sporadic heavy rainfalls. They dammed the temporary lakes (termed *wadis*) created by these rainfalls and built ditches to convey the water to fields, rather than allowing it simply to flow off onto the desert. Sometimes this wadi irrigation involved a whole series of small dams down the course of rivers that ran only after storms. Besides providing water, wadi irrigation also built up terraces because the rivers carried soil with them.

The earliest water systems were for crop irrigation, but people also began to demand good drinking water. In many parts of the ancient world, the demand for drinking water led to the setting up of a second system because river water that is suitable for irrigation may be brackish, unpleasant, or even unhealthful to drink. In southern Europe, where lakes were often not far from growing cities, people solved the problem by building channels made of timber, stone, or clay earthenware to carry water from the lakes to the city. These channels might be open or closed, depending on the terrain and the level of technical development of the culture that built them. Generally they relied on gravity flow and fed into underground tanks or reservoirs in the city; the oldest known water channels are in Jerusalem and date from about 1000 B.C. The construction of such systems, which demanded even more technical expertise than the building of irrigation ditches, provoked additional legal problems about ownership of the right to this clean, cool water.

When lakes were not located close enough to make aboveground channels feasible, people had to rely on water from *aquifers*, underground water-bearing layers of gravel or porous rock. The water could be obtained from wells drilled in the ground, but wells could supply only a small amount of water at a time. Once an aquifer had been discovered, however, a horizontal channel could be dug to lead the water to an outside channel or reservoir. A horizontal channel worked only in hilly areas where the aquifer stood higher than a nearby valley, but such channels, called *qanats*, have been found in Iran, Syria, Egypt, and Turkey that are over 2,000 years old. If the amount of water it yielded was large enough, the qanat could be used for irrigation as well as drinking water.

When the Romans conquered the Middle East and North Africa in the second century B.C., they inherited irrigation systems that in some cases had already been in existence for more than 2,000 years. The Romans carried many ideas to other parts of their empire and made innovations as the terrain or distance required. Most of the European territory in the Roman Empire received adequate rainfall for farming without irrigation, but many Roman cities, especially Rome itself, experienced a chronic shortage of drinking water. The Romans solved this problem by building *aqueducts,* covered or uncovered channels that brought water into the cities from lakes and springs. The first of these in Rome was built in 312 B.C., and the system expanded continuously up to about A.D. 150. Over 300 miles of aqueducts served the city of Rome alone, with extensive systems in the outlying provinces as well. Although Roman engineers went to great lengths to avoid valleys, they were occasionally forced to construct enormous bridges to carry the aqueducts over valleys. Some of these bridges were over 150 feet high, and a few, such as the bridge-aqueduct in Segovia, Spain, still bring water to city residents. The Romans' sophisticated architectural and construction techniques—the arch and water-resistant cement, for example—enabled them to build water systems undreamed of in Mesopotamia and Egypt. Legal problems were not as easily solved, however, and disputes about water rights recur frequently throughout the long history of Rome.

Supplying cities with water was not simply a technological problem; it had economic, legal, and political implications. Through their solutions to these complex problems, ancient societies created what we call civilization. Your task in this chapter will be to use both visual and written evidence of ancient water systems to answer the question, How did the need for a steady supply of water shape civilization?

SOURCES AND METHOD

Historians use a wide variety of sources when examining ancient irrigation and water supply systems. Many of these systems were created before the development of writing, so archaeological evidence is extremely important, especially in examining technological development. This evidence may be the actual remains of ancient ditches, machines, or aqueducts, but in many areas these have completely disappeared. This does not mean that they have left no trace, however, for the ancient uses of modern landscapes are often revealed through patterns of depressions and discoloration.

The easiest way to see these patterns is through aerial photography. Analyzing aerial photographs can be a difficult task, however, and learning how to read ancient land-use patterns through the overlay of modern development takes a great deal of training. Occasionally the older patterns can be quite clear, however, and only a small amount of additional information is necessary for you to begin to decode them. The first piece of evidence, Source 1, is an aerial photograph of the site of a pre-Roman city in Italy. Examine the picture carefully. Can you see the old grid pattern of irrigation ditches, which shows up as light and dark marsh grass? The dark lines are the outlines of ancient irrigation ditches, the lighter squares are ancient fields, and the white parallel lines superimposed on the top are part of a modern drainage system. To examine the an-

cient system, you will need to strip away the modern system mentally. What do you think the broader black strip at the top left is? Does this system look like basin or perennial irrigation? Look at the flatness of the landscape. Would silting be a problem?

A more sophisticated type of aerial photography involves the use of satellites rather than airplanes. Satellites can take extremely detailed pictures of the earth's surface that reveal natural and artificially constructed features, both ancient and contemporary. The sharpest images are produced by high-resolution military satellites whose pictures are not available to the public. Low-power images produced by LANDSAT, the only U.S. commercial imaging satellite system, are adequate for most archaeological and historical purposes, however. Source 2 is a map of the major ancient irrigation ditches between the Tigris and Euphrates rivers that were identifiable in a recent LANDSAT image. What does the size of the system reveal about Mesopotamian technology? What does it imply about the political systems in this area—would you expect, for example, the cities in Mesopotamia to be hostile to one another? New technologies such as LANDSAT imagery not only provide answers to questions, but also guide future research. How could you use this map to plan further investigations of irrigation systems?

Aerial photography provides visual evidence of entire irrigation systems but not of the specific tools and machines used to lift water to the fields. For these we must look to the remains of the tools themselves or to depictions of them in tomb paintings, mosaics, and pottery. Comparing these pictures with machines still in use today shows that many techniques for lifting water have remained virtually unchanged for thousands of years.

Sources 3 through 6 show four different machines for raising water that we know were in use in ancient times and are still in use in many parts of the world today: the shaduf, saqiya, Archimedes' screw,[1] and noria. To assess their role and importance, you must consider a number of different factors while carefully examining the four diagrams. Some of these factors are technical: How complicated is the machine to build? Does it have many moving parts that must all be in good repair? How much water can it lift? How high can it lift the water? Can it work with both flowing and stationary water? Some factors are economic: Does the machine require a person to operate it, thus taking that person away from other types of labor? Does it require a strong adult, or can it be operated by a child? Does it require an animal, which must be fed and cared for? Some factors are both economic and political: Does the machine require a variety of raw materials to build, more than one family might possess? Does it require any raw materials, like metal, that would have to be imported? (Such questions are political because someone has to decide which families get the raw materials necessary for their fields.) Some factors are legal: Does the machine raise

so much water that laws about distribution would become necessary? At this point, you may want to make a chart summarizing your assessment of the advantages and disadvantages of each machine, which will help you in making your final conclusions.

We will now turn from visual to written sources. Because water is such a vital commodity, mention of water systems appears very early in recorded human history. The next five sources are written accounts of the construction or operation of water systems. Source 7 contains sections from the Code of Hammurabi, a Babylonian legal code dating from 1750 B.C., that refer to irrigation. Source 8 is a description of the Roman aqueduct system written by Vitruvius during the first century B.C., and Source 9 is a description of the water-system projects undertaken by Emperor Claudius during his reign (A.D. 41–54), written by the Roman historian Suetonius. The next selection is a discussion of some of the problems associated with Rome's water system written about A.D. 100 by Frontinus, who was commissioner of the water supply. The last is a proclamation issued by Emperor Theodosius in 438 as part of his code of laws, an edict that had probably been in effect for many earlier decades as well.

As you read these sources, notice first of all the technical issues that the authors are addressing. What problems in tapping, transportation, and storage of water do they discuss? What solutions do they suggest? Then look at legal problems, which you can find most clearly stated in the selection by Frontinus and the law codes

1. Archimedes (287–212 B.C.) was a Greek mathematician and inventor who is credited with inventing this machine.

of Hammurabi and Theodosius. Keep in mind when you are reading the law codes that laws are generally written to address those problems that already exist, not those the lawmakers are simply anticipating. The presence of a law, especially one that is frequently repeated, is often a good indication that the prohibited activity was probably happening, and happening often. How did people misuse or harm the water systems? What penalties were provided for those who did? Who controlled the legal use of water, and who decided how water was to be distributed?

The written sources also include information about political and economic factors in ancient water supply systems that is nearly impossible to gain from archaeological evidence. Careful reading can reveal who paid for the construction of such systems and who stood to gain financially from them once they were built. What reasons, other than the simple need for water, might rulers have had for building water systems? What political and economic factors entered into decisions about the ways in which water was to be distributed?

THE EVIDENCE

Source 1 from Leo Deuel, Flights into Yesterday: The Story of Aerial Archeology *(New York: St. Martin's Press, 1969), p. 236. Photo by Fotoaerea Valvassori, Ravenna.*

1. Aerial Photograph of Pre-Roman City in Italy

Source 2 from Robert MaC. Adams, Heartland of Cities; Surveys of Ancient Settlements and Land Use on the Central Floodplains of the Euphrates *(Chicago: University of Chicago Press, 1981), p. 34.*

2. Major Ancient Levees Identifiable in LANDSAT Imagery

Sources 3 through 6 adapted from sketches by Merry E. Wiesner.

3. Shaduf

4. Saqiya

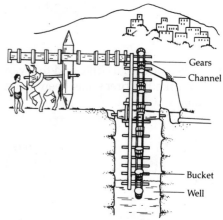

5. Archimedes' Screw

6. Noria

Source 7 from Robert F. Harper, The Code of Hammurabi *(Chicago: University of Chicago Press, 1904).*

7. Sections from the Code of Hammurabi Referring to Irrigation, 1750 B.C.

53. If a man neglects to maintain his dike and does not strengthen it, and a break is made in his dike and the water carries away the farmland, the man in whose dike the break has been made shall replace the grain which has been damaged.

54. If he is not able to replace the grain, they shall sell him and his goods and the farmers whose grain the water has carried away shall divide [the results of the sale].

55. If a man opens his canal for irrigation and neglects it and the water carries away an adjacent field, he shall pay out grain on the basis of the adjacent field.

56. If a man opens up the water and the water carries away the improvements of an adjacent field, he shall pay out ten *gur* of grain per *bur* [of damaged land]. . . .

66. If a man has stolen a watering-machine from the meadow, he shall pay five shekels of silver to the owner of the watering-machine.

Sources 8 and 9 from Naphtali Lewis and Meyer Reinhold, editors and translators, Roman Civilization *(New York: Columbia University Press, 1955), pp. 304–306; pp. 151–152. Reprinted with permission of Columbia University Press, 562 W. 113th St., New York, NY 10025, via Copyright Clearance Center, Inc.*

8. Vetruvius's Description of the Roman Aqueduct System, first century B.C.

The supply of water is made by three methods: by channels through walled conduits, or by lead pipes, or by earthenware pipes. And they are arranged as follows. In the case of conduits, the structure must be very solid; the bed of the channel must be leveled with a fall of not less than half a foot in 100 feet. The walled conduits are to be arched over so that the minimum amount of sun may strike the water. When it comes to the city walls, a reservoir is to be made. To this reservoir a triple distribution tank is to be joined to receive the water; and three pipes of equal size are to be placed in the reservoir, leading to the adjoining tanks, so that when there is an overflow from the two outer tanks, it may deliver into the middle tank. From the middle tank pipes will be laid to all basins and fountains; from the second tank to the baths, in order to furnish an annual revenue to the treasury; to avoid a deficiency in the public supply, private houses are to be supplied from the third, for private persons will not be able to divert the water, since they have their own limited supply from the distribution sources. Another reason why I have made these divisions is that those who take private supplies into their houses may by their taxes paid through tax farmers contribute to the maintenance of the water supply.

If, however, there are hills between the city and the source, we must proceed as follows: underground channels are to be dug and leveled to the fall mentioned above. If the bed is of tufa or stone, the channel may be cut in it; but if it is of soil or sand, the bed of the channel and the walls with the vaulting must be constructed, and the water should be thus conducted. Air shafts are to be so constructed that they are 120 feet apart.

But if the supply is to be by lead pipes, first of all a reservoir is to be built at the source. Then the opening of the pipe is to be determined in accordance with the amount of water, and these pipes are to be laid from the source reservoir to a reservoir which is inside the city.

When an aqueduct is to be made with lead pipes it is to have the following arrangement. If there is a fall from the source to the city and the intervening hills are not high enough to interrupt the supply, then if there are valleys, we must build substructures to bring it up to a level, as in the case of channels and conduits. If the way round the valley is not long, a circuit should be used; but if the valleys are expansive, the course will be directed down the hill, and when it reaches the bottom it is carried on a low substructure so that the level there may continue as far as possible. This will form a "belly," which the Greeks call *koilia.* When the "belly" comes to the hill opposite, and the long distance of the "belly" makes the water slow in welling up, the water is to be forced to the height of the top of the hill. . . .

Again, it is not without advantage to put reservoirs at intervals of 24,000 feet, so that if a break occurs anywhere neither the whole load of water nor the whole structure need be disturbed, and the place where it has occurred may be more easily found. But these reservoirs are to be neither in the descent nor on the level portion of the "belly," nor at risings, nor anywhere in a valley, but on unbroken level ground.

But if we wish to employ a less expensive method, we must proceed as follows. Earthenware pipes are to be made not less than two inches thick, but these pipes should be so tongued at one end that they can fit into and join one another. The joints are to be coated with quicklime mixed with oil. . . . Everything also is to be fixed as for lead pipes. Further, when the water is first let in from the source, ashes are to be put in beforehand, so that if any joints are not sufficiently coated they may be lined with the ashes.

Water supply by earthenware pipes has these advantages. First, in the construction: if a break occurs, anybody can repair it. Again, water is much more wholesome from earthenware pipes than from lead pipes. For it seems to be made injurious by lead, because white lead is produced by it; and this is said to be harmful to the human body. So if what is produced by anything is injurious, there is no doubt that the thing itself is not wholesome. We can take an example from the workers in lead who have complexions affected by pallor. For when lead is smelted in casting, the fumes from it settle on the members of the body and, burning them, rob the limbs of the virtues of the blood. Therefore it seems that water should by no means be brought in lead pipes if we desire to have it wholesome. Everyday life can be used to show that the flavor from earthenware pipes is better, because everybody (even those who load their table with silver vessels) uses earthenware to preserve the purity of water.

But if we are to create springs from which the water supplies come, we must dig wells.

But if the soil is hard, or if the veins of water lie too deep, then supplies of water are to be collected from the roofs or higher ground in concrete cisterns. . . . If the cisterns are made double or triple, so that they can be changed by percolation, they will make the supply of water much more wholesome. For when the sediment has a place to settle in, the water will be more limpid and will keep its taste without any smell. If not, salt must be added to purify it.

9. Suetonius's Description of the Water Projects Undertaken by Emperor Claudius (r. A.D. 41–54)

The public works which Claudius completed were great and essential rather than numerous; they were in particular the following: an aqueduct begun by Caligula; also the drainage channel of Lake Fucine and the harbor at Ostia, although in the case of the last two he knew that Augustus had refused the former to the Marsians in spite of their frequent requests, and that the latter had often been considered by the deified Julius but given up because of its difficulty. He brought to the city on stone arches the cool and abundant springs of the Claudian aqueduct . . . and at the same time the channel of the New Anio, distributing them into many beautifully ornamented fountains. He made the attempt on the Fucine Lake as much in the hope of gain as of glory, inasmuch as there were some who offered to drain it at their own cost provided the land that was drained be given them. He finished the drainage canal, which was three miles in length, partly by leveling and partly by tunneling a mountain, a work of great difficulty requiring eleven years, although he had 30,000 men at work all the time without interruption.

Source 10 from B. K. Workman, editor and translator, They Saw It Happen in Classical Times *(New York: Barnes & Noble, 1964), pp. 179–181. Reprinted by permission of Littlefield, Adams & Company and Basil Blackwell Publishers.*

10. Frontinus's Discussion of Rome's Water System, ca A.D. 100

The New Anio[2] is drawn from the river in the district of Sinbrinum, at about the forty-second milestone along the Via Sublacensis. On either side of the river at this point are fields of rich soil which make the banks less firm, so that the water in the aqueduct is discoloured and muddy even without the damage done by storms. So a little way along from the inlet a cleansing basin was built where the water could settle and be purified between the river and the conduit. Even so, in the event of rain, the water reaches the city in a muddy state. The length of the New Anio is about 47 miles, of which over 39 are underground and more than 7 carried on structures above the ground. In the upper reaches a distance of about two miles in various sections is carried on low structures or arches. Nearer the city, from the seventh Roman mile-stone, is half a mile on substructures and five miles on arches. These arches are very high, rising in certain places to a height of 109 feet.

. . . All the aqueducts reach the city at different levels. So some serve the higher districts and some cannot reach loftier ground. For the hills of Rome have gradually increased in height because of the rubble from frequent fires. There are five aqueducts high enough at entrance to reach all the city, but they supply water at different pressures. . . .

Anyone who wants to tap water for private consumption must send in an application and take it, duly signed by the Emperor, to the Commissioner. The latter must take immediate action on Caesar's grant, and enroll one of the Imperial freedmen to help him in the business. . . . The right to water once granted cannot be inherited or bought, and does not go with the property, though long ago a privilege was extended to the public baths that their right should last in perpetuity. . . . When grants lapse, notice is given and record made in the ledgers, which are consulted so that future applicants can be given vacant supplies. The previous custom was to cut off these lapsed supplies at once, to make some profit by a temporary sale to the landowners or even to outsiders. Our Emperor felt that property should not suddenly be left without water, and that it would be fairer to give thirty days' notice for other arrangements to be made by the interested party. . . .

Now that I have explained the situation with regard to private supply, it will be pertinent to give some examples of the ways in which men have broken these very sound arrangements and have been caught red-handed. In some reservoirs I have found larger valves in position than had been granted,

2. An aqueduct completed under the emperor Claudius in A.D. 52.

and some have not even had the official stamp on them. When a stamped valve exceeds the legal dimensions, then the private advantage of the controller who stamped it is uncovered. When a valve is not even stamped, then both parties are clearly liable, chiefly the purchaser, but also the controller. Sometimes stamped valves of the correct dimensions open into pipes of a larger cross-section. The result is that the water is not kept in for the legal distance, but forced through a short, narrow pipe and easily fills the larger one which is joined to it. So care must be taken that, when a valve is stamped, the pipes connected to it should be stamped as of the correct length ordered by Senatorial decree. For then and only then will the controller be fully liable when he knows that only stamped pipes must be positioned.

When valves are sited, good care must be taken to see that they are placed in a horizontal line, not one above the other. A lower inlet gets a greater pressure of water, the upper one less, because the supply of water is taken by the lower. In some pipes no valves are positioned at all. These are called "free" pipes, and are opened and closed to suit the watermen.

Another of the watermen's intolerable practices is to make a new outlet from the cistern when a water-grant is transferred to a new owner, leaving the old one for themselves. I would say that it was one of the Commissioner's chief duties to put a stop to this. For it affects not only the proper protection of the supply, but also the upkeep of the reservoir which would be ruined if needlessly filled with outlets.

Another financial scheme of the watermen, which they call "puncturing," must also be abolished. There are long separate stretches all over the city through which the pipes pass hidden under the pavement. I found out that these pipes were being tapped everywhere by the "puncturers," from which water was supplied by private pipe to all the business premises in the area, with the result that only a meagre amount reached the public utilities. I can estimate the volume of water stolen in this way from the amount of lead piping which was removed when these branch pipes were dug up.

Source 11 from Naphtali Lewis and Meyer Reinhold, editors and translators, Roman Civilization *(New York: Columbia University Press, 1955), pp. 479–480. Reprinted with permission of Columbia University Press, 562 W. 113th St., New York, NY 10025, via Copyright Clearance Center, Inc.*

11. Proclamation of Emperor Theodosius, A.D. 438

It is our will that the landholders over whose lands the courses of aqueducts pass shall be exempt from extraordinary burdens, so that by their work the aqueducts may be cleansed when they are choked with dirt. The said landholders shall not be subject to any other burden of a superindiction,[3] lest they be occupied in other matters and not be present to clean the aqueducts. If they neglect this duty, they shall be punished by the forfeiture of their landholdings; for the fisc[4] will take possession of the landed estate of any man whose negligence contributes to the damage of the aqueducts. Furthermore, persons through whose landed estates the aqueducts pass should know that they may have trees to the right and left at a distance of fifteen feet from the aqueducts, and your[5] office shall see to it that these trees are cut out if they grow too luxuriantly at any time, so that their roots may not injure the structure of the aqueduct.

QUESTIONS TO CONSIDER

Now that you have looked at both visual and written evidence, you will need to put together the information you have gathered from each type of source to achieve a more complete picture. Because sources for the earliest period of human development are so scanty, we need to use every shred of information available and use it somewhat creatively, making speculations where no specific evidence exists.

Take all the evidence about technical problems first. Keeping in mind that the ancient world had no power equipment and no tools more elaborate than axes, hammers, saws, and drills (the Romans also had planes and chisels), what would you judge to be the most difficult purely technical problem involved in constructing water systems? In keeping them operating? The four diagrams of the water-raising machines are arranged in chronological order of their development: The shaduf may be as old as 2500 B.C., and the other three did not appear until 1,000 years later. Looking at your chart on the advantages and disadvantages of each machine, in what ways did the later machines improve on the shaduf? What additional problems might these improvements have produced? What types of technological experimentation did the need for water encourage?

Technological advance is not always an unmitigated blessing. For example, water standing in irrigation ditches can become brackish, providing a good breeding ground for mosquitoes and other carriers of disease. Cities that depend on irrigation suffer food shortages and famine when ditches cannot be kept clear or when river levels are low. The diversion of large quantities of water for irrigation makes rivers much smaller when they finally reach their deltas, which means

3. That is, any special taxes.

4. **fisc:** the imperial treasury.

5. This proclamation was addressed to the administrator of the water supply, the same office that Frontinus held earlier.

that the deltas become increasingly salty from seawater and unable to support the types of plant and animal life they originally fostered. Judging by the aerial photograph and the LANDSAT map, would you expect any of these problems in ancient Italy or Mesopotamia? Do you find evidence in the written sources for problems in the later Roman water systems that were caused by technical advances? Do the written sources offer suggestions for solving these problems?

Now consider what you have learned about the economic issues associated with water systems. You have doubtless noticed that tremendous numbers of people were needed to construct irrigation ditches and aqueducts. Some of the written sources, such as the extract from Suetonius, provide exact figures. The size and complexity of the systems in the other sources also imply a substantial work force, given the lack of elaborate equipment. The rulers of Mesopotamia and Rome saw the need for a large labor force as no problem; it was, rather, a solution to the greater problem of unemployment. According to a story told about the Roman emperor Vespasian, when he was offered a labor-saving machine, he refused to allow its use because that would put people out of work and lead to social problems in Rome. We might regard this concern for full employment as a positive social attitude, but it should also tell you something about the value of labor in ancient societies. What would you expect wages to be for construction workers? What class of people would you expect to find working on these water systems?

Large numbers of workers were needed not only to build but also to maintain irrigation systems and to operate water-lifting machines. What does this fact tell you about the value of labor? What would happen with a sudden drop in the population, such as that caused by a famine or epidemic? How would a loss of workers affect the available food supply?

The sources also reveal information about political factors associated with water systems. What does the construction of these systems indicate about the power of rulers to coerce or hire labor? How do rulers control the building and maintenance of machines and ditches? How might their control affect the power and independence of local communities or of individual families? What does this tell you about the role of water in expanding centralized political power?

Finally, the sources provide evidence of alterations in the law made necessary by the search for water. Previously unrestricted and unregulated actions now came under the control of public authorities, which meant that the number of enforcement agents and courts had to increase. What would this do to taxation levels? In what ways would political concerns shape the regulations?

Political issues affect not only the types of laws to be passed, but also the stringency or selectivity with which those laws are enforced. We have very little information about how rigidly law codes were implemented in ancient societies, for few legal documents have survived; law codes were frequently recopied and reissued, but the outcome of individual cases was not. It is therefore dangerous to assume that the prescribed penalties were actually levied or that the law was regularly obeyed. (Think for a minute the mistake a person 2,000 years from now would make in describing traffic patterns in twentieth-century America if he or she assumed that the posted speed limit described the actual speed at which traffic moved!) Looking again at the law codes of Hammurabi and Theodosius, would you expect the penalties to be carried out, or do they appear to serve more as a strong warning? How would the penalties differ in their effects on poor and rich people?

You are now ready to answer the question posed at the beginning of the chapter. How did the need for a steady supply of water affect the development of civilization in the West?

EPILOGUE

The irrigation and water supply systems of the ancient world not only required huge amounts of labor, but also made necessary a strong central authority to coerce or hire that labor and to enforce laws to keep the channels flowing. At first, each Mesopotamian city managed its own irrigation system, but the wealthy and advanced cities were attractive targets for foreign conquerors. The political history of ancient Mesopotamia was one of wave after wave of conquerors coming down from the north—the Akkadians, Babylonians, Assyrians, Persians, Greeks, and finally the Romans. Most of these conquerors realized the importance of irrigation and ordered the conquered residents to maintain or expand their systems. When the Muslims invaded the region in the seventh century, they also learned Mesopotamian techniques and spread these westward into North Africa and Spain, where Roman irrigation systems had in many places fallen apart.

Irrigation could also be overdone, however, and during periods of political centralization many areas were overirrigated, which led to salinization, making the land useless for farming. This, combined with the rivers of Mesopotamia changing their courses, meant that many cities could not survive. Centuries of irrigation combined with too little fertilization made even land that was not salinized less and less productive.

The benefits and problems produced by irrigation are not limited to the ancient world, however; they can be seen in many modern societies. One of the best modern examples comes from the same part of the world we have been studying in this chapter. Throughout the twentieth century, Egypt has expanded its irrigation system watered by the Nile with a series of dams, culminating in the Aswan High Dam; this dam, begun in 1960, was designed to provide hydroelectric power and limit the free flow of water at the height of the flood season. The enormous reservoir formed by the dam can also be tapped at low-water times to allow for perennial irrigation. The Aswan Dam serves all its intended purposes very well, but it has also created some unexpected problems. The river's regular flooding had brought new fertile soil to the Nile Valley and carried away the salts that resulted from evaporation. Once the dam stopped the flooding, Egyptian fields needed artificial fertilizer to remain productive, a commodity many farmers could not afford. The soil of the Nile Valley has a high clay content, rendering drainage difficult, and a steady supply of water makes many fields waterlogged and unusable. The large reservoir created by the dam sits in the middle of the Sahara, allowing a tremendous amount of evaporation and significantly decreasing the total flow of water in the Nile; it has also put many acres of farmland under water and forced the relocation of tens of thousands of people. The drought in North Africa has further lowered the Nile's level, decreasing the amount of hydroelectric power the river can produce. Ending the flooding also allowed snails carrying bilharzia or schistosomiasis—an intestinal parasite that makes people very weak—to proliferate in the fields and irrigation ditches. The high water table resulting from the dam is destroying many ancient monuments, such as the temples of Luxor and Karnak, that have survived for millennia. Thus, like the lead pipes that brought water to the Romans, the Aswan High Dam has proved a mixed blessing in modern Egypt.

As you reflect on what you have discovered in this chapter, you may want to think about problems associated with the distribution of water in your own region. How does the need for water affect the political and economic structures of your city or state? What technological solutions has your region devised, and how have these worked?

CHAPTER TWO

THE IDEAL AND THE REALITY

OF CLASSICAL ATHENS

THE PROBLEM

Athens during the fifth century B.C. is often identified as one of the main sources of Western values and standards. Later Europeans and Americans regarded the Athenians as the originators of democracy, drama, representational or realistic art, history, philosophy, and science. At different times over the past 2,500 years they have attempted to imitate this "Golden Age" of classical Athens in everything from buildings to literature. Many U.S. state capitols and government buildings are modeled on the Parthenon or other temples, complete with statuary of former governers in the manner of Greek gods. We still divide drama into tragedies and comedies in the same way the Athenians did, though now we sometimes use a prerecorded laugh track instead of grinning masks to indicate that a given work is a comedy. During some historical periods, such as the Renaissance, thinkers and writers made conscious attempts to return to classical ideals in all areas of life, combing the works of Athenian authors for previously overlooked material in their quest to draw guidance and learn everything possible from this unique flowering of culture.

Even more than as a model for literature and art, classical Athens has continued to serve as a relevant source for answers to basic questions about human existence. Though all cultures have sought to identify the ultimate aim and meaning of human life, the ancient Greeks, especially the Athenians, were the first in the West to provide answers that were not expressed in religious or mythological terms. Their thoughts on these matters grew out of speculations on the nature of the universe made by earlier Greeks, particularly Thales and his followers Anaximander and Heraclitus. These thinkers, living in the seventh and sixth centuries B.C., theorized about how the universe had been formed and what it was made of by means of rational explanations drawn from observation rather than from myth or religious tradition. Because they believed the natural universe could be explained in other than supernatural terms, they are often termed the first true scientists or first philosophers.

During the fifth century B.C., several Athenian thinkers turned their attention from the world around them to the human beings living in that world. They used this new method of philosophical inquiry to question the workings of the human mind and the societies humans create. They asked such questions as, How do we learn things? What should we try to learn? How do we know what is right or wrong, good or bad? If we can know what is good, how can we create things that are good? What kind of government is best? This type of questioning is perhaps most often associated with Socrates (469–399 B.C.) and his pupil Plato (427?–347 B.C.), who are generally called the founders of Western philosophy. Thales and his followers are thus known as the pre-Socratics; and a twentieth-century philosopher, Alfred North Whitehead, noted—only half jokingly—that "the European philosophical tradition . . . consists of a series of footnotes to Plato."

Both Socrates and Plato believed that goodness is related to knowledge and that excellence could be learned. For Plato especially, true knowledge was gained not by observation of the world but by contemplation of what an ideal world would be like. In their view, to understand goodness, justice, or beauty, it is necessary to think about what pure and ultimate goodness, justice, or beauty means. Plato thus introduced into Western thought a strong strain of *idealism* and was the first to write works on what an ideal society or set of laws would look like. He also described the education required to train citizens for governing this ideal state and the social and economic structure necessary to keep them at their posts. Though he probably recognized that these standards could never be achieved, he believed that the creation of ideals was an important component of the discipline of philosophy, a sentiment shared by many Western thinkers after him.

Plato's most brilliant pupil, Aristotle (384–322 B.C.), originally agreed with his teacher but then began to depart somewhat from idealism. Like the pre-Socratics, Aristotle was fascinated by the world around him, and many of his writings on scientific subjects reveal keen powers of observation. Even his treatises on standards of human behavior, such as those concerning ethics and politics, are based on close observation of Athenian society and not simply on speculation. Aristotle further intended that these works should not only describe ideal human behavior or political systems, but also provide suggestions about how to alter current practice to conform more closely to the ideal. Thus, although Aristotle was still to some degree an idealist, both the source and the recipient of his ideals was the real world.

In classical Athens, human nature was a subject contemplated not only by scientists and philosophers, but also by historians, such as Herodotus and Thucydides. They, too, searched for explanations about the natural order that did not involve the gods. For Herodotus and Thucydides, the Persian and Peloponnesian wars were caused by human failings, not by actions of vengeful gods such as those that Homer, following tradition, depicted in the *Iliad* as causing the Trojan War. Like Aristotle, they were interested in describing real events and finding explanations for them; like Plato, they were also interested in the possible as well as the actual. History, in their opinion, was the best arena for observing the true worth of various ideals to human society.

To the Athenians, war was the ultimate test of human ideals, morals, and values, but these could also be tested and observed on a much smaller scale in the way people conducted their everyday lives. Although for Plato the basis of an ideal government was the perfectly trained ruler or group of rulers, for Aristotle and other writers it was the perfectly managed household, which they regarded as a microcosm of society. Observing that the household was the smallest economic and political unit in Athenian society, Aristotle began his consideration of the ideal governmental system with thoughts on how households should be run. Other writers on politics and economics followed suit, giving advice after observing households they regarded as particularly well managed.

Whereas Plato clearly indicated that he was describing an ideal, in the case of Aristotle and other Athenians, it is sometimes difficult to determine whether they were attempting to describe reality, what they wished were reality, or a pure ideal. Your task in this chapter will be to examine the relationship between ideal and reality in the writings of several Athenian philosophers, historians, and commentators and in architectural diagrams of Athenian buildings and houses. What ideals do the writers set forth for the individual, the household, and the government? How are these ideals reflected in more realistic descriptions of life in Athens and in the way Athenians built their houses and their city?

SOURCES AND METHOD

All the written sources we will use come from Athenians who lived during the classical period and are thus what we term original or primary sources. They differ greatly from modern primary sources, however, in that their textual accuracy cannot be checked. Before the development of the printing press, the only way to obtain a copy of a work was to write it out by hand yourself or hire someone to do so. Therefore, each manuscript copy might be slightly different. Because the originals of the works of Aristotle or Thucydides have long since disappeared, what we have to work with are translations of composites based on as many of the oldest copies still in existence after 2,500 years that the translators could find.

The problem of accuracy is further complicated with some of the authors we will read because they did not actually write the works attributed to them. Many of Aristotle's works, for instance, are probably copies of his students' notes combined with (perhaps) some of his own. If you think of the way in which you record your own instructors' remarks, you can see why we must be cautious about assuming that these secondhand works contain everything Aristotle taught exactly as he intended it. Socrates, in fact, wrote nothing at all; all his ideas and words come to us through his pupil Plato. Scholars have long debated how much of the written record represents Socrates and how much represents Plato, especially when we consider that Socrates generally spoke at social gatherings or informally while walking around Athens, when Plato was not taking notes. These problems do not mean that we should discount these sources, they simply mean that we should realize that they differ from the printed documents and tape-recorded speeches of later eras.

We will begin our investigation with what is probably the most famous description of classical Athens: a funeral speech delivered by Pericles. Pericles, one of the leaders of Athens when the Peloponnesian War opened, gave this speech in 430 B.C. in honor of those who had died during the first year of the war. It was recorded by Thucydides and, though there is some disagreement over who actually wrote it, reflects Pericles' opinions. Read the speech carefully. Is Pericles describing an ideal he hopes Athens will achieve or reality as he sees it? How does he depict Athenian democracy and the Athenian attitude toward wealth? How does he compare Athens with Sparta? How does Athens treat its neighbors? What role does Pericles see for Athenian women? Before going on to the next readings, jot down some words that you feel best describe Athens and the Atheni-

ans. Would you want to live in the Athens Pericles describes?

Source 2 comes from a later section of Thucydides' *Peloponnesian War*, and it describes Athenian actions in the sixteenth year of the war. As you read it, think about the virtues that Pericles ascribed to the Athenians. Are these virtues reflected in the debate with the Melians or in the actions against them? How do the Athenians justify their actions? After reading this selection, jot down a few more words that you think describe the Athenians. Would you now erase some entries from your first list?

Source 3 is taken from the first book of Aristotle's *The Politics*. In this selection, he describes the proper functioning of a household and the role of each person in it. As you read it, you will notice that Aristotle is concerned equally with the economic role of household members and their moral status. What qualities does he see as important in the ideal head of household? the ideal wife or child? the ideal slave? How does he justify the differences between household members? How do these qualities compare with those described by Pericles or exhibited by the Athenians in their contact with the Melians? Add a few more words to your list describing the Athenians.

The fourth selection, by an unknown author, presents another view of Athenian democracy and the Athenian empire. This passage was written about five years after the speech made by Pericles and about ten years before the Melian debate. How does this author view democracy and Athens's relations with its neighbors?

[23]

What words might he add to your list to describe his fellow Athenians? How do you think he would have responded had he been in the audience listening to Pericles' funeral speech?

The fifth selection is a discussion of household management cast in the form of a dialogue, from a treatise by Xenophon called *The Economist*. What does the main speaker, whose name is Ischomachus, see as the main roles of husband and wife? Would he have agreed with Aristotle's conclusions about the qualities necessary in an ideal husband and wife? What suggestions does he make for encouraging ideal behavior in wives and slaves? Does he appear to be describing an actual or an ideal marital relationship? What words would you now add to or subtract from your list?

The sixth selection is a very small part of *The Republic*, in which Plato sets out his views on the ideal government. Plato did not favor democracy; he advocated training a group of leaders, whom he called *guardians*, to work for the best interests of all. What qualities does Plato feel are most important in the guardians? What economic and family structures does he feel will help them maintain these qualities? How does his description of the ideal female guardian compare with Pericles' and Xenophon's descriptions of the ideal Athenian wife? Do the qualities he finds important in guardians match up with any of those on your list?

Once you have read all the selections carefully, go back to Pericles' speech and read it again. Do you still have the same opinion about whether he is describing ideal or reality? Which of the words describing Athens that were on your original list are left?

Now look at the two diagrams, which are based on archaeological discoveries. They are thus clear representations of physical reality in classical Greece, but they tell us something about ideals as well, for people construct the space they live in according to their ideas about how society should operate. The first diagram, Source 7, is the floor plan of a house from fifth-century B.C. Olynthus. Does the actual house correspond to the one described by Xenophon? How does the layout of the house reinforce the roles prescribed for the ideal husband and wife? The second diagram, the eighth selection, is a plan of the Athenian *agora*, the open square in the center of Athens that served as both the political and commercial center of the city. The west side of the agora was a line of government buildings, including the *bouleuterion*, where the council met. The agora was bordered by several *stoa*, roofed-over open colonnades in front of lines of shops and offices. Because the climate of Greece is mild a good part of the year, much business could take place outside or in one of the stoa. What qualities from your list does the openness of the agora encourage? As you can see from the diagram, the agora was bordered by buildings with religious, governmental, and commercial functions. What does the placement of these buildings indicate about how Athenians valued the different areas of their lives?

Sources 1 and 2 from Thucydides, History of the Peloponnesian War, *translated by Richard Crawley (New York: Modern Library, 1951), pp. 103–106; p. 109.*

1. Pericles' Funeral Speech,
430 B.C.

That part of our history which tells of the military achievements which gave us our several possessions, or of the ready valour with which either we or our fathers stemmed the tide of Hellenic or foreign aggression, is a theme too familiar to my hearers for me to dilate on, and I shall therefore pass it by. But what was the road by which we reached our position, what the form of government under which our greatness grew, what the national habits out of which it sprang; these are questions which I may try to solve before I proceed to my panegyric upon these men: since I think this to be a subject upon which on the present occasion a speaker may properly dwell, and to which the whole assemblage, whether citizens or foreigners, may listen with advantage.

Our constitution does not copy the laws of neighbouring states; we are rather a pattern to others than imitators ourselves. Its administration favours the many instead of the few; this is why it is called a democracy. If we look to the laws, they afford equal justice to all in their private differences; if to social standing, advancement in public life falls to reputation for capacity, class considerations not being allowed to interfere with merit; nor again does poverty bar the way, if a man is able to serve the state, he is not hindered by the obscurity of his condition. The freedom which we enjoy in our government extends also to our ordinary life. There, far from exercising a jealous surveillance over each other, we do not feel called upon to be angry with our neighbour for doing what he likes, or even to indulge in those injurious looks which cannot fail to be offensive, although they inflict no positive penalty. But all this ease in our private relations does not make us lawless as citizens. Against this fear is our chief safeguard, teaching us to obey the magistrates and the laws, particularly such as regard the protection of the injured, whether they are actually on the statute book, or belong to that code which, although unwritten, yet cannot be broken without acknowledged disgrace.

Further, we provide plenty of means for the mind to refresh itself from business. We celebrate games and sacrifices all the year round, and the elegance of our private establishments forms a daily source of pleasure and helps to banish the spleen; while the magnitude of our city draws the produce of the world into our harbour, so that to the Athenian the fruits of other countries are as familiar a luxury as those of his own.

If we turn to our military policy, there also we differ from our antagonists. We throw open our city to the world, and never by alien acts exclude foreigners from any opportunity of learning or observing, although the eyes of an enemy may occasionally profit by our liberality; trusting less in system and policy than to the native spirit of our citizens; while in education, where our rivals from their very cradles by a painful discipline seek after manliness, at Athens we live exactly as we please, and yet are just as ready to encounter every legitimate danger. In proof of this it may be noticed that the Lacedæmonians[1] do not invade our country alone, but bring with them all their confederates; while we Athenians advance unsupported into the territory of a neighbour, and fighting upon a foreign soil usually vanquish with ease men who are defending their homes. Our united force was never yet encountered by any enemy, because we have at once to attend to our marine and to despatch our citizens by land upon a hundred different services; so that, wherever they engage with some such fraction of our strength, a success against a detachment is magnified into a victory over the nation, and a defeat into a reverse suffered at the hands of our entire people. And yet if with habits not of labour but of ease, and courage not of art but of nature, we are still willing to encounter danger, we have the double advantage of escaping the experience of hardships in anticipation and of facing them in the hour of need as fearlessly as those who are never free from them.

Nor are these the only points in which our city is worthy of admiration. We cultivate refinement without extravagance and knowledge without effeminacy; wealth we employ more for use than for show, and place the real disgrace of poverty not in owning to the fact but in declining the struggle against it. Our public men have, besides politics, their private affairs to attend to, and our ordinary citizens, though occupied with the pursuits of industry, are still fair judges of public matters; for, unlike any other nation, regarding him who takes no part in these duties not as unambitious but as useless, we Athenians are able to judge at all events if we cannot originate, and instead of looking on discussion as a stumbling-block in the way of action, we think it an indispensable preliminary to any wise action at all. Again, in our enterprises we present the singular spectacle of daring and deliberation, each carried to its highest point, and both united in the same persons; although usually decision is the fruit of ignorance, hesitation of reflexion. But the palm of courage will surely be adjudged most justly to those, who best know the difference between hardship and pleasure and yet are never tempted to shrink from danger. In generosity we are equally singular, acquiring our friends by conferring not by receiving favours. Yet, of course, the doer of the favour is the firmer friend of the two, in order by continued kindness to keep the recipient in his debt; while the debtor feels less keenly from the very consciousness that the return he makes will be a payment, not a free gift. And it is only the Athenians who,

---

1. **Lacedæmonians:** Spartans.

fearless of consequences, confer their benefits not from calculations of expediency, but in the confidence of liberality.

In short, I say that as a city we are the school of Hellas; while I doubt if the world can produce a man, who where he has only himself to depend upon, is equal to so many emergencies, and graced by so happy a versatility as the Athenian. And that this is no mere boast thrown out for the occasion, but plain matter of fact, the power of the state acquired by these habits proves. For Athens alone of her contemporaries is found when tested to be greater than her reputation, and alone gives no occasion to her assailants to blush at the antagonist by whom they have been worsted, or to her subjects to question her title by merit to rule. Rather, the admiration of the present and succeeding ages will be ours, since we have not left our power without witness, but have shown it by mighty proofs; and far from needing a Homer for our panegyrist, or other of his craft whose verses might charm for the moment only for the impression which they gave to melt at the touch of fact, we have forced every sea and land to be the highway of our daring, and everywhere, whether for evil or for good, have left imperishable monuments behind us. Such is the Athens for which these men, in the assertion of their resolve not to lose her, nobly fought and died; and well may every one of their survivors be ready to suffer in her cause. . . .

[I]f I must say anything on the subject of female excellence to those of you who will now be in widowhood, it will be all comprised in this brief exhortation. Great will be your glory in not falling short of your natural character; and greatest will be hers who is least talked of among the men whether for good or for bad.

My task is now finished. I have performed it to the best of my ability, and in words, at least, the requirements of the law are now satisfied. If deeds be in question, those who are here interred have received part of their honours already, and for the rest, their children will be brought up till manhood at the public expense: the state thus offers a valuable prize, as the garland of victory in this race of valour, for the reward both of those who have fallen and their survivors. And where the rewards for merit are greatest, there are found the best citizens.

And now that you have brought to a close your lamentations for your relatives, you may depart.

2. The Melian Debate, 415 B.C.

The Athenians also made an expedition against the isle of Melos with thirty ships of their own, six Chian, and two Lesbian vessels, sixteen hundred heavy infantry, three hundred archers, and twenty mounted archers from Athens, and about fifteen hundred heavy infantry from the allies and the islanders. The

Melians are a colony of Lacedæmon[2] that would not submit to the Athenians like the other islanders, and at first remained neutral and took no part in the struggle, but afterwards upon the Athenians using violence and plundering their territory, assumed an attitude of open hostility. Cleomedes, son of Lycomedes, and Tisias, son of Tisimachus, the generals, encamping in their territory with the above armament, before doing any harm to their land, sent envoys to negotiate. These the Melians did not bring before the people, but bade them state the object of their mission to the magistrates and the few; upon which the Athenian envoys spoke as follows: . . .

ATHENIANS: We will now proceed to show you that we are come here in the interest of our empire, and that we shall say what we are now going to say, for the preservation of your country; as we would fain exercise that empire over you without trouble, and see you preserved for the good of us both.

MELIANS: And how, pray, could it turn out as good for us to serve as for you to rule?

ATHENIANS: Because you would have the advantage of submitting before suffering the worst, and we should gain by not destroying you.

MELIANS: So that you would not consent to our being neutral, friends instead of enemies, but allies of neither side.

ATHENIANS: No; for your hostility cannot so much hurt us as your friendship will be an argument to our subjects of our weakness, and your enmity of our power.

MELIANS: Is that your subjects' idea of equity, to put those who have nothing to do with you in the same category with peoples that are most of them your own colonists, and some conquered rebels?

ATHENIANS: As far as right goes they think one has as much of it as the other, and if any maintain their independence it is because they are strong, and that if we do not molest them it is because we are afraid; so that besides extending our empire we should gain in security by your subjection; the fact that you are islanders and weaker than others rendering it all the more important that you should not succeed in baffling the masters of the sea.

MELIANS: But do you consider that there is no security in the policy which we indicate? For here again if you debar us from talking about justice and invite us to obey your interest, we also must explain ours, and try to persuade you, if the two happen to coincide. How can you avoid making enemies of all existing neutrals who shall look at our case and conclude from it that one day or another you will attack them? And what is this but to make greater the enemies that you have already, and to force others to become so who would otherwise have never thought of it?

ATHENIANS: Why, the fact is that continentals generally give us but little alarm; the liberty which they enjoy will long prevent their taking precautions against us; it is rather islanders like yourselves, outside our empire, and sub-

---

2. **Lacedæmon:** Sparta.

jects smarting under the yoke, who would be the most likely to take a rash step and lead themselves and us into obvious danger.

MELIANS: Well then, if you risk so much to retain your empire, and your subjects to get rid of it, it were surely great baseness and cowardice in us who are still free not to try everything that can be tried, before submitting to your yoke.

ATHENIANS: Not if you are well advised, the contest not being an equal one, with honour as the prize and shame as the penalty, but a question of self-preservation and of not resisting those who are far stronger than you are. . . .

Of the gods we believe, and of men we know, that by a necessary law of their nature they rule wherever they can. And it is not as if we were the first to make this law, or to act upon it when made: we found it existing before us, and shall leave it to exist for ever after us; all we do is to make use of it, knowing that you and everybody else, having the same power as we have, would do the same as we do. . . . You will surely not be caught by that idea of disgrace, which in dangers that are disgraceful, and at the same time too plain to be mistaken, proves so fatal to mankind; since in too many cases the very men that have their eyes perfectly open to what they are rushing into, let the thing called disgrace, by the mere influence of a seductive name, lead them on to a point at which they become so enslaved by the phrase as in fact to fall wilfully into hopeless disaster, and incur disgrace more disgraceful as the companion of error, than when it comes as the result of misfortune. This, if you are well advised, you will guard against; and you will not think it dishonourable to submit to the greatest city in Hellas, when it makes you the moderate offer of becoming its tributary ally, without ceasing to enjoy the country that belongs to you; nor when you have the choice given you between war and security, will you be so blinded as to choose the worse. And it is certain that those who do not yield to their equals, who keep terms with their superiors, and are moderate towards their inferiors, on the whole succeed best. Think over the matter, therefore, after our withdrawal, and reflect once and again that it is for your country that you are consulting, that you have not more than one, and that upon this one deliberation depends its prosperity or ruin.

The Athenians now withdrew from the conference; and the Melians, left to themselves, came to a decision corresponding with what they had maintained in the discussion, and answered, 'Our resolution, Athenians, is the same as it was at first. We will not in a moment deprive of freedom a city that has been inhabited these seven hundred years; but we put our trust in the fortune by which the gods have preserved it until now, and in the help of men, that is, of the Lacedæmonians; and so we will try and save ourselves. Meanwhile we invite you to allow us to be friends to you and foes to neither party, and to retire from our country after making such a treaty as shall seem fit to us both. . . .

The Athenian envoys now returned to the army; and the Melians showing no signs of yielding, the generals at once betook themselves to hostilities, and drew a line of circumvallation[3] round the Melians, dividing the work among the different states. Subsequently the Athenians returned with most of their army, leaving behind them a certain number of their own citizens and of the allies to keep guard by land and sea. The force thus left stayed on and besieged the place. . . .

Meanwhile the Melians attacked by night and took the part of the Athenian lines over against the market, and killed some of the men, and brought in corn and all else that they could find useful to them, and so returned and kept quiet, while the Athenians took measures to keep better guard in future.

Summer was now over. The next winter . . . the Melians again took another part of the Athenian lines which were but feebly garrisoned. Reinforcements afterwards arriving from Athens in consequence, under the command of Philocrates, son of Demeas, the siege was now pressed vigorously; and some treachery taking place inside, the Melians surrendered at discretion to the Athenians, who put to death all the grown men whom they took, and sold the women and children for slaves, and subsequently sent out five hundred colonists and inhabited the place themselves.

Source 3 from Aristotle, The Politics, *translated by T. A. Sinclair and revised by Trevor J. Saunders (Baltimore: Penguin, 1962, 1981), pp. 26–27, 31, 34, 50–53. Copyright © the estate of T. A. Sinclair, 1962; revised material copyright © Trevor J. Saunders, 1981. Reprinted with permission.*

3. From Aristotle, *The Politics*

We shall, I think, in this as in other subjects, get the best view of the matter if we look at the natural growth of things from the beginning. . . .

It was out of the association formed by men with these two, women and slaves, that the first household was formed; and the poet Hesiod was right when he wrote, "Get first a house and a wife and an ox to draw the plough." (The ox is the poor man's slave.) This association of persons, established according to the law of nature and continuing day after day, is the household. . . .

Now property is part of a household and the acquisition of property part of the economics of a household; for neither life itself nor the good life is possible without a certain minimum standard of wealth. Again, for any given craft the existence of the proper tools will be essential for the performance of its task. Tools may be animate as well as inanimate; a ship's captain uses a lifeless rudder, but a living man for watch; for the worker in a craft is, from the point of view of the craft, one of its tools. So any piece of property can be regarded as a tool enabling a man to live; and his property is an assemblage of such tools, including his slaves; and a slave, being a living creature like any other servant, is a tool worth many tools. . . .

3. **circumvallation:** ramparts and walls.

The "slave by nature" then is he that can and therefore does belong to another, and he that participates in the reasoning faculty so far as to understand but not so as to possess it. For the other animals serve their owner not by exercise of reason but passively. The use, too, of slaves hardly differs at all from that of domestic animals; from both we derive that which is essential for our bodily needs. . . . It is clear then that in household management the people are of greater importance than the material property, and their quality of more account than that of the goods that make up their wealth, and also that free men are of more account than slaves. About slaves the first question to be asked is whether in addition to their value as tools and servants there is some other quality or virtue, superior to these, that belongs to slaves. Can they possess self-respect, courage, justice, and virtues of that kind, or have they in fact nothing but the serviceable quality of their persons?

The question may be answered in either of two ways, but both present a difficulty. If we say that slaves have these virtues, how then will they differ from free men? If we say that they have not, the position is anomalous, since they are human beings and capable of reason. Roughly the same question can be put in relation to wife and child: Have not these also virtues? Ought not a woman to be self-respecting, brave, and just? Is not a child sometimes naughty, sometimes good? . . .

This mention of virtue leads us straightaway to a consideration of the soul; for it is here that the natural ruler and the natural subject, whose virtue we regard as different, are to be found. In the soul the difference between ruler and ruled is that between the rational and the nonrational. It is therefore clear that in other connexions also there will be natural differences. And so generally in cases of ruler and ruled; the differences will be natural but they need not be the same. For rule of free over slave, male over female, man over boy, are all natural, but they are also different, because, while parts of the soul are present in each case, the distribution is different. Thus the deliberative faculty in the soul is not present at all in a slave; in a female it is inoperative, in a child undeveloped. We must therefore take it that the same conditions prevail also in regard to the ethical virtues, namely that all must participate in them but not all to the same extent, but only as may be required by each for his proper function. The ruler then must have ethical virtue in its entirety; for his task is simply that of chief maker and reason is chief maker. And the other members must have what amount is appropriate to each. So it is evident that each of the classes spoken of must have ethical virtue. It is also clear that there is some variation in the ethical virtues; self-respect is not the same in a man as in a woman, nor justice, nor courage either, as Socrates thought; the one is courage of a ruler, the other courage of a servant, and likewise with the other virtues.

If we look at the matter in greater detail it will become clearer. For those who talk in generalities and say that virtue is "a good condition of the soul," or that it is "right conduct" or the like, delude themselves. Better than those who look for general definitions are those who, like Gorgias, enumerate the different virtues. So the poet Sophocles singles out "silence" as "bringing

[31]

credit to a woman," but that is not so for a man. This method of assessing virtue according to function is one that we should always follow. Take the child: he is not yet fully developed and his function is to grow up, so we cannot speak of his virtue as belonging absolutely to him, but only in relation to the progress of his development and to whoever is in charge of him. So too with slave and master; we laid it down that a slave's function is to perform menial tasks; so the amount of virtue required will not be very great, only enough to ensure that he does not neglect his work through loose living or mere fecklessness.

Source 4 from B. K. Workman, editor and translator, They Saw It Happen in Classical Times *(New York: Barnes & Noble, 1964), pp. 32–34. Reprinted by permission of Littlefield, Adams & Company and Basil Blackwell, Publishers.*

4. An Unknown Author's View of Athenian Democracy

Insolent conduct of slaves and resident aliens is everywhere rife in Athens. You cannot strike a slave there, and he will not get out of your way in the street. There is good reason for this being the local custom. If the law allowed a free-born citizen to strike a slave, an alien, or a freedman, then you would often strike an Athenian citizen in the mistaken impression that he was a slave. For the common people dress as poorly as slaves or aliens and their general appearance is no better. . . .

The common people take no supervisory interest in athletic or aesthetic shows, feeling that it is not right for them, since they know that they have not the ability to become expert at them. When it is necessary to provide men to put on stageshows or games or to finance and build triremes,[4] they know that impresarios come from the rich, the actors and chorus from the people. In the same way, organizers and ship-masters are the rich, while the common people take a subordinate part in the games and act as oarsmen for the triremes. But they do at least think it right to receive pay for singing or running or dancing or rowing in the fleet, to level up the incomes of rich and poor. The same holds good for the law courts as well; they are more interested in what profit they can make than in the true ends of justice. . . .

Of the mainland cities in the Athenian Empire, the large ones are governed by fear, the small ones by want. For all states must import and export, and this they cannot do unless they remain subject to the mistress of the seas.

4. **trireme:** standard Greek warship, about 120 feet long and rowed by 150 to 175 men; a ram on the bow was the trireme's main weapon.

Source 5 from Julia O'Faolain and Lauro Martines, editors, Not in God's Image: Women in History from the Greeks to the Victorians *(New York: Harper & Row, 1973), pp. 20–22. Adapted from several translations. Copyright © 1973 by Julia O'Faolain and Lauro Martines. Reprinted with permission of HarperCollins Publishers, Inc.*

5. From Xenophon, *The Economist*

"Here's another thing I'd like to ask you," said I. "Did you train your wife yourself or did she already know how to run a house when you got her from her father and mother?"

"What could she have known, Socrates," said he, "when I took her from her family? She wasn't yet fifteen. Until then she had been under careful supervision and meant to see, hear, and ask as little as possible. Don't you think it was already a lot that she should have known how to make a cloak of the wool she was given and how to dole out spinning to the servants? She had been taught to moderate her appetites, which, to my mind, is basic for both men's and women's education."

"So, apart from that," I asked, "it was you, Ischomachus, who had to train and teach her her household duties?"

"Yes," said Ischomachus, "but not before sacrificing to the gods. . . . And she solemnly swore before heaven that she would behave as I wanted, and it was clear that she would neglect none of my lessons."

"Tell me what you taught her first. . . ."

"Well, Socrates, as soon as I had tamed her and she was relaxed enough to talk, I asked her the following question: 'Tell me, my dear,' said I, 'do you understand why I married you and why your parents gave you to me? You know as well as I do that neither of us would have had trouble finding someone else to share our beds. But, after thinking about it carefully, it was you I chose and me your parents chose as the best partners we could find for our home and our children. Now, if God sends us children, we shall think about how best to raise them, for we share an interest in securing the best allies and support for our old age. For the moment we only share our home. . . .' "

"My wife answered, 'But how can I help? What am I capable of doing? It is on you that everything depends. My duty, my mother said, is to be well behaved.' "

" 'Oh, by Zeus,' said I, 'my father said the same to me. But the best behavior in a man and woman is that which will keep up their property and increase it as far as may be done by honest and legal means.' "

" 'And do you see some way,' asked my wife, 'in which I can help in this?' "

" '. . . It seems to me that God adapted women's nature to indoor and man's to outdoor work. . . . As Nature has entrusted woman with guarding the household supplies, and a timid nature is no disadvantage in such a job, it has endowed woman with more fear than man. . . . It is more proper for a woman

[33]

to stay in the house than out of doors and less so for a man to be indoors instead of out. If anyone goes against the nature given him by God and leaves his appointed post . . . he will be punished. . . . You must stay indoors and send out the servants whose work is outside and supervise those who work indoors, receive what is brought in, give out what is to be spent, plan ahead what should be stored and ensure that provisions for a year are not used up in a month. When the wool is brought in, you must see to it that clothes are made from it for whoever needs them and see to it that the corn is still edible. . . . Many of your duties will give you pleasure: for instance, if you teach spinning and weaving to a slave who did not know how to do this when you got her, you double her usefulness to yourself, or if you make a good housekeeper of one who didn't know how to do anything. . . . ' Then I took her around the family living rooms, which are pleasantly decorated, cool in summer and warm in winter. I pointed out how the whole house faces south so as to enjoy the winter sun. . . . I showed her the women's quarters which are separated from the men's by a bolted door to prevent anything being improperly removed and also to ensure that the slaves should not have children without our permission. For good slaves are usually even more devoted once they have a family; but good-for-nothings, once they begin to cohabit, have extra chances to get up to mischief."

Source 6 from B. Jowett, translator, The Dialogues of Plato, *revised edition, vol. 3 (Oxford: Oxford University Press, 1895, revised 1924), pp. 58, 100–101, 103, 106, 140–142, 147–148, 151, 159.*

6. From Plato, *The Republic*

Is not the love of learning the love of wisdom, which is philosophy?

They are the same, he replied.

And may we not say confidently of man also, that he who is likely to be gentle to his friends and acquaintances, must by nature be a lover of wisdom and knowledge?

That we may safely affirm.

Then he who is to be a really good and noble guardian of the State will require to unite in himself philosophy and spirit and swiftness and strength?

Undoubtedly.

Then we have found the desired natures; and now that we have found them, how are they to be reared and educated? Is not this an enquiry which may be expected to throw light on the greater enquiry which is our final end—How do justice and injustice grow up in States?

Adeimantus thought that the enquiry would be of great service to us. . . .

Come then, and let us pass a leisure hour in storytelling, and our story shall be the education of our heroes.

By all means.

And what shall be their education? Can we find a better than the traditional sort?—and this has two divisions, gymnastic for the body, and music[5] for the soul.

True. . . .

Very good, I said; then what is the next question? Must we not ask who are to be rulers and who subjects?

Certainly.

There can be no doubt that the elder must rule the younger.

Clearly.

And that the best of these must rule.

That is also clear.

Now, are not the best husbandmen those who are most devoted to husbandry?

Yes.

And as we are to have the best of guardians for our city, must they not be those who have most the character of guardians?

Yes. . . .

Then there must be a selection. Let us note among the guardians those who in their whole life show the greatest eagerness to do what is for the good of their country, and the greatest repugnance to do what is against her interests.

Those are the right men.

And they will have to be watched at every age, in order that we may see whether they preserve their resolution, and never, under the influence either of force or enchantment, forget or cast off their sense of duty to the State. . . . And he who at every age, as boy and youth and in mature life, has come out of the trial victorious and pure, shall be appointed a ruler and guardian of the State; he shall be honoured in life and death, and shall receive sepulture[6] and other memorials of honour, the greatest that we have to give. But him who fails, we must reject. I am inclined to think that this is the sort of way in which our rulers and guardians should be chosen and appointed. I speak generally, and not with any pretension to exactness.

And, speaking generally, I agree with you, he said. . . .

Then let us consider what will be their way of life, if they are to realize our idea of them. In the first place, none of them should have any property of his own beyond what is absolutely necessary; neither should they have a private house or store closed against any one who has a mind to enter; their provisions should be only such as are required by trained warriors, who are men of temperance and courage; they should agree to receive from the citizens a fixed rate of pay, enough to meet the expenses of the year and no more; and

5. By "music," the Athenians meant all that was sacred to the **muses**, the patron goddesses of the arts and sciences.

6. **sepulture:** a special burial ceremony.

[35]

they will go to mess and live together like soldiers in a camp. Gold and silver we will tell them that they have from God; the diviner metal is within them, and they have therefore no need of the dross which is current among men, and ought not to pollute the divine by any such earthly admixture; for that commoner metal has been the source of many unholy deeds, but their own is undefiled. And they alone of all the citizens may not touch or handle silver or gold, or be under the same roof with them, or wear them, or drink from them. And this will be their salvation, and they will be the saviours of the State. But should they ever acquire homes or lands or moneys of their own, they will become housekeepers and husbandmen instead of guardians, enemies and tyrants instead of allies of the other citizens; hating and being hated, plotting and being plotted against, they will pass their whole life in much greater terror of internal than of external enemies, and the hour of ruin, both to themselves and to the rest of the State, will be at hand. For all which reasons may we not say that thus shall our State be ordered, and that these shall be the regulations appointed by us for our guardians concerning their houses and all other matters?

Yes, said Glaucon. . . .

The part of the men has been played out, and now properly enough comes the turn of the women. Of them I will proceed to speak, and the more readily since I am invited by you.

For men born and educated like our citizens, the only way, in my opinion, of arriving at a right conclusion about the possession and use of women and children is to follow the path on which we originally started, when we said that the men were to be the guardians and watchdogs of the herd.

True.

Let us further suppose the birth and education of our women to be subject to similar or nearly similar regulations; then we shall see whether the result accords with our design.

What do you mean?

What I mean may be put into the form of a question, I said: Are dogs divided into hes and shes, or do they both share equally in hunting and in keeping watch and in the other duties of dogs? or do we entrust to the males the entire and exclusive care of the flocks, while we leave the females at home, under the idea that the bearing and suckling their puppies is labour enough for them?

No, he said, they share alike; the only difference between them is that the males are stronger and the females weaker.

But can you use different animals for the same purpose, unless they are bred and fed in the same way?

You cannot.

Then, if women are to have the same duties as men, they must have the same nurture and education?

Yes. . . .

My friend, I said, there is no special faculty of administration in a state which a woman has because she is a woman, or which a man has by virtue of his sex, but the gifts of nature are alike diffused in both; all the pursuits of men are the pursuits of women also, but in all of them a woman is inferior to a man.

Very true.

Then are we to impose all our enactments on men and none of them on women?

That will never do.

One woman has a gift of healing, another not; one is a musician, and another has no music in her nature?

Very true.

And one woman has a turn for gymnastic and military exercises, and another is unwarlike and hates gymnastics?

Certainly.

And one woman is a philosopher, and another is an enemy of philosophy; one has spirit, and another is without spirit?

That is also true.

Then one woman will have the temper of a guardian, and another not. Was not the selection of the male guardians determined by differences of this sort?

Yes.

Men and women alike possess the qualities which make a guardian; they differ only in their comparative strength or weakness.

Obviously.

And those women who have such qualities are to be selected as the companions and colleagues of men who have similar qualities and whom they resemble in capacity and in character?

Very true. . . .

The law, I said, which is the sequel of this and of all that has preceded, is to the following effect—"that the wives of our guardians are to be common, and their children are to be common, and no parent is to know his own child, nor any child his parent."

Yes, he said, that is a much greater wave than the other; and the possibility as well as the utility of such a law are far more questionable. . . .

Both the community of property and the community of families, as I am saying, tend to make them more truly guardians; they will not tear the city in pieces by differing about "mine" and "not mine"; each man dragging any acquisition which he has made into a separate house of his own, where he has a separate wife and children and private pleasures and pains; but all will be affected as far as may be by the same pleasures and pains because they are all of one opinion about what is near and dear to them, and therefore they all tend towards a common end.

Certainly, he replied.

Source 7 adapted from Orestis B. Doumanis and Paul Oliver, editors, Shelter in Greece *(Athens: Architecture in Greece Press, 1974), p. 25.*

7. Floor Plan of a House from Olynthus, 5th century B.C.

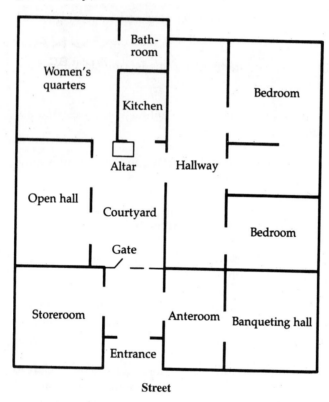

Source 8 adapted from A. W. Lawrence, Greek Architecture *(Baltimore: Penguin Books, 1957), p. 257.*

8. The Athenian Agora, 4th century B.C.

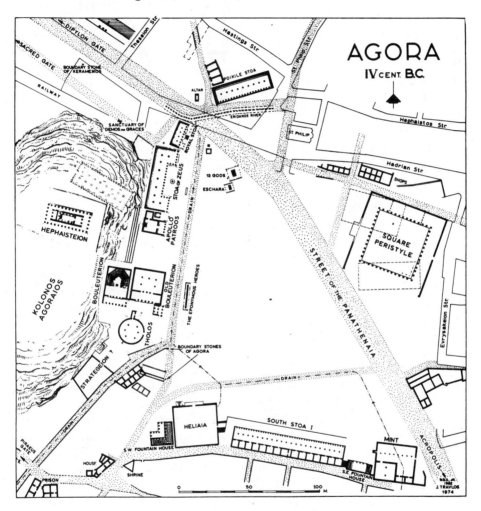

QUESTIONS TO CONSIDER

Before you start to think about the questions in this section, you may want to turn to your text to read (or reread) the section on Athens during the classical period. This can give you more background on the authors and on the political events that might have affected what they wrote.

Though some of the written selections in this chapter clearly describe ideals and others reality, still others blend realism and idealism, creating an idealized view of actual persons or situations. Which selections would you put in this last category? Why would these authors describe reality in an idealized manner? (To answer this question, you need to think about both the purpose of each selection and whether the author truly thought that what he was describing actually existed—in other words, whether this was a conscious or unconscious alteration of reality.)

Once you have labeled the written sources as ideals, reality, and idealizations of reality, go back to your list of the personal qualities of Athenians. Which qualities would you put in each of these three categories? Now that you know you are describing only an ideal or real characteristic, would you add any further qualities? The next step is to divide your list into categories of persons, for it is clear that most of the authors make great distinctions between male and female, adult and child, slave and free. Do all the authors agree on the qualities important in an ideal man, woman, or slave? Which authors have

opposing ideas? Why might this be so? Sometimes distinctions between categories are not clearly set out by the author; when Pericles, for instance, uses the words *person* and *people* in his funeral oration, one might think he was talking about all Athenians. Looking at your list divided into categories, of whom is Pericles speaking when he says "person" and "people"? Do any of the authors make distinctions between individuals of the same category based on such factors as wealth or education; for example, do they describe wealthy men differently from poor men, or set out different ideals for women who are interested in learning than for those who are not? If Athenians lived up to the ideals prescribed for them, what types of people would you expect to meet in the agora? What types of people would you not expect to meet?

Turning from the individual to social units, what qualities should the ideal Athenian household possess? How might real households work to emulate these ideals? Judging from information in the selections and in your text about Athenian marriage patterns, family life, and social life in general, did real Athenian households approach the ideal at all? How did their beliefs about the way households should be run affect the way Athenians designed their houses? How did the layout of a house work to make reality correspond with those ideals?

The qualities of governments as presented in the selections may also be classified as real, ideal, or idealized. Were any of the words you used to describe the Athenian government after first reading Pericles included in your final list? Does his idealized view of Athens come closer to the realistic view provided in the Melian debate or to the purely ideal view of Plato? After reading all the selections, would you put the quality "democracy" into the real or the ideal column for Athens? How would Athenians define democracy? How does the layout of the agora reflect this definition? Do all the authors agree that democracy is a desirable form of government? Judging from information in your text about politics in Athens in the fifth century, why would authors disagree on this matter? If you put democracy in the ideal column, what changes in existing conditions would have been necessary for it to become a reality?

The selections you have read offer varying opinions on a great many subjects, including the benefits of wealth and private property, the relationship between dominant and dependent states and between dominant and dependent individuals, the reasons for the differences between men and women, the role of naval power in foreign policy, and the causes of imperialism. All these issues have both ideal and real components, and you may want to think about them before you draw your final conclusions about classical Athens. How well did Athens live up to the ideals it set for itself? How did the different ideals held up for different categories of persons affect their participation in Athenian life?

EPILOGUE

We can find the ideals of the Athenians expressed not only in their philosophy, history, and architecture, as you have discovered here, but also in their drama, poetry, and sculpture. Indeed, most of the original sources we have from Athens are not realistic descriptions but either thoughts about ideals or idealizations of actual persons and episodes. That they are idealizations may be very clear to us as modern skeptical readers, but for a long time the statements in these sources were taken as literal truth. To give you an example, here is a quotation from Edith Hamilton, one of the

foremost historians of Greece, published in 1930:

> For a hundred years Athens was a city where the great spiritual forces that war in men's minds flowed together along in peace; law and freedom, truth and religion, beauty and goodness, the objective and the subjective—there was a truce to their eternal warfare, and the result was the balance and clarity, the harmony and completeness, that the word Greek has come to stand for.[7]

Given what you have just read, would you agree with her? Do you

7. Edith Hamilton, *The Greek Way* (New York: Norton, 1930), p. 206.

think everyone living in classical Athens would have agreed with her?

No matter how you have judged the relationship between ideal and reality in classical Athens, the ideals for the individual and state created there have significantly shaped the development of Western philosophy and social institutions. Roman philosophers closely studied Plato's *Republic,* and medieval philosophers were strongly influenced by Aristotle's *Politics.* Writers from the Renaissance to the present have invented ideal societies, "utopias" guided by wise leaders like Plato's guardians. Occasionally small groups of people have actually tried to set up working replicas of these ideal societies, frequently forbidding private property and the nuclear family as Plato did. Educational theorists have devised "perfect" school systems that, if not entirely successful when put into practice, have had their effect on real-life pedagogy. The Athenian ideal of

government by the people is reflected in the constitutions of modern democratic states, with the category "people" now including groups unthinkable to Pericles.

In terms of Athenian history, democracy was an extremely short-lived phenomenon. Widespread revolt broke out in the Athenian empire, and Sparta ultimately defeated Athens, bringing the Peloponnesian War to a close after twenty-seven years. This did not end warfare in Greece, however, as the city-states continued to battle among themselves. Finally, in 338 B.C., Greece was conquered by Philip of Macedon, and Athens became simply one small part of a much larger empire. From that point on, Athenian ideals of individual behavior would be emulated in Western culture, but democratic government would not again be attempted as an experiment in the real world for another 2,000 years.

CHAPTER THREE

THE ACHIEVEMENTS

OF AUGUSTUS

For many centuries, the seat of power in Rome was the senate, a body of men drawn from the most powerful and prominent Roman families that made all major political and military decisions. Under the leadership of the senate, Rome had gradually taken control of the entire Italian peninsula. It then conquered southern France and much of Spain, and, after defeating Carthage in the Punic Wars, occupied northern Africa. These territorial conquests altered the nature of power in Rome, however, because the armies that conquered and held the new territories pledged loyalty to their military leaders and not to the senate. During the first century before Christ, several of these semi-independent armies challenged the senate's power, and civil war erupted in many parts of the Roman territory. The city itself was plundered several times by rival legions, and trade and communications were frequently dis-

rupted. In 60 B.C., three army generals—Pompey, Crassus, and Julius Caesar—decided to form a political alliance, the triumvirate, leaving the senate intact but without much actual power.

All three of these generals were ambitious men who were unwilling to share power with anyone for very long. The senate was especially worried about Julius Caesar, who was gathering an increasingly larger army in Gaul (present-day France), and decided to put its trust in Pompey, whose base of power lay in Greece. (Crassus had meanwhile died in battle.) It ordered Caesar to disband his army and not to return to Rome, setting the Rubicon River near Ravenna in northern Italy as the line he must not cross. In 49 B.C., Caesar crossed the Rubicon (an expression we still use for an irrevocable decision), directly challenging the power of the senate and of Pompey. His armies quickly defeated those of the senate in Italy, and within a few months he held the entire Italian peninsula. From there Caesar turned his attention to Pompey's army, which his forces also defeated in 48 B.C., leaving him in control of all the Roman territory. Though he did not disband the senate, he did begin to shape the government to his liking, appointing officials and army officers and directly overseeing the administration of the provinces. He increased the size of the senate from 600 to 900 members by padding it with his followers, many of whom came from the provinces.

Caesar's meteoric and extralegal rise to power created great resentment among many Roman senators. Intensely proud of Roman traditions and of their own families' long-standing political power, they felt that Caesar was degrading the senate by adding unsophisticated rural representatives. A group of senators, led by Brutus and Cassius, decided to assassinate Caesar, which they did on the steps of the Roman senate on March 15, 44 B.C. The conspirators had not thought much beyond this act, however, and Caesar's death led not to peace but to a renewal of civil war. Some of the army was loyal to the assassins; some to Mark Antony, an associate of Caesar's; and some to Caesar's nephew and adopted son, Octavian. At first Mark Antony and Octavian cooperated to defeat the assassins, but then they turned against each other. The war dragged on for over a decade, with Octavian's forces gradually gaining more territory. Octavian won the support of many Romans by convincing them that Antony was plotting with Cleopatra, queen of Egypt, and in 31 B.C. his forces decisively de-

feated those of Antony at the naval battle of Actium. Antony and his ally Cleopatra committed suicide, leaving Octavian sole ruler of the Mediterranean world.

The problem now facing Octavian was the same one Julius Caesar had confronted twelve years earlier: how to transform a state won by military force into a stable political system. Caesar's answer—personal, autocratic rule—had led to his assassination at the hands of disgruntled senators. This lesson was not lost on Octavian, who realized that directly opposing the strong republican tradition in Rome could be very dangerous.

This tradition had arisen from both political reality—the senate had held actual power for many generations—and Roman political theory. The Romans held that their form of government had been given to them by the gods, who had conferred authority on Romulus, the mythical founder of Rome. That authority was later passed on to the senate, whose original function was to consult the gods about actions Rome should take. The senate in turn passed on authority to the rest of the government bureaucracy and to male heads of household, for in Rome households were considered, as in Athens, the smallest unit of government. Only male heads of household could sit in the senate, for only such individuals were regarded as worthy enough to consult the gods on matters of great importance to the state. This meant that Roman society was extremely patriarchal, with fathers having (at least in theory) absolute control over their wives, children, and servants.

This divinely ordained authority could always be distributed downward as the political bureaucracy grew, but to do away with existing institutions was extremely dangerous. Any radical transformation of the structure of government, especially any change in the authority of the senate, would have been regarded as impious.

Octavian had himself grown up in this tradition and at least to some degree shared these ideas about authority and the divine roots of the Roman political system. He realized that he could be more effective—and probably would live longer—if he worked through, rather than against, existing political institutions. Moreover, serious problems existed that had to be faced immediately, and after years of civil war, the government bureaucracy was no longer firmly in place to deal with them. Octavian needed to appoint officials and governors and reestablish law and order throughout Roman territory without offending the senate by acting like an autocrat or dictator.

In the eyes of many of his contemporaries, Octavian accomplished this admittedly difficult task very well. The senate conferred on him the name he is usually known by, Augustus, meaning "blessed" or "magnificent." Later historians regarded Augustus, rather than Julius Caesar, as the creator of the Roman Empire. Your task in this chapter will be to evaluate these judgments. How did Augustus transform the Roman republic into an empire? Why was he successful where Julius Caesar had not been?

SOURCES AND METHOD

As you think about these questions, you can see that they involve two somewhat different components: the process by which Augustus made changes and the results of these changes, or what we might term the *means* and the *ends*. Both are important to consider in assessing the achievements of any political leader, and both have been used by the contemporaries of Augustus, later Roman writers, and modern historians in evaluating the first Roman emperor's reign.

One of the best sources for observing the process of political change is laws, especially basic laws such as constitutions that set out governmental structure. Rome was a society in which law was extremely important and was explicitly written down, unlike many early societies, in which laws were handed down orally from generation to generation. As the Romans conquered Europe and the Mediterranean, they brought their legal system with them; consequently, Roman law forms the basis of most modern Western legal systems, with England and thus the United States the most notable exceptions.

We encounter some serious difficulties in using laws as our source material for the reign of Augustus, however. Given Roman ideas about authority and the strength of Roman tradition, would you expect him to have made major legal changes? Augustus, after all, described his aims and his actions as restoring republican government; if we use only the constitution of Rome as a source, we might be tempted to believe him. No new office was created for the emperor. Instead, he carefully preserved all traditional offices while gradually taking over many of them himself. Augustus was both a consul and a tribune, although the former office was usually reserved for a patrician and the latter for a plebeian. Later the senate appointed him *imperator,* or commander-in-chief of the army, and gave him direct control of many of the outlying provinces. These provinces furnished grain supplies essential to the people of Rome as well as soldiers loyal to Augustus rather than to the senate. The senate also gave him the honorary title of *princeps* (or "first citizen"), the title he preferred, which gradually lost its republican origins and gained the overtones of "monarch" evident in its modern English derivative, "prince." Augustus recognized the importance of religion to most Romans, and in 12 B.C. he had himself named *pontifex maximus,* or "supreme priest." He encouraged the building of temples dedicated to "Rome and Augustus," laying the foundations for the growth of a ruler cult closely linked with patriotic loyalty to Rome.

None of these innovations required any alteration in the basic constitution of Rome. What did change, however, was the tone of many laws, particularly those from the outlying provinces, where Augustus could be more open about the transformation he was working without bringing on the wrath of the senate. Our first two selections, then, are decrees and laws from Roman territories, where we can perhaps see some hint of the gradual development of the republic into an empire.

Source 1 is a decree by Augustus himself, an inscription dated 4 B.C. from the Greek city of Cyrene. Like all laws, it was passed in response to a perceived problem. What problem does the decree confront? What procedure does it provide to solve this problem? What complications does it anticipate, and how does it try to solve them? You will notice that the decree itself is set within a long framework giving the reasons it was issued. This is true for many laws, including the American Constitution, which begins, "We the people of the United States, in order to form a more perfect union, establish justice, insure domestic tranquillity." Why does Augustus say he is passing this law? This framework can also give you clues to the relationship between Augustus and the senate. How is this relationship described, and what does Augustus's attitude appear to be?

The second law is an inscription dated A.D. 11 from an altar in the city of Narbonne in southern France. This law was passed by the local government, not the central Roman authorities. What does it order the population to do? Although the law itself does not state why it was passed, what might some reasons have been? What does the law indicate about attitudes toward Augustus and toward Roman authorities?

Another valuable source for examining the achievements of Augustus consists of the comments of his contemporaries and later Roman historians. Because Romans had such a strong sense of their own traditions, they were fascinated by history and were ever eager to point out how the hand of the gods operated in a way that allowed Rome to conquer most of the Western world. In the century before Augustus took over, it looked to many Romans as if the gods had forgotten Rome, leaving its citizens to kill each other in revolutions and civil wars. Augustus's military successes and political acumen seemed to show that he had the gods on his side, so writers delighted in extolling his accomplishments. Augustus's astuteness also extended to the world of literature and the arts, and he hired writers, sculptors, architects, and painters to glorify Rome, causing his own reputation no harm in the process. Many of the poems and histories are blatant hero worship, others communicate a more balanced view, and, because Augustus was not totally successful at winning everyone over to his side, some authors are openly critical.

Sources 3 through 6 are assessments by various Romans of Augustus's rule. As you read them, first try to gauge each author's basic attitude toward Augustus. What does he find to praise or blame? Does his judgment appear overly positive or negative? Does he sound objective? In answering these questions, you will need to pay attention not only to the content of the selection but also to the specific words each author chooses. What kinds of adjectives does he use to describe Augustus's person and political actions? Once you have as-

sessed the basic attitude of each author, identify what he regards as important in Augustus's reign. To what factors does he attribute Augustus's success? How does he describe the process by which the Roman republic was turned into an empire? What reasons does he give for Augustus's success and Julius Caesar's failure?

A bit of background on each of these selections will help you put them in better perspective. Source 3 was written by Horace, a poet living at the court of Augustus. This is an excerpt from his *Odes,* a literary rather than a primarily historical work. Source 4, an excerpt from Suetonius's biography of Augustus, was composed during the first half of the second century. Suetonius, private secretary to the emperor Hadrian, was keenly interested in the private as well as the public lives of the Roman emperors. Source 5 is taken from the long history of Rome by the politician and historian Dio Cassius (ca 150–235). Source 6 is drawn from the *Annals* of Tacitus, an orator and historian from a well-to-do Roman family. Sources 4 through 6 were written between one and two centuries after the events they present and are thus "history" as we know it, describing events after they happened.

Source 7 is a third type of evidence, namely, Augustus's own description of his rule. Usually called the *Res Gestae Divi Augusti,* it is an inscription he composed shortly before the end of his life. In this piece, following a long Roman tradition of inscriptions commemorating distinguished citizens, he describes the honors conferred on him as well as his accomplishments. Like all autobiographical statements, it is intended not simply as an objective description of a ruler's deeds but specifically as a vehicle for all that Augustus most wanted people to remember about this reign. Even though it is subjective, the *Res Gestae* is unique and invaluable as a primary source because it gives us Augustus's own version of the transformations he wrought in Roman society. As you read it, compare Augustus's descriptions of his deeds with those of the historians you have just read. What does Augustus regard as his most important accomplishments?

Many of the best sources for Augustus, of course, as for all of ancient history, are not written but archaeological. In fact, two of the sources we have looked at so far, the decree issued by Augustus and the inscription from Narbonne (Sources 1 and 2), are actually archaeological as well as written sources because they are inscriptions carved in stone. Thus, unlike other texts from the ancient world, including such basic ones as Plato's *Republic,* we have the original text and not a later copy.

Inscriptions are just one of many types of archaeological evidence. As the Romans conquered land after land, they introduced not only their legal code but their monetary system as well. Roman coins have been found throughout all of Europe and the Near East, far beyond the borders of the Roman Empire. *Numismatics,* the study of coins, can thus provide us with clues available from no other source, for coins have the great advantage of being both durable and valuable. Though their value sometimes

works to render them less durable—people melt them down to make other coins or to use the metal in other ways—it also makes them one of the few material goods that people hide in great quantities. Their owners intend to dig them up later, of course, but die or forget where they have buried them, leaving great caches of coins for later archaeologists and historians.

Roman coins differ markedly from modern coins in some respects. Though the primary function of both is to serve as a means of exchange, Roman coins were also transmitters of political propaganda. One side usually displayed a portrait of the emperor, chosen very carefully by the emperor himself to emphasize certain qualities. The reverse side often depicted a recent victory, anniversary, or other important event, or the personification of an abstract quality of virtue such as health or liberty. Modern coins also feature portraits, pictures, and slogans, but they tend to stay the same for decades, and so we pay very little attention to what is on them. Roman emperors, on the other hand, issued new coins frequently, expecting people to look at them. Most of the people who lived in the Roman Empire were illiterate, with no chance to read about the illustrious deeds of the emperor, but they did come into contact with coins nearly every day. From these coins they learned what the emperor looked like, what he had recently done, or what qualities to associate with him, for even illiterate people could identify the symbols for such abstract virtues as liberty or victory. Over one hundred different portraits of Augustus have been found on coins, providing us with additional clues about the achievements he most wanted to emphasize.

Once you have read the written documents, look at the two illustrations of coins, Sources 8 and 9. On the first, issued in 2 B.C., the lettering reads CAESAR AUGUSTUS DIVI F PATER PATRIAE, or "Augustus Caesar, son of a God, Father of the Fatherland." (Julius Caesar had been deified by the senate after his assassination, which is why Augustus called himself "son of a God.") Augustus is crowned with what appears to be a wreath of wheat stalks; this crown was the exclusive right of the priests of one of Rome's oldest religious groups that honored agricultural gods. The second coin, issued between 20 and 16 B.C., shows Augustus alongside the winged figure of the goddess Victory in a chariot atop a triumphal arch that stands itself on top of a viaduct; the inscription reads QUOD VIAE MUN SUNT, "because the roads have been reinforced." Think about the message Augustus was trying to convey with each of these coins. Even if you could not read the words, what impression of the emperor would you have from coins like these?

Issuing coins was one way for an emperor to celebrate and communicate his achievements; building was another. As you have read in Augustus's autobiography, he had many structures—stadiums, marketplaces, and temples—built for various purposes. He, and later Roman emperors, also built structures that were purely symbolic, the most impressive of which were celebratory arches,

built to commemorate an achievement or a military victory. The second coin shows Augustus standing on top of such an arch; Source 10 is a photograph of the arch of Augustus that still stands at Rimini. This arch was built at one end of the Flaminian Way, which Augustus reconstructed, as you have read in his autobiography; a similar arch was built at the other end in Rome. As you did when looking at the coins, think about the message such an arch conveys. It was put up with the agreement of the senate; does it give you a sense of republicanism or empire?

Roads are another prime archaeological source, closely related to the aqueducts we examined in Chapter 1. The Romans initially built roads to help their army move more quickly; once built, however, the road system facilitated trade and commerce as well. Roads are thus symbols of power as well as a means to maintain and extend it. Archaeologists have long studied the expansion of the Roman road system, and their findings can most easily be seen diagrammed on maps. Though maps do not have the immediacy of actual archaeological remains, they are based on such remains and enable us to detect patterns and make comparisons over time.

Selections 11 and 12 are maps of the major Roman roads existing before the reign of Augustus, those built or reconstructed during his reign, and the Roman road system at its farthest extent. Compare the first map with the information you have obtained from Augustus himself about his expansion of the frontiers of

Rome (Source 7, paragraph 26). Notice that he mentions only the western part of the Roman Empire; do the roads built during his reign reflect this western orientation? What do the later road-building patterns shown in Source 12 tell us about the goals and successes of later Roman emperors?

THE EVIDENCE

Sources 1 through 3 from Naphtali Lewis and Meyer Reinhold, editors and translators, Roman Civilization, *vol. 2,* The Empire *(New York: Columbia University Press, 1955), pp. 39–42; p. 62; p. 20. Reprinted with permission of Columbia University Press, 562 W. 113th St., New York, NY 10025, via Copyright Clearance Center, Inc.*

1. Decree Issued by Emperor Augustus, 4 B.C.

The Emperor Caesar Augustus, *pontifex maximus*, holding the tribunician power for the nineteenth year, declares:

A decree of the senate was passed in the consulship of Gaius Calvisius and Lucius Passienus, with me as one of those present at the writing. Since it affects the welfare of the allies of the Roman people, I have decided to send it into the provinces, appended to this my prefatory edict, so that it may be known to all who are under our care. From this it will be evident to all the inhabitants of the provinces how much both I and the senate are concerned that none of our subjects should suffer any improper treatment or any extortion.

DECREE OF THE SENATE

Whereas the consuls Gaius Calvisius Sabinus and Lucius Passienus Rufus spoke "Concerning matters affecting the security of the allies of the Roman people which the Emperor Caesar Augustus, our *princeps*, following the recommendation of the council which he had drawn by lot from among the senate, desired to be brought before the senate by us," the senate passed the following decree:

Whereas our ancestors established legal process for extortion so that the allies might more easily be able to take action for any wrongs done them and recover moneys extorted from them, and whereas this type of process is sometimes very expensive and troublesome for those in whose interest the law was enacted, because poor people or persons weak with illness or age are dragged from far-distant provinces as witnesses, the senate decrees as follows:

If after the passage of this decree of the senate any of the allies, desiring to recover extorted moneys, public or private, appear and so depose before one of the magistrates who is authorized to convene the senate, the magistrate—except where the extorter faces a capital charge—shall bring them before the senate as soon as possible and shall assign them any advocate they themselves request to speak in their behalf before the senate; but no one who has in accordance with the laws been excused from this duty shall be required to serve as advocate against his will. . . .

The judges chosen shall hear and inquire into only those cases in which a man is accused of having appropriated money from a community or from private parties; and, rendering their decision within thirty days, they shall order him to restore such sum of money, public or private, as the accusers prove was taken from them. Those whose duty it is to inquire into and pronounce judgment in these cases shall, until they complete the inquiry and pronounce their judgment, be exempted from all public duties except public worship. . . .

The senate likewise decrees that the judges who are selected in accordance with this decree of the senate shall pronounce in open court each his several finding, and what the majority pronounces shall be the verdict.

2. Inscription from the City of Narbonne, A.D. 11

In the consulship of Titus Statilius Taurus and Lucius Cassius Longinus, September 22. Vow taken to the divine spirit of Augustus by the populace of the Narbonensians in perpetuity: "May it be good, favorable, and auspicious to the Emperor Caesar Augustus, son of a god, father of his country, *pontifex maximus*, holding the tribunician power for the thirty-fourth year; to his wife, children, and house; to the Roman senate and people; and to the colonists[1] and residents of the Colonia Julia Paterna of Narbo Martius,[2] who have bound themselves to worship his divine spirit in perpetuity!"

The populace of the Narbonensians has erected in the forum at Narbo an altar at which every year on September 23—the day on which the good fortune of the age bore him to be ruler of the world—three Roman *equites*[3] from the populace and three freedmen shall sacrifice one animal each and shall at their own expense on that day provide the colonists and residents with incense and wine for supplication to his divine spirit. And on September 24 they shall likewise provide incense and wine for the colonists and residents. Also on January 1 they shall provide incense and wine for the colonists and residents. Also on January 7, the day on which he first entered upon the command of the world, they shall make supplication with incense and wine, and

---

1. The word *colonist* has a very specific meaning in Roman history. **Colonists** were Romans, often retired soldiers, who were granted land in the outlying provinces in order to build up Roman strength there. They were legally somewhat distinct from native residents, which is why this law uses the phrase "colonists and residents" to make it clear that both groups were required to follow its provisions.

2. The long phrase "Colonia Julia Pasterna of Narbo Martius" is the official and complete Roman name for the town of Narbo, which we now call Narbonne.

3. **equites:** cavalry of the Roman army.

shall sacrifice one animal each, and shall provide incense and wine for the colonists and residents on that day. And on May 31, because on that day in the consulship of Titus Statilius Taurus and Manius Aemilius Lepidus he reconciled the populace to the decurions,[4] they shall sacrifice one animal each and shall provide the colonists and residents with incense and wine for supplication to his divine spirit. And of these three Roman *equites* and three freedmen one . . . [The rest of this inscription is lost.]

3. From Horace, *Odes*

Thine age, O Caesar, has brought back fertile crops to the fields and has restored to our own Jupiter the military standards stripped from the proud columns of the Parthians;[5] has closed Janus' temple[6] freed of wars; has put reins on license overstepping righteous bounds; has wiped away our sins and revived the ancient virtues through which the Latin name and the might of Italy waxed great, and the fame and majesty of our empire were spread from the sun's bed in the west to the east. As long as Caesar is the guardian of the state, neither civil dissension nor violence shall banish peace, nor wrath that forges swords and brings discord and misery to cities. Not those who drink the deep Danube shall violate the orders of Caesar, nor the Getae, nor the Seres,[7] nor the perfidious Parthians, nor those born by the Don River. And we, both on profane and sacred days, amidst the gifts of merry Bacchus, together with our wives and children, will first duly pray to the gods; then, after the tradition of our ancestors, in songs to the accompaniment of Lydian flutes we will hymn leaders whose duty is done.

Source 4 from Suetonius, The Lives of the Twelve Caesars, *edited and translated by Joseph Gavorse (New York: Modern Library, 1931), p. 89.*

4. From Suetonius, *Life of Augustus*

The whole body of citizens with a sudden unanimous impulse proffered him the title of "father of his country"—first the plebs, by a deputation sent to

4. **decurion:** member of a town council.

5. The Parthians were an empire located in the region occupied by present-day Iraq. They had defeated Roman armies led by Mark Antony and had taken the Roman military standards, that is, the flags and banners of the army they defeated. Augustus recovered these standards, an important symbolic act, even though he did not conquer the Parthians.

6. This was a small temple in Rome that was ordered closed whenever peace reigned throughout the whole Roman Empire. During the reign of Augustus it was closed three times.

7. The Getae and the Seres were people who lived in the regions occupied by present-day Romania and Ukraine.

Antium, and then, because he declined it, again at Rome as he entered the theater, which they attended in throngs, all wearing laurel wreaths; the senate afterwards in the senate house, not by a decree or by acclamation, but through Valerius Messala. He, speaking for the whole body, said: "Good fortune and divine favor attend thee and thy house, Caesar Augustus; for thus we feel that we are praying for lasting prosperity for our country and happiness for our city. The senate in accord with the Roman people hails thee 'Father of thy Country.' " Then Augustus with tears in his eyes replied as follows (and I have given his exact words, as I did those of Messala): "Having attained my highest hopes, members of the senate, what more have I to ask of the immortal gods than that I may retain this same unanimous approval of yours to the very end of my life?"

Sources 5 through 7 from Naphtali Lewis and Meyer Reinhold, editors and translators, Roman Civilization, *vol. 2,* The Empire *(New York: Columbia University Press, 1955), pp. 4–8; p. 4; pp. 9–10, 12, 14–16, 17, 19. Reprinted with permission of Columbia University Press, 562 W. 113th St., New York, NY 10025, via Copyright Clearance Center, Inc.*

5. From Dio Cassius, *Roman History*

In this way the power of both people and senate passed entirely into the hands of Augustus, and from this time there was, strictly speaking, a monarchy; for monarchy would be the truest name for it, even if two or three men later held the power jointly. Now, the Romans so detested the title "monarch" that they called their emperors neither dictators nor kings nor anything of this sort. Yet, since the final authority for the government devolves upon them, they needs must be kings. The offices established by the laws, it is true, are maintained even now, except that of censor; but the entire direction and administration is absolutely in accordance with the wishes of the one in power at the time. And yet, in order to preserve the appearance of having this authority not through their power but by virtue of the laws, the emperors have taken to themselves all the offices (including the titles) which under the Republic possessed great power with the consent of the people—with the exception of the dictatorship. Thus, they very often become consuls, and they are always styled proconsuls whenever they are outside the *pomerium*.[8] The title *imperator* is held by them for life, not only by those who have won victories in battle but also by all the rest, to indicate their absolute power, instead of the title "king" or "dictator." These latter titles they have never assumed since they fell out of use in the constitution, but the actuality of those offices is secured to them by the appellation *imperator*. By virtue of the titles named, they secure the right to make levies, collect funds, declare war, make peace, and

8. **pomerium:** the city limits of Rome.

rule foreigners and citizens alike everywhere and always—even to the extent of being able to put to death both *equites* and senators inside the *pomerium*—and all the other powers once granted to the consuls and other officials possessing independent authority; and by virtue of holding the censorship they investigate our lives and morals as well as take the census, enrolling some in the equestrian and senatorial orders and removing others from these orders according to their will. By virtue of being consecrated in all the priesthoods and, in addition, from their right to bestow most of them upon others, as well as from the fact that, even if two or three persons rule jointly, one of them is *pontifex maximus*, they hold in their own hands supreme authority over all matters both profane and sacred. The tribunician power, as it is called, which once the most influential men used to hold, gives them the right to nullify the effects of the measures taken by any other official, in case they do not approve, and makes their persons inviolable; and if they appear to be wronged in even the slightest degree, not merely by deed but even by word, they may destroy the guilty party as one accursed, without a trial.

Thus by virtue of these Republican titles they have clothed themselves with all the powers of the government, so that they actually possess all the prerogatives of kings without the usual title. For the appellation "Caesar" or "Augustus" confers upon them no actual power but merely shows in the one case that they are the successors of their family line, and in the other the splendor of their rank. The name "Father" perhaps gives them a certain authority over us all—the authority which fathers once had over their children; yet it did not signify this at first, but betokened honor and served as an admonition both to them to love their subjects as they would their children; and to their subjects to revere them as they would their fathers. . . .

The senate as a body, it is true, continued to sit in judgment as before, and in certain cases transacted business with embassies and envoys from both peoples and kings; and the people and the plebs, moreover, continued to come together for the elections; but nothing was actually done that did not please Caesar. At any rate, in the case of those who were to hold office, he himself selected and nominated some; and though he left the election of others in the hands of the people and the plebs, in accordance with the ancient practice, yet he took care that no persons should hold office who were unfit or elected as the result of factious combinations or bribery.

Such were the arrangements made, generally speaking, at that time; for in reality Caesar himself was destined to have absolute power in all matters for life, because he was not only in control of money matters (nominally, to be sure, he had separated the public funds from his own, but as a matter of fact he spent the former also as he saw fit) but also in control of the army. At all events, when his ten-year period came to an end, there was voted him another five years, then five more, after that ten, and again another ten, and then ten for the fifth time, so that by the succession of ten-year periods he continued to be sole ruler for life. And it is for this reason that the subsequent monarchs, though no longer appointed for a specified period but for their whole life once for all, nevertheless always held a celebration every ten years, as if then renewing their sovereignty once more; and this is done even at the present day.

Now, Caesar had received many privileges previously, when the question of declining the sovereignty and that of apportioning the provinces were under discussion. For the right to fasten laurels to the front of the imperial residence and to hang the civic crown above the doors was then voted him to symbolize the fact that he was always victorious over enemies and savior of the citizens. The imperial palace is called Palatium, not because it was ever decreed that this should be its name but because Caesar dwelt on the Palatine and had his military headquarters there. . . . Hence, even if the emperor resides somewhere else, his dwelling retains the name of Palatium.

And when he had actually completed the reorganization, the name Augustus was at length bestowed upon him by the senate and by the people. . . . He took the title of Augustus, signifying that he was more than human; for all most precious and sacred objects are termed *augusta*. For which reason they called him also in Greek *sebastos* . . . meaning an august person.

6. From Tacitus, *Annals*

After the death of Brutus and Cassius, there was no longer any army loyal to the Republic. . . . Then, laying aside the title of triumvir and parading as a consul, and professing himself satisfied with the tribunician power for the protection of the plebs, Augustus enticed the soldiers with gifts, the people with grain, and all men with the allurement of peace, and gradually grew in power, concentrating in his own hands the functions of the senate, the magistrates, and the laws. No one opposed him, for the most courageous had fallen in battle or in the proscription. As for the remaining nobles, the readier they were for slavery, the higher were they raised in wealth and offices, so that, aggrandized by the revolution, they preferred the safety of the present to the perils of the past. Nor did the provinces view with disfavor this state of affairs, for they distrusted the government of the senate and the people on account of the struggles of the powerful and the rapacity of the officials, while the protection afforded them by the laws was inoperative, as the provinces were repeatedly thrown into confusion by violence, intrigue, and finally bribery. . . .

At home all was peaceful; the officials bore the same titles as before. The younger generation was born after the victory of Actium, and even many of the older generation had been born during the civil wars. How few were left who had seen the Republic!

Thus the constitution had been transformed, and there was nothing at all left of the good old way of life. Stripped of equality, all looked to the directives of a *princeps* with no apprehension for the present, while Augustus in the vigorous years of his life maintained his power, that of his family, and peace.

7. From Augustus, *Res Gestae Divi Augusti*

1. At the age of nineteen, on my own initiative and at my own expense, I raised an army by means of which I liberated the Republic, which was oppressed by the tyranny of a faction. For which reason the senate, with honorific decrees, made me a member of its order in the consulship of Gaius Pansa and Aulus Hirtius, giving me at the same time consular rank in voting, and granted me the *imperium.* It ordered me as propraetor, together with the consuls, to see to it that the state suffered no harm. Moreover, in the same year, when both consuls had fallen in the war, the people elected me consul and a triumvir for the settlement of the commonwealth.

2. Those who assassinated my father I drove into exile, avenging their crime by due process of law; and afterwards when they waged war against the state, I conquered them twice on the battlefield.

3. I waged many wars throughout the whole world by land and by sea, both civil and foreign, and when victorious I spared all citizens who sought pardon. Foreign peoples who could safely be pardoned I preferred to spare rather than to extirpate. . . . Though the Roman senate and people unitedly agreed that I should be elected soul guardian of the laws and morals with supreme authority, I refused to accept any office offered me which was contrary to the traditions of our ancestors. . . .

9. The senate decreed that vows for my health should be offered up every fifth year by the consuls and priests. In fulfillment of those vows, games were often celebrated during my lifetime, sometimes by the four most distinguished colleges of priests, sometimes by the consuls. Moreover, the whole citizen body, with one accord, both individually and as members of municipalities, prayed continuously for my health at all the shrines.

10. My name was inserted, by decree of the senate, in the hymn of the Salian priests. And it was enacted by law that I should be sacrosanct in perpetuity and that I should possess the tribunician power as long as I live. I declined to become *pontifex maximus* in place of a colleague while he was still alive, when the people offered me that priesthood, which my father had held. A few years later, in the consulship of Publius Sulpicius and Gaius Valgius, I accepted this priesthood, when death removed the man who had taken possession of it at a time of civil disturbance; and from all Italy a multitude flocked to my election such as had never previously been recorded at Rome. . . .

17. Four times I came to the assistance of the treasury with my own money, transferring to those in charge of the treasury 150,000,000 sesterces. And in the consulship of Marcus Lepidus and Lucius Arruntius I transferred out of my own patrimony 170,000,000 sesterces to the soldiers' bonus fund, which was

established on my advice for the purpose of providing bonuses for soldiers who had completed twenty or more years of service.

18. From the year in which Gnaeus Lentulus and Publius Lentulus were consuls, whenever the provincial taxes fell short, in the case sometimes of 100,000 persons and sometimes of many more, I made up their tribute in grain and in money from my own grain stores and my own patrimony. . . .

20. I repaired the Capitol and the theater of Pompey with enormous expenditures on both works, without having my name inscribed on them. I repaired the conduits of the aqueducts which were falling into ruin in many places because of age, and I doubled the capacity of the aqueduct called Marcia by admitting a new spring into its conduit. I completed the Julian Forum and the basilica which was between the temple of Castor and the temple of Saturn, works begun and far advanced by my father, and when the same basilica was destroyed by fire, I enlarged its site and began rebuilding the structure, which is to be inscribed with the names of my sons; and in case it should not be completed while I am still alive, I left instructions that the work be completed by my heirs. In my sixth consulship I repaired eighty-two temples of the gods in the city, in accordance with a resolution of the senate, neglecting none which at that time required repair. In my seventh consulship I reconstructed the Flaminian Way from the city as far as Ariminum,[9] and also all the bridges except the Mulvian and the Minucian. . . .

22. I gave a gladiatorial show three times in my own name, and five times in the names of my sons or grandsons; at these shows about 10,000 fought. Twice I presented to the people in my own name an exhibition of athletes invited from all parts of the world, and a third time in the name of my grandson. I presented games in my own name four times, and in addition twenty-three times in the place of other magistrates. On behalf of the college of fifteen, as master of that college, with Marcus Agrippa as my colleague, I celebrated the Secular Games[10] in the consulship of Gaius Furnius and Gaius Silanus. In my thirteenth consulship I was the first to celebrate the Games of Mars, which subsequently the consuls, in accordance with a decree of the senate and a law, have regularly celebrated in the succeeding years. Twenty-six times I provided for the people, in my own name or in the names of my sons or grandsons, hunting spectacles of African wild beasts in the circus or in the Forum or in the amphitheaters; in these exhibitions about 3,500 animals were killed.

9. Present-day Rimini, Italy.

10. The Secular Games were an enormous series of athletic games, festivals, and banquets that Augustus ordered held in 17 B.C. Though called "secular," they were held in honor of the gods and were directed by the College of Fifteen, a board that oversaw sacrifices to the gods. All adult Roman citizens were expected to view the games out of religious duty.

23. I presented to the people an exhibition of a naval battle across the Tiber where the grove of the Caesars now is, having had the site excavated 1,800 feet in length and 1,200 feet in width. In this exhibition thirty beaked ships, triremes or biremes, and in addition a great number of smaller vessels engaged in combat. On board these fleets, exclusive of rowers, there were about 3,000 combatants. . . .

26. I extended the frontiers of all the provinces of the Roman people on whose boundaries were peoples subject to our empire. I restored peace to the Gallic and Spanish provinces and likewise to Germany, that is, to the entire region bounded by the Ocean from Gades to the mouth of the Elbe River. I caused peace to be restored in the Alps, from the region nearest to the Adriatic Sea as far as the Tuscan Sea, without undeservedly making war against any people. My fleet sailed the Ocean from the mouth of the Rhine eastward as far as the territory of the Cimbrians,[11] to which no Roman previously had penetrated either by land or by sea. . . .

34. In my sixth and seventh consulships, after I had put an end to the civil wars, having attained supreme power by universal consent, I transferred the state from my own power to the control of the Roman senate and people. For this service of mine I received the title of Augustus by decree of the senate, and the doorposts of my house were publicly decked with laurels, the civic crown was affixed over my doorway, and a golden shield was set up in the Julian senate house, which, as the inscription on this shield testifies, the Roman senate and people gave me in recognition of my valor, clemency, justice, and devotion. After that time I excelled all in authority, but I possessed no more power than the others who were my colleagues in each magistracy.

35. When I held my thirteenth consulship, the senate, the equestrian order, and the entire Roman people gave me the title of "father of the country" and decreed that this title should be inscribed in the vestibule of my house, in the Julian senate house, and in the Augustan Forum on the pedestal of the chariot which was set up in my honor by decree of the senate. At the time I wrote this document I was in my seventy-sixth year.

11. Near present-day Hamburg, Germany.

Sources 8 and 9 from The American Numismatic Society, New York.

8. Roman Coin Issued 2 B.C.

9. Roman Coin Issued 20–16 B.C.

Source 10 from Alinari/Art Resource. Photo by Stab D. Anderson, 1931.

10. Arch of Augustus at Rimini

Source 11 adapted from sketches by Merry E. Wiesner.

11. Main Roman Roads, 31 B.C.–A.D. 14

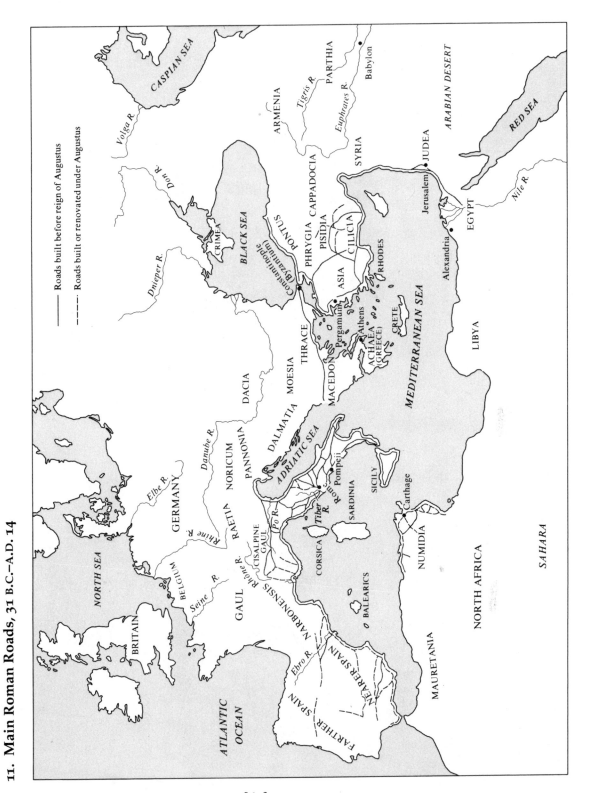

Roads built before reign of Augustus

Roads built or renovated under Augustus

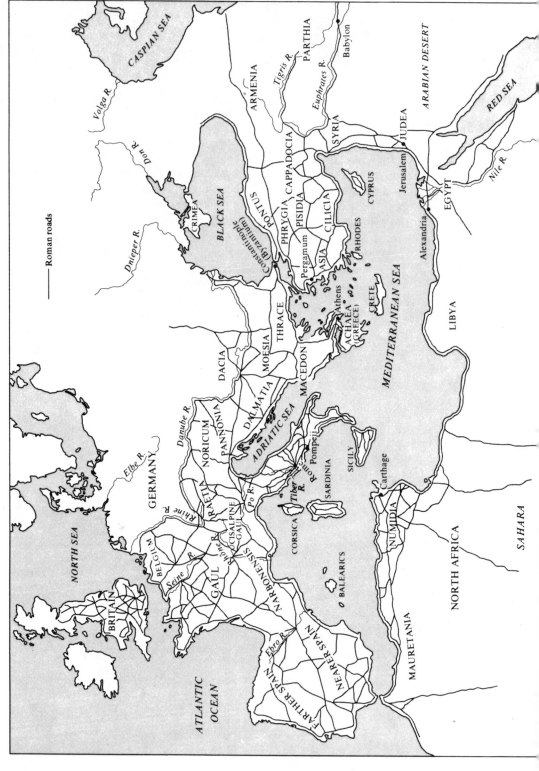

Source 12 from Victor W. Von Hagen, The Roads That Led to Rome *(Cleveland and New York: World Publishing Co., © 1967 by George Weidenfeld and Nicolson, London), pp. 18–19.*

12. Main Roman Roads at Their Greatest Extent, A.D. 180

Roman roads

CASPIAN SEA

Volga R.

Don R.

ARMENIA

PARTHIA

Babylon

Tigris R.

Euphrates R.

ARABIAN DESERT

RED SEA

SYRIA

JUDEA

Jerusalem

Nile R.

EGYPT

Alexandria

PHRYGIA CAPPADOCIA

PISIDIA

CILICIA

CYPRUS

RHODES

Pergamum

ASIA

Dnieper R.

CRIMEA

BLACK SEA

Constantinople
(Byzantium)

PONTUS

THRACE

MACEDON

Athens

ACHAEA
(GREECE)

CRETE

MEDITERRANEAN SEA

LIBYA

MOESIA

DACIA

DALMATIA

ADRIATIC SEA

Danube R.

PANNONIA

NORICUM

Rome
Pompeii

Tiber R.

SICILY

SARDINIA

Carthage

NUMIDIA

NORTH AFRICA

SAHARA

MAURETANIA

BALEARICS

CORSICA

CISALPINE GAUL

Po R.

RAETIA

Rhine R.

GERMANY

Elbe R.

NORTH SEA

BRITAIN

ATLANTIC OCEAN

BELGIUM

GAUL

Seine R.

Loire R.

Rhône R.

NARBONENSIS

Ebro R.

NEARER SPAIN

FARTHER SPAIN

[62]

QUESTIONS TO CONSIDER

Now that you have examined various pieces of evidence, you need to put them together to arrive at a conclusion that you can support. Do not worry about not having all the evidence you need; no historian can ever discover "all" the facts about an event or person. He or she makes conclusions on the basis of the evidence available, alters those conclusions when new material is discovered, and uses those conclusions as a framework for further research. In this respect, historians operate just like physicists learning how the universe works. Do not worry if some of your sources disagree; ten people who witness an auto accident often come up with ten quite contradictory accounts of the event. Why might accounts of Augustus's rule be even more contradictory?

The sources have made you aware of the operation of Roman government on two levels: that of the formal constitution, which remained a republic, and that of the actual locus of power, which was increasingly the emperor. The changes that Augustus instituted thus took place at the second level, and in many areas we can ignore the formal constitution of Rome in describing the process of change. Comparing all the sources, how would you describe the means by which Augustus transformed the republic into a different type of government? Which steps were most important? Which observers seemed to have the clearer view of this process, Augustus himself and those living during his lifetime, or later histori-

ans? In considering this last question, you need to think about the advantages and disadvantages of eyewitness reports versus later, secondary accounts.

The second question concerns results, not process: Why was Augustus successful? To answer this, we must consider not only the changes themselves, but people's perceptions of them. A ruler's place in history depends not only on real accomplishments but also on how these accomplishments are perceived and judged by later generations. Rulers perceived as good or successful are often given credit for everything good that happened during their reigns, even if they had nothing to do with it. Conversely, rulers regarded as unsuccessful, weak, or bad get blamed for many things that were not their fault. A reputation is generally based on actual achievements, but occasionally it is also determined by a ruler's successful manipulation of public opinion, and sometimes by that manipulation alone.

Augustus clearly recognized the importance of public opinion, which in Rome was tied to upholding tradition. How does he make use of Roman traditions in the laws and coins he issues? How do other observers judge his connection with tradition? Many of Rome's traditions were incorporated into public rituals and ceremonies. What sorts of ceremonies did Romans participate in or view? How did Augustus use these ceremonies to demonstrate his power or his personal connections with Roman tradition? Along with rituals, titles are also important demonstrations of power. What does Augustus call himself and what do others call him, both in the written documents and on the coins? Why is there so much discussion of his accepting or not accepting various titles?

Now that you have considered the opinions of a range of commentators, assessed some actual legal changes and road-building patterns, examined some coins, and heard from Augustus himself, you are ready to answer the questions: How did Augustus transform the Roman republic into an empire? Why was he successful? Once you have made your assessment, think about how you would use it to structure future research. What other evidence would be useful in supporting your conclusions? Where might you go to find that evidence?

EPILOGUE

Though Augustus said that his aim was a restoration of the republic, in reality he transformed Roman government into an empire ruled by one individual. His reign is generally termed the *Principate,* a word taken from Augustus's favorite title *princeps,* but the rulers of Rome after him did not hesitate to use the title *emperor.* Like him, they also retained the titles *pontifex maximus,* supreme priest, and *imperator,* commander-in-chief. It is interesting to see how many of our words denoting aspects of royal rule come from Augustus: not only *prince, emperor,* and *czar* (the Russian variant of "Caesar") but also *palace,* from Palatine, the hill where Augustus had his house.

The emperors who came after Augustus built on his achievements, both literally and figuratively. They extended the borders of the Roman Empire even farther, so that at its largest it would stretch from Scotland to the Sudan and from Spain to Syria. The Roman road system was expanded to over 50,000 miles, longer than the current interstate highway system in the United States; some of those roads are still usable today. Roman coins continued to be stamped with the emperor's picture and have been found as far away as southern India. Later emperors continued Augustus's building projects in Rome and throughout the empire. Vespasian built the Colosseum, which could seat 50,000 people; Trajan, the Forum with a number of different buildings and an enormous 125-foot column with his statue on top; Hadrian, the Pantheon and a wall dividing England and Scotland. The emperor Nero may have even ordered part of Rome burned to make room for his urban renewal projects.

Augustus's successors also continued his centralization of power. His stepson Tiberius stripped the assemblies of their right to elect magistrates, and later emperors took this power away from the senate as well. Bureaucrats appointed by the emperor oversaw the grain trade, the army, and the collection of taxes, with the senate gradually dwindling into a rubber stamp for the emperor's decisions. New territories were ruled directly by the emperor through governors and generals; in these jurisdictions, the senate did not have even the pretense of power.

The cult of ruler worship initiated somewhat tentatively in the provinces under Augustus grew enormously after his death, when, like Julius Caesar, he was declared a god. Though Romans officially deified only the *memory* of deceased emperors, some emperors were not willing to wait that long. Caligula declared himself a god at the age of twenty-five, spent much of his time in the temple of Castor and Pollux, and talked to the statue of Jupiter as an equal. Though Caligula was probably insane and later was stabbed to death, ruler worship in general was serious business for most Romans, closely linked as it was to tradition and patriotism. Groups like the Christians who did not offer sacrifices to the emperor or at least to the emperor's "genius" were felt to be unpatriotic, disloyal, and probably traitorous.

Thus in many ways Augustus laid the foundation for the success and durability of his empire. Historians have always been fascinated with the demise of the Roman Empire, but considering the fact that it lasted more than 400 years after Augustus in western Europe—and, in a significantly altered form, almost 1,500 years in eastern Europe—a more appropriate question might be why it lasted so long. Though the weaknesses that led to the empire's eventual collapse were also outgrowths of the reign of Augustus, the latter still represents a remarkable success story.

We must be careful of attributing too much to one man, however. As we have seen, Augustus had an extremely effective network of supporters and advisers, including Rome's most important men of letters. Their rendering of the glories of Roman civilization and the brilliance of Augustus has shaped much of what has been written about Rome since; you may only need to check the adjectives used in your text to describe Augustus to confirm this. Myths or exaggerations told about a ruler die hard, especially those that have been repeated for nearly 2,000 years.

CHAPTER FOUR

PHILOSOPHY AND FAITH:

THE PROBLEM OF ANCIENT SUICIDE

THE PROBLEM

Life itself is our most precious possession, and every civilization has viewed suicide, representing as it does the rejection of all human society, as an act of supreme importance, charged with religious, philosophical, and even legal significance. Indeed, the French philosopher Albert Camus (1913–1960) wrote, "There is only one truly philosophical problem, and that is suicide. Judging whether life is or is not worth living amounts to answering the fundamental question of philosophy."[1] Camus was only one of the most recent in a long line of thinkers, extending back at least to the civilization of ancient Egypt, who have written on the fundamental issues raised by the act of self-destruction. This extensive discourse on suicide can afford us a revealing glimpse of the intellectual life of past civilizations by allowing us to compare the evolution of their thinkers' ideas on this important act.

In the twentieth century, for example, most of us understand suicide in terms defined by the modern social, psychological, and medical sciences. Emile Durkheim (1858–1917), the pioneering French sociologist, identified several kinds of suicide, but concentrated particularly on the role of modern society in eroding the integrative and regulative aspects of traditional society, resulting, he claimed, in an increase in suicide. We now know that Durkheim's statistical evidence for the increase in suicide in modern times was defective, but his conclusion that suicide is a particular side effect of modern society has endured, even though deprived of its statistical support. Sigmund Freud (1856–1940), the father of modern psychoanalysis, and others of his discipline focused modern attention on the psychological problems that often produce suicide. And since the work of the German physician Emil Kraepelin (1865–1926), medical professionals have sought to treat the organic

1. Albert Camus, *The Myth of Sisyphus and Other Essays,* translated by Justin O'Brien (New York: Vintage Books, 1991), p. 3.

causes of depressive disorders that can end in self-destruction.

The earliest Western societies, on the other hand, lacking our modern scientific knowledge, viewed the act of self-destruction in very different, often spiritual terms. Such societies certainly condemned suicide because it robbed their ranks of productive members. But primitive peoples also believed that the spirits of those who took their own lives would not rest in the world of the dead, but would return to haunt the realm of the living.

In the present chapter we will examine the thought of the ancient world on suicide. The practice was common for much of the period, and ancients seem to have taken their lives for a number of reasons. One had to do with personal honor. Examples abound of ancients extolled in the literature of their time for their nobility in ending their lives to preserve their honor. Perhaps the most famous of these suicides was that of Cato the Younger (95–46 B.C.), a leader of the senatorial opposition to Julius Caesar's attempt to control Rome. With his forces defeated in the field, and facing Caesar's imminent attack on Utica, the stronghold under his command, Cato assured the escape of his followers and took his own life rather than surrender to the man he regarded as a tyrant. Other ancients took their own lives to avoid the pains of old age, perhaps because they saw mental and physical decline as diminishing their honor. Thus, the Greek philosopher Zeno (ca 334–ca 262) took his own life at the age of seventy-two when breaking a bone in a minor accident seemed to convince him of impending physical decline. Love for a dead spouse also led to suicide. Portia, the daughter of Cato and the wife of Caesar's assassin, Brutus, took her own life after her husband's suicide upon his defeat by Caesar's heir, Octavian, in 42 B.C. Ancients also took their lives in the belief that their deaths could advance a cause, and we will look at such an act in the death of Samson. Indeed, we will examine ancient thought on such acts of self-destruction among the Greeks, the Romans, the Hebrews of the Old Testament, and early Christians.

Historians date Hellenic, or classical Greek, civilization from about 800 B.C., when growing commercial wealth and the development of an efficient writing system promoted the economic and intellectual flowering of Greek city-states on the Greek mainland, the islands of the Aegean, Asia Minor (modern Turkey), and the shores of the Black Sea. The epics of Homer helped to shape early Hellenic culture, with the heroes providing role models for young Greeks and the tales of the gods forming the basis for early belief in a cluster of deities, presided over by Zeus, inhabiting the heights of Mount Olympus. These religious beliefs of the Greeks had little of the creedal structure of modern religion, but emphasized instead the duty of citizens of an independent city-state (as most Greeks were) to live in accord with the community. For the early Greeks, as for most Mediterranean peoples of that period, death simply represented the spirit's journey to a shadowy realm of the dead.

The greatest accomplishment of Hellenic intellectuals was to begin to transcend this traditional Greek religion—which explained events in this life in terms of divine action—and to apply reason to their understanding of natural phenomena and human events. As they replaced myth with reason, the Greeks first attempted to explain the physical world around them. The Cosmologists, thinkers concerned with the origins, structure, and operation of the universe, including Thales (ca 624–548 B.C.), Anaximander (ca 611–547 B.C.), and Pythagoras (ca 580–507 B.C.), sought natural explanations for the origins of the universe and advanced the concept that the physical world operates according to mathematical, scientific laws. Greek philosophers also evaluated human society, examining political and ethical problems through the use of reason. Socrates (ca 469–399 B.C.) and Plato (ca 429–347 B.C.), philosophers we will study in this chapter, in particular led the Greek inquiry into ethical problems.

A political event fundamentally transformed the Hellenic age, however. In 338 B.C. King Philip of Macedon (382–336 B.C.), a primitive state in northern Greece, conquered the city-states of Greece and ended their independence by subjecting them to the rule of his growing empire. Philip planned further military campaigns; these were carried out after his death by his son, Alexander the Great (356–323 B.C.). Alexander conquered Greece's historic enemy, the Persian Empire, and created an empire that stretched to the borders of India.

Although Alexander's empire dissolved into several smaller monarchies after his death, his conquests began a new Hellenistic age. Greek became the language of administration and intellectual life in the eastern Mediterranean world, and contact with eastern ideas reshaped Hellenic thought. Hellenistic philosophy reflected a search for intellectual peace for the individual in a world far less democratic and secure than that of the independent city-states of the Hellenic age.

Epicurus (342–270 B.C.) began to teach philosophy in Athens in the late fourth century, creating Epicureanism, one of the great schools of Hellenistic philosophy. Seeking intellectual tranquillity in a much less secure age, Epicurus urged his followers to withdraw from public affairs and civic responsibilities, which had been central to the earlier period of city-states. He also taught his students to abandon pursuit of worldly success. The wise person, Epicurus taught, would seek spiritual tranquillity instead, and he taught his students not to fear even divine interruptions of that peace. He affirmed the gods' existence, but held that they played no role in human affairs. Adopting the thought of the Cosmologist Democritus (ca 460–370 B.C.), Epicurus taught that the physical world consisted of matter made up of atoms governed by mechanical principles and unaffected by divine action. Death released the atoms making up the human form to constitute new matter, and so the peace Epicurus sought to instill in his followers was very much one of this world.

Zeno, who, as we have seen, committed suicide, founded a second school of Hellenistic philosophy. He taught on the *stoa poecile* (the "painted porch") near the agora, or marketplace, of Athens. As a consequence, his ideas came to be called Stoicism. Stoics accepted the new realities of the Greek and, later, Roman worlds by emphasizing the universality of human society. As expressed by Zeno, "All men should regard themselves as members of one city and people, having one life and order as a herd feeding together on a common pasture."[2] Stoics believed that the universe inhabited by such a society received order from divine reason, or Logos. Animals followed this divine order by instinct, and inanimate objects necessarily adhered to the physical laws of the universe—for example, those governing the regular movements of the heavenly bodies. Humans, however, had free will and could choose to reject the divine plan. But Stoics taught that the virtuous person could achieve happiness only by living in harmony with the Logos, subjecting personal emotions to reason, and accepting life's trials as part of the overall plan of the universe.

While Epicureans withdrew from the world and Stoics sought to live in accord with the Logos, the Cynics, a third group of Hellenistic philosophers led by Diogenes of Sinope (ca 412–323 B.C.), rejected social conventions. They urged their followers to give up material possessions and the complexities of human society and live lives of self-sufficiency and high personal ethics. Because material matters meant little to Cynics, they were prepared to commit suicide if anything blocked their quest for the virtuous life. Indeed, Diogenes reportedly said that the conduct of life required either reason or the noose.

Imperial expansion fundamentally shaped Roman civilization. Thus, in the fourth century B.C., the Romans came into contact with the Greek settlements in the south of their native Italy, and Roman equivalents of the Greek deities soon replaced traditional Roman religion, which was centered on the gods of home and family. In philosophy, the Romans similarly embraced Hellenistic Epicureanism and Stoicism. But, ultimately, the fundamental force reshaping Roman thought as the empire conquered the Mediterranean world was religious. Rome's world empire only increased the sense of alienation and personal insecurity that we identified in the Hellenistic age, and while educated Romans adopted Stoicism and other rational solutions to these problems, others often sought religious answers. Popular among such people were the mystery religions, so called because they involved secret rituals known only to initiates. These religions, whose attraction only grew as the Roman Empire weakened, offered their adherents spiritual immortality in an afterlife. But the greatest religious force transforming Rome was Christianity, whose roots we must seek in the Jewish experience beginning in

2. Quoted in D. Brendan Nagle, *The Ancient World: A Social and Cultural History* (Englewood Cliffs, N.J.: Prentice-Hall, 1979), p. 206.

[69]

the Middle East in the late second millennium B.C.

The founders of this religious tradition, the Hebrews, originated a faith that was unique in the ancient Middle East. By the late second millennium B.C., their Judaism was a monotheistic religion centered on the deity Yahweh, who demanded ethical behavior of his followers. In this ethical monotheism of the early Hebrews, Yahweh enforced his laws by divine intervention in this life. There was no belief in a last judgment, and afterlife beliefs were quite similar to those of the Greeks; the Jews' Sheol was a dark underworld of the dead.

By the first century B.C., new ideas were taking root among the Jews of Palestine, dividing them into four main sects. The Sadducees, often drawn from the elite of Jewish society, maintained traditional beliefs and ceremonies and the letter of ancient religious law dating back to the days of the lawgiver Moses. The Pharisees, quite possibly representing the majority of Jews in Palestine, challenged the Sadducees by their willingness to admit the law to interpretation and by their acceptance of the eastern idea of a life after death, with the possibility of spiritual salvation through resurrection. The Essenes, the third group within first-century Judaism, also accepted the idea of resurrection, but formed a monastic-style community near the Dead Sea where they awaited the imminent establishment of the Kingdom of God on earth. The fourth sect, the Zealots, refused to accept Roman conquest of their homeland and engaged in violent resistance, culminating in a Jewish revolt in Palestine in A.D. 66.

A widely held belief among first-century Jews in Palestine was that they would be delivered from foreign domination by a Messiah. Many Jews conceived of the Messiah as a military leader, but when a peaceful figure, Jesus of Nazareth (ca 4 B.C.–ca A.D. 29), declared that he was the Messiah, many Jews saw him as fulfilling their expectation, and Jesus soon had a growing following. Grounded in Jewish monotheism, Jesus' teachings called on his followers to repent their sins in order to enter the Kingdom of God and thus achieve spiritual salvation in a life after death. But to conservative Jews like the Sadducees, Jesus was defying traditional religious law, and they turned him over to Roman authorities. In a difficult province of their empire, these officials certainly saw Jesus as an unsettling presence who counted Zealots among his closest followers, and they ordered his execution.

Jesus' followers proclaimed his resurrection three days after his death as fulfillment of his teachings, and the nature of his following shortly began to change. More and more Gentiles, or non-Jews, joined Jesus' original Jewish followers, as Saint Paul (ca 5–ca A.D. 67) emphasized that adherence to traditional Jewish law, including dietary rules and circumcision, was not required for membership in the Christian community. In the Hellenized culture of the Middle East, Jesus increasingly was referred to as "Christ," from the Greek *Christos*, or "the Anointed," a translation of the

Hebrew word *Messiah*. Thus, a new faith, Christianity, quite distinct from Judaism, emerged and grew steadily because of its promise of otherworldly rewards in a society already seeking such spiritual comfort in the mystery religions. Soon the Christian community grew large enough to attract the attention of Roman authorities to a faith that seemed subversive in its nonviolence and refusal even superficially to conform to the Roman civic practice of venerating the emperor. Imperial authorities responded with sporadic, often brutal, persecutions of Christians, beginning in A.D. 64. But the continued growth of the new faith led first to its legalization under Emperor Constantine in A.D. 313 and finally to its elevation to the status of Rome's official religion by Emperor Theodosius I in A.D. 392.

As it achieved legitimacy, Christianity also defined its belief system in an atmosphere of theological controversy. Many theologians whose ideas came to be viewed by the Church as false doctrines, or heresies, sought to promote their ideas in the Christian community. Thus, the followers of Arius (A.D. 250–326), a Greek priest of Alexandria, denied the absolute divinity of Christ, who had declared that he was the son of God. Arians, who taught that Christ was certainly no mere mortal but that

neither was he God's equal, received the Church's condemnation at the Council of Nicaea in A.D. 325. Another heretical group was the Donatists, who rejected the idea, held by the majority of Christians, that the Church should be a universal, or catholic, church embracing all, sinners as well as those meriting salvation. Donatists believed that the Church should include only the elect. Other heresies also spread, but the work of a group of theologians remembered as Church Fathers eventually imposed doctrinal uniformity on the early Church.

Your goal in this chapter is to analyze the thought of these ancient peoples on three levels defined by the central questions of this chapter. The first is very specific to the issue of suicide: What does the author of each selection say about suicide? The second asks you to place these ideas in their intellectual context: How do each author's ideas on self-destruction represent his own thought system and the intellectual outlook of the society in which he lived? The third requires that you perform one of the essential tasks of the historian and examine change over an extended period of time: What change in attitudes toward self-destruction do you see over the extended time period covered by these selections?

SOURCES AND METHOD

This chapter, like Chapter 2, offers us ancient primary sources that present certain analytical challenges. Again,

we must recognize that the absolute accuracy of these texts cannot be verified the way records of modern scholars' writings can be checked in their printed works or in recordings or transcripts of their lectures.

Products of a pre-print age, the handwritten originals of most of these sources have long ago disappeared, and students must rely on texts based on ancient scribes' transcriptions of the originals, which may not always be entirely faithful to the authors' precise words. Furthermore, because much ancient writing has failed to survive, it is often difficult to determine whether a given work represents all that its author had to say on a subject.

We also will encounter again sources that are not actually the work of those to whom they are attributed. As we saw in Chapter 2, we can know the thought of Socrates, who wrote nothing, only through the work of his student Plato, and scholars still disagree as to which ideas in the latter's writings are his own and which are those of his teacher. Such considerations require some analysis for all our sources in this chapter.

Source 1 is the work of Plato, an Athenian philosopher who, in the course of his long career, wrote on just about all the philosophical problems that have occupied Western thinkers since his death. His surviving works include letters and a number of dialogues. The dialogues replicate in written form the teaching method of Socrates. Socrates particularly concerned himself with the search for the values by which he and his fellow Athenians might live lives of moral excellence. Socrates believed that these values were not imparted to humanity by a deity, but rather that the individual could discover them through rational inquiry, and

he devised a mode of inquiry, dialectics, to facilitate that search. As practiced by Socrates and his followers, dialectics represented a logical discussion, propelled by the teacher's questions to the student, that forced the student to clarify and justify his thought. Thus, in Source 1, from Plato's dialogue *The Phaedo*, questions are posed by Socrates.

Many scholars divide Plato's dialogues into two chief categories, according to the order in which they probably were written. They call the earlier dialogues, including *The Apology, The Meno*, and *The Gorgias*, "Socratic" because they seem to express chiefly the ideas of Socrates. The later dialogues, including *The Phaedo*, seem more nearly to express the ideas of Plato himself.

Plato divided knowledge into two realms. One of these was knowledge of the material world, which can be gathered through sensory perceptions. The other, higher realm of knowledge was that of absolute reality and perfect virtues, the realm of forms or ideas for Plato, which could be achieved only intellectually.

In Source 1, one of the most dramatic episodes of ancient literature, Plato describes the execution of Socrates. Plato's teacher had employed his dialectic method not only with his students, but with his fellow citizens as well, in the hope of leading them to more ethical lives. Indeed, he became the Athenians' "gadfly," and he made more than a few enemies. When Athens lost the Peloponnesian War with Sparta, many of those enemies led Athenians who were seeking an explanation for their defeat to charge Socrates with having had a role in the military disaster. Indeed, several of Socrates' former students had betrayed their city in the war, and his enemies charged him with having led the youth of Athens away from the traditional gods and thereby contributed to the Spartan victory.

As was customary in Athens, the trial of Socrates took place before a jury with wide-ranging powers; the jury not only judged guilt or innocence but also determined the sentence. Plato's accounts of the procedure in *The Apology* make it clear that Socrates could have escaped serious penalty by going into voluntary exile before trial or, perhaps after conviction, by admitting error and promising to stop teaching. But when the jury found him guilty and asked him to suggest a punishment, Socrates almost mockingly proposed what amounted to civic honors. Even though he subsequently suggested a fine, the jury clearly took offense at his remarks; more jurors voted for the penalty of death by taking poison (hemlock) than had voted for the verdict of guilty.

Socrates' behavior at his trial and his subsequent refusal to approve the efforts of his friends Simmias and Cebes, who arrived with money to finance an escape from confinement, suggest to many scholars a sort of death wish. These scholars propose that the philosopher's end represented not so much an execution as a suicide. Indeed, self-destruction figures prominently in *The Phaedo*, which opens on Socrates' execution day (which had been delayed by Athenian religious observances). Socrates spent that day surrounded by friends, and one of these, Cebes, asked Socrates, on behalf of the poet Evenus, why he had lately taken to writing poetry. Socrates replied that he had no wish to rival Evenus, but simply wrote in response to a dream demanding that he "make music"; he wrote only so as to leave no duty undone as he met his end. Our selection from The Phaedo opens in the midst of the discussion of poetry. In that selection, why does Socrates think that philosophers in particular should welcome death? How should death open to philosophers the realm of ideas or forms? Does Socrates suggest any divine limitation on an individual's right to self-destruction? What suggests to you that Socrates believed that a divine necessity now permitted his death and that he welcomed his end as a remedy for the problems of this life? What in the thought of Socrates strikes you as characteristic of a philosopher who was a free citizen of a democratic city-state? What about Plato's thought might suggest to you that he was less optimistic than his teacher about finding perfection in this life?

While important portions of Plato's work have survived for modern study, the work of some other ancient philosophers comes to us less directly. This is the case with both Epicurus (ca 341–270 B.C.), of whose vast writings only fragments have survived, and Epictetus (ca 50–ca A.D.

138), whose thought survives only in writings of a disciple, Arrian, based on notes of Epictetus' words.

Much of what we know of the life and thought of Epicurus comes from *Lives of Eminent Philosophers* by Diogenes Laertius, an author about whom scholars know very little. He wrote this history of ancient philosophers in Greek, and the contents of the book suggest that he composed it early in the third century after the birth of Christ. *Lives of Eminent Philosophers* is a remarkable source for ancient history because Diogenes Laertius included many writings that subsequently were lost and, therefore, are available nowhere else. The author illustrated his accounts of philosophers' lives with quotations from their philosophical writings as well as from decrees, letters, wills, and epitaphs. Indeed, Source 2 opens with a letter from Epicurus and concludes with a brief portion of the maxims that he expected his students to memorize, all drawn from *Lives of Eminent Philosophers*.

In the excerpts from the works of Epicurus in Source 2, what aim in life does he urge on his followers? How are they to attain that goal? Why will death be "nothing" to Epicureans? How did his thought relate to self-destruction? Why did the Roman thinker Cicero (106–43 B.C.) write the following passage?

For my part I think that in life we should observe the rule which is followed at Greek banquets:—"Let him either drink," it runs, "or go!" And rightly; for either he should enjoy the pleasure of tippling along with the oth-ers or get away early, that a sober man may not be a victim to the violence of those who are heated with wine. Thus by running away one can escape the assaults of fortune which one cannot face. This is the same advice as Epicurus gives.[3]

How does this quotation embody developments we have examined in the Hellenistic and Roman worlds?

Source 3 presents a selection from the *Discourses* of Epictetus recorded by Arrian (ca A.D. 95–175), who was a cosmopolitan figure indeed. A Greek born in Asia Minor, he entered Roman service and combined success as a governor and general with scholarship. Writing in Greek, he was the author of several histories, including one of Alexander the Great, and as a student of philosophy, Arrian wrote the only record of the thought of his teacher, Epictetus.

Like Arrian a Greek born in Asia Minor, Epictetus was the son of a slave woman and was a slave himself for many years. Taken to Rome as a youth, he studied philosophy there; once freed, perhaps at his master's death, he taught first in the imperial capital and then at Nicopolis in Greece. The teaching of Epictetus reflected this former slave's love of freedom and placed him in the ranks of the foremost Stoics.

Stoicism proved particularly attractive to the Romans, many of whom believed that their empire represented the Stoic ideal of a universal

3. Cicero, *Tusculan Disputations*, translated by J. E. King (Cambridge, Mass.: Harvard University Press, 1960), pp. 543–545.

human community. For Roman audiences, Epictetus called Logos "God" in Source 3. What evidence do you find of the philosopher's love of freedom? What is the concern of "the good and excellent man" in life? When may such a person terminate his life? What similarity do you find between these circumstances and those in which Plato found suicide justifiable? How does the thought of Epictetus perhaps reflect problems of the Roman world?

With Sources 4 through 9, we move from the classical tradition of Greece and Rome to the roots of the Judeo-Christian heritage in Palestine. Sources 4 through 8 are from the thirty-nine books of the Hebrew scriptures that Jews refer to as *Tanak* and that Christians call the Old Testament of the Bible. Written between the thirteenth and second centuries B.C., the Hebrew scriptures provide a remarkable record of the experience of the Jewish people before the birth of Christ, and we must examine their utility as a work of history.

The compilers of the Old Testament were not historians but religious thinkers concerned with Jewish faith, law, and literature, as well as history. The Old Testament thus is the foundation of the modern Jewish and Christian faiths. Students of history find the Old Testament an invaluable source, but they also find that this work of religious inspiration sometimes contains historical contradictions and occasional factual errors, and so scholars must verify biblical accounts of events against records in other sources. Nevertheless, the Old Testament, a collection of works by many authors, contains a consistent expression of values and belief and is our best source for understanding the religion of the Hebrews, and it is from that perspective that we will consider Sources 4 through 8.

We draw Sources 4 through 8 from the Hebrew scriptures' books of Judges, 1 and 2 Samuel, and 1 Kings, books that recount the teachings and careers of the great Hebrew prophets and leaders. These books contain all the acts of self-destruction that are found in the Hebrew scriptures. Sources 4 and 5 come from the Book of Judges, which describes the period in Hebrew history between the deaths of Moses and Joshua—who had led their people out of captivity in Egypt and into the promised land of Canaan—and the advent of kings as rulers among the Hebrews. Source 4 is from the Book of Judges' account of political instability among the Hebrews as they evolved from nomadic tribesmen into a more settled people who needed nontribal, permanent institutions of government. In search of that government, they offered the crown to the prophet Gideon, who rejected the overture, proclaiming that God alone should rule. After Gideon's death, his son Abimelech slew all but one of his brothers and seized the crown his father had rejected. Established as king, Abimelech brutally put down rebellions against his authority and, as told in Source 4, engaged in an attack on the rebellious city of Thebez. How did Abimelech meet his end? Why may we consider this suicide? Beyond the statement that Abimelech's death represented divine retribution, do you find any textual condemnation of the death of Abimelech?

Source 5 also comes from the Book of Judges; it is part of the account of the mighty Samson, a judge, or leader, of the Hebrews. According to this account, Samson possessed extraordinary strength, which he used against the pagan Philistines, who were enemies of the Hebrews. Samson's long hair represented his vows of devotion to God, and when the woman Delilah learned of this, she cut his hair, depriving Samson of his strength. The Philistines then captured Samson, blinded him, and enslaved him. But his hair grew back, and with it his strength, a fact unnoticed by the Philistines when they put him on display in a temple to their god, Dagon. What does Source 5 show Samson doing in the temple? While this is an act of martyrdom, why must it also be considered a suicide? Understanding that among many ancient peoples, burial in the family tomb was an honor, what can you conclude about the Hebrews' perception of Samson's death?

In Source 6 we have an account of the first anointed king of the Hebrews, Saul. Selected as king by the great judge Samuel, Saul disobeyed God's commands, and Samuel designated David as the new and rightful king. Nevertheless, Saul retained the crown, fighting David in a civil war, while continuing to battle the historic enemies of the Hebrews, the Philistines. What action did Saul, facing defeat by the Philistines atop Mount Gilboa, take in Source 6? Why must you conclude that Saul's death was a suicide? What is the reaction of

the Hebrews to Saul's death? How does the following response of David to the death of Saul and his son Jonathan reinforce your conclusion about the Hebrews' reaction to Saul's self-destruction?

Thy glory, O Israel, is slain upon
   thy high places!
How are the mighty fallen!
    . . . . .
Saul and Jonathan, beloved and
   lovely!
In life and death they were not
   divided;
They were swifter than eagles,
   they were stronger than lions.[4]

Saul's death allowed David to gain the crown, but David's rule did not go unchallenged. He faced a rebellion by his son Absalom and his former counselor, Ahithophel. The advice of Ahithophel was highly esteemed, for "in those days the counsel which Ahithophel gave was as if one consulted the oracle of God."[5] Nevertheless, Absalom rejected the strategy proposed by Ahithophel, "For the Lord had ordained to defeat the good counsel of Ahithophel, so that the Lord might bring evil on Absalom."[6] What does Source 7 indicate was Ahithophel's response to Absalom's humiliating him by ignoring his advice? What happened to Ahithophel's remains? What response does this in-

4. 2 Samuel 1:19, 23, in *The Oxford Annotated Bible with the Apocrypha* (New York: Oxford University Press, 1965), p. 375.

5. 2 Samuel 16:23, in *The Oxford Annotated Bible*, p. 397.

6. 2 Samuel 17:14, in *The Oxford Annotated Bible*, p. 398.

dicate that Ahithophel's contemporaries had to his death?

After the death of King David's son and heir, Solomon, the Hebrew kingdom divided into Israel and Judah, and Source 8 recounts an event in Israel. Zimri, a powerful military leader, killed King Elah and seized the throne. Zimri's coup did not go unopposed, however, and the forces of the army commander, Omri, besieged the usurper in the city of Tirzah. What end overtook Zimri, according to Source 8? While the text certainly suggests that God's punishment was a factor in Zimri's death, did the author in any way condemn the act of suicide?

Source 9 also is a biblical selection, but it comes from the writings commonly known among Christians as the New Testament. These Christian scriptures consist of the twenty-seven books that recount the life of Jesus Christ and record his teachings and those of his followers. They are central to the belief of all Christians. Source 9 describes the death of one of the twelve apostles of Jesus, Judas Iscariot. For thirty silver coins, Judas had betrayed Jesus' location to priests of the Temple in Jerusalem who opposed his teachings. Christ was arrested and executed by crucifixion, a mode of punishment commonly employed by the Roman authorities. Source 9 describes the suicide of Judas. Why, according to this account, did Judas take his own life? Is there any textual condemnation of this act of self-destruction? What response to suicide seems common to both Hebrew and Christian texts?

Source 10 is the work of Josephus, one of the greatest ancient historians. Josephus (37–ca A.D. 100) was a complex individual, and we require an understanding of his background in order to interpret his writings. A Jew born in Jerusalem, his early studies led Josephus to join the Pharisees. When Palestine erupted in a Jewish rebellion against Roman rule in A.D. 66, the scholarly Josephus took an active role, commanding rebel forces in Galilee. Roman legions eventually crushed the rebellion, and Josephus won the favor of their commander, Titus Flavius Vespasian; he even added "Flavius" to his own name. Vespasian went on to become emperor of Rome, and Josephus Flavius enjoyed imperial patronage in the capital. There he wrote in Greek several important histories, including *Jewish Antiquities,* a history of the Jews from Adam and Eve to the first century A.D., and *The Jewish War,* a history of the Jewish rebellion against Roman rule in Palestine.

Scholars detect many influences on Josephus that we must identify before reading his work. Certainly he was a devout Jewish Pharisee whose work represented an apology of sorts for his people's rebellion. At the same time, Josephus was a Roman citizen who had been thoroughly imbued with the Greco-Roman culture of the first century A.D. And we must not forget that Josephus enjoyed an imperial pension, which might have affected his portrayal of events in his histories.

Source 10 presents perhaps the most famous event in the Jewish rebellion, the last stand of the Zealots at the mountain fortress of Masada in 73 A.D. Faced with inevitable defeat, what step did the Zealots' leader, Eleazar, urge upon them? How did the garrison respond? How many persons perished, according to Josephus? How does he portray this mass suicide? How does this portrayal replicate reactions to suicide in other ancient sources?

Our final source, Source 11, is the work of Saint Augustine (A.D. 354–430), one of the greatest early Church Fathers. Saint Augustine lived in turbulent times, when the Roman Empire in the West was in marked decline and heretical ideas challenged Christian doctrine. Raised as a Christian in his native North Africa, Augustine abandoned that faith during a rather dissolute period as a young man and adopted the Manichaean heresy, an eastern belief system founded upon the idea that the world was a battleground between the forces of good and evil deities. Eventually, in Milan, Italy, Augustine encountered the eloquent preaching of another Church Father, Saint Ambrose, bishop of Milan, which helped to win him back to Christianity.

Augustine returned to North Africa, became bishop of Hippo, and produced a large body of writings that helped to define Christian doctrine and to defend it against the numerous heresies of the day. *The City of God Against the Pagans,* excerpted in Source 11, is the most important of these. Saint Augustine wrote it in response to the sack of Rome by the Visigoths in 410. Non-Christians blamed this disaster on the Christianity that had won over much of the

empire in the fourth century A.D. They saw the event as the revenge of the old gods that had been abandoned by many Romans and as the result of Christians' refusal to perform military service. Saint Augustine denied such charges and reasoned that, while imperial Rome was the greatest city that humanity could realize, the true object of the Christian life should be attainment to the heavenly City of God. In short, the rise and fall of empires was unimportant compared to the individual's spiritual journey to heavenly salvation.

Saint Augustine also used *The City of God* to further his mission of defending Christian doctrine. An issue that particularly concerned him was how his contemporaries, Christians and heretics alike, fulfilled Christ's injunction in Mark 8:34–35: "If any man would come after me, let him deny himself and take up his cross and follow me. For whoever would save his life will lose it; and whoever loses his life for my sake and the gospel's will save it."[7] Early Christians sometimes actually sought martyrdom at the hands of Roman officers assigned to enforce the superficial rites of official veneration of the emperor. Such suicidal self-sacrifice especially occurred among Donatists.

This enthusiastic martyrdom caused several early Christian thinkers to distinguish between true martyrdom and suicide. Saint Augustine takes up this theme in Source 11 as part of his discussion of the plunder of Rome in 410, when a number of women committed suicide rather than suffer sex-

7. *The Oxford Annotated Bible,* p. 1225.

ual assault by the Visigothic attackers. How does Saint Augustine view suicide? How does Saint Augustine's interpretation of the deaths of Samson and Judas differ from the accounts in Sources 5 and 9? In what circumstances would Saint Augustine permit suicide? What religious change did these conditions reflect? What new approach to suicide did Saint Augustine introduce?

Using this background on ancient philosophy and theology, now examine the evidence. As you read each source, you should seek answers for the central questions of this chapter. What does the author of each selection say about suicide? How do each author's ideas on self-destruction represent his own thought system and the intellectual outlook of the society in which he lived? What change in attitude toward self-destruction do you observe over the extended time period covered by these selections?

THE EVIDENCE

Source 1 from Plato with English Translation, *vol. 1,* Euthyphro, Apology, Crito, Phaedo, Phaedrus, *translated by Harold North Fowler (Cambridge, Mass.: Harvard University Press, 1953), pp. 213–233, 399–403. Reprinted with permission of the publishers and the Loeb Classical Library.*

1. Plato, *The Phaedo*

"So tell Evenus that, Cebes, and bid him farewell, and tell him, if he is wise, to come after me as quickly as he can. I, it seems, am going to-day; for that is the order of the Athenians."

And Simmias said, "What a message that is, Socrates, for Evenus! I have met him often, and from what I have seen of him, I should say that he will not take your advice in the least if he can help it."

"Why so?" said he. "Is not Evenus a philosopher?"

"I think so," said Simmias.

"Then Evenus will take my advice, and so will every man who has any worthy interest in philosophy. Perhaps, however, he will not take his own life, for they[8] say that is not permitted." And as he spoke he put his feet down on the ground and remained sitting in this way through the rest of the conversation.

Then Cebes asked him: "What do you mean by this, Socrates, that it is not permitted to take one's life, but that the philosopher would desire to follow after the dying?" . . .

8. **they:** Socrates refers here to the Pythagorean philosophers, including Philolaus, who opposed suicide. Pythagoreans believed that the soul was imprisoned in the body as punishment for sins in an earlier life. Thus, self-destruction was akin to a prison escape and was unacceptable to them.

"Why in the world do they say that it is not permitted to kill oneself, Socrates? I heard Philolaus, when he was living in our city, say the same thing you just said, and I have heard it from others, too, that one must not do this; but I never heard anyone say anything definite about it."

"You must have courage," said he, "and perhaps you might hear something. But perhaps it will seem strange to you that this alone of all laws is without exception, and it never happens to mankind, as in other matters, that only at some times and for some persons it is better to die than to live; and it will perhaps seem strange to you that these human beings for whom it is better to die cannot without impiety do good to themselves, but must wait for some other benefactor."

And Cebes, smiling gently, said, "Gawd knows it doos," speaking in his own dialect.

"It would seem unreasonable, if put in this way," said Socrates, "but perhaps there is some reason in it. Now the doctrine that is taught in secret about this matter, that we men are in a kind of prison and must not set ourselves free or run away, seems to me to be weighty and not easy to understand. But this at least, Cebes, I do believe is sound, that the gods are our guardians and that we men are one of the chattels of the gods. Do you not believe this?"

"Yes," said Cebes, "I do."

"Well, then," said he, "if one of your chattels should kill itself when you had not indicated that you wished it to die, would you be angry with it and punish it if you could?"

"Certainly," he replied.

"Then perhaps from this point of view it is not unreasonable to say that a man must not kill himself until god sends some necessity upon him, such as has now come upon me."

"That," said Cebes, "seems sensible. But what you said just now, Socrates, that philosophers ought to be ready and willing to die, that seems strange if we were right just now in saying that god is our guardian and we are his possessions. For it is not reasonable that the wisest men should not be troubled when they leave that service in which the gods, who are the best overseers in the world, are watching over them. A wise man certainly does not think that when he is free he can take better care of himself than they do. A foolish man might perhaps think so, that he ought to run away from his master, and he would not consider that he must not run away from a good master, but ought to stay with him as long as possible; and so he might thoughtlessly run away; but a man of sense would wish to be always with one who is better than himself. And yet, Socrates, if we look at it in this way, the contrary of what we just said seems natural; for the wise ought to be troubled at dying and the foolish to rejoice." . . .

. . . "I wish now to explain to you, my judges, the reason why I think a man who has really spent his life in philosophy is naturally of good courage when he is to die, and has strong hopes that when he is dead he will attain the greatest blessings in that other land. So I will try to tell you, Simmias, and Cebes, how this would be.

"Other people are likely not to be aware that those who pursue philosophy aright study nothing but dying and being dead. Now if this is true, it would be absurd to be eager for nothing but this all their lives, and then to be troubled when that came for which they had all along been eagerly practising."

And Simmias laughed and said, "By Zeus, Socrates, I don't feel much like laughing just now, but you made me laugh. For I think the multitude, if they heard what you just said about the philosophers, would say you were quite right, and our people at home would agree entirely with you that philosophers desire death, and they would add that they know very well that the philosophers deserve it."

"And they would be speaking the truth, Simmias, except in the matter of knowing very well. For they do not know in what way the real philosophers desire death, nor in what way they deserve death, nor what kind of a death it is. Let us then," said he, "speak with one another, paying no further attention to them. Do we think there is such a thing as death?"

"Certainly," replied Simmias.

"We believe, do we not, that death is the separation of the soul from the body, and that the state of being dead is the state in which the body is separated from the soul and exists alone by itself and the soul is separated from the body and exists alone by itself? Is death anything other than this?" "No, it is this," said he.

"Now, my friend, see if you agree with me; for, if you do, I think we shall get more light on our subject. Do you think a philosopher would be likely to care much about the so-called pleasures, such as eating and drinking?"

"By no means, Socrates," said Simmias.

"How about the pleasures of love?"

"Certainly not."

"Well, do you think such a man would think much of the other cares of the body—I mean such as the possession of fine clothes and shoes and the other personal adornments? Do you think he would care about them or despise them, except so far as it is necessary to have them?"

"I think the true philosopher would despise them," he replied.

"Altogether, then, you think that such a man would not devote himself to the body, but would, so far as he was able, turn away from the body and concern himself with the soul?"

"Yes."

"To begin with, then, it is clear that in such matters the philosopher, more than other men, separates the soul from communion with the body?"

"It is." ...

"Now, how about the acquirement of pure knowledge? Is the body a hindrance or not, if it is made to share in the search for wisdom? What I mean is this: Have the sight and hearing of men any truth in them, or is it true, as the poets are always telling us, that we neither hear nor see anything accurately? And yet if these two physical senses are not accurate or exact, the rest are not likely to be, for they are inferior to these. Do you not think so?"

"Certainly I do," he replied.

"Then," said he, "when does the soul attain to truth? For when it tries to consider anything in company with the body, it is evidently deceived by it."

"True."

"In thought, then, if at all, something of the realities becomes clear to it?"

"Yes."

"But it thinks best when none of these things troubles it, neither hearing nor sight, nor pain nor any pleasure, but it is, so far as possible, alone by itself, and takes leave of the body, and avoiding, so far as it can, all association or contact with the body, reaches out toward the reality."

"That is true."

"In this matter also, then, the soul of the philosopher greatly despises the body and avoids it and strives to be alone by itself?"

"Evidently."

"Now how about such things as this, Simmias? Do we think there is such a thing as absolute justice or not?"

"We certainly think there is."

"And absolute beauty and goodness."

"Of course."

"Well, did you ever see anything of that kind with your eyes?"

"Certainly not," said he.

"Or did you ever reach them with any of the bodily senses? I am speaking of all such things, as size, health, strength, and in short the essence or under-lying quality of everything. Is their true nature contemplated by means of the body? Is it not rather the case that he who prepares himself most carefully to understand the true essence of each thing that he examines would come near-est to the knowledge of it?"

"Certainly."

"Would not that man do this most perfectly who approaches each thing, so far as possible, with the reason alone, not introducing sight into his reasoning nor dragging in any of the other senses along with his thinking, but who em-ploys pure, absolute reason in his attempt to search out the pure, absolute essence of things, and who removes himself, so far as possible, from eyes and ears, and, in a word, from his whole body, because he feels that its compan-ionship disturbs the soul and hinders it from attaining truth and wisdom? Is not this the man, Simmias, if anyone, to attain to the knowledge of reality?"

"That is true as true can be, Socrates," said Simmias.

"Then," said he, "all this must cause good lovers of wisdom to think and say one to the other something like this: 'There seems to be a short cut which leads us and our argument to the conclusion in our search that so long as we have the body, and the soul is contaminated by such an evil, we shall never attain completely what we desire, that is, the truth. . . .

. . . "For, if pure knowledge is impossible while the body is with us, one of two thing[s] must follow, either it cannot be acquired at all or only when we are dead; for then the soul will be by itself apart from the body, but not before. And while we live, we shall, I think, be nearest to knowledge when we avoid, so far as possible, intercourse and communion with the body, except what is absolutely necessary, and are not filled with its nature, but keep ourselves pure from it until God himself sets us free. And in this way, freeing ourselves from the foolishness of the body and being pure, we shall, I think, be with the pure and shall know of ourselves all that is pure—and that is, perhaps, the truth. For it cannot be that the impure attain the pure.' Such words as these, I think, Simmias, all who are rightly lovers of knowledge must say to each other and such must be their thoughts. Do you not agree?"

"Most assuredly, Socrates."

"Then," said Socrates, "if this is true, my friend, I have great hopes that when I reach the place to which I am going, I shall there, if anywhere, attain fully to that which has been my chief object in my past life, so that the journey which is now imposed upon me is begun with good hope; and the like hope exists for every man who thinks that his mind has been purified and made ready." . . .

Thereupon Crito nodded to the boy who was standing near. The boy went out and stayed a long time, then came back with the man who was to administer the poison, which he brought with him in a cup ready for use. And when Socrates saw him, he said: "Well, my good man, you know about these things; what must I do?" "Nothing," he replied, "except drink the poison and walk about till your legs feel heavy; then lie down, and the poison will take effect of itself."

At the same time he held out the cup to Socrates. He took it, and very gently, Echecrates, without trembling or changing colour or expression, but looking up at the man with wide open eyes, as was his custom, said: "What do you say about pouring a libation[9] to some deity from this cup? May I, or not?" "Socrates," said he, "we prepare only as much as we think is enough." "I understand," said Socrates; "but I may and must pray to the gods that my departure hence be a fortunate one; so I offer this prayer, and may it be granted." With these words he raised the cup to his lips and very cheerfully and quietly drained it. Up to that time most of us had been able to restrain our tears fairly well, but when we watched him drinking and saw that he had drunk the poison, we could do so no longer. . . . He walked about and, when he said his legs were heavy, lay down on his back, for such was the advice of the attendant. The man who had administered the poison laid his hands on him and after a while examined his feet and legs, then pinched his foot hard and asked if he

9. **libation:** the ritual pouring out of wine or holy oil as an offering to a deity.

felt it. He said "No"; then after that, his thighs; and passing upwards in this way he showed us that he was growing cold and rigid. And again he touched him and said that when it reached his heart, he would be gone. The chill had now reached the region about the groin, and uncovering his face, which had been covered, he said—and these were his last words—"Crito, we owe a cock to Aesculapius.[10] Pay it and do not neglect it." "That," said Crito, "shall be done; but see if you have anything else to say." To this question he made no reply, but after a little while he moved; the attendant uncovered him; his eyes were fixed. And Crito when he saw it, closed his mouth and eyes.

Such was the end, Echecrates, of our friend, who was, as we may say, of all those of his time whom we have known, the best and wisest and most righteous man.

Source 2 from Diogenes Laertius, Lives of Eminent Philosophers, *vol. 2, translated by Robert Drew Hicks (New York: G. P. Putnam's Sons, 1925), pp. 651–653, 657, 665.*

2. Epicurus on the Meaning of Death

[From a letter]

"Accustom thyself to believe that death is nothing to us, for good and evil imply sentience,[11] and death is the privation of all sentience; therefore a right understanding that death is nothing to us makes the mortality of life enjoyable, not by adding to life an illimitable time, but by taking away the yearning after immortality. For life has no terrors for him who has thoroughly apprehended that there are no terrors for him in ceasing to live. Foolish, therefore, is the man who says that he fears death, not because it will pain when it comes, but because it pains in the prospect. Whatsoever causes no annoyance when it is present, causes only a groundless pain in the expectation. Death, therefore, the most awful of evils, is nothing to us, seeing that, when we are, death is not come, and, when death is come, we are not. It is nothing, then, either to the living or to the dead, for with the living it is not and the dead exist no longer. But in the world, at one time men shun death as the greatest of all evils, and at another time choose it as a respite from the evils in life. The wise man does not deprecate life nor does he fear the cessation of life. The thought of life is no offence to him, nor is the cessation of life regarded as an evil. And even as men choose of food not merely and simply the larger portion, but the more pleas-

10. **Aesculapius:** sometimes also rendered "Asclepius," this was the chief god of healing. It was common in the ancient world to offer animal sacrifices to deities as part of prayerful entreaties or as offerings of thanks.

11. **sentience:** the capacity for feeling or sensation.

ant, so the wise seek to enjoy the time which is most pleasant and not merely that which is longest. . . .

"When we say, then, that pleasure is the end and aim, we do not mean the pleasures of the prodigal or the pleasures of sensuality, as we are understood to do by some through ignorance, prejudice, or wilful misrepresentation. By pleasure we mean the absence of pain in the body and of trouble in the soul. It is not an unbroken succession of drinking-bouts and of revelry, not sexual love, not the enjoyment of the fish and other delicacies of a luxurious table, which produce a pleasant life; it is sober reasoning, searching out the grounds of every choice and avoidance, and banishing those beliefs through which the greatest tumults take possession of the soul. Of all this the beginning and the greatest good is prudence. Wherefore prudence is a more precious thing even than philosophy; from it spring all the other virtues, for it teaches that we cannot lead a life of pleasure which is not also a life of prudence, honour, and justice; nor lead a life of prudence, honour, and justice, which is not also a life of pleasure. For the virtues have grown into one with a pleasant life, and a pleasant life is inseparable from them. . . .

[*From the maxims*]

Death is nothing to us; for the body, when it has been resolved into its elements, has no feeling, and that which has no feeling is nothing to us.

Source 3 from Epictetus, The Discourses as Reported by Arrian, the Manual, and Fragments, *vol. 2, translated by W(illiam) A(bbott) Oldfather (New York: G. P. Putnam's Sons, 1926), pp. 215–217.*

3. Epictetus on Ending Life

For this reason the good and excellent man, bearing in mind who he is, and whence he has come, and by whom he was created, centres his attention on this and this only, how he may fill his place in an orderly fashion, and with due obedience to God. "Is it Thy will that I should still remain? I will remain as a free man, as a noble man, as Thou didst wish it; for Thou hast made me free from hindrance in what was mine own. And now hast Thou no further need of me? Be it well with Thee. I have been waiting here until now because of Thee and of none other, and now I obey Thee and depart." "How do you depart?" "Again, as Thou didst wish it, as a free man, as Thy servant, as one who has perceived Thy commands and Thy prohibitions. But so long as I continue to live in Thy service, what manner of man wouldst Thou have me be? An official or a private citizen, a senator or one of the common people, a soldier or a general, a teacher or the head of a household? Whatsoever station and post Thou assign me, I will die ten thousand times, as Socrates says, or

[85]

ever I abandon it.[12] And where wouldst Thou have me be? In Rome, or in Athens, or in Thebes, or in Gyara? Only remember me there. If Thou sendest me to a place where men have no means of living in accordance with nature, I shall depart this life, not in disobedience to Thee, but as though Thou wert sounding for me the recall. I do not abandon Thee—far be that from me! but I perceive that Thou hast no need of me. Yet if there be vouchsafed a means of living in accordance with nature, I will seek no other place than that in which I am, or other men than those who are now my associates."

Sources 4 through 9 from the Revised Standard Version of the Bible, pp. 307–308; p. 316; p. 373; p. 399; p. 441; p. 1209. Copyright 1946, 1952, 1971 by the Division of Christian Education of the National Council of the Churches of Christ in the U.S.A. Used by permission.

4. The Death of Abimelech
(Judges 9:50–56)

Then Abim'elech went to Thebez, and encamped against Thebez, and took it. But there was a strong tower within the city, and all the people of the city fled to it, all the men and women, and shut themselves in; and they went to the roof of the tower. And Abim'elech came to the tower, and fought against it, and drew near to the door of the tower to burn it with fire. And a certain woman threw an upper millstone upon Abim'elech's head, and crushed his skull. Then he called hastily to the young man his armor-bearer, and said to him, "Draw your sword and kill me, lest men say of me, 'A woman killed him.' " And his young man thrust him through, and he died. And when the men of Israel saw that Abim'elech was dead, they departed every man to his home. Thus God requited the crime of Abim'elech, which he committed against his father in killing his seventy brothers.

5. The Death of Samson
(Judges 16:23–31)

Now the lords of the Philistines gathered to offer a great sacrifice to Dagon their god, and to rejoice; for they said, "Our god has given Samson our enemy into our hand." And when the people saw him, they praised their god; for they said, "Our god has given our enemy into our hand, the ravager of our country, who has slain many of us." And when their hearts were merry, they said, "Call Samson, that he may make sport for us." So they called Samson out of the prison, and he made sport before them. They made him stand between the pillars; and Samson said to the lad who held him by the hand, "Let me feel

---

12. This is a paraphrase of the words of Socrates in Plato's dialogue *The Apology,* which recounts the philosopher's defense at his trial.

the pillars on which the house rests, that I may lean against them." Now the house was full of men and women; all the lords of the Philistines were there, and on the roof there were about three thousand men and women, who looked on while Samson made sport.

Then Samson called to the LORD and said, "O Lord GOD, remember me, I pray thee, and strengthen me, I pray thee, only this once, O God, that I may be avenged upon the Philistines for one of my two eyes." And Samson grasped the two middle pillars upon which the house rested, and he leaned his weight upon them, his right hand on the one and his left hand on the other. And Samson said, "Let me die with the Philistines." Then he bowed with all his might; and the house fell upon the lords and upon all the people that were in it. So the dead whom he slew at his death were more than those whom he had slain during his life. Then his brothers and all his family came down and took him and brought him up and buried him between Zorah and Esh'ta-ol in the tomb of Mano'ah his father. He had judged Israel twenty years.

6. The Deaths of Saul and His Armor-Bearer (1 Samuel 31:1–13)

Now the Philistines fought against Israel; and the men of Israel fled before the Philistines, and fell slain on Mount Gilbo'a. And the Philistines overtook Saul and his sons; and the Philistines slew Jonathan and Abin'adab and Mal'chishu'a, the sons of Saul. The battle pressed hard upon Saul, and the archers found him; and he was badly wounded by the archers. Then Saul said to his armor-bearer, "Draw your sword, and thrust me through with it, lest these uncircumcised come and thrust me through, and make sport of me." But his armor-bearer would not; for he feared greatly. Therefore Saul took his own sword, and fell upon it. And when his armor-bearer saw that Saul was dead, he also fell upon his sword, and died with him. Thus Saul died, and his three sons, and his armor-bearer, and all his men, on the same day together. And when the men of Israel who were on the other side of the valley and those beyond the Jordan saw that the men of Israel had fled and that Saul and his sons were dead, they forsook their cities and fled; and the Philistines came and dwelt in them.

On the morrow, when the Philistines came to strip the slain, they found Saul and his three sons fallen on Mount Gilbo'a. And they cut off his head, and stripped off his armor, and sent messengers throughout the land of the Philistines, to carry the good news to their idols and to the people. They put his armor in the temple of Ash'taroth; and they fastened his body to the wall of Beth-shan. But when the inhabitants of Ja'besh-gil'ead heard what the Philistines had done to Saul, all the valiant men arose, and went all night, and took the body of Saul and the bodies of his sons from the wall of

Beth-shan; and they came to Jabesh and burnt them there. And they took their bones and buried them under the tamarisk tree in Jabesh, and fasted seven days.

7. The Death of Ahithophel
(2 Samuel 17:23)

When Ahith'ophel saw that his counsel was not followed, he saddled his ass, and went off home to his own city. And he set his house in order, and hanged himself; and he died, and was buried in the tomb of his father.

8. The Death of Zimri
(1 Kings 16:18–19)

And when Zimri saw that the city was taken, he went into the citadel of the king's house, and burned the king's house over him with fire, and died, because of his sins which he committed, doing evil in the sight of the LORD, walking in the way of Jerobo'am,[13] and for his sin which he committed, making Israel to sin.

9. The Death of Judas
(Matthew 27:1–8)

When morning came, all the chief priests and the elders of the people took counsel against Jesus to put him to death; and they bound him and led him away and delivered him to Pilate the governor.

When Judas, his betrayer, saw that he was condemned, he repented and brought back the thirty pieces of silver to the chief priests and the elders, saying, "I have sinned in betraying innocent blood." They said, "What is that to us? See to it yourself." And throwing down the pieces of silver in the temple, he departed; and he went and hanged himself. But the chief priests, taking the pieces of silver, said, "It is not lawful to put them into the treasury, since they are blood money." So they took counsel, and bought with them the potter's field, to bury strangers in. Therefore that field has been called the Field of Blood to this day.

13. **Jeroboam:** a traitor and idolater in the Old Testament who led an unsuccessful revolt of the north of the Hebrew state against King David's son, Solomon. He later led a successful rebellion against Solomon's son, King Rehoboam, and established an independent state in which he encouraged the worship of idols, not Yahweh.

Source 10 from Josephus with English Translation, vol. 3, The Jewish War, Books IV–VII, *translated by Henry St. John Thackeray (New York: G. P. Putnam's Sons, 1928), pp. 595–603, 613–619.*

10. Josephus on Mass Suicide at Masada, 73 A.D.

However, neither did Eleazar himself contemplate flight, nor did he intend to permit any other to do so. Seeing the wall consuming in the flames, unable to devise any further means of deliverance or gallant endeavour, and setting before his eyes what the Romans, if victorious, would inflict on them, their children and their wives, he deliberated on the death of all. And, judging, as matters stood, this course the best, he assembled the most doughty of his comrades and incited them to the deed by such words as these:

"Long since, my brave men, we determined neither to serve the Romans nor any other save God, for He alone is man's true and righteous Lord; and now the time is come which bids us verify that resolution by our actions. At this crisis let us not disgrace ourselves; we who in the past refused to submit even to a slavery involving no peril, let us not now, along with slavery, deliberately accept the irreparable penalties awaiting us if we are to fall alive into Roman hands. For as we were the first of all to revolt, so are we the last in arms against them. Moreover, I believe that it is God who has granted us this favour, that we have it in our power to die nobly and in freedom—a privilege denied to others who have met with unexpected defeat. Our fate at break of day is certain capture, but there is still the free choice of a noble death with those we hold most dear. For our enemies, fervently though they pray to take us alive, we can no more prevent this than we can now hope to defeat them in battle. . . .

. . . Let our wives thus die undishonoured, our children unacquainted with slavery; and, when they are gone, let us render a generous service to each other, preserving our liberty as a noble winding-sheet. But first let us destroy our chattels and the fortress by fire; for the Romans, well I know, will be grieved to lose at once our persons and the lucre. Our provisions only let us spare; for they will testify, when we are dead, that it was not want which subdued us, but that, in keeping with our initial resolve, we preferred death to slavery."

Thus spoke Eleazar; but his words did not touch the hearts of all hearers alike. Some, indeed, were eager to respond and all but filled with delight at the thought of a death so noble,[14] but others, softer-hearted, were moved with

14. Scholars disagree about the precise translation of the original Greek text at this point. Some render "filled with delight at the thought of a death so noble" as "filled with pleasure supposing such a death to be noble." The latter translation significantly modifies the meaning of Josephus.

compassion for their wives and families, and doubtless also by the vivid prospect of their own end, and their tears as they looked upon one another revealed their unwillingness of heart. Eleazar, seeing them flinching and their courage breaking down in face of so vast a scheme, feared that their whimpers and tears might unman even those who had listened to his speech with fortitude. Far, therefore, from slackening in his exhortation, he roused himself and, fired with mighty fervour, essayed a higher flight of oratory on the immortality of the soul. Indignantly protesting and with eyes intently fixed on those in tears, he exclaimed:

"Deeply, indeed, was I deceived in thinking that I should have brave men as associates in our struggles for freedom—men determined to live with honour or to die. But you, it seems, were no better than the common herd in valour or in courage, you who are afraid even of that death that will deliver you from the direst ills, when in such a cause you ought neither to hesitate an instant nor wait for a counsellor. For from of old, since the first dawn of intelligence, we have been continually taught by those precepts, ancestral and divine—confirmed by the deeds and noble spirit of our forefathers—that life, not death, is man's misfortune. For it is death which gives liberty to the soul and permits it to depart to its own pure abode, there to be free from all calamity; but so long as it is imprisoned in a mortal body and tainted with all its miseries, it is, in sober truth, dead, for association with what is mortal ill befits that which is divine. . . .

. . . Unenslaved by the foe let us die, as free men with our children and wives let us quit this life together! This our laws enjoin, this our wives and children implore of us. The need for this is of God's sending, the reverse of this is the Romans' desire, and their fear is lest a single one of us should die before capture. Haste we then to leave them, instead of their hoped-for enjoyment at securing us, amazement at our death and admiration of our fortitude."

He would have pursued his exhortation but was cut short by his hearers, who, overpowered by some uncontrollable impulse, were all in haste to do the deed. Like men possessed they went their way, each eager to outstrip his neighbour and deeming it a signal proof of courage and sound judgement not to be seen among the last: so ardent the passion that had seized them to slaughter their wives, their little ones and themselves. . . . They had died in the belief that they had left not a soul of them alive to fall into Roman hands; but an old woman and another, a relative of Eleazar, superior in sagacity and training to most of her sex, with five children, escaped by concealing themselves in the subterranean aqueducts, while the rest were absorbed in the slaughter. The victims numbered nine hundred and sixty, including women and children; and the tragedy occurred on the fifteenth of the month Xanthicus.[15]

15. May 2, A.D. 73.

The Romans, expecting further opposition, were by daybreak under arms and, having with gangways formed bridges of approach from the earthworks, advanced to the assault. Seeing none of the enemy but on all sides an awful solitude, and flames within and silence, they were at a loss to conjecture what had happened. At length, as if for a signal to shoot, they shouted, to call forth haply any of those within. The shout was heard by the women-folk, who, emerging from the caverns, informed the Romans how matters stood, one of the two lucidly reporting both the speech and how the deed was done. But it was with difficulty that they listened to her, incredulous of such amazing fortitude; meanwhile they endeavoured to extinguish the flames and soon cutting a passage through them entered the palace. Here encountering the mass of slain, instead of exulting as over enemies, they admired the nobility of their resolve and the contempt of death displayed by so many in carrying it, unwavering, into execution.

Source 11 from Saint Augustine, The City of God Against the Pagans, *translated by George E. McCracken (Cambridge, Mass.: Harvard University Press, 1957), pp. 77–79, 91–101, 109–113. Reprinted by permission of the publishers and the Loeb Classical Library.*

11. Saint Augustine, *The City of God*, Book I

XVII

ON SUICIDE CAUSED BY FEAR OF PUNISHMENT OR DISGRACE.

For if it is not right on individual authority to slay even a guilty man for whose killing no law has granted permission, certainly a suicide is also a homicide, and he is guilty, when he kills himself, in proportion to his innocence of the deed for which he thought he ought to die. If we rightly execrate Judas' deed, and truth pronounces that when he hanged himself, he increased rather than expiated the crime of that accursed betrayal, since by despairing of God's mercy, though he was at death repentant, he left himself no place for a saving repentance, how much more should the man who has no guilt in him to be punished by such means refrain from killing himself!

When Judas killed himself, he killed an accursed man, and he ended his life guilty not only of Christ's death but also of his own, because, though he was killed to atone for his crime, the killing itself was another crime of his. Why, then, should a man who has done no evil do evil to himself, and in doing away with himself do away with an innocent man so as not to suffer from the crime of another, and perpetrate upon himself a sin of his own, so that another's may not be perpetrated on him?

[91]

XX
THAT THERE IS NO AUTHORITY THAT ALLOWS CHRISTIANS IN ANY CASE THE RIGHT TO DIE OF THEIR OWN WILL.

Not for nothing is it that in the holy canonical books no divinely inspired order or permission can be found authorizing us to inflict death upon ourselves, neither in order to acquire immortality nor in order to avert or divert some evil. For we must certainly understand the commandment as forbidding this when it says: "Thou shalt not kill,"[16] particularly since it does not add "thy neighbour," as it does when it forbids false witnessing. . . .

On this basis some try to extend this commandment even to wild and domestic animals and maintain that it is wrong to kill any of them. Why not then extend it also to plants and to anything fixed and fed by roots in the earth? For things of this kind, though they have no feeling, are said to live, and therefore can also die, and hence, when violence is exercised, be slain. Thus the Apostle, when he speaks of seeds of this sort, says: "That which thou sowest is not quickened except it die,"[17] and we find in a psalm, "He killed their vines with hail."[18] Do we from this conclude, when we hear "Thou shalt not kill," that it is wrong to pull up a shrub? Are we so completely deranged that we assent to the Manichaean error?

Hence, putting aside these ravings, if when we read, "Thou shalt not kill," we do not understand this phrase to apply to bushes, because they have no sensation, nor to the unreasoning animals that fly, swim, walk or crawl, because they are not partners with us in the faculty of reason, the privilege not being given them to share it in common with us—and therefore by the altogether righteous ordinance of the Creator both their life and death are a matter subordinate to our needs—the remaining possibility is to understand this commandment, "Thou shalt not kill," as meaning man alone, that is, "neither another nor thyself," for in fact he who kills himself kills what is no other than a man.

XXI
WHAT CASES OF HOMICIDE ARE EXCEPTED FROM THE CHARGE OF MURDER?

This very same divine law, to be sure, made certain exceptions to the rule that it is not lawful to kill a human being. The exceptions include only such persons as God commands to be put to death, either by an enacted law or by special decree applicable to a single person at the given time—but note that the man who is bound to this service under orders, as a sword is bound to be the tool of him who employs it, is not himself the slayer, and consequently there is no breach of this commandment, which says, "Thou shalt not kill," in the case of those who by God's authorization have waged wars, or, who, repre-

16. Exodus 20:16. Saint Augustine makes frequent biblical references in his text.
17. 1 Corinthians 15:36.
18. Psalms 78:46.

senting in their person the power of the state, have put criminals to death in accordance with God's law, being vested, that is, with the imperial prerogative of altogether righteous reason. Abraham too not only was not blamed for cruelty, but was even praised for piety, because he resolved to slay his son, not with criminal motives but in obedience to God. And it is properly a question whether we should regard it as equivalent to a command of God when Jephthah slew his daughter who ran to meet him after he had vowed to sacrifice to God the first victim that met him as he returned victorious from battle.[19] Nor is Samson acquitted of guilt on any other plea, inasmuch as he crushed himself by the collapse of the house along with his enemies, than the plea that the Spirit who through him had been working miracles,[20] had secretly ordered this. With these exceptions then, those slain either by application of a just law or by command of God, the very fount of justice, whoever kills a human being, either himself or no matter who, falls within the meshes of the charge of murder.

XXII
WHETHER SUICIDE IS EVER A SIGN OF GREATNESS OF MIND.

Those who have laid violent hands upon themselves are perhaps to be admired for the greatness of their souls, but not to be praised for the soundness of their wisdom. If, however, you take reason more carefully into account, you will not really call it greatness of soul which brings anyone to suicide because he or she lacks strength to bear whatever hardships or sins of others may occur. For the mind is rather detected in weakness, if it cannot bear whether it be the harsh enslavement of its own body, or the stupid opinion of the mob; and a mind might better be called greater that can endure instead of fleeing from a distressful life, and that can in the light of pure conscience despise the judgement of men, especially that of the mob, which as a rule is wrapped in a fog of error.

Therefore, if suicide can be thought to be a great-souled act, this quality of greatness of soul was possessed by that Theombrotus[21] of whom they say that, when he had read Plato's book containing a discussion of the immortality of the soul,[22] he hurled himself headlong from a wall and so departed from this life to that which he thought a better. He was not urged to this act by any calamity of fortune or accusation, false or true, that he had not strength to bear and so made away with himself. Nay, his sole motive for seeking death and breaking the sweet bonds of this life was his greatness of soul. Nevertheless, this Plato himself whom he had read could have borne witness that he

---

19. Judges 11:29–40.
20. Judges 16:28–30.
21. **Theombrotus:** a philosopher of Ambracia, Greece.
22. Plato's dialogue *The Phaedo*.

acted greatly rather than well, for assuredly Plato would have made this act the first step and the most important step he took himself, and might well have pronounced in favour of it too, had he not, with that intellect by which he saw the soul's immortality, reached the conclusion that suicide should not be committed, nay more, should be forbidden.

Yet in fact many have killed themselves to prevent falling into the hands of the enemy. We are not now asking whether this was done but whether it should have been done. Sound reasoning, naturally, is to be preferred even to precedents, but there are precedents for that matter not discordant with reason—such, be it noted, as are precedents the more worthy of imitation as they are more outstanding in piety. No case of suicide occurred among patriarchs, among prophets, among apostles, seeing that the Lord Christ himself, when he advised them, if they suffered persecution, to flee from city to city,[23] might then have advised them to lay hands upon themselves to avoid falling into the hands of their persecutors. Furthermore, granted that he gave no command or advice to His disciples to employ this means of departing from life, though he promised that he would prepare everlasting mansions for them when they departed, then, no matter what precedents are brought forward by heathen that know not God, it is obvious that suicide is unlawful for those who worship the one true God.

XXVI

WHAT EXPLANATION WE SHOULD ADOPT TO ACCOUNT FOR THE SAINTS' DOING CERTAIN THINGS THAT THEY ARE KNOWN TO HAVE DONE WHICH IT IS NOT LAWFUL TO DO.

But, they say, in time of persecution certain saintly women, to avoid the pursuers of their chastity, cast themselves into a river that would ravish and drown them, and in that way they died and their memorial shrines are frequented by great numbers who venerate them as martyrs in the Catholic Church.

With regard to these women I dare not give any rash judgement. I do not know whether the divine authority has counselled the church by some trustworthy testimonies to honour their memory in this, and it may be so. For what if the women acted as they did, not by human misconception, but by divine command, and they did not go astray in their act, but were obedient? Compare the case of Samson, where it would be sin to hold any other view. When God, moreover, gives a command and makes it clear without ambiguity that he gives it, who can summon obedience to judgement? Who can draw up a brief against religious deference to God? . . .

. . . Let anyone, therefore, who is told that he has no right to kill himself, do the deed if he is so ordered by him whose orders must not be slighted. There is just one proviso: he must be sure that his divine command is not made pre-

23. Matthew 10:5–15.

carious by any doubt. It is through the ear that we take note of men's thoughts; we do not arrogate to ourselves any right to judge such as are kept secret. No one "knows what goes on in a man except the spirit of the man that is in him."[24]

This we say, this we declare, this we by all means endorse: that no man ought to inflict on himself a voluntary death, thinking to escape temporary ills, lest he find himself among ills that are unending; that no one ought to do so because of another's sins, lest by the very act he bring into being a sin that is his own, when he would not have been polluted by another's; that on one ought to do so on account of any past sins, inasmuch as he needs this life the more to make possible their healing by repentance; that no one ought to do so thinking to satisfy his hunger for the better life for which we hope after death, inasmuch as the better life after death does not accept those who are guilty of their own death.

24. 1 Corinthians 2:11.

QUESTIONS TO CONSIDER

The evidence in this chapter all deals with the central issue of suicide, but it comes from sources originating over an extraordinarily long period, about a millennium and one-half of the ancient period. Our objective in spanning such a period is to examine the continuities and changes in ancient thought on the subject of self-destruction by asking you to address three progressively more probing central questions based on the sources.

The first question asks that you consider each of the selections individually by identifying every author's thought on the suicide that was common in much of the ancient world. How do all of the authors, except Saint Augustine, implicitly or more directly accept suicide as justifiable? What sort of ethical considera-

tions does the act raise for each author? What limitations, if any, does each place on self-destruction?

The second question requires that you place each of the sources in the intellectual context within which its author wrote. You must consider the religious beliefs and philosophical outlook of each period represented in the sources: the Hellenic and Hellenistic ages, the Roman Empire, Old and New Testament Palestine, and the early Christian era. How did the ideas of the various thinkers reflect the religious and philosophical orientations of their respective ages?

The third question asks that you examine the evolution of ancient ideas on suicide over an extended period of time. What basic continuities on this subject do you note in ancient thought? At what point did ancient thought on suicide change? What aspects of Christian doctrine and the controversies surrounding this faith in the third and fourth centuries A.D. promoted the viewpoint advanced by Saint Augustine? On what basis did he deny that the acts of self-destruction in the Bible were true suicides? Why might you assume that Saint Augustine's theology heavily influenced Western attitudes toward suicide in the Christian era that emerged from the decline and fall of the Roman Empire?

As you consider your answers to these questions, you should better comprehend the ancients' views on suicide, but even more importantly, you should understand the philosophical and theological foundations for those ideas.

EPILOGUE

Very few ancient thinkers unconditionally condemned the act of self-destruction, although as we have seen, Socrates noted one such group, the Pythagoreans. [We must add that Neoplatonists like Plotinus (205–270) also condemned suicide. They held that since one's standing in the afterlife rested on the state of one's soul at death, suicide was inadmissible because the possibility of moral improvement existed as long as life endured.] Thus, Saint Augustine's general condemnation of suicide reflected a distinct break with the past. Indeed, his dictum that suicide was murder, reaffirmed by later theologians, including Saint Thomas Aquinas (1225–1274), shaped the religious and legal response of the Christian West to the act of self-destruction into the twentieth century.[25]

Religiously, Saint Augustine's condemnation of all forms of suicide, perhaps reinforced by primitive suicide taboos among the Germanic tribes overwhelming late ancient Rome, became part of canon law. That law always relieved persons of diminished psychological capacity from the spiritual consequence of suicide. But for suicides of apparently sound mind, the act of self-destruction incurred severe spiritual penalties. Theologians believed suicides by such individuals represented despair and thus rejection of the Christian message, perhaps reflecting Satanic possession. Thus at the Council of Braga in 563, the Roman Catholic Church denied religious burial to these persons, a practice many Protestant groups perpetuated after the Reformation of the sixteenth century.

---

25. Indeed, the very word *suicide* did not exist in Western languages prior to the early seventeenth century, and some variation of the phrase "murder of oneself" described the act of self-destruction in most European tongues. The word *suicide* seems first to have appeared in a work of the Englishman Sir Thomas Browne, *Religio medici*, published in 1642. The use of the term slowly gained ground in English usage, and in the eighteenth century it found its way into French, Italian, Portuguese, and Spanish lexicons. Literally translated from its Latin roots as "to strike oneself mortally," the word itself is highly significant because it eschews the more condemnatory term *murder*.

Legally, most medieval and early modern Western states reflected canon law by adopting statutes recognizing suicide as a form of murder. Thus, persons taking their own lives might incur worldly as well as spiritual penalties if a postmortem judicial proceeding determined that they had, indeed, ended their own lives while in a sound mental state. Worldly penalties typically included two elements. The first was financial in nature. Under laws dating from at least as early as the thirteenth century in England and France, the state confiscated the property of the successful suicide. In the second form of punishment, the authorities desecrated the corpse of the suicide in ceremonies that included the spiritual penalty of denied burial. Thus, in Catholic France prior to the Revolution, judicial authorities dragged suicides' corpses through the streets, frequently displayed the remains to the public, and disposed of the bodies without burial rites, often as refuse. In England, after the Reformation, the authorities buried suicides' remains without religious sacraments at crossroads. Because of popular fears that the spirits of suicides might return to the world of the living, the authorities often drove stakes through the bodies and into the ground to prevent the return of the deceased from their graves. Other Western countries engaged in similar practices that long endured, and attempted suicide was a capital offense in many legal codes for centuries.

Only in the late seventeenth and eighteenth centuries, in a process that historians have called a "secularization of suicide,"[26] did many Western thinkers begin to view the act of self-destruction as a social, psychological, or medical problem rather than the moral and theological issue defined by Saint Augustine. Nevertheless, the law long reflected this earlier attitude, and the act of suicide persistently excited basic religious and philosophical controversies. Suicide remained a crime in France until 1791, and the last English crossroads burial occurred in 1823. Attempted suicide continued to be a crime in England until 1961, and until that same year, those of sound mind who took their own lives might be denied burial rites by the Church of England. Attempted suicide remains a criminal offense in a small number of American states today.

26. This terminology was introduced by the work of Michael MacDonald and Terence Murphy, *Sleepless Souls: Suicide in Early Modern England* (Oxford: Oxford University Press, 1990).

CHAPTER FIVE

SLAVE LAW IN ROMAN AND

GERMANIC SOCIETY

In all the cultures of the ancient Mediterranean, some people were slaves, owned as property by other people. In Mesopotamia and Egypt, people became slaves in a variety of ways, and the earliest law codes, such as that of Hammurabi (ca 1780 B.C.), include provisions regarding slavery. Many slaves were war captives, brought into the area from outside along with other types of booty. Some were criminals, for whom slavery was the punishment for a crime. Some had been sold into slavery by their parents or had sold themselves into slavery in times of economic hardship. Others became slaves to repay debts, a condition that was often temporary. In these cultures, slaves performed a variety of tasks, from farming to highly skilled professional and administrative work, but the proportion of slaves in the population was not very great and most work was carried out by free persons. Thus, historians describe Mesopotamia and Egypt as slave-using but not slave societies.

By contrast, republican Rome was truly a slave society, in which a significant proportion of the population were slaves—perhaps one-quarter or one-third by the second century B.C.—and in which slaves did much of the productive labor. The military conquests of Rome during the second and first centuries B.C. provided many new war captives and also increased the wealth of Rome's elite, who invested in huge agricultural estates (termed *latifundia*). These estates were too large to be worked by single peasant families—who were often migrating to the cities in any case—and so an increasing share of agricultural production was carried on by large labor gangs of slaves under the supervision of overseers, who might themselves be slaves. The owners of both the land and the slaves were often absentee, living in Rome or another urban center rather than out on the latifundia themselves. This system of agricultural slavery continued into the Roman Empire, although the influx of new slaves lessened somewhat as military expansion slowed and laws were passed prohibiting the enslavement of subjects of the Empire. In addition, urban slaves who worked as household servants, artisans, teachers, gladiators, or shopkeepers continued to be very common.

The Germanic tribes that gradually migrated into the Roman Empire beginning in the second century were also slave-owning cultures, although the relative number of slaves among them was probably less than that in Rome. When they conquered Roman lands, they generally took a proportion of the slaves and the land for themselves, leaving the rest to the existing Roman proprietors. However, the breakdown in communication and political control that accompanied the disintegration of the Roman Empire in the West made it increasingly difficult for absentee owners to control their estates and to ship their products safely to distant markets. Thus, like many other aspects of life during this period, slavery became increasingly localized and less economically significant than it had been earlier in these areas, although it did not disappear.

Slavery in both Roman and Germanic societies was based not on racial distinctions but on notions of personal freedom that could be very complex. At the heart of this complexity was the issue that a slave was both a person, able to engage in relationships with other persons and to act on his or her own, and a thing, owned by another person. Law codes developed by both Romans and Germans had to balance these two aspects of being a slave, as well as regulate other matters concerning slaves and slavery. They had to establish and protect the boundaries between slave and free, but also establish ways in which those boundaries could be crossed, as slavery was not necessarily a permanent status. Your task in this chapter will be to investigate Roman and Germanic laws regarding slavery during the period 400 to 1000, in order to answer the following questions: How were legal distinctions between slave and free established, structured, and maintained, and how could they be overcome? What similarities and differences are there in Roman and Germanic laws regarding slavery?

SOURCES AND METHOD

When historians investigate legal developments, they often use law codes in conjunction with court records and other documents to examine the actual workings of the law, or to contrast legal theory with reality. For the period we are investigating in this chapter, sources describing actual legal practice in central and western Europe are virtually nonexistent, and so our focus will be strictly on the law codes. (Other sources regarding slavery in the Roman Empire do exist, such as economic treatises, histories of slave revolts, and philosophical discussions of slavery, but there are no parallel sources for early Germanic societies.) We must thus keep in mind that everything we read is essentially legal theory, describing what is supposed to happen rather than what actually does happen. Law codes are not written in a vacuum, however. They reflect not only the ideals of the legal and political authorities who were their authors, but also these authorities' assumptions about what people—in this case slaves, their owners, and people who came into contact with slaves and their owners—might actually do. In some cases laws also explicitly describe actual conduct, generally as a preamble to a prohibition of this conduct, or a succession of laws implies actual conduct, as prohibitions are made more specific or penalties are made more stringent.

It is important in this chapter, then, to keep in mind the limitations of using law codes as a source, and it is also important to recognize that the law codes we will be using come from two cultures that had very different notions concerning the origin, function, and purpose of law. Roman law began during the republican period as a set of rules governing the private lives of citizens, and was later expanded to include the handling of disputes between Romans and non-Romans and between foreigners under Roman jurisdiction. The first written codification, the Twelve Tables, was made in the middle of the fifth century B.C. and posted publicly, giving at least those Romans who could read direct access to it. Legal interpreters called *praetors* and judges

called *judices* made decisions based on explicit statutes and also on their own notions of what would be fair and equitable, which gave them a great deal of flexibility. Praetors generally followed the laws set by their predecessors, announcing publicly at the beginning of their terms of office that they would do this, but they also added to the body of law as new issues arose. Thus Roman law was adaptable to new conditions, with jurists in the Empire regarding their work as building on that of earlier centuries rather than negating it. Ultimately all those living within the boundaries of the Roman Empire were regarded as subject to the same law, the *ius gentium,* or "law of peoples."

Roman law regarding slavery—like all Roman law—for most of the republican and imperial periods was a mixture of senatorial statutes, edicts of elected officials, opinions of learned jurists, imperial decrees, and rulings by lesser officials. Under Emperor Theodosius II (r. 408–450), an attempt was made to compile some of the actual imperial decrees, and the resultant Theodosian Code promulgated in 435–438 contained all of the imperial laws issued since the time of the emperor Constantine (r. 311–337) that were still in effect, including those on slavery. Theodosius ruled the eastern half of the Roman Empire (which later came to be called the Byzantine Empire), but his laws were promulgated for both the eastern and western halves. The Theodosian Code was expanded under the direction of the Byzantine Emperor Justinian (r. 527–565), with older and newer laws and the opinions of jurists added. Justinian's Code, promulgated in 529–533 and officially termed the *Corpus Juris Civilis,* became the basis of Byzantine legal procedure for nearly a millennium.

In contrast to Roman written statutory law, Germanic law remained a body of traditions handed down orally for almost a thousand years after the first codification of Roman law. Like all systems of customary law around the world, it was regarded as binding because it represented the immemorial customs of a specific tribe. The ultimate authority in this legal system was not an abstract body of laws or a group of legal interpreters, but the king, whose chief legal function was to "speak the law"—that is, to decide cases based on existing oral tradition; neither the king nor anyone else could (at least in theory) make new laws. This body of custom was regarded as the inalienable possession of all members of a tribe, no matter where they happened to be, and was thus attached to persons rather than to geographic areas the way Roman (and today's) statutory law codes were.

At roughly the same time that codifications of Roman law were promulgated by the emperors Theodosius and Justinian, Germanic kings in western Europe supported the initial written codifications of what had been oral customary law. These codes usually bore the name of the tribe, such as the Lombard Law, the Burgundian Law, or the Salic Law (the law of the Salian Franks). On the continent of Europe, such law codes were written down in Latin, often by Roman jurists employed by Germanic kings, so that they sometimes included Roman legal tradition as well as Germanic customs, particularly in southern Europe, where Roman culture was strongest. In northern Europe and in England—where the laws were initially written in the West Saxon dialect that became Old English—Roman influences were weaker, making the codes of these areas, such as those of the Frisians and the Anglo-Saxons, more purely customary in origin.

When the Germanic tribes came into the Empire, these two notions of the law—statutory and geographic versus customary and personal—came into direct conflict. The problem was solved initially by letting Romans be judged according to written Roman law while non-Romans were judged by their own oral customs. As the Germanic kingdoms became more firmly established, their rulers saw the merits of a written code, but two legal systems—one for Romans and one for Germanic people—often existed side by side for centuries in these areas. Only in cases that involved a conflict between a Roman and a German was the former expected to follow the new Germanic code. As noted above, however, Roman principles did shape these Germanic codes to some degree. Though the initial codifications claimed to be simply the recording of long-standing customs, in reality the laws often modified customs that no longer fit the needs of the Germanic peoples as they became more settled and adopted some aspects of the more sophisticated Roman culture. Later kings were also not hesitant to make new laws when situations demanded it and to state explicitly that this is what they were doing. Thus Germanic codes gradually evolved from records of tribal customs based on moral sanctions and notions of a common tradition into collections of royal statutes based on the political authority of kings. They remained more closely linked to the ruler than Roman law and never included the opinions of legal commentators the way Justinian's Code did, but, like Roman law, they were eventually tied to a geographic area rather than to a group of people.

There were thus significant differences between Roman and Germanic societies in the function and complexity of law, but the legal codes of all these societies included provisions regarding slavery. The sources for this chapter come from seven different law codes, two from Roman tradition—the Theodosian Code and Justinian's Code—and five from Germanic tradition—Burgundian, Salic, Lombard, Alemannic, and Anglo-Saxon. Many of these law codes exist in multiple manuscript versions, with the earliest extant version often dating from centuries after the code was first compiled. This provides much fuel for scholarly disagreement about exactly when they were drawn up, exactly which sections date from the initial codification and which from later revisions, and exactly how certain sections are supposed to read. (Scholars can often trace the path manuscripts followed by noting which errors were recopied by subse-

quent scribes; often this does not help in determining which versions are more "authentic," however.) For this chapter, we have used the version of these codes most widely accepted by recent scholarship, but you should be aware that any edition or translation of texts like these from manuscript cultures involves a decision on the part of the editor as to which version to use.

To explore the legal definitions of and boundaries between slavery and freedom, we will be examining four basic issues in this chapter: (A) How could a person become a slave, or a slave become free? (B) How were slaves valued, in comparison to other things a person might own, and what limits were placed on the treatment of slaves by their owners? (C) How were personal relationships between slave and free regulated? (D) How were slaves differentiated from free persons in terms of criminal actions committed by them or against them? To assist you in working through the issues in this chapter, provisions in the laws have been grouped according to these four topics rather than being presented in the order in which they appear in the codes. (In many of these codes, particularly the Germanic ones, laws are arranged completely haphazardly in any case, so that the order makes no difference.) Thus, as you are taking notes on the sources, it would be a good idea to draw up a chart for each issue. Other than this, your basic method in this chapter is careful reading.

Source 1 includes selections from the Theodosian Code. According to the selections in Source 1A, what are some of the ways in which one could become a slave in the late Roman Empire? What are some ways in which slaves could become free? According to 1B, what would happen to a master who beat his slaves? According to 1C, what would happen to a woman who had sexual relations with or married one of her slaves? To a man who had sexual relations with one of his slaves? To a decurion (a man who was a member of a local municipal council) who did so? According to 1D, what would happen to rebellious slaves?

Source 2 contains selections from Justinian's Code, which was itself divided into three parts: the *Codex*, actual imperial legislation, including much that was contained in the Theodosian Code; the *Digest*, the opinions of various jurists from throughout the history of Rome; and the *Institutes*, an officially prescribed course for first-year law students, in which some of the opinions found in the *Digest* are repeated. The legal opinions included in the *Digest* sometimes refer to specific imperial statutes, and sometimes simply describe what the commentator saw as Roman tradition in regard to legal categories or procedures. Like legal opinions today, however, the judgments of these jurists shaped the handling of cases, for later judges and lawyers looked to earlier precedents and opinions when making their decisions. They are thus much more important than the opinion of a private person on an issue would be, and all the selections included here come from the *Digest*. According to Source 2A, what were some of the ways in which one could

become a slave or become free? Would becoming free remove all obligations a slave had toward his master? According to 2C, did slaves have family relationships? According to 2D, what would happen to someone who killed a slave? To slaves whose master was killed while they were within earshot? To runaway slaves and those who protected them?

Putting the information from Sources 1 and 2 together, you can begin to develop an idea about the legal status of slaves in the later Roman Empire. What are some of the ways one could cross from slave to free? From free to slave? Is this a hard boundary, as the writers of the *Digest* imply in 2A, or are there intermediate steps? How do restrictions on slave/free sexual relationships help to maintain the boundaries? Why do you think there are gender differences in such restrictions? In what ways do the laws in 1D and 2D regard the slave as a thing? In what ways as a person?

Sources 3 through 7 are selections from Germanic law codes, which were often written down under the reign of one king and then expanded under his successors. Compared with Roman law, Germanic codes were extremely short and consist solely of statements of law, with no juristic opinions such as those contained in the *Digest*. They thus offer a less full picture of slave life than does Roman law, but slaves are mentioned in many of their clauses. In Germanic society, murder, injuries, or insults to honor had resulted in feuds between individuals and families, but by the time the law codes were written down, a system of monetary compensatory payments—called *wergeld* in the case of murder or *composition* in the case of lesser injuries—was being devised as a substitute. These compensatory payments were set according to the severity of the loss or injury, and also according to the social status of the perpetrator and the victim.

Source 3 comes from one of the earliest Germanic law codes, the Law of Gundobad, drawn up for his Burgundian subjects by King Gundobad (r. 474–516), who ruled the Burgundian kingdom in what is now southeastern France. (Following the principle that customary law applied to persons and not territories, Gundobad also drew up a separate code for his Roman subjects, the *Lex Romana Burgundionem*, at about the same time.) According to the laws in Source 3A, what were some of the ways in which one could become a slave or be freed if one were a slave? According to 3C, what were the penalties for rape of freewomen and slaves? For women who willingly had sexual relations with slaves? According to 3D, what was the relative value of slaves as compared to that of free persons and freedmen (former slaves), at least in regard to their teeth and female honor?

Source 4 comes from the Germanic tribe known as the Franks, who conquered the Burgundian kingdom in 534. The original Frankish code, the *Pactus Legis Salicae,* was issued by King Clovis in about 510 and was amended and revised by many of his successors. (Like all Germanic codes,

it did not apply to everyone living under Frankish overlordship; Burgundians living within the Frankish kingdom continued to be judged by Burgundian law for centuries after the conquest.) It includes no laws on how one becomes a slave or is released from slavery, but it does include sections on sexual relations with slaves, and on slaves who steal or run away. According to the laws in Source 4C, in the first group, what would happen to a freeman or freewoman who marries or has sexual intercourse with a slave? To a slave who marries or has sexual intercourse with a free person or another slave? According to 4D, how were the slave's owners' rights balanced against those of the person from whom the slave stole? How were those who encouraged slaves to run away to be punished? How does this punishment compare with that set for slaves who steal?

Source 5 contains selections from the Lombard Laws, written down between 643 and 755 under the direction of various Lombard kings, including King Rothair (issued in 643), King Luitprand (issued 713–735), and King Aistulf (issued 750–755). The Lombards invaded Italy in 568, after the Franks, Burgundians, and other tribes had already established successor kingdoms in parts of the old Roman Empire, and established a kingdom in central and northern Italy that lasted until 774, when it was conquered by the Frankish ruler Charlemagne. Like Burgundian law, Lombard law remained in force for Lombards within Frankish territory for centuries—in fact, until the city-states of Italy began to adopt Roman legal principles and the *Corpus Juris Civilis* in the twelfth century. Lombard law was more comprehensive than the Burgundian and Frankish codes, and included provisions regarding all of the issues we are investigating in this chapter. According to the laws in Source 5A, what were some of the ways in which a person could become a slave in Lombard society? How could a slave be freed? According to 5B, what was the relative value of slaves as compared to horses? According to 5C, how were marriages between slaves, freed persons, and free people to be handled? According to 5D, how were fugitive slaves and slaves who revolted to be handled?

Source 6 comes from the Germanic tribe known as the Alamans, who settled in what is now southern Germany and Switzerland in the third century A.D. and wrote their law codes between 613 and 713. Like other Germanic codes, Alamannic law set compensatory payments for various injuries and actions, and also used slavery as a punishment for certain crimes. According to Source 6A, what was one of the ways in which people could become slaves? According to 6B, were there limits on a master's treatment of slaves? According to 6C, what would happen to a freewoman who married a slave? According to 6D, what were the relative values placed on men and women from the three basic social groups, free persons, freedpersons, and slaves? How was the rape of slaves to be compensated?

Source 7, the final source for this chapter, contains provisions from Anglo-Saxon law codes from the various kingdoms of England, dating from the sixth through the tenth centuries. These codes were written in Old English, not in Latin, and show no signs of Roman influence, although many of their provisions are similar to those we have seen in other Germanic codes. According to Source 7A, laws issued by Edward the Elder (dated between 901 and 925), what was one way in which a person could become a slave? According to 7B, from the laws of Ine (688–695), what were some of the limitations on a master's treatment of his slaves? According to 7D, laws of Aethelbert of Kent (565–604) and Alfred (890–899), what was the punishment for rape of a slave? How did this differ depending on the status of the slave and the perpetrator?

You now need to put together the Germanic material in the same way that you did the Roman. How could people in Germanic society move from free to slave? From slave to free? Are there intermediate steps between these two, and how do the rights of these people differ from those of free people and slaves? What are the consequences of various types of slave/free sexual relationships? Are there hierarchies of status and value among slaves? On what are these based? Do the laws regarding crimes against slaves and crimes committed by slaves tend to view slaves as things or as persons?

THE EVIDENCE

Source 1 from Clyde Pharr, editor, The Theodosian Code *(Princeton, N.J.: Princeton University Press, 1952), Sections 3.3.1; 4.6.7; 5.6.3; 5.9.1; 7.13.16; 7.18.4; 9.12.1–2; 9.9.1–3, 6; 10.10.33; 14.18.1. Copyright © 1952 by Clyde Pharr, Princeton University Press. Renewed 1980 by Roy Pharr. Reprinted by permission of Princeton University Press.*

1. Theodosian Code

A. Slave to Free/Free to Slave

[3.3.1] All those persons whom the piteous fortune of their parents has consigned to slavery while their parents thereby were seeking sustenance shall be restored to their original status of free birth. Certainly no person shall demand repayment of the purchase price, if he has been compensated by the slavery of a freeborn person for a space of time that is not too short.

INTERPRETATION: If a father, forced by need, should sell any freeborn child whatsoever, the child cannot remain in perpetual slavery, but if he has made compensation by his slavery, he shall be restored to his freeborn status without even the repayment of the purchase price.

[4.6.7] We sanction that the name of natural children shall be placed upon those who have been begotten and brought into this world as the result of a lawful union without an honorable performance of the marriage ceremony. But it is established that children born from the womb of a slave woman are slaves, according to the law . . . [I]f natural children have been born from a slave woman and have not been manumitted by their master, they are reckoned among the slaves belonging to his inheritance.

[5.6.3] We have subjected the Scyrae, a barbarian nation, to Our power after We had routed a very great force of Chuni, with whom they had allied themselves. Therefore We grant to all persons the opportunity to supply their own fields with men of the aforesaid race.

[5.9.1] If any person should take up a boy or a girl child that has been cast out of its home with the knowledge and consent of its father or owner, and if he should rear this child to strength with his own sustenance, he shall have the right to keep the said child under the same status as he wished it to have when he took charge of it, that is, as his child or as a slave, whichever he should prefer.

[14.18.1] If there should be any persons who adopt the profession of mendicancy[1] and who are induced to seek their livelihood at public expense, each of

---

1. **mendicancy:** begging.

them shall be examined. The soundness of body and the vigor of years of each one of them shall be investigated. In the case of those who are able, the necessity shall be placed upon them that the zealous and diligent informer shall obtain the ownership of those beggars who are held bound by their servile status, and such informer shall be supported by the right to the perpetual colonate[2] of those beggars who are attended by only the liberty of their birth rights, provided that the informer should betray and prove such sloth.

[7.13.16] In the matter of defense against hostile attacks,[3] We order that consideration be given not only to the legal status of soldiers, but also to their physical strength. Although We believe that freeborn persons are aroused by love of country, We exhort slaves[4] also, by the authority of this edict, that as soon as possible they shall offer themselves for the labors of war, and if they receive their arms as men fit for military service, they shall obtain the reward of freedom, and they shall also receive two solidi each for travel money. Especially, of course, do We urge this service upon the slaves of those persons who are retained in the armed imperial service, and likewise upon the slaves of federated allies and of conquered peoples, since it is evident that they are making war also along with their masters.

[7.18.4] [In the case of deserters,] if a slave should surrender such deserter, he shall be given freedom. If a freeborn person of moderate status should surrender such deserter, he shall gain immunity.[5]

B. Value and Treatment of Slaves

[9.12.1–2] If a master should beat a slave with light rods or lashes or if he should cast him into chains for the purpose of custody, he shall not endure any fear of criminal charges if the slave should die, for We abolish all consideration of time limitations and legal interpretation.[6] The master shall not, indeed, use his own right immoderately, but he shall be guilty of homicide if he should kill the slave voluntarily by a blow of a club or of a stone, at any rate if he should use a weapon and inflict a lethal wound or should order the slave to be hanged by a noose, or if he should command by a shameful order that he be thrown from a high place or should administer the virus of a poison or should lacerate his body by public punishments,[7] that is, by cutting through

---

2. **colonate:** forced labor on farms.

3. At this time the Roman Empire was gradually crumbling from the attacks of the barbarians.

4. In violation of long-established Roman custom.

5. From compulsory public services, including taxes.

6. The references seem to be to preceding laws, which specified distinctions depending on whether a slave died immediately or after a period of time, and which contained various technicalities.

7. Types of punishment that were inflicted for certain public crimes.

his sides with the claws of wild beasts[8] or by applying fire and burning his body, or if with the savagery of monstrous barbarians he should force bodies and limbs weakening and flowing with dark blood, mingled with gore, to surrender their life almost in the midst of tortures.

Whenever such chance attends the beating of slaves by their masters that the slaves die, the masters shall be free from blame if by the correction of very evil deeds they wished to obtain better conduct on the part of their household slaves. . . .

INTERPRETATION: If a slave should die while his master is punishing a fault, the master shall not be held on the charge of homicide, because he is guilty of homicide only if he is convicted of having intended to kill the slave. For disciplinary correction is not reckoned as a crime.

C. Slave/Free Relations

[9.9.1–6] If any woman is discovered to have a clandestine love affair with her slave, she shall be subject to the capital sentence, and the rascally slave shall be delivered to the flames. All persons shall have the right to bring an accusation of this public crime; office staffs shall have the right to report it; even a slave shall have permission to lodge information, and freedom shall be granted to him if the crime is proved, although punishment threatens him if he makes a false accusation. 1. If a woman has been so married[9] before the issuance of this law, she shall be separated from such an association, shall be deprived not only of her home but also of participation in the life of the province, and shall mourn the absence of her exiled lover. 2. The children also whom she bears from this union shall be stripped of all the insignia of rank. They shall remain in bare freedom, and neither through themselves nor through the interposition of another person shall they receive anything under any title of a will from the property of the woman. 3. Moreover, the inheritance of the woman, in case of intestacy, shall be granted either to her children, if she has legitimate ones, or to the nearest kinsmen and cognates, or to the person whom the rule of law admits, so that whatever of their own property her former lover and the children conceived from him appear by any chance to have had shall be joined to the property of the woman and may be vindicated by the aforesaid successors. . . .

6. For after the issuance of this law We punish by death those persons who commit this crime. But those who have been separated in accordance with this

8. Implements of torture, actually made of metal.

9. A loose use of the word *marriage,* as slaves could not enter legally recognized marriages (*conubia*) because those were contracts available only to free persons. Instead they were joined in less formal unions termed *contubernia*.

law and secretly come together again and renew the forbidden union and who are convicted by the evidence of slaves or that of the office of the special investigator or also by the information of nearest kinsmen shall sustain a similar penalty.

INTERPRETATION: If any freeborn woman should join herself secretly to her own slave, she shall suffer capital punishment. A slave also who should be convicted of adultery with his mistress shall be burned by fire. Whoever wishes shall have it in his power to bring accusation of a crime of this kind. Even slaves or maidservants, if they should bring an accusation of this crime, shall be heard, on this condition, however, that they shall obtain their freedom if they prove their accusation; that if they falsify, they shall be punished. The inheritance of a woman who defiles herself with such a crime shall be granted either to her children, if they were conceived from her husband, or to those near kinsmen who succeed according to law.

[12.1.6] Although it appears unworthy for men, even though not endowed with any high rank, to descend to sordid marriages with slave women, nevertheless this practice is not prohibited by law; but a legal marriage cannot exist with servile persons, and from a slave union of this kind, slaves are born. We command, therefore, that decurions shall not be led by their lust to take refuge in the bosom of the most powerful houses. For if a decurion should be secretly united with any slave woman belonging to another man and if the overseers and procurators should not be aware of this, We order that the woman shall be cast into the mines through sentence of the judge, and the decurion himself shall be deported to an island; his movable property and his urban slaves shall be confiscated; his landed estates and rustic slaves shall be delivered to the municipality of which he had been a decurion, if he had been freed from paternal power and has no children or parents, or even close kinsmen, who may be called to his inheritance, according to the order of the law. But if the overseers or procurators of the place in which the disgraceful act was committed were aware of it and were unwilling to divulge this crime of which they were aware, they shall be cast into the mines. But if the master permitted such offense to be committed of afterwards learned of the deed and concealed it, and if indeed, it was perpetrated on his farm, the farm with the slaves and flocks and all other things which are used in rural cultivation shall be [confiscated].

D. Criminal Actions
by/toward Slaves

[10.10.33] The lawful distinction between slavery and freedom shall stand firm. We sanction the rights of masters by the restitution of their slaves, who shall not rebel with impunity.

Source 2 from S. P. Scott, translator, Corpus Juris Civilis: The Civil Law (Cincinnati, Ohio: The Central Trust, 1932), Sections 1.5.4–5; 9.2.2; 11.4.1; 29.5.1; 37.14.1, 19; 38.10.10; 40.1.5.

2. Selections from the *Digest* of Justinian's Code

A. *Slave to Free/Free to Slave*

[1.5.4] Liberty is the natural power of doing whatever anyone wishes to do unless he is prevented in some way, by force or by law.

(1) Slavery is an institution of the Law of Nations by means of which anyone may subject one man to the control of another, contrary to nature.

(2) Slaves are so called for the reason that military commanders were accustomed to sell their captives, and in this manner to preserve them, instead of putting them to death.

(3) They are styled *mancipia*, because they are taken by the hands [*manus*] of their enemies.

[1.5.5] One condition is common to all slaves; but of persons who are free some are born such, and others are manumitted.

(1) Slaves are brought under our ownership either by the Civil Law or by that of Nations. This is done by the Civil Law where anyone who is over twenty years of age permits himself to be sold for the sake of sharing in his own price. Slaves become our property by the Law of Nations when they are either taken from the enemy, or are born of our female slaves.

(2) Persons are born free who are born from a free mother, and it is sufficient for her to have been free at the time when her child was born, even though she may have been a slave when she conceived; and, on the other hand, if she was free when she conceived, and was a slave when she brought forth, it has been established that her child is born free, nor does it make any difference whether she conceived in a lawful marriage or through promiscuous intercourse; because the misfortune of the mother should not be a source of injury to her unborn child.

(3) Hence the following question arose, where a female slave who was pregnant, has been manumitted, and is afterwards again made a slave, or, after having been expelled from the city, should bring forth a child, whether that child should be free or a slave? It was very properly established that it was born free; and that it is sufficient for a child who is unborn that its mother should have been free during the intermediate time.

[40.1.5] If a slave should allege that he was purchased with his own money, he can appear in court against his master, whose good faith he impugns, and complain that he has not been manumitted by him; but he must do this at Rome, before the Urban Prefect, or in the provinces before the Governor, in accordance with the Sacred Constitutions of the Divine Brothers; under the penalty, however, of being condemned to the mines, if he should attempt this and not prove his case; unless his master prefers that he be restored to him, and then it should be decided that he will not be liable to a more severe penalty.

(1) Where, however, a slave is ordered to be free after having rendered his accounts, an arbiter between the slave and his master, that is to say, the heir, shall be appointed for the purpose of having the accounts rendered in his presence.

[37.14.1] Governors should hear the complaints of patrons against their freedmen, and their cases should be tried without delay; for if a freedman is ungrateful, he should not go unpunished. Where, however, the freedman fails in the duty which he owes to his patron, his patroness, or their children, he should only be punished lightly, with a warning that a more severe penalty will be imposed if he again gives cause for complaint, and then be dismissed. But if he is guilty of insult or abuse of his patrons, he should be sent into temporary exile. If he offers them personal violence, he must be sentenced to the mines.

[37.14.19] A freedman is ungrateful when he does not show proper respect for his patron, or refuses to manage his property, or undertake the guardianship of his children.

C. Slave/Free Relations

[38.10.10] We make use of this term, that is to say, cognates, even with reference to slaves. Therefore, we speak of the parents, the children, and the brothers of slaves; but cognation is not recognized by servile laws.

D. Criminal Actions
by/toward Slaves

[11.4.1] He who conceals a fugitive slave is a thief.

(1) The Senate decreed that fugitive slaves shall not be admitted on land or be protected by the superintendents or agents of the possessors of the same, and prescribed a fine. But, if anyone should, within twenty days, restore fugitive slaves to their owners, or bring them before magistrates, what they had previously done will be pardoned; but it was afterwards stated in the same Decree of the Senate that immunity is granted to anyone who restores fugitive slaves to their masters, or produces them before a magistrate within the prescribed time, when they are found on his premises. . . .

(4) And the magistrates are very properly notified to detain them carefully in custody to prevent their escape. . . .

(7) Careful custody permits the use of irons.

[9.2.2] It is provided by the first section of the *Lex Aquilia* that, "Where anyone unlawfully kills a male or female slave belonging to another, or a quadruped included in the class of cattle, let him be required to pay a sum equal to the greatest value that the same was worth during the past year."

[29.5.1] As no household can be safe unless slaves are compelled, under peril of their lives, to protect their masters, not only from persons belonging to his family, but also from strangers, certain decrees of the Senate were enacted with reference to putting to public torture all the slaves belonging to a household in case of the violent death of their master . . . , for the reason that slaves are punished whenever they do not assist their master against anyone who is guilty of violence towards him, when they are able to do so. . . . Whenever slaves can afford assistance to their master, they should not prefer their own safety to his. Moreover, a female slave who is in the same room with her mistress can give her assistance, if not with her body, certainly by crying out, so that those who are in the house or the neighbors can hear her; and this is evident even if she should allege that the murderer threatened her with death if she cried out. She ought, therefore, to undergo capital punishment, to prevent other slaves from thinking that they should consult their own safety when their master is in danger.

Source 3 from Katherine Fischer Drew, translator, The Burgundian Code *(Philadelphia: University of Pennsylvania Press, 1972), Sections 26, 30, 33, 35, 88, Constitutiones Extravagentes 21.9. Copyright © University of Pennsylvania Press. Reprinted by permission of the publisher.*

3. Selections from
The Burgundian Code

A. Slave to Free/Free to Slave

[Constitutiones Extravagantes, 21.9] If anyone shall buy another's slave from the Franks, let him prove with suitable witnesses how much and what sort of price he paid and when witnesses have been sworn in, they shall make oath in the following manner: "We saw him pay the price in our presence, and he who purchased the slave did not do so through any fraud or connivance with the enemy." And if suitable witnesses shall give oaths in this manner, let him receive back only the price which he paid; and let him not seek back the cost of support and let him return the slave without delay to his former owner.

[88] Since the title of emancipation takes precedence over the law of possession, great care must be exercised in such matters. And therefore it should be observed, that if anyone wishes to manumit a slave, he may do so by giving him his liberty through a legally competent document; or if anyone wishes to give freedom to a bondservant without a written document, let the manumis-

sion thus conferred by confirmed with the witness of not less than five or seven native freemen, because it is not fitting to present a smaller number of witnesses than is required when the manumission is in written form.

C. Slave/Free Relations

[30] OF WOMEN VIOLATED.

1. Whatever native freeman does violence to a maidservant, and force can be proved, let him pay twelve solidi to him to whom the maidservant belongs.
2. If a slave does this, let him receive a hundred fifty blows.

[35] OF THE PUNISHMENT OF SLAVES WHO COMMIT A CRIMINAL ASSAULT ON FREEBORN WOMEN.

1. If any slave does violence to a native freewoman, and if she complains and is clearly able to prove this, let the slave be killed for the crime committed.
2. If indeed a native free girl unites voluntarily with a slave, we order both to be killed.
3. But if the relatives of the girl do not wish to punish their own relative, let the girl be deprived of her free status and delivered into servitude to the king.

D. Criminal Actions
by/toward Slaves

[26] OF KNOCKING OUT TEETH.

1. If anyone by chance strikes out the teeth of a Burgundian of the highest class, or of a Roman noble, let him be compelled to pay fifteen solidi.
2. For middle-class freeborn people, either Burgundian or Roman, if a tooth is knocked out, let composition be made in the sum of ten solidi.
3. For persons of the lowest class, five solidi.
4. If a slave voluntarily strikes out the tooth of a native freeman, let him be condemned to have a hand cut off; if the loss which has been set forth above has been committed by accident, let him pay the price for the tooth according to the status of the person.
5. If any native freeman strikes out the tooth of a freedman, let him pay him three solidi. If he strikes out the tooth of another's slave, let him pay two solidi to him to whom the slave belongs.

[33] OF INJURIES WHICH ARE SUFFERED BY WOMEN.

1. If any native freewoman has her hair cut off and is humiliated without cause (when innocent) by any native freeman in her home or on the road, and

this can be proved with witnesses, let the doer of the deed pay her twelve so-lidi, and let the amount of the fine be twelve solidi.

2. If this was done to a freedwoman, let him pay her six solidi.

3. If this was done to a maidservant, let him pay her three solidi, and let the amount of the fine be three solidi.

4. If this injury (shame, disgrace) is inflicted by a slave on a native free-woman, let him receive two hundred blows; if a freedwoman, let him receive a hundred blows; if a maidservant, let him receive seventy-five blows.

5. If indeed the woman whose injury we have ordered to be punished in this manner commits fornication voluntarily (i.e., if she yields), let nothing be sought for the injury suffered.

Source 4 from Katherine Fischer Drew, translator, The Laws of the Salian Franks *(Philadel-phia: University of Pennsylvania Press, 1991), Sections 25, 39, 40, 98. Copyright © 1991 Uni-versity of Pennsylvania Press. Reprinted by permission of the publisher.*

4. Selections from Salic Law

C. Slave/Free Relations

[25] ON HAVING INTERCOURSE WITH SLAVE GIRLS OR BOYS

1. The freeman who has intercourse with someone else's slave girl, and it is proved against him . . . , shall be liable to pay six hundred denarii (i.e., fifteen solid[i]) to the slave girl's lord.

2. The man who has intercourse with a slave girl belonging to the king and it is proved against him . . . , shall be liable to pay twelve hundred denarii (i.e., thirty solidi).

3. The freeman who publicly joins himself with (i.e., marries) another man's slave girl, shall remain with her in servitude.

4. And likewise the free woman who takes someone else's slave in marriage shall remain in servitude.

5. If a slave has intercourse with the slave girl of another lord and the girl dies as a result of this crime, the slave himself shall pay two hundred forty denarii (i.e., six solidi) to the girl's lord or he shall be castrated; the slave's lord shall pay the value of the girl to her lord.

6. If the slave girl has not died . . . , the slave shall receive three hundred lashes or, to spare his back, he shall pay one hundred twenty denarii (i.e., three solidi) to the girl's lord.

7. If a slave joins another man's slave girl to himself in marriage without the consent of her lord . . . , he shall be lashed or clear himself by paying one hun-dred twenty denarii (i.e., three solidi) to the girl's lord.

[98] CONCERNING THE WOMAN WHO JOINS HERSELF TO HER SLAVE

1. If a woman joins herself in marriage with her own slave, the fisc[10] shall acquire all her possessions and she herself will be outlawed.

2. If one of her relatives kills her, nothing may be required from that relative or the fisc for her death. The slave shall be placed in the most severe torture, that is, he shall be placed on the wheel. And if one of the relatives of the woman gives her either food or shelter, he shall be liable to pay fifteen solidi.

D. Criminal Actions by/toward Slaves

[40] CONCERNING THE SLAVE ACCUSED OF THEFT

1. In the case where a slave is accused of theft, if [it is a case where] a freeman would pay six hundred denarii (i.e., fifteen solidi) in composition, the slave stretched on a rack shall receive one hundred twenty blows of the lash.

2. If he [the slave] confesses before torture and it is agreeable to the slave's lord, he may pay one hundred twenty denarii (i.e., three solidi) for his back [i.e., to avoid the lashes]; and the slave's lord shall return the value of the property stolen to its owner. . . .

4. . . . If indeed he [the slave] confessed in the earlier torture, i.e., before the one hundred twenty lashes were completed, let him [the slave] be castrated or pay two hundred forty denarii (i.e., six solidi); the lord should restore the value of the property stolen to its owner.

5. If he [the slave] is guilty of a crime for which a freeman or a Frank would be liable to pay eight thousand denarii (i.e., two hundred solidi), let the slave compound fifteen solidi (i.e., six hundred denarii). If indeed the slave is guilty of a more serious offense—one for which a freeman would be liable to pay eighteen hundred denarii (i.e., forty-five solidi)—and the slave confessed during torture, he shall be subjected to capital punishment. . . .

11. If indeed it is a female slave accused of an offense for which a male slave would be castrated, then she should be liable to pay two hundred forty denarii (i.e., six solidi)—if it is agreeable for her lord to pay this—or she should be subjected to two hundred forty lashes.

[39] ON THOSE WHO INSTIGATE SLAVES TO RUN AWAY

1. If a man entices away the bondsmen of another man and this is proved against him . . . , he shall be liable to pay six hundred denarii (i.e., fifteen solidi) [in addition to return of the bondsmen plus a payment for the time their labor was lost] .

10. **fisc:** king's treasury.

Source 5 from Katherine Fischer Drew, translator, The Lombard Laws *(Philadelphia: University of Pennsylvania Press, 1973), Sections Rothair 156, 217, 221, 222, 267, 280, 333, 334; Luitprand 55, 63, 80, 140, 152. Copyright © 1973 University of Pennsylvania Press. Reprinted with permission of the publisher.*

5. Selections from Lombard Laws

A. Slave to Free/Free to Slave

[Rothair 156]   In the case of a natural son who is born to another man's woman slave, if the father purchases him and gives him his freedom by the formal procedure . . . , he shall remain free. But if the father does not free him, the natural son shall be a slave to him to whom the mother slave belongs.

[Luitprand 63] He who renders false testimony against anyone else, or sets his hand knowingly to a false charter, and this fraud becomes evident, shall pay his wergeld as composition,[11] half to the king and half to him whose case it is. If the guilty party does not have enough to pay the composition, a public official ought to hand him over as a slave to him who was injured, and he [the offender] shall serve him as a slave.

[Luitprand 80] In connection with thieves, each judge shall make a prison underground in his district. When a thief has been found, he shall pay composition for his theft, and then the judge shall seize him and put him in prison for two or three years, and afterwards shall set him free.

   If the thief is such a person that he does not have enough to pay the composition for theft, the judge ought to hand him over to the man who suffered the theft, and that one may do with him as he pleases.

   If afterwards the thief is taken again in theft, he [the judge] shall shave . . . and beat him for punishment as befits a thief, and shall put a brand on his forehead and face. If the thief does not correct himself and if after such punishment he has again been taken in theft, then the judge shall sell him outside the province, and the judge shall have his sale price provided, nevertheless, that it be a proved case for the judge ought not to sell the man without certain proof.

[Luitprand 152] If the man who is prodigal or ruined, or who has sold or dissipated his substance, or for other reasons does not have that with which to pay composition, commits theft or adultery or a breach of the peace . . . or injures another man and the composition for this is twenty solidi or more, then a public representative ought to hand him over as a slave to the man who suffered such illegal acts.

---

11. **composition:** restitution.

[Luitprand 55] If anyone makes his slave folkfree and legally independent . . . or sets him free from himself in any manner by giving him into the hand of the king or by leading him before the altar of a church, and if afterwards that freedman [continues] to serve at the will of his patron, the freedman ought at frequent intervals to make clear his liberty to the judge and to his neighbors and [remind them] of the manner in which he was freed.

Afterward the patron or his heirs may at no time bring complaints against him who was freed by saying that because [he continues to serve] he ought still to obey, for it was only on account of the goodness of his lord that the former slave continued to serve his commands of his own free will. He shall remain permanently free.

[Luitprand 140] If a freeman has a man and woman slave, or aldius and aldia,[12] who are married, and, inspired by hatred of the human race, he has intercourse with that woman whose husband is the slave or with the aldia whose husband is the aldius, he has committed adultery and we decree that he shall lose that slave or aldius with whose wife he committed adultery and the woman as well. They shall go free where they wish and shall be as much folkfree . . . as if they had been released by the formal procedure for alienation . . .—for it is not pleasing to God that any man should have intercourse with the wife of another.

B. Value and Treatment of Slaves

[Rothair 333] On mares in foal. He who strikes a mare in foal and causes a miscarriage shall pay one solidus as composition. If the mare dies, he shall pay as above for it and its young.

[Rothair 334] On pregnant woman slaves. He who strikes a woman slave large with child and causes a miscarriage shall pay three solidi as composition. If, moreover, she dies from the blow, he shall pay composition for her and likewise for the child who died in her womb.

C. Slave/Free Relations

[Rothair 217] On the aldia who marries a slave. The aldia or freedwoman who enters another man's house to a husband and marries a slave shall lose her liberty. But if the husband's lord neglects to reduce her to servitude, then when her husband dies she may go forth together with her children and all the property which she brought with her when she came to her husband. But

12. **aldius** and **aldia:** freedman and freedwoman.

she shall have no more than this as an indication of her mistake in marrying a slave.

[Rothair 221] The slave who dares to marry a free woman or girl shall lose his life. With regard to the woman who consented to a slave, her relatives have the right to kill her or to sell her outside the country and to do what they wish with her property. And if her relatives delay in doing this, then the king's gastald or schultheis[13] shall lead her to the king's court and place her there in the women's apartments among the female slaves.

[Rothair 222] On marrying one's own woman slave. If any man wishes to marry his own woman slave, he may do so. Nevertheless he ought to free her, that is, make her worthy born . . . , and he ought to do it legally by the proper formal procedure. . . . She shall then be known as a free and legal wife and her children may become the legal heirs of their father.

D. Criminal Actions
by/toward Slaves

[Rothair 267] The boatman who knowingly transports fugitive bondsmen, and it is proved, shall search for them and return them together with any properties taken with them to their proper owner. If the fugitives have gone elsewhere and cannot be found, then the value of those bondsmen together with the sworn value of the property which they carried with them shall be paid by that ferryman who knowingly transported the fugitives. In addition, the ferryman shall pay twenty solidi as composition to the king's fisc.

[Rothair 280] On seditious acts committed by field slaves. If, for any reason, rustics[14] . . . associate together for plotting or committing seditious acts such as, when a lord is trying to take a bondsman or animal from his slave's house, blocking the way or taking the bondsman or animal, then he who was at the head of these rustics shall either be killed or redeem his life by the payment of a composition equal to that amount at which he is valued. And each of those who participated in this evil sedition shall pay twelve solidi as composition, half to the king and half to him who bore the injury or before whom he presumed to place himself. And if that one who was trying to take his property endures blows or suffers violence from these rustics, composition for such blows or violence shall be paid to him just as is stated above, and the rustics shall suffer such punishment as is noted above for this presumption. If one of the rustics is killed no payment shall be required because he who killed him did it while defending himself and in protecting his own property.

13. **gastald** and **schultheis:** royal officials.
14. **rustics:** field slaves.

Source 6 from Theodore John Rivers, translator, Laws of the Alamans and Bavarians *(Philadelphia: University of Pennsylvania Press, 1977), Alamannic Law, Sections 17, 18, 37, 39, 75. Copyright © 1977 University of Pennsylvania Press. Reprinted by permission of the publisher.*

6. Laws of the Alamans

A. Slave to Free/Free to Slave

[39] We prohibit incestuous marriages. Accordingly, it is not permitted to have as wife a mother-in-law, daughter-in-law, step-daughter, step-mother, brother's daughter, sister's daughter, brother's wife, or wife's sister. Brother's children and sister's children are under no pretext to be joined together. If anyone acts against this, let them [the married pair] be separated by the judges in that place, and let them lose all their property, which the public treasury shall acquire. If there are lesser persons who pollute themselves through an illicit union, let them lose their freedom; let them be added to the public slaves.

B. Value and Treatment of Slaves

[37] 1. Let no one sell slaves . . . outside the province, whether among pagans or Christians, unless it is done by the order of the duke.

C. Slave/Free Relations

[17] 1. Concerning maidservants.[15] If a freewoman was manumitted by a charter or in a church, and after this she married a slave, let her remain permanently a maidservant of the church.

2. If, however, a free Alamannic woman marries a church slave and refuses the servile work of a maidservant, let her depart. If, however, she gives birth to sons or daughters there, let them remain slaves and maidservants permanently, and let them not have the right of departure.

D. Criminal Actions by/toward Slaves

[18] 1. Concerning waylayers . . . , [if a man blocks the way of a freeman] , let him pay six solidi.

2. If it is a freedman [who is blocked] , let the perpetrator pay four solidi.

3. If it is a slave, three solidi.

4. If he does this to a free Alamannic woman, let him compensate with twelve solidi.

15. **maidservants:** here, female slaves.

5. If it is a freedwoman, let him compensate with eight solidi.

6. If it is a maidservant, let him pay four solidi.

7. If a man seizes her hair, [let him compensate similarly].

[75] 1. If anyone lies with another's chambermaid against her will, let him compensate with six solidi.

2. And if anyone lies with the first maid of the textile workshop against her will, let him compensate with six solidi.

3. If anyone lies with other maids of the textile workshop against their will, let him compensate with three solidi.

Source 7 from F. L. Attenborough, editor, Laws of the Earliest English Kings, *Laws of Edward the Elder, Section 6; Laws of Ine, Section 3. Laws of Aethelbert, Sections 10, 11, 16; Laws of Alfred, Section 25.*

7. Laws of Anglo-Saxon Kings

A. Slave to Free/Free to Slave

[Edward the Elder 6] If any man, through [being found guilty of] an accusation of stealing, forfeits his freedom and gives up his person to his lord, and his kinsmen forsake him, and he knows no one who will make legal amends for him, he shall do such servile labour as may be required, and his kinsmen shall have no right to his wergeld [if he is slain].

B. Value and Treatment of Slaves

[Ine 3] If a slave works on Sunday by his lord's command, he shall become free, and the lord shall pay a fine of 30 shillings.

§1. If, however, the slave works without the cognisance of his master, he shall undergo the lash or pay the fine in lieu thereof.

§2. If, however, a freeman works on that day, except by his lord's command, he shall be reduced to slavery, or [pay a fine of] 60 shillings. A priest shall pay a double fine.

D. Criminal Actions
by/toward Slaves

[Aethelbert 10] If a man lies with a maiden belonging to the king, he shall pay 50 shillings compensation.

[Aethelbert 11] If she is a grinding slave, he shall pay 25 shillings compensation. [If she is of the] third [class], [he shall pay] 12 shillings compensation.

[Aethelbert 16] If a man lies with a commoner's serving maid, he shall pay 6 shillings compensation; [if he lies] with a slave of the second class, [he shall pay] 50 sceattas[16] [compensation] ; if with one of the third class, 30 sceattas.

[Alfred 25] If anyone rapes the slave of a commoner, he shall pay 5 shillings to the commoner, and a fine of 60 shillings.[17]

§1. If a slave rapes a slave, castration shall be required as compensation.

16. 20 sceattas = one shilling.
17. The 60 shillings went to the king's treasury.

QUESTIONS TO CONSIDER

The central questions for this chapter ask you to do two things: investigate the boundaries between slave and free in various law codes, and then compare these issues in Roman and Germanic cultures. Your answers to the second question are based, of course, on your answers to the first, and the Sources and Method section suggests some of the questions you might ask yourself about slave law in each of these two cultures.

In addition to these, in the Roman codes, what role does military conquest play in the determination of slave and free? Does conquest simply provide slaves, or does it also offer them opportunities? What limitations were placed on a male owner's treatment of his slaves? On a female owner's treatment of her slaves? What obligations does—or could— the status of freedman or freedwoman entail? Do these obligations make this status appear closer to that of a slave or that of a free person? How are family relationships among slaves regarded legally? The provision in Justinian's Code (Source 2D) that slaves who did not prevent a master's being killed were to be killed themselves may seem very harsh. Why do you think this was part of Roman slave law? What other provisions strike you as especially harsh, and why might these have been enacted? Given the role of slavery in the Roman economy, why were there such strong provisions about runaway slaves? Other than the restrictions on those who aided runaways, what laws discuss actions by those who were neither owners nor slaves? How might these have shaped general attitudes toward slavery and slaves?

Turning now to the Germanic codes, what are the hierarchies you find among slaves based on? Given the nature of Germanic society, in which tribes often moved around a great deal, why do you think there was so much concern about not taking slaves away to other areas, even if it was their owners who were taking them? Historians often point out the importance of personal honor in Germanic societies. Do you find evidence of this? Do slaves have honor?

Do any of their actions affect the honor of others in ways that the actions of free people do not? A close examination of the laws indicates that the only nonpunishable sexual relation between slave and free was a man marrying his own slave among the Lombards, mentioned in Source 5C. Why do you think this was allowed? What must a man do before he does this, and why do you think this was important?

You are now ready to investigate some comparative questions: In what ways do the different notions of the law in Roman and Germanic cultures—territorial versus personal, statutory versus traditional—emerge in laws regarding slavery? When comparing Germanic culture to Roman, historians often point to the relative propensity to interpersonal violence and the importance of the family among the Germans. Do the laws regarding slavery from these two cultures provide evidence of these factors? What evidence do you see of the different economic structures in the two cultures, i.e., of the greater complexity of the Roman economic system?

Comparing two cultures involves exploring continuities along with contrasts. One of the issues in slave systems was how to punish slaves without harming their owners. How do the laws handle this? Do you see much difference between Roman and Germanic cultures in this? How do the laws handle the issue that slaves do not own property? How are the actions and obligations of freed slaves toward their former masters handled in both cultures? Why do you think it was important in both cultures to have an intermediate status between slave and free? Do you see much difference with regard to laws concerning sexual relations between slaves and free in the two cultures? Why might there have been continuity in this?

After putting all of this material together, you are now ready to answer the central questions for this chapter: How were legal distinctions between slave and free established, structured, and maintained, and how could they be overcome? What similarities and differences are there in Roman and Germanic law regarding slavery?

EPILOGUE

During the Renaissance, scholars and thinkers began to divide the history of Europe into three stages, ancient, medieval, and modern, a division that has persisted until today. They viewed the end of the Roman Empire as a dramatic break in history, and saw the Germanic successor states as sharply different from Rome. This view is increasingly being modified today as historians point to a number of continuities between late ancient and early medieval society.

As you have discovered in this chapter, the slave system was one of those continuities, for slavery did not disappear from the European scene with the fall of Rome, nor did the spread of Christianity lead to an end of slavery. (Christianity did not oppose slavery on moral grounds, although it did praise those who chose to free their slaves and pushed for slaves being allowed to marry in legally binding ceremonies.) Gradually, however, more people came to occupy the intermediate stage between slave and free that you have seen in these laws, which became known as serfdom. Serfdom was a legal condition in which people were personally free—not owned by another individual as slaves were—but were bound to the land, unable to move and owing labor obligations to their lord. For former slaves, serfdom was a step up; for others, however, it was a step down, for the bulk of the serfs in Europe probably came from families that had originally been free peasants, but had traded their labor and freedom to move in return for protection. In any case, serfdom did not immediately replace slavery; both continued side by side for centuries, and the laws you have seen here regarding slaves often shaped later laws regarding serfs. Law codes alone, of course, cannot tell us about relative numbers of slaves or serfs, and they sometimes hide major changes. The transformation of slave to serf was so gradual that it occasioned little comment in the codes, which had, as we have seen, long included discussion of intermediate stages between slave and free and of hierarchies among slaves.

The laws you have seen here also had great influence beyond Europe.

As you have discovered, Germanic law did not break sharply with Roman on many issues regarding slavery, indicating that Justinian's Code probably influenced some early medieval Germanic codes. Justinian's Code was also rediscovered in western Europe in the eleventh century, and became the basis of legal education at the law schools that were established in southern Europe in the twelfth century. It influenced national and local codes in this era of expanding states and growing cities, and ultimately all of the legal systems of western Europe except for that of England became based on Roman law. When Portugal and Spain set up slave systems extending into the New World, Roman law was the basis of many provisions regarding slavery. Thus, two of the New World's most heavily slave societies—the French Caribbean and Brazil—based their systems on Roman law.

The other slave societies in the New World—the British Caribbean and the southern United States before the Civil War—did not base their laws as directly on those of Rome, but their laws did grow out of Germanic codes such as those you have seen here. Though these systems were different from the Roman and Germanic systems in that slavery came to be based on race, many of the laws—those concerning owners' freedom to treat slaves as they wished, sexual relations between slave and free, punishment of those who aided runaway slaves—were remarkably similar. Once slavery came to be racially based, however, the permeable boundary between slave and free that you have traced in this chapter, with slavery not necessarily being a permanent status, became much harder to cross. Poverty, begging, theft, debt, capture in war, false testimony, or incest did not make a white person a slave, nor did turning in deserters, marriage to an owner, or—except in rare instances—military service make a black person free.

CHAPTER SIX

THE DEVELOPMENT OF

THE MEDIEVAL STATE

The governments of medieval Europe are generally described as *feudal,* a word that perhaps confuses more than it clarifies. The term *feudalism* was unknown in the Middle Ages; it was invented only later to describe the medieval system of landholding and government. Used correctly, feudalism denotes a system of reciprocal rights and obligations, in which individuals who fight (knights) promise their loyalty, aid, and assistance to a king or other powerful noble, becoming what were termed *vassals* of that lord. The lord in turn promises his vassals protection and material support, which in the Early Middle Ages was often board and room in the lord's own household. As their vassals became more numerous or lived farther away, lords increasingly gave them grants of land as recompense for their allegiance. This piece of land, termed a *fief* (*feudum* in Latin), theoretically still belonged to the lord, with the vassal obtaining only the use of it. Thus feudalism involved a mixture of personal and property ties. Unlike the systems of property ownership in the Roman Empire or most modern governments, it did not involve any ties to an abstract state or governmental system, but was simply a personal agreement between individuals.

This promise of allegiance and support could be made only by free individuals, so that the slaves we examined in the last chapter or serfs who were tied to the land were not actually part of the feudal system. In the economic structure of medieval Europe, estates or *manors* of various sizes were worked by slaves, serfs, and free peasants. The whole economic system is termed *manorialism.* Fiefs were generally made up of manors and included the peasants who lived on them, but manorialism and feudalism are not synonymous.

Though serfs were not included in the feudal system, Church officials were. Rulers rewarded Church officials with fiefs for their spiritual services or promises of allegiance. In addition, the Church held pieces of land on its own, and granted fiefs in return for promises of assistance from knightly vassals. Abbots and abbesses of monasteries, bishops, and archbishops were either lords[1] or vassals in many feudal arrangements. In addition, both secular and clerical vassals further subdivided their fiefs, granting land to people who became their vassals, a process known as *subinfeudation*. Thus the same person could be a lord in one relationship and a vassal in another.

This system could easily become chaotic, particularly as it was easy to forget, once a family had held a piece of land for several generations, that the land actually belonged to the lord. This is more or less what happened from 700 until 1050, with political power becoming completely decentralized and vassals ruling their fiefs quite independently. About 1050 this began to change, however, and rulers started to manipulate feudal institutions to build up rather than diminish their power.

The rulers of England after the Norman Conquest in 1066 were particularly successful at manipulating feudal institutions to build up their own power. William the Conqueror (1066–1087) and Henry II (1154–1189) dramatically increased royal authority, as did later rulers of France, especially Philip II Augustus (1180–

1223), and of Germany, especially Frederick Barbarossa (1152–1190). Gradually the feudal system was transformed into one that is sometimes termed *feudal monarchy*. Because monarchs in the High Middle Ages had so much more power than they had had in the Early Middle Ages, however, some historians no longer term such governments feudal at all, but simply monarchies, and see in them the origins of the modern state.

In asserting their power, the rulers of western Europe had to suppress or limit the independent powers of two groups in medieval society— their noble vassals and Church officials. The challenge provided by each group was somewhat different. Noble vassals often had their own armies, and the people living on their fiefs were generally more loyal to– or afraid of—them than to any faraway ruler. During the period before the mid-eleventh century, vassals often supervised courts, which heard cases and punished crimes, and regarded themselves as the supreme legal authority in their fief. Though they were vassals of the ruler, Church officials also owed allegiance to an independent, international power— the papacy in Rome. Throughout the Middle Ages, the pope and higher Church officials claimed that all Church personnel, down to village priests and monks, were not subject to any secular legal jurisdiction, including that of a ruler. They also argued that the spiritual hierarchy of Western Christianity, headed by the pope, was elevated by God over all secular hierarchies, so that

---

1. Because abbesses and, in some parts of Europe, noblewomen who inherited land could grant fiefs and have vassals, the word *lord* in the context of feudalism did not always mean a man. It simply means "the person who holds the rights of lordship."

every ruler was subject to papal authority.

In this chapter we will be exploring the ways in which medieval monarchs asserted their authority over their vassals and the Church. We will use both visual and written evidence in answering the question, How did the rulers of the High Middle Ages overcome challenges to their power and begin the process of recentralization of power?

SOURCES AND METHOD

Traditionally, political history has been seen as the history of politics, and has used as its sources laws, decrees, parliamentary debates, and other written documents that give information about political changes. These are still important, but recently political history has been seen more broadly as the history not only of politics but of all relations involving power, and a wider range of sources is now used to understand the power relationships in past societies. Picking up techniques from anthropologists, political historians now use objects as well as written documents to explore the ways in which power is externally expressed and symbolized as well as the ways in which it is manipulated in relationships. The rulers of medieval western Europe were aware of the power of symbols, and along with actual military and legal moves to increase their authority, they also demonstrated that authority symbolically.

A symbol is basically something that stands for something else, that has a meaning beyond the actual object or words. Symbols can be used consciously or unconsciously, and can be interpreted differently by different observers or readers. Anthropologists have pointed out that symbols can often be read at many different levels, so understanding them in all their meanings can be very complicated. The symbols we will be looking at here are less complicated than many, however, because they were consciously employed by rulers and officials who wanted to be very sure that their correct meaning was understood. Since many of the observers were not highly educated or even literate, rulers chose simple symbols and repeated them so that their meaning would certainly be grasped. Because many of these symbols have much the same meaning to us today, you will find them easier to analyze than the symbols from unfamiliar cultures that are often the focus of anthropologists' studies. As we explore the ways in which rulers asserted their authority, then, we must keep in mind both the tactical and the symbolic impact of their actions.

The first four sources all provide evidence of one of the ways in which William the Conqueror and his successors gained power over the English nobility. Source 1 is from a history of England written in the early twelfth century by Ordericus Vitalis, a monk who was half Anglo-Saxon and half Norman. The author provides a relatively unbiased account of William's reign, and here describes how William subdued one of the many rebellions against him. Read the selection carefully. Rather than simply sending out armies, what does William do to establish royal power? Why does Ordericus feel this was effective in ending the rebellion?

Visual depictions of Norman castles may help you judge whether Ordericus's opinion about their importance was valid, so turn to the next three sources. Sources 2 and 3 are photographs of castles built by English kings. The first was begun at Richmond in 1089, and the second was built at Harlech between 1283 and 1290. Source 4 is a map of all the castles built in England by William the Conqueror during his reign, from 1066 to 1087. Many of these were wooden fortifications rather than the enormous stone castles shown in Sources 2 and 3, but William's successors expanded these simpler castles into larger stone ones as quickly as time and resources permitted. As you look at these, try to imagine yourself as a vassal or subject confronted by castles that looked like these in all the places you see on the map. What message would you get about the power of the king? What strategic value is gained by placing a castle on a hill? How would this also increase the castle's symbolic value? What other features of the castles depicted increase either their strategic value as fortresses or their symbolic value? The map indicates that the castles built by William were not evenly distributed. Given what your text tells you about the Norman Con-

quest and the problems that William faced, why might he have built his castles where he did? Does this pattern of castle building surprise you? (A clue here is to keep in mind that castles are both symbols of power and a means to enforce that power, and that these castles may not all have been built for the same reason.)

Source 5 provides evidence of another way in which William and his successors both gained and demonstrated authority over their vassals. It is an excerpt from *The Anglo-Saxon Chronicle* describing William's requirement in 1086 that all vassals swear loyalty to him in what became known as the Salisbury Oath. Rulers such as William recognized that people regarded oaths as very serious expressions of their duties as Christians, and so they required their vassals to swear allegiance regularly in person in ceremonies of *homage* (allegiance) and *fealty* (loyalty). They expanded the ceremonies of knighthood, impressing on young knights their duties of obedience and loyalty. After you read this short selection, think about how the fact that the vassals had to leave their fiefs to swear the Oath might have also helped increase royal power.

After William, Henry II was the most innovative fashioner of royal power in medieval England. In 1166, he issued the Assize[2] of Clarendon (the location of the king's hunting lodge), which set up inquest juries to report to the king's sheriff or traveling judges the name of anyone sus-

---

2. **assize:** a decree made by an assembly.

pected of having committed a major crime. Source 6 gives you some of the clauses from the Assize of Clarendon. As you read it, note the ways in which the independent powers of the vassals in their territories are restricted. Who does it state is the ultimate legal authority? Who gains financially from these provisions?

Henry II directly limited not only the legal power of his vassals, but also that of the Church in England. Two years before the Assize of Clarendon, he issued the Constitutions of Clarendon, which purported to be a codification of existing practices governing relations between the Church and the state. Source 7 is an extract from this document. Read it carefully, noting first under whose authority Henry issues it. Who does he say has agreed to its provisions? How do these provisions limit the legal power of the Church over its own clergy? Over laypeople? What role is the king to play in the naming of Church officials? In hearing cases involving clergy? How are Church officials to be reminded of their duties as the king's vassals?

The Constitutions of Clarendon are perhaps the strongest statement of the power of a secular ruler over the Church to emerge from the Middle Ages, and, as we will see in the epilogue to this chapter, they were quickly opposed by the Church. This was not the only time a ruler asserted his power over the Church, however, for on the Continent German kings and emperors also claimed extensive powers over all aspects of Church life up to and including the papacy. Source 8 gives an example of this as-sertion of power. It is a selection from the biography of the German emperor Frederick Barbarossa (1152–1190), begun by Bishop Otto of Freising. Otto was Frederick's uncle, so though he is a bishop of the Church, he is quite favorably inclined toward the emperor. In this selection, Otto describes Frederick's coronation and some later responses by the emperor to papal ambassadors. What roles do Church officials play in Frederick's coronation? What does Otto view as a further symbol of Frederick's right to rule? What role does Otto report that the pope claimed to have played in granting Frederick power? What, in contrast to this, does Frederick view as the source of his authority? What does he see to be his religious duties as emperor?

Along with actions such as constructing castles or requiring oaths of loyalty, both of which combined tactical with symbolic assertions of power, medieval rulers also demonstrated their power over vassals and the Church in purely symbolic ways. The final sources in this chapter provide examples of some of these. Source 9 is a description of the coronation ceremony of Richard the Lionhearted, Henry II's son, in 1189. More than the much shorter description of Frederick Barbarossa's coronation, which you have already read, it gives evidence of the way in which kings and other territorial rulers expanded their coronation ceremonies, turning them into long, spectacular celebrations of royal wealth and power. As you read it, look first for things that symbolize power relationships. What titles are used to

[129]

describe the participants? What objects are used in the ceremonies? Who is in attendance, and what roles do they play? What actions are required of the various participants, either during the ceremony or as part of their later duties?

Living in the media age as we do, we are certainly used to the manipulation of symbols to promote loyalty and allegiance. Indeed, given the barrage of symbols accompanying the celebrations of the anniversaries of the Constitution, the Statue of Liberty, and the Bill of Rights, we may even be a bit jaded by flag-waving and military bands. Medieval people did not live in a world as full of visual stimulation, so the ceremonies surrounding a monarch were truly extraordinary.

Coronation ceremonies were rare events, and rulers also used symbols in more permanent visual demonstrations of their power, such as paintings and statuary, which they commissioned or which were designed in a way to gain their approval. The next three sources all depict rulers. Source 10 is a manuscript-illumination portrait of the German emperor Otto III (983–1002) seated on his throne. Source 11 is a section of the Bayeux tapestry showing on the left King Harold of England (1053–1066) seated on the throne. In the center, Englishmen acclaim him as king and point up to Halley's Comet (identified in the tapestry as a star). Source 12 is a tomb sculpture of Duke Henry of Brunswick in Germany and his wife, Matilda, dating from about 1240, shortly after they died. The Church that Henry holds in his right hand is

Brunswick Cathedral, which he completed and which houses his tomb. Because we no longer live in a world of royal authority, you may need some assistance in interpreting the meaning of the objects shown with the rulers, although medieval people would have understood them immediately. Many of these objects had both a secular and a religious meaning: the crown represented royal authority (the points symbolized the rays of the sun) and the crown of thorns worn by Jesus before the Crucifixion; the orb (the ball surmounted by a cross) represented the ruler's domination of the land and protection of the Church; the scepter also represented Church and state power by being ornamented with both religious and secular designs. Seeing a monarch in full regalia or a portrait of a monarch would impress on anyone that this was not just the greatest of the nobles, but also someone considered sacred, whose authority was supported by Scripture. Monarchs also demonstrated the sacred aspects of their rule with purely religious symbols, such as crosses and chalices.

Now look carefully at the pictures. What symbols are used to depict the sources of royal authority? How do these communicate the ruler's secular and religious authority? What types of individuals are shown with the ruler? What does this indicate about the relationship between lord and vassal, and between Church and state? Why might the appearance of the heavenly body that came to be known as Halley's Comet have been viewed as an appropriate symbol of monarchy?

You have now examined evidence of a number of ways in which rulers increased their own authority, decreased that of their noble vassals and Church officials, and expressed their greater power symbolically. As you assess how all of these helped rulers overcome challenges to their authority, it will be useful to recognize that symbols are not just passive reflections of existing power relationships, but are actively manipulated to build up or decrease power. Therefore it is often difficult to separate what we might term the real or tactical effect of an action or legal change from the symbolic. As you answer the central question in this chapter, then, think about the ways in which symbols and real change are interwoven.

Source 1 from Ordericus Vitalis, The Ecclesiastical History of England and Normandy, *trans. Thomas Forester (London: Henry G. Bohn, 1854). This source taken from a reprint of this edition (New York: AMS Press, 1968), vol. 2, pp. 17–20.*

1. From Ordericus Vitalis's *Ecclesiastical History of England and Normandy*

The same year [1068], Edwin and Morcar, sons of Earl Algar, and young men of great promise, broke into open rebellion, and induced many others to fly to arms, which violently disturbed the realm of Albion.[3] King William, however, came to terms with Edwin, who assured him of the submission of his brother and of nearly a third of the kingdom, upon which the king promised to give him his daughter in marriage. Afterwards, however, by a fraudulent decision of the Normans, and through their envy and covetousness, the king refused to give him the princess who was the object of his desire, and for whom he had long waited. Being, therefore, much incensed, he and his brother again broke into rebellion, and the greatest part of the English and Welsh followed their standard. The two brothers were zealous in the worship of God, and respected good men. They were remarkably handsome, their relations were of high birth and very numerous, their estates were vast and gave them immense power, and their popularity great. The clergy and monks offered continual prayers on their behalf, and crowds of poor daily supplications. . . .

At the time when the Normans had crushed the English, and were overwhelming them with intolerable oppressions Blethyn, king of Wales, came to

3. **Albion:** England.

the aid of his uncles, at the head of a large body of Britons. A general assembly was now held of the chief men of the English and Welsh, at which universal complaints were made of the outrages and tyranny to which the English were subjected by the Normans and their adherents, and messengers were dispatched into all parts of Albion to rouse the natives against their enemies, either secretly or openly. All joined in a determined league and bold conspiracy against the Normans for the recovery of their ancient liberties. The rebellion broke out with great violence in the provinces beyond the Humber. The insurgents fortified themselves in the woods and marshes, on the estuaries, and in some cities. York was in a state of the highest excitement, which the holiness of its bishop was unable to calm. Numbers lived in tents, disdaining to dwell in houses lest they should become enervated; from which some of them were called savages by the Normans.

In consequence of these commotions, the king carefully surveyed the most inaccessible points in the country, and, selecting suitable spots, fortified them against the enemy's excursions. In the English districts there were very few fortresses, which the Normans call castles; so that, though the English were warlike and brave, they were little able to make a determined resistance. One castle the king built at Warwick, and gave it into the custody of Henry, son of Roger de Beaumont.[4] Edwin and Morcar, now considering the doubtful issue of the contest, and not unwisely preferring peace to war, sought the king's favour, which they obtained, at least, in appearance. The king then built a castle at Nottingham, which he committed to the custody of William Peverell.

When the inhabitants of York heard the state of affairs, they became so alarmed that they made hasty submission, in order to avoid being compelled by force; delivering the keys of the city to the king, and offering him hostages. But, suspecting their faith, he strengthened the fortress within the city walls, and placed in it a garrison of picked men. At this time, Archill, the most powerful chief of the Northumbrians, made a treaty of peace with the king, and gave him his son as a hostage. The bishop of Durham, also being reconciled to King William, became the mediator for peace with the king of the Scots, and was the bearer into Scotland of the terms offered by William. Though the aid of Malcolm had been solicited by the English, and he had prepared to come to their succour with a strong force, yet when he heard what the envoy had to propose with respect to a peace, he remained quiet, and joyfully sent back ambassadors in company with the bishop of Durham, who in his name swore fealty to King William. In thus preferring peace to war, he best consulted his own welfare, and the inclinations of his subjects; for the people of Scotland, though fierce in war, love ease and quiet, and are not disposed to disturb themselves about their neighbours' affairs, loving rather religious exercises than those of arms. On his return from this expedition, the king erected castles at Lincoln, Huntingdon, and Cambridge, placing in each of them garrisons composed of his bravest soldiers.

4. **Roger de Beaumont:** a Norman noble.

Source 2 from The British Tourist Authority.

2. **Richmond Castle, Begun in 1089**

Source 3: Photograph courtesy of the British Tourist Authority. Ground plan courtesy of the Ministry of Public Building and Works.

3. View and Ground Plan of Harlech Castle, Built by Edward I Between 1283 and 1290

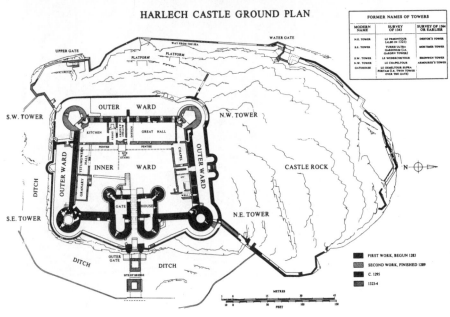

HARLECH CASTLE GROUND PLAN

FORMER NAMES OF TOWERS		
MODERN NAME	SURVEY OF 1343	SURVEY OF 1564 OR EARLIER
N.E. TOWER	LE PRISONTOUR (ALSO IN 1321)	DESTON'S TOWER
S.E. TOWER	TURRIS ULTRA GARDINUM (I.E. GARDEN TOWER)	MORTIMER TOWER
S.W. TOWER	LE WEDERCOKTOUR	BRONWEN TOWER
N.W. TOWER	LE CHAPELTOUR	ARMOURER'S TOWER
GATEHOUSE	LE GEMELTOUR SUPRA PORTAM (I.E. TWIN TOWER OVER THE GATE)	

FIRST WORK, BEGUN 1283
SECOND WORK, FINISHED 1289
C. 1295
1323-4

Source 4 adapted from map in H. C. Darby, Domesday England *(Cambridge: Cambridge University Press, 1977), p. 316.*

4. Major Royal Castles Built During the Reign of William the Conqueror, 1066–1087

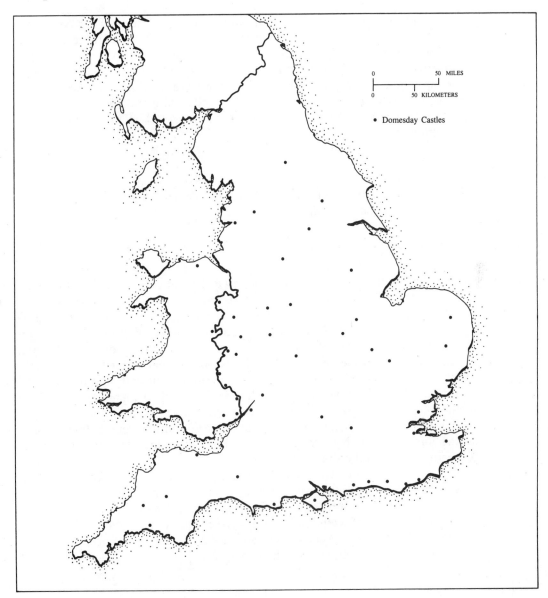

Source 5 from The Anglo-Saxon Chronicle *(London: Eyre and Spottiswoode, 1961, and New Brunswick, N.J.: Rutgers University Press), p. 162.*

5. From *The Anglo-Saxon Chronicle*

1086—In this year the king wore his crown and held his court at Winchester for Easter, and travelled so as to be at Westminster for Whitsuntide, and there dubbed his son, Henry, a knight. Then he travelled about so as to come to Salisbury at Lammas,[5] and there his councillors came to him, and all the people occupying land who were of any account all over England, no matter whose vassals they might be; and they all submitted to him and became his vassals, and swore oaths of allegiance to him, that they would be loyal to him against all other men. . . .

Sources 6 and 7 from Edward P. Cheyney, editor, "English Constitutional Documents," Translations and Reprints from the Original Sources of European History *(Philadelphia: University of Pennsylvania, 1900), vol. I, no. 6, pp. 22–25; pp. 26–30.*

6. Assize of Clarendon

Here begins the Assize of Clarendon, made by King Henry II, with the assent of the archbishops, bishops, abbots, earls and barons of all England.

1. In the first place, the aforesaid King Henry, with the consent of all his barons, for the preservation of the peace and the keeping of justice, has enacted that inquiry should be made through the several counties and through the several hundreds,[6] by twelve of the most legal men of the hundred and by four of the most legal men of each manor, upon their oath that they will tell the truth, whether there is in their hundred or in their manor, any man who has been accused or publicly suspected of himself being a robber, or murderer, or thief, or of being a receiver of robbers, or murderers, or thieves, since the lord king has been king. And let the justices make this inquiry before themselves, and the sheriffs before themselves.

2. And let any one who has been found by the oath of the aforesaid to have been accused or publicly suspected of having been a robber, or murderer, or thief, or a receiver of them, since the lord king has been king, be arrested and go to the ordeal of water and let him swear that he has not been a robber, or murderer, or thief, or receiver of them since the lord king has been king, to the value of five shillings, so far as he knows. . . .

5. **Lammas:** the wheat-harvest festival, August 1.

6. **hundred:** a division of a county.

4. And when a robber, or murderer, or thief, or receiver of them shall have been seized through the above-mentioned oath, if the justices are not to come very soon into that country where they have been arrested, let the sheriffs send word to the nearest justice by some intelligent man that they have arrested such men, and the justices will send back word to the sheriffs where they wish that these should be brought before them; and the sheriffs shall bring them before the justices; and along with these they shall bring from the hundred and the manor where they have been arrested, two legal men to carry the record of the county and of the hundred as to why they were seized, and there before the justice let them make their law.

5. And in the case of those who have been arrested through the aforesaid oath of this assize, no one shall have court, or judgment, or chattels,[7] except the lord king in his court before his justices, and the lord king shall have all their chattels. In the case of those, however, who have been arrested, otherwise than through this oath, let it be as it has been accustomed and ought to be. . . .

17. And if any sheriff shall have sent word to any other sheriff that men have fled from his county into another county, on account of robbery or murder or theft, or the reception of them, or for outlawry or for a charge concerning the forest of the king, let him arrest them. And even if he knows of himself or through others that such men have fled into his county, let him arrest them and hold them until he shall have secured pledges from them.

18. And let all sheriffs cause a list to be made of all fugitives who had fled from their counties; and let them do this in the presence of their county courts, and they will carry the written names of these before the justices when they come first before these, so that they may be sought through all England, and their chattels may be seized for the use of the king. . . .

7. Constitutions of Clarendon

In the year of the incarnation of the Lord, 1164, of the papacy of Alexander, the fourth year, of the most illustrious king of the English, Henry II, the tenth year, in the presence of the same king, has been made this memorial or acknowledgment of a certain part of the customs and franchises and dignities of his predecessors, that is to say of King Henry, his grandfather, and of other kings, which ought to be observed and held in the kingdom. And on account of the discussions and disputes which have arisen between the clergy and the justices of our lord and king and the barons of the kingdom concerning the customs and dignities, this acknowledgment is made in the presence of the archbishops and bishops and clergy and earls and barons and principal men of the kingdom. And these customs, acknowledged by

7. **chattels:** all items of property and goods except land.

the archbishops and bishops and earls and barons, and by the most noble
and ancient of the kingdom, Thomas, archbishop of Canterbury, and Roger,
archbishop of York, . . . [plus 12 bishops and 38 named barons] and many
others of the principal men and nobles of the kingdom, as well clergy as
laity.

Of these acknowledged customs and dignities of the realm, a certain part
is contained in the present writing. Of this part the heads are as follows:

1. If any controversy has arisen concerning the advowson[8] and presentation of churches between laymen and ecclesiastics, or between ecclesiastics,
it is to be considered or settled in the courts of the lord king.

2. Churches of the fee of the lord king cannot be given perpetually without
his assent and grant.

3. Clergymen charged and accused of anything, when they have been
summoned by a justice of the king shall come into his court, to respond
there to that which it shall seem good to the court of the king for them to
respond to, and in the ecclesiastical court to what it shall seem good should
be responded to there; so that the justice of the king shall send into the court
of holy church to see how the matter shall be treated there. And if a clergyman shall have been convicted or has confessed, the church ought not to
protect him otherwise.

4. It is not lawful for archbishops, bishops, and persons of the realm to
go out of the realm without the permission of the lord king. And if they go
out, if it please the lord king, they shall give security that neither in going
nor in making a stay nor in returning will they seek evil or loss to the king
or the kingdom. . . .

7. No one who holds from the king in chief, nor any one of the officers of
his demesnes shall be excommunicated, nor the lands of any one of them
placed under an interdict, unless the lord king, if he is in the land, first agrees,
or his justice, if he is out of the realm, in order that he may do right concerning
him; . . .

8. Concerning appeals, if they should occur, they ought to proceed from the
archdeacon to the bishop, from the bishop to the archbishop. And if the archbishop should fail to show justice, it must come to the lord king last, in order
that by his command the controversy should be finally terminated in the
court of the archbishop, so that it ought not to proceed further without the assent of the lord king. . . .

10. If any one who is of a city or a castle or a borough or a demesne manor
of the lord king has been summoned by the archdeacon or the bishop for any
offence for which he ought to respond to them, and is unwilling to make
answer to their summons, it is fully lawful to place him under an interdict,
but he ought not to be excommunicated before the principal officer of the lord

8. **advowson:** the right to recommend candidates for vacant church positions that carried with
them capital assets.

king for that place agrees, in order that he may adjudge him to come to the answer. And if the officer of the king is negligent in this, he himself will be at the mercy of the lord king, and afterward the bishop shall be able to coerce the accused man by ecclesiastical justice.

11. Archbishops, bishops, and all persons of the realm, who hold from the king in chief, have their possessions from the lord king as a barony, and are responsible for them to the justices and officers of the king, and follow and perform all royal rules and customs; and just as the rest of the barons ought to be present at the judgment of the court of the lord king along with the barons, at least till the judgment reaches to loss of limbs or to death.

12. When an archbishopric or bishopric or abbacy or priorate of the demesne of the king has become vacant, it ought to be in his hands, and he shall take thence all its rights and products just as demesnes. And when it has come to providing for the church, the lord king ought to summon the more powerful persons of the church, and the election ought to be made in the chapel of the lord king himself, with the assent of the lord king and with the agreement of the persons of the realm whom he has called to do this. And there the person elected shall do homage and fealty to the lord king as to his liege lord, concerning his life and his limbs and his earthly honor, saving his order, before he shall be consecrated. . . .

This acknowledgment of the aforesaid royal customs and dignities has been made by the aforesaid archbishops, and bishops, and earls, and barons, and the more noble and ancient of the realm, at Clarendon, on the fourth day before the Purification of the Blessed Mary, perpetual Virgin, Lord Henry being there present with his father, the lord king. There are, however, many other and great customs and dignities of holy mother church and of the lord king, and of the barons of the realm, which are not contained in this writing. These are preserved to holy church and to the lord king and to his heirs and to the barons of the realm, and shall be observed inviolably forever.

First document in Source 8 from Gesta Friderici, G. Waitz, editor, and J. B. Ross, translator (Hanover, 1884) in James Bruce Ross and Mary Martin McLaughlin, The Portable Medieval Reader (New York: Viking, 1949), pp. 262–264. Copyright 1949 by Viking Penguin, Inc. Copyright renewed © 1976 by James Bruce Ross and Mary Martin McLaughlin. Second document from Otto of Freising, "The Deeds of Frederick Barbarossa," Records of Civilization, trans. C. C. Mierow (New York: Columbia University Press, 1953), vol. 49, pp. 180, 183–184, 185–186. Reprinted with permission of Columbia University Press, 562 W. 113th St., New York, NY 10025, via Copyright Clearance Center, Inc.

8. Coronation of Emperor Frederick Barbarossa, 1152

[*From* Gesta Friderici]

In the year . . . 1152, after the most pious King Conrad had died in the spring . . . in the city of Bamberg . . . there assembled in the city of Frankfort from the vast expanse of the transalpine kingdom [Germany], marvellous to tell, the whole strength of the princes, not without certain of the barons from Italy, in one body, so to speak. Here, when the primates were taking counsel about the prince to be elected—for the highest honour of the Roman Empire claims this point of law for itself, as if by special prerogative, namely, that the kings do not succeed by heredity but are created by the election of the princes—finally Frederick, duke of Swabia, son of Duke Frederick, was desired by all, and with the approval of all, was raised up as king. . . .

When the king had bound all the princes who had assembled there in fealty and homage, he, together with a few whom he had chosen as suitable, having dismissed the others in peace, took ship with great joy on the fifth day and, going by the Main and Rhine, he landed at the royal palace of Sinzig. There, taking horse, he came to Aachen on the next Saturday; on the following day, Sunday [March 9th] . . . led by the bishops from the palace to the church of the blessed Virgin Mary, and with the applause of all present, crowned by Arnold, archbishop of Cologne, assisted by the other bishops, he was set on the throne of the Franks, which was placed in the same church by Charles the Great. Many were amazed that in such a short space of time not only so many of the princes and nobles of the kingdom had assembled but also that not a few had come even from western Gaul, where, it was thought, the rumour of this event could not yet have penetrated. . . .

Nor should I pass over in silence that on the same day in the same church the bishop-elect of Münster, also called Frederick, was consecrated as bishop by the same bishops who had consecrated the king; so that in truth the highest king and the priest believed this to be a sort of prognostication[9] in the present joyfulness that, in one church, one day saw the unction[10] of two persons, who

9. **prognostication:** prophecy.

10. **unction:** anointing.

alone are anointed sacramentally with the institution of the old and new dispensations and are rightly called the anointed of Christ. . . .

[*From "The Deeds of Frederick Barbarossa"*]

In the middle of the month of October (1157) the emperor set out for Burgundy to hold a diet at Besançon. . . . We must speak of the ambassadors of the Roman pontiff, Hadrian. . . . The personnel of the embassy consisted of Roland, cardinal priest of the title of St. Mark and chancellor of the Holy Roman Church, and Bernard, cardinal priest of the title of St. Clement, both distinguished for their wealth, their maturity of view, and their influence, and surpassing in prestige almost all others in the Roman Church. . . . When this letter had been read and carefully set forth by Chancellor Rainald in a faithful interpretation, the princes who were present were moved to great indignation, because the entire content of the letter appeared to have no little sharpness and to offer even at the very outset an occasion for future trouble. But what had particularly aroused them all was the fact that in the aforesaid letter it had been stated, among other things, that the fullness of dignity and honor had been bestowed upon the emperor by the Roman pontiff, that the emperor had received from his hand the imperial crown, and that he would not have regretted conferring even greater benefits (*beneficia*) upon him. . . . And the hearers were led to accept the literal meaning of these words and to put credence in the aforesaid explanation because they knew that the assertion was rashly made by some Romans that hitherto our kings had possessed the imperial power over the City, and the kingdom of Italy, by gift of the popes, and that they made such representations and handed them down to posterity not only orally but also in writing and in pictures. . . .

They returned without having accomplished their purpose, and what had been done by the emperor was published throughout the realm in the following letter (October, 1157):

"Whereas the Divine Sovereignty, from which is derived all power in heaven and on earth, has entrusted unto us, His anointed, the kingdom and the empire to rule over, and has ordained that the peace of the churches is to be maintained by the imperial arms, not without the greatest distress of heart are we compelled to complain to Your Benevolence that from the head of the Holy Church, on which Christ has set the imprint of his peace and love, there seem to be emanating causes of dissentions and evils, like a poison, by which, unless God avert it, we fear the body of the Church will be stained, its unity shattered, and a schism created between the temporal and spiritual realms. . . . And since, through election by the princes, the kingdom and the empire are ours from God alone, Who at the time of the passion of His Son Christ subjected the world to dominion by the two swords, and since the apostle Peter taught the world this doctrine: 'Fear God, honor the king,' whosoever says that we received the imperial crown as a benefice (*pro beneficio*) from the lord pope contradicts the divine ordinance and the doctrine of Peter and is guilty of a lie. . . ."

Source 9 from J. A. Giles, translator and editor, Roger of Wendover's Flowers of History (London: H. G. Bohn, 1849), vol. II, pp. 79–81.

9. Coronation of Richard the Lionhearted, 1189

Duke Richard, when all the preparations for his coronation were complete, came to London, where were assembled the archbishops of Canterbury, Rouen, and Treves, by whom he had been absolved for having carried arms against his father after he had taken the cross. The archbishop of Dublin was also there, with all the bishops, earls, barons, and nobles of the kingdom. When all were assembled, he received the crown of the kingdom in the order following: First came the archbishops, bishops, abbots, and clerks, wearing their caps, preceded by the cross, the holy water, and the censers, as far as the door of the inner chamber, where they received the duke, and conducted him to the church of Westminster, as far as the high altar, in a solemn procession. In the midst of the bishops and clerks went four barons carrying candlesticks with wax candles, after whom came two earls, the first of whom carried the royal sceptre, having on its top a golden cross; the other carried the royal sceptre, having a dove on its top. Next to these came two earls with a third between them, carrying three swords with golden sheaths, taken out of the king's treasury. Behind these came six earls and barons carrying a chequer,[11] over which were placed the royal arms and robes, whilst another earl followed them carrying aloft a golden crown. Last of all came Duke Richard, having a bishop on the right hand, and a bishop on the left, and over them was held a silk awning. Proceeding to the altar, as we have said, the holy Gospels were placed before him together with the relics of some of the saints, and he swore, in presence of the clergy and people, that he would observe peace, honour, and reverence, all his life, towards God, the holy Church and its ordinances: he swore also that he would exercise true justice towards the people committed to his charge, and abrogating all bad laws and unjust customs, if any such might be found in his dominions, would steadily observe those which were good. After this they stripped him of all his clothes except his breeches and shirt, which had been ripped apart over his shoulders to receive the unction. He was then shod with sandals interwoven with gold thread, and Baldwin archbishop of Canterbury anointed him king in three places, namely, on his head, his shoulders, and his right arm, using prayers

11. **chequer:** a small table.

composed for the occasion: then a consecrated linen cloth was placed on his head, over which was put a hat, and when they had again clothed him in his royal robes with the tunic and gown, the archbishop gave into his hand a sword wherewith to crush all the enemies of the Church; this done, two earls placed his shoes upon his feet, and when he had received the mantle, he was adjured by the archbishop, in the name of God, not to presume to accept these honours unless his mind was steadily purposed to observe the oaths which he had made: and he answered that, with God's assistance, he would faithfully observe everything which he had promised. Then the king taking the crown from the altar gave it to the archbishop, who placed it upon the king's head, with the sceptre in his right hand and the royal wand in his left; and so, with his crown on, he was led away by the bishops and barons, preceded by the candles, the cross and the three swords aforesaid. When they came to the of-fertory of the mass, the two bishops aforesaid led him forwards and again led him back. At length, when the mass was chanted, and everything finished in the proper manner, the two bishops aforesaid led him away with his crown on, and bearing in his right hand the sceptre, in his left the royal wand, and so they returned in procession into the choir, where the king put off his royal robes, and taking others of less weight, and a lighter crown also, he proceeded to the dinner-table, at which the archbishops, bishops, earls, and barons, with the clergy and people, were placed, each according to his rank and dignity, and feasted splendidly, so that the wine flowed along the pavement and walls of the palace.

Source 10 from Hirmer Fotoarchiv.

10. Portrait of Emperor Otto III

Source 11 from Giraudon/Art Resource, NY.

11. Portion of the Bayeux Tapestry Showing King Harold Seated on the Throne of England, with Halley's Comet Above

Source 12 from Erwin Panofsky, Tomb Sculpture *(New York: Harry N. Abrams), fig. 222.*
Photograph from Foto Marburg/Art Resource, NY.

12. Tomb Sculpture of Duke Henry of Brunswick and His Wife, Matilda

QUESTIONS TO CONSIDER

The power relationships we have been investigating involve three main groups in medieval society: the nobles, the Church, and the rulers. To understand changes in the balance of power among them, you will need to extract information from each of the sources about them, and then compare your findings.

Take the nobles first. How would you compare the role of the nobles in the ceremonies of homage such as the Salisbury Oath with their role in the coronation ceremonies? How is their relationship to the ruler expressed in the pictures of Otto III and Harold? How does this compare with the way this relationship is expressed in the Assize of Clarendon? What differences do you see in the role of the nobles in Germany and those in England, as expressed in the coronation accounts?

Turning to the Church, what types of religious objects appear in the ceremonies and depictions of rulers? Do they serve to express the power of the Church as an institution or of someone else? What do they reveal to you about medieval religious beliefs and practices? What do the pictures of Otto III and Harold indicate about the relationship between the ruler and Church officials? How does this compare with the expression of this relationship in the Constitutions of Clarendon?

The most prominent group in the sources are rulers. How would you compare the three visual depictions of rulers? Might any of the differ-ences you see be explained by differences in the function of these depictions, that is, the fact that the last one is a tomb sculpture? Why might rulers wish to express certain aspects of their rule while they are still living, and make sure others are stressed for posterity after they are dead?

The claim of rulers such as Henry II and Frederick Barbarossa to religious authority was accompanied in the High Middle Ages by changes in the theory underlying kingship. In the Early Middle Ages, the king was viewed as simply the greatest of the nobles, whose power derived from the agreements he had made with his vassals. This idea continued into the High Middle Ages, but alongside it developed the idea that the king got his power from God as well. Rulers were increasingly viewed not only as the apex of a pyramid of vassals, but also as the representative to God for their entire kingdom. They were not regarded as divine in the way that ancient rulers such as the Egyptian pharaohs and Roman emperors had been, for Christianity would not allow this, but they were considered sacred in some ways. What evidence of this new idea of kingship can you find in either the Constitutions of Clarendon or the statements of Frederick Barbarossa? The two coronation ceremonies, Sources 8 and 9, are from the period of the building up of the monarchy. What evidence do you see in them of both the older idea of the king as the greatest of the nobles, and the newer idea of the king as ordained by God?

Remember that most literate people in the Middle Ages were clerics, so that all of the documents included here were probably written by priests or monks. How might this have affected their account of the events?

Given what you have read and looked at here, what actions would you now regard as most significant in the creation of the medieval state?

EPILOGUE

The moves undertaken by rulers to increase their power during the High Middle Ages did not go unchallenged. The Constitutions of Clarendon were immediately opposed by Church officials, including Henry II's friend Thomas Becket, whom Henry had made the Archbishop of Canterbury. The controversy between them grew very bitter, and ended with Becket's murder by several of Henry's nobles. After this the Constitutions were officially withdrawn, but Henry continued to enforce many of their provisions anyway.

In the area ruled by the German emperors, the Church was better able to assert its independent power; in fact, constant disputes with the pope were one of the reasons that the German emperors were not successful at establishing a unified country. Church officials patterned themselves after secular rulers and began in the twelfth century to demand regular oaths of homage and loyalty. They made sure that Church power was clearly symbolized in any royal ceremony and in all ceremonies of knighthood. As rulers built castles, they built cathedrals, permanent monuments in stone to both the glory of God and the authority of the Church. The consecrations of churches and cathedrals rivaled the coronations of

monarchs in splendor and pomp. The Church was fortunate in this regard, for opportunities for special ceremonies and celebrations were much more frequent than they were for secular rulers. Even the regular mass could be used to convey the Church's might to all who observed it. The king may have had sacred authority, but Church officials wanted to make sure that everyone knew that they did as well.

Nobles in England also opposed the growth of royal power, and were more effective than the Church in enforcing limits to royal authority. The most famous of these was the Magna Carta in 1215, which King John was forced to sign at a meeting in Runnymede, giving the higher nobles of England the right to participate in government. This document said nothing about the rights of the vast majority of English people, but it is still unusual in its limitation of the power of the king, though John immediately refuted it once he left Runnymede.

Despite opposition, however, the expansion of royal power at the expense of the nobles and Church continued, for this expansion had only begun during the High Middle Ages. Monarchs in the later Middle Ages, the Renaissance, and the early modern period continued to build up their power, devising new methods of taxation to raise revenue, creating a centralized legal system under firm royal control, reducing the role of or doing away with feudal assemblies of nobles, hiring middle-class lawyers and bureaucrats as their advisers and officials, and forbidding the nobles to maintain their own armies while building up royal armies led by generals whom they chose for loyalty.

This expansion of royal power was made easier in many countries in the sixteenth century because of the Protestant Reformation. Many rulers, such as Henry VIII of England, resented any independent power of the Church; they thus found Protestant theology, which declared the papacy to be evil and the ruler the proper source of all religious authority, very attractive. Some rulers became Protestant out of sincere religious conviction, but for others the chance to take over Church property and appoint Church officials was the strongest motivation.

The growth of actual royal power was accompanied, as you would expect after working through this chapter, by changes in the theory underlying kingship and in the symbols used to portray the king. Political theorists developed the idea of the divine right of kings, whereby kings got their power directly and pretty much only from God, and so were not answerable to their subjects for their behavior. You can see this idea beginning in the documents you have just read, and it would be developed to its furthest extent in seventeenth-century absolutism.

Centralized monarchy did not develop in all parts of Europe, however. Germany and Italy remained divided, and in fact did not become unified nations until the late nineteenth century, just a little over a hundred years ago. From the description of Frederick Barbarossa's coronation, you can see one reason for this, the fact that the emperorship was elected rather than hereditary. The lack of strong central governments in Germany and Italy was one reason for their decreasing political importance in the early modern period. The rulers of western Europe had much greater financial resources, and so could field larger armies and encourage economic development. After the voyages of the Portuguese and Spanish revealed new lands and new ways to the East, these rulers also supported exploration and colonization, which further increased royal and national power. Some type of feudal structure existed in most parts of western Europe in the High Middle Ages, but it was the rulers of France, England, and Spain who were most successful at manipulating both actual power and the symbols of that power to build up their own authority and end the feudal system.

CHAPTER SEVEN

LIFE AT A

MEDIEVAL UNIVERSITY

Centers of learning grew up in several European cities—particularly Paris and Bologna, Italy—during the twelfth and thirteenth centuries. In Paris, scholars, drawn by excellent teachers such as Peter Abelard, gathered at the bishop's cathedral school. Because only an official of the bishop, called the *scholasticus* or chancellor, had the authority to issue licenses to teach, students and teachers clustered around the cathedral of Notre Dame, located on an island in the Seine. This educational community soon grew so large that it required additional housing on the left bank of the river, which came to be known as the "Latin Quarter" after the official academic language. Special residence halls for students, called *colleges,* were opened, though the teachers themselves had no classrooms and simply rented rooms on their own for lecturing.

As the number of students in Paris increased, the teachers joined together into a "universal society of teachers," or *university* for short. Be-

lieving that the chancellor often either granted the right to teach to unqualified parties or simply sold licenses outright, they began to require that prospective teachers pass an examination set by the university besides getting the chancellor's approval. This certificate to teach was the earliest form of academic degree, granting the holder one of the titles, *master* or *doctor,* that we still use today. (Bachelor's degrees were to come later.) Most of the students studied theology, and Paris became the model for later universities such as Oxford and Cambridge in England and Heidelberg in Germany.

Colleges at many universities changed their character over the centuries. Originally no more than residence halls, the colleges gradually began to sponsor lectures and arrange for courses, and the university became simply the institution that granted degrees. This process was especially noticeable at the English universities of Oxford and Cambridge. When colleges were first established in the United States, they generally modeled themselves on the colleges of Oxford and Cambridge; because they were not part of larger universities, the colleges also granted degrees themselves. Thus modern U.S. colleges may be either completely independent institutions or part of a university, such as the College of Engineering or the College of Letters and Science found at many universities. In most cases, colleges that are part of modern universities have completely lost their original function as residences.

The University of Bologna had somewhat different roots and a different emphasis. Professional schools for the training of notaries and lawyers had grown up in Bologna in the twelfth century because the city, located at the crossing of the main trade routes in northern Italy, was a center of commerce. The university developed from these professional schools, and consequently the students were older and more sophisticated than those at Paris. Here, the students themselves banded into a university; they determined the fees teachers would be paid, the hours of classes, and the content of lectures. The most important course of study at Bologna was law. Bologna became the model for European universities such as Orleans or Padua, where students have retained their traditional power through modern times.

Because all those associated with the universities were literate, a great many records survive detailing every aspect of university life, both inside and outside the classroom. We can observe the process by which universities were established, read the rules students were required to live by, and learn what they were supposed to be studying (as well as what they actually spent time doing!). Much of medieval university life will seem familiar to us, for modern colleges and universities have inherited a great deal from their medieval predecessors. Indeed, most of the universities that had their beginning in the Middle Ages are still thriving today, making universities one of the few medieval institutions we can evaluate to some extent as insiders, rather than the outsiders we are when we look at such vanished social forms as serfdom or feudalism.

Because of the many parallels between medieval and modern universities, your task in this chapter will be twofold. First, you will be asked to use a variety of records to answer this question: What was life like for students at a medieval university? You can then use this description and your own experiences as a student to answer the second question: How would you compare medieval with modern student life, and what factors might account for the differences?

SOURCES AND METHOD

You will be using four types of sources in this chapter. The first type (Sources 1 through 4) consists of rules for university or college life issued by the founders. These are prescriptive documents, setting forth standards of functioning and behavior. The second type (Sources 5 through 8), written by teachers at medieval universities, describes their methods of teaching or presents the area on which they concentrated. The third type (Source 9) is a critique of university teaching by an individual outside the university structure. These sources provide us with information about how and what students studied or were supposed to study and so have both prescriptive and descriptive qualities. Selections of the fourth type (Sources 10 through 13) describe actual student life or were written by students themselves. These sources are thus fully descriptive, recounting real events or the problems and desires of real students.

As you read each selection, keep in mind the identity of its author and his position in the university. (No women were allowed to attend medieval universities in any capacity, so we can be sure that all authors, even anonymous students, were male.) Then as now, the perspective of administrators, those who established and ran the universities, was very different from that of students and faculty. It is also important to identify the source as prescriptive or descriptive. Prescriptive rules were often written in response to real problems, but the standards they laid down should never be mistaken for reality.

Begin your analysis of medieval university life with a careful reading of Sources 1 through 4. Source 1 describes privileges granted to the students at the University of Paris by the king of France in 1200. Though the University of Paris was originally started by the teachers themselves, the king took the scholars under his special protection and guaranteed

them certain extraordinary rights. What privileges are they granted in this document?

Source 2 consists of the statutes issued for the University of Paris by Cardinal Robert Courçon in 1215. Courçon, a representative of Pope Innocent III, took a special interest in the university and approved rules governing academic life. Innocent had been a student at Paris himself and wanted to ensure the university's tradition of theological orthodoxy and high levels of scholarship and behavior. As you read the selection, note the restrictions placed on those allowed to teach the arts. What restrictions are placed on teachers of theology? Why would Innocent be stricter about theology? What other areas did he believe important to regulate? What matters were the masters and students allowed to decide for themselves?

Source 3 contains further statutes issued for the University of Paris by Pope Gregory XI in 1231. What rules did he set for the chancellor's granting of teaching licenses? What issues was the university permitted to decide for itself? What special legal protections did students and teachers have? As pope, Gregory was particularly concerned with the manner in which theology was taught. What special restrictions did he lay down for students and teachers of theology? How would you compare these rules with the earlier ones established by Innocent III?

Source 4 is a series of rules governing life in one of the residential colleges, not the university as a whole. They were issued by Robert de Sorbon, the chaplain of King Louis IX, who established the college in the thirteenth century. This college was originally a residence hall for students of theology. By the sixteenth century, however, the word *Sorbonne* was used to describe the faculty of theology; since the nineteenth century the entire University of Paris has been called the Sorbonne.

As you can see from Source 4, Sorbon's establishment was simply a residence hall, with none of the broader functions that colleges later assumed. What aspects of student life did he regulate? What qualities did he attempt to encourage in the students living at his college?

By reading these four prescriptive sources, you have gained some information about the structure of one university (Paris), the hierarchy of authority, special student privileges, daily life in a residential college, and the handling of rule infractions. You have also learned something about the ideals held by authorities and patrons, for the popes and Sorbon established these rules because they held certain beliefs about how students should behave. What qualities would their ideal student exhibit? What did they see as the ultimate aim of the university? You can also use these sources to assess how church and secular leaders reacted to scholars, students, and the university in general. How would you describe their attitude—patronizing, respectful, hostile? How might their opinions about members of the university community have influenced other citizens of these university towns?

Besides informing us of standards, rules can also expose real-life problems because those who set the regulations were often responding to events in their environment. Which rules were specifically aimed at halting acts that were already taking place? Which rules seem most likely to have been a response to actual behavior? What kinds of acts did the authorities appear most upset about? Why do you think they believed these acts were important? Judging by the information in these sources, how would you describe relations between university students and the other residents of Paris? Before you go on to the next selections, write a brief description of medieval university life as you now see it. What types of sources would help you test whether your assumptions at this point are correct?

You have probably realized that so far you do not know very much about what or how students actually studied, other than those writings the popes recommended or forbade. The next four selections provide specific academic information. Sources 5 and 6 were written by teachers of theology and philosophy at Paris; Sources 7 and 8, by teachers of law at Bologna. Source 5 is the introduction to Peter Abelard's *Sic et Non,* a philosophical treatise introducing students and other readers to the *scholastic method* of inquiry, which applied logic to Christian theology. Source 6 is a demonstration of the scholastic method by one philosopher, Anselm of Canterbury, to prove the existence of God. If you are not familiar with philosophical works, you will need to read these excerpts very carefully, with special attention to the author's main points and the way in which logic is used to advance arguments. Because scholastic philosophers regarded logic as the most important aid to human understanding, it is fair for you to be critical if you see any flaws in their own logic. In making this analysis, you will be engaging in an activity that students in medieval universities both did themselves and were encouraged to do.

Begin with Abelard's introduction. How did he suggest to students that they read the works of the church fathers? How were they to handle seeming contradictions? Was all literature to be treated in this way? What, for Abelard, was the most important quality a student could possess? How was education supposed to strengthen this quality? Proceed to Anselm's proof, which you may need to read a number of times. Do you see any flaws in the logic? If you were a student disputing his proof, where would you begin?

Source 7 is an announcement of lectures in law by Odofredus, a teacher at the University of Bologna, written about 1250. Although later in the thirteenth century the city of Bologna began to pay teachers in order to control the university faculty more closely, at this point teachers were still paid directly by their students, and so Odofredus did not simply announce his course, he advertised it in a way that would make it attractive. What did he see as the positive qualities of his teaching method? How did he propose to handle a text? What specific skills was he trying to teach his students?

Source 8 is the introduction to the *Digest*, the main part of the collection of laws and commentaries made by the Emperor Justinian in the sixth century and one of the basic legal texts taught by Odofredus and his colleagues at Bologna. Like many textbooks, it opens with definitions of what would be taught. What distinctions among types of law does it present? What is the ultimate aim of legal education to be? Return to the description of university life you wrote after reading the first group of sources. What can you now add about the way teachers approached their subjects or the way in which material was taught? What do you now know about the content of courses in medieval universities?

Though teachers of theology and law used both logic and reason as means of analysis, there were some thinkers in the Middle Ages who questioned their value, particularly in matters of theology. Source 9 is an excerpt from two letters of St. Bernard of Clairvaux (1090–1153), a very influential French abbot, mystic, and adviser to the papacy. What does Bernard object to in Abelard's teaching? Why does he view Abelard's ideas as dangerous? What is his opinion of the scholastic method being developed at that time in the universities?

Students did not spend all their time studying, nor did they always behave in the ways popes or patrons hoped they would. The final group of sources come from students themselves or describe what might be termed their extracurricular activities. Source 10 is an anonymous account of a riot in Oxford in 1298, and Source 11 is a description of student life at Paris written by Jacques de Vitry, a high-minded scholar and historian who had studied at Paris himself. Source 12 consists of two letters, one from a student at Oxford to his father and another from a father to his son, a student at Orleans; Source 13 contains three anonymous short poems written originally in Latin by twelfth-century students.

The account of the riot is relatively straightforward and objective, like a story you might read in a newspaper today. What does this incident indicate about the relations between university scholars and townspeople? Whom did the two sets of disputants ask to decide the matter?

The other selections are more subjective than this account, so you must keep the point of view and the intent of the authors in mind as you read them. What kind of language does Vitry use to describe students? With what authority did he criticize their actions? How would you describe his general opinion of university life?

How would you compare his critique of logic and the philosophers who used it with Bernard's? What tactics did the student use to convince his father to send money? How would you compare the father's attitude with Vitry's?

Most medieval student poetry was written by young scholars who wandered from university to university and took much longer at their studies than normal, if they ever finished at all. It is important when reading from this genre to remember that the authors were not describing the daily grind but celebrating their wild escapades, in the same way you might talk about an academic year in terms of homecoming parties, weekend bashes, and early morning cramming for exams. This does not mean that we should reject their poetry as a valid historical source; rather, we must simply be aware of its intent and limitations. Keeping this in mind, how do the poets describe themselves and their problems? How does this description of student life reinforce or change what you have learned so far?

Return to your original description of university life. What would you add now?

Sources 1 through 3 from Dana Carleton Munro, editor and translator, Translations and Reprints from the Original Sources of European History, *vol. 2, no. 3 (Philadelphia: University of Pennsylvania Press, no date), pp. 4–5; pp. 12–15; pp. 7–11.*

1. Royal Privileges Granted to the University of Paris by the King of France, 1200

In the Name of the sacred and indivisible Trinity, amen. Philip, by the grace of God, King of the French. . . .

Concerning the safety of the students at Paris in the future, by the advice of our subjects we have ordained as follows: we will cause all the citizens of Paris to swear that if any one sees an injury done to any student by any layman, he will testify truthfully to this, nor will any one withdraw in order not to see [the act]. And if it shall happen that any one strikes a student, except in self-defense, especially if he strikes the student with a weapon, a club or a stone, all laymen who see [the act] shall in good faith seize the malefactor or malefactors and deliver them to our judge; nor shall they withdraw in order not to see the act, or seize the malefactor, or testify to the truth. Also, whether the malefactor is seized in open crime or not, we will make a legal and full examination through clerks or laymen or certain lawful persons; and our count and our judges shall do the same. And if by a full examination we or our judges are able to learn that he who is accused, is guilty of the crime, then we or our judges shall immediately inflict a penalty, according to the quality and nature of the crime; notwithstanding the fact that the criminal may deny the deed and say that he is ready to defend himself in single combat, or to purge himself by the ordeal by water.

Also, neither our provost nor our judges shall lay hands on a student for any offence whatever; nor shall they place him in our prison, unless such a crime has been committed by the student, that he ought to be arrested. And in that case, our judge shall arrest him on the spot, without striking him at all, unless he resists, and shall hand him over to the ecclesiastical judge, who ought to guard him in order to satisfy us and the one suffering the injury. And if a serious crime has been committed, our judge shall go or shall send to see what is done with the student.

2. Statutes for the University of Paris Issued by Robert Courçon, 1215

R., servant of the cross of Christ, by the divine mercy cardinal priest of the title of St. Stephen in Monte Celio and legate of the apostolic seat, to all the masters and scholars at Paris—eternal safety in the Lord.

Let all know, that having been especially commanded by the lord pope to devote our energy effectively to the betterment of the condition of the students at Paris, and wishing by the advice of good men to provide for the tranquillity of the students in the future, we have ordered and prescribed the following rules:

No one is to lecture at Paris in arts before he is twenty-one years old. He is to listen in arts at least six years, before he begins to lecture. He is to promise that he will lecture for at least two years, unless he is prevented by some good reason, which he ought to prove either in public or before the examiners. He must not be smirched by any infamy. When he is ready to lecture, each one is to be examined according to the form contained in the letter of lord P. bishop of Paris (in which is contained the peace established between the chancellor and the students by the judges appointed by the lord pope, approved and confirmed namely by the bishop and deacon of Troyes and by P., the bishop, and J., the chancellor of Paris).

The treatises of Aristotle on logic, both the old and the new, are to be read in the schools in the regular and not in the extraordinary courses. The two Priscians,[1] or at least the second, are also to be read in the schools in the regular courses. On the feast-days nothing is to be read except philosophy, rhetoric, *quadrivialia*,[2] the Barbarism, the Ethics, if they like, and the fourth book of the Topics. The books of Aristotle on Metaphysics or Natural Philosophy, or the abridgements of these works, are not to be read, nor the writings of Master David of Dinant, the heretic Amauri, or the Spaniard Mauricius.[3]

In the promotions and meetings of the masters and in the confutations or arguments of the boys or youths there are to be no festivities. But they may call in some friends or associates, but only a few. We also advise that donations of garments and other things be made, as is customary or even to a greater extent, and especially to the poor. No master lecturing in arts is to

---

1. **Priscian:** a Roman grammarian whose two works presented models of correct letters and legal documents.

2. **quadrivialia:** the four more advanced fields of study within the seven liberal arts, arithmetic, geometry, astronomy, and music.

3. Aristotle's treatises on metaphysics and natural philosophy were forbidden by the pope because they stated that the world was eternal (rather than created by God) and that the human soul was not immortal. The last three authors the Church regarded as heretics.

[157]

wear anything except a cope,[4] round and black and reaching to the heels—at least, when it is new. But he may well wear a pallium.[5] He is not to wear under the round cope embroidered shoes and never any with long bands.

If anyone of the students in arts or theology dies, half of the masters of arts are to go to the funeral one time, and the other half to the next funeral. They are not to withdraw until the burial is completed, unless they have some good reason. If any master of arts or theology dies, all the masters are to be present at the vigils, each one is to read the psalter or have it read. Each one is to remain in the church, where the vigils are celebrated, until midnight or later, unless prevented by some good reason. On the day when the master is buried, no one is to lecture or dispute.

We fully confirm to them the meadow of St. Germain in the condition in which it was adjudged to them.

Each master is to have jurisdiction over his scholars. No one is to receive either schools or a house without the consent of the occupant, if he is able to obtain it. No one is to receive a license from the chancellor or any one else through a gift of money, or furnishing a pledge or making an agreement. Also, the masters and students can make among themselves or with others agreements and regulations, confirmed by a pledge, penalty or oath, about the following matters: namely, if a student is killed, mutilated or receives some outrageous injury—if justice is not done; for fixing the prices of lodgings; concerning the dress, burial, lectures and disputations; in such a manner, however, that the university is not scattered or destroyed on this account.

We decide concerning the theologians, that no one shall lecture at Paris before he is thirty-five years old, and not unless he has studied at least eight years, and has heard the books faithfully and in the schools. He is to listen in theology for five years, before he reads his own lectures in public. No one of them is to lecture before the third hour on the days when the masters lecture. No one is to be received at Paris for the important lectures or sermons unless he is of approved character and learning. There is to be no student at Paris who does not have a regular master.

3. Statutes for the University of Paris Issued by Pope Gregory XI, 1231

Gregory, the bishop, servant of the servants of God, to his beloved sons, all the masters and students of Paris—greeting and apostolic benediction. . . .

---

4. **cope:** a long cloak or cape.

5. **pallium:** a white stole usually worn by popes and archbishops as a symbol of their authority. In this case, a master teacher was allowed to wear one as an indication of his level of academic achievement and its corresponding institutional authority; the pallium thus served a function similar to the master's or doctoral hood.

Concerning the condition of the students and schools, we have decided that the following should be observed: each chancellor, appointed hereafter at Paris, at the time of his installation, in the presence of the bishop, or at the command of the latter in the chapter at Paris—two masters of the students having been summoned for this purpose and present in behalf of the university—shall swear that, in good faith, according to his conscience, he will not receive as professors of theology and canon law any but suitable men, at a suitable place and time, according to the condition of the city and the honor and glory of those branches of learning; and he will reject all who are unworthy without respect to persons or nations. Before licensing anyone, during three months, dating from the time when the license is requested, the chancellor shall make diligent inquiries of all the masters of theology present in the city, and of all other honest and learned men through whom the truth can be ascertained, concerning the life, knowledge, capacity, purpose, prospects and other qualities needful in such persons; and after the inquiries, in good faith and according to his conscience, he shall grant or deny the license to the candidate, as shall seem fitting and expedient. The masters of theology and canon law, when they begin to lecture, shall take a public oath that they will give true testimony on the above points. The chancellor shall also swear, that he will in no way reveal the advice of the masters, to their injury; the liberty and privileges being maintained in their full vigor for the canons at Paris, as they were in the beginning. Moreover, the chancellor shall promise to examine in good faith the masters in medicine and arts and in the other branches, to admit only the worthy and to reject the unworthy.

In other matters, because confusion easily creeps in where there is no order, we grant to you the right of making constitutions and ordinances regulating the manner and time of lectures and disputations, the costume to be worn, the burial of the dead; and also concerning the bachelors,[6] who are to lecture and at what hours, and on what they are to lecture; and concerning the prices of the lodgings or the interdiction of the same; and concerning a fit punishment for those who violate your constitutions or ordinances, by exclusion from your society. And if, perchance, the assessment of the lodgings is taken from you, or anything else is lacking, or an injury or outrageous damage, such as death or the mutilation of a limb, is inflicted on one of you; unless through a suitable admonition satisfaction is rendered within fifteen days, you may suspend your lectures until you have received full satisfaction. And if it happens that any one of you is unlawfully imprisoned, unless the injury ceases on a remonstrance from you, you may, if you judge it expedient, suspend your lectures immediately.

We command, moreover, that the bishop of Paris shall so chastise the excesses of the guilty, that the honor of the students shall be preserved and evil

---

6. **bachelor:** a student who had his first degree and could teach beginning-level subjects.

deeds shall not remain unpunished. But in no way shall the innocent be seized on account of the guilty; nay rather, if a probable suspicion arises against anyone, he shall be detained honorably and on giving suitable bail he shall be freed, without any exactions from the jailors. But if, perchance, such a crime has been committed that imprisonment is necessary, the bishop shall detain the criminal in his prison. The chancellor is forbidden to keep him in his prison. We also forbid holding a student for a debt contracted by another, since this is interdicted by canonical and legitimate sanctions. Neither the bishop, nor his official, nor the chancellor shall exact a pecuniary penalty for removing an excommunication or any other censure of any kind. Nor shall the chancellor demand from the masters who are licensed an oath, or obedience, or any pledge; nor shall he receive any emolument[7] or promise for granting a license, but be content with the above-mentioned oath.

Also, the vacation in summer is not to exceed one month, and the bachelors, if they wish, can continue their lectures in vacation time. Moreover, we prohibit more expressly the students from carrying weapons in the city, and the university from protecting those who disturb the peace and study. And those who call themselves students but do not frequent the schools, or acknowledge any master, are in no way to enjoy the liberties of the students.

Moreover, we order that the masters in arts shall always read one lecture on Priscian, and one book after the other in the regular courses. Those books on natural philosophy which for a certain reason were prohibited in a provincial council, are not to be used at Paris until they have been examined and purged of all suspicion of error. The masters and students in theology shall strive to exercise themselves laudably in the branch which they profess; they shall not show themselves philosophers, but they shall strive to become God's learned. And they shall not speak in the language of the people, confounding the sacred language with the profane. In the schools they shall dispute only on such questions as can be determined by theological books and the writings of the holy fathers.

It is not lawful for any man whatever to infringe this deed of our provision, constitution, concession, prohibition and inhibition or to act contrary to it, from rash presumption. If anyone, however, should dare to attempt this, let him know that he incurs the wrath of almighty God and of the blessed Peter and Paul, his apostles.

Given at the Lateran, on the Ides of April [April 13], in the fifth year of our pontificate.

---

7. **emolument:** fee.

Source 4 from Lynn Thorndike, editor and translator, University Records and Life in the Middle Ages *(New York: Columbia University Press, 1944), pp. 88–98. Reprinted with permission of Columbia University Press, 562 W. 113th St., New York, NY 10025, via Copyright Clearance Center, Inc.*

4. Robert de Sorbon's
Regulations for His College,
Before 1274

I wish that the custom which was instituted from the beginning in this house by the counsel of good men may be kept, and if anyone ever has transgressed it, that henceforth he shall not presume to do so.

No one therefore shall eat meat in the house on Advent, nor on Monday or Tuesday of Lent, nor from Ascension Day to Pentecost.

Also, I will that the community be not charged for meals taken in rooms. If there cannot be equality, it is better that the fellow eating in his room be charged than the entire community.

Also, no one shall eat in his room except for cause. If anyone has a guest, he shall eat in hall. If, morever, it shall not seem expedient to the fellow to bring that guest to hall, let him eat in his room and he shall have the usual portion for himself, not for the guest. If, moreover, he wants more for himself or his guest, he should pay for it himself. . . .

Also, the fellows should be warned by the bearer of the roll that those eating in private rooms conduct themselves quietly and abstain from too much noise, lest those passing through the court and street be scandalized and lest the fellows in rooms adjoining be hindered in their studies. . . .

Also, the rule does not apply to the sick. If anyone eats in a private room because of sickness, he may have a fellow with him, if he wishes, to entertain and wait on him, who also shall have his due portion. What shall be the portion of a fellow shall be left to the discretion of the dispenser. If a fellow shall come late to lunch, if he comes from classes or a sermon or business of the community, he shall have his full portion, but if from his own affairs, he shall have bread only. . . .

Also, all shall wear closed outer garments, nor shall they have trimmings of vair or grise[8] or of red or green silk on the outer garment or hood.

Also, no one shall have loud shoes or clothing by which scandal might be generated in any way.

Also, no one shall be received in the house unless he shall be willing to leave off such and to observe the aforesaid rules.

Also, no one shall be received in the house unless he pledges faith that, if he happens to receive books from the common store, he will treat them carefully as if his own and on no condition remove or lend them out of the

---

8. **vair:** squirrel fur. **grise:** any type of gray fur.

house, and return them in good condition whenever required or whenever he leaves town.

Also, let every fellow have his own mark on his clothes and one only and different from the others. And let all the marks be written on a schedule and over each mark the name of whose it is. And let that schedule be given to the servant so that he may learn to recognize the mark of each one. And the servant shall not receive clothes from any fellow unless he sees the mark. And then the servant can return his clothes to each fellow. . . .

Also, for peace and utility we propound that no secular person living in town—scribe, corrector, or anyone else—unless for great cause eat, sleep in a room, or remain with the fellows when they eat, or have frequent conversation in the gardens or hall or other parts of the house, lest the secrets of the house and the remarks of the fellows be spread abroad.

Also, no outsider shall come to accountings or the special meetings of the fellows, and he whose guest he is shall see to this.

Also, no fellow shall bring in outsiders frequently to drink at commons, and if he does, he shall pay according to the estimate of the dispenser.

Also, no fellow shall have a key to the kitchen.

Also, no fellow shall presume to sleep outside the house in town, and if he did so for reason, he shall take pains to submit his excuse to the bearer of the roll. . . .

Also, no women of any sort shall eat in the private rooms. If anyone violates this rule, he shall pay the assessed penalty, namely, sixpence.[9] . . .

Also, no one shall form the habit of talking too loudly at table. Whoever after he has been warned about this by the prior shall have offended by speaking too loudly, provided this is established afterwards by testimony of several fellows to the prior, shall be held to the usual house penalty, namely two quarts of wine.

The penalty for transgression of statutes which do not fall under an oath is twopence, if the offenders are not reported by someone, or if they were, the penalty becomes sixpence in the case of fines. I understand "not reported" to mean that, if before the matter has come to the attention of the prior, the offender accuses himself to the prior or has told the clerk to write down twopence against him for such an offence, for it is not enough to say to the fellows, "I accuse myself."

9. This was a substantial amount for most students to pay.

Source 5 from James Harvey Robinson, editor and translator, Readings in European History, *vol. 1 (Boston: Ginn, 1904), pp. 450–452.*

5. Introduction to Peter
Abelard's *Sic et Non,* ca 1122

There are many seeming contradictions and even obscurities in the innumerable writings of the church fathers. Our respect for their authority should not stand in the way of an effort on our part to come at the truth. The obscurity and contradictions in ancient writings may be explained upon many grounds, and may be discussed without impugning the good faith and insight of the fathers. A writer may use different terms to mean the same thing, in order to avoid a monotonous repetition of the same word. Common, vague words may be employed in order that the common people may understand; and sometimes a writer sacrifices perfect accuracy in the interest of a clear general statement. Poetical, figurative language is often obscure and vague.

Not infrequently apocryphal works are attributed to the saints. Then, even the best authors often introduce the erroneous views of others and leave the reader to distinguish between the true and the false. Sometime, as Augustine confesses in his own case, the fathers ventured to rely upon the opinions of others.

Doubtless the fathers might err; even Peter, the prince of the apostles, fell into error; what wonder that the saints do not always show themselves inspired? The fathers did not themselves believe that they, or their companions, were always right. Augustine found himself mistaken in some cases and did not hesitate to retract his errors. He warns his admirers not to look upon his letters as they would upon the Scriptures, but to accept only those things which, upon examination, they find to be true.

All writings belonging to this class are to be read with full freedom to criticise, and with no obligation to accept unquestioningly; otherwise the way would be blocked to all discussion, and posterity be deprived of the excellent intellectual exercise of debating difficult questions of language and presentation. But an explicit exception must be made in the case of the Old and New Testaments. In the Scriptures, when anything strikes us as absurd, we may not say that the writer erred, but that the scribe made a blunder in copying the manuscripts, or that there is an error in interpretation, or that the passage is not understood. The fathers make a very careful distinction between the Scriptures and later works. They advocate a discriminating, not to say suspicious, use of the writings of their own contemporaries.

In view of these considerations, I have ventured to bring together various dicta of the holy fathers, as they came to mind, and to formulate certain questions which were suggested by the seeming contradictions in the

statements. These questions ought to serve to excite tender readers to a zealous inquiry into truth and so sharpen their wits. The master key of knowledge
is, indeed, a persistent and frequent questioning. Aristotle, the most clear-
sighted of all the philosophers, was desirous above all things else to arouse
this questioning spirit, for in his *Categories* he exhorts a student as follows:
"It may well be difficult to reach a positive conclusion in these matters unless
they be frequently discussed. It is by no means fruitless to be doubtful on
particular points." By doubting we come to examine, and by examining we
reach the truth.

> [*Abelard provides arguments for and
> against 158 different philosophical or
> theological propositions. The following are
> a few of the questions he discusses.*]

Should human faith be based upon reason, or no?
Is God one, or no?
Is God a substance, or no?
Does the first Psalm refer to Christ, or no?
Is sin pleasing to God, or no?
Is God the author of evil, or no?
Is God all-powerful, or no?
Can God be resisted, or no?
Has God free will, or no?
Was the first man persuaded to sin by the devil, or no?
Was Adam saved, or no?
Did all the apostles have wives except John, or no?
Are the flesh and blood of Christ in very truth and essence present in the
    sacrament of the altar, or no?
Do we sometimes sin unwillingly, or no?
Does God punish the same sin both here and in the future, or no?
Is it worse to sin openly than secretly, or no?

Source 6 from Roland H. Bainton, The Medieval Church *(Princeton, N.J.: D. VanNostrand,
1962), pp. 128–129.*

6. St. Anselm's Proof of the Existence of God, from His *Monologium*, ca 1070

I sought if I might find a single argument which would alone suffice to
demonstrate that God exists. This I did in the spirit of faith seeking
understanding. . . . Come now, O Lord my God, teach my heart where and

how it may seek Thee. O Lord, if Thou art not here where shall I seek Thee absent, and if Thou art everywhere why do I not see Thee present? Surely Thou dwellest in light inaccessible. When wilt Thou enlighten our eyes? I do not presume to penetrate Thy profundity but only in some measure to understand Thy truth, which my heart believes and loves, for I seek not to understand that I may believe, but I believe in order that I may understand.

Now the fool will admit that there can be in the mind something than which nothing greater can be conceived. This, being understood, is in the mind, but it cannot be only in the mind, because it is possible to think of something which exists also in reality and that would be greater. If, therefore, that than which nothing greater can be conceived is only in the mind, that than which a greater cannot be conceived is that than which a greater can be conceived and this certainly cannot be. Consequently, without doubt, that than which nothing greater can be conceived exists both in the mind and in reality. This, then, is so sure that one cannot think of its not being so. For it is possible to think of something which one cannot conceive not to exist which is greater than that which cannot be conceived can be thought not to exist, it is not that a greater than which cannot be conceived. But this does not make sense. Therefore, it is true that something than which a greater cannot be conceived is not able to be conceived as not existing. This art Thou, O Lord, my God.

Source 7 from Lynn Thorndike, editor and translator, University Records and Life in the Middle Ages *(New York: Columbia University Press, 1944), pp. 66–67. Reprinted with permission of Columbia University Press, 562 W. 113th St., New York, NY 10025, via Copyright Clearance Center, Inc.*

7. Odofredus Announces His Law Lectures at Bologna, ca 1255

If you please, I will begin the *Old Digest*[10] on the eighth day or thereabouts after the feast of St. Michael[11] and I will finish it entire with all ordinary and extraordinary, Providence permitting, in the middle of August or thereabouts. The *Code*[12] I will always begin within about a fortnight of the feast of St. Michael and I will finish it with all ordinary and extraordinary, Providence permitting, on the first of August or thereabouts. The extraordinary lectures used not to be given by the doctors. And so all scholars including the

10. **Old Digest:** the first part of the *Digest*, the emperor Justinian's collation of laws, commentaries, and interpretations of laws by Roman jurists.

11. **feast of St. Michael:** September 29.

12. **Code:** another part of Justinian's collation of laws reflecting the additions to Roman law that came about after Christianity became the official religion of the empire.

unskilled and novices will be able to make good progress with me, for they will hear their text as a whole, nor will anything be left out, as was once done in this region, indeed was the usual practice. For I shall teach the unskilled and novices but also the advanced students. For the unskilled will be able to make satisfactory progress in the position of the case and exposition of the letter; the advanced students can become more erudite in the subtleties of questions and contrarieties. I shall also read all the glosses, which was not done before my time. . . .

For it is my purpose to teach you faithfully and in a kindly manner, in which instruction the following order has customarily been observed by the ancient and modern doctors and particularly by my master, which method I shall retain. First, I shall give you the summaries of each title before I come to the text. Second, I shall put forth well and distinctly and in the best terms I can the purport of each law. Third, I shall read the text in order to correct it. Fourth, I shall briefly restate the meaning. Fifth, I shall solve conflicts, adding general matters (which are commonly called *brocardica*) and subtle and useful distinctions and questions with the solutions, so far as divine Providence shall assist me. And if any law is deserving of a review by reason of its fame or difficulty, I shall reserve it for an afternoon review.

Source 8 from Anders Piltz, The World of Medieval Learning, *translated by David Jones (Totowa, N.J.: Barnes & Noble, 1981), p. 97.*

8. Introduction to *Digest* of Emperor Justinian, 6th century

Public law is the legislation which refers to the Roman state, *private law* on the other hand is of value to the individual. Common law contains statutes about sacrifices, the priesthood and civil servants. Private law can be divided into three parts: it comprises regulations based on natural law and regulations governing the intercourse of nations and of individuals. *Natural law* is what is taught to all living creatures by nature itself, laws which apply not only to mankind but to every living creature on the earth, in the heavens or in the seas. It is this that sanctions the union of man and woman, which is called marriage, and likewise the bearing and upbringing of children: we can see that other living creatures also possess understanding of this law. *International law* is the [commonly recognized set of] laws applied by every nation of the world. As can be seen it differs from natural law in that the latter is the same for all living creatures whereas the former only concerns human intercourse. . . . *Civil law* does not deviate completely from natural law but neither is it subordinate to it. . . . It is either written or unwritten. . . . Its sources are laws, popular decisions, decisions of the senate, the decrees of princes and the opinions of jurists. . . . *Justice* is the earnest and steadfast desire to give every man the rights he is entitled to. The injunctions of the law are these: live honestly, do no man injury, give to every man what he is entitled to.

Jurisprudence is knowledge of divine and human things, the study of right and wrong.

Source 9 from The Letters of St. Bernard of Clairvaux, *translated by Bruno Scott James (Chicago: Henry Regnery Company, 1953), pp. 321, 328.*

9. Extracts from the Letters of St. Bernard of Clairvaux, 1140

Master Peter Abelard is a monk without a rule, a prelate without responsibility. . . . He speaks iniquity openly. He corrupts the integrity of the faith and the chastity of the Church. He oversteps the landmarks placed by our Fathers in discussing and writing about faith, the sacraments, and the Holy Trinity; he changes each thing according to his pleasure, adding to it or taking from it. In his books and in his works he shows himself to be a fabricator of falsehood, a coiner of perverse dogmas, proving himself a heretic not so much by his error as by his obstinate defence of error. He is a man who does not know his limitations, making void the virtue of the cross by the cleverness of his words. Nothing in heaven or on earth is hidden from him, except himself. . . . He has defiled the Church; he has infected with his own blight the minds of simple people. He tries to explore with his reason what the devout mind grasps at once with a vigorous faith. Faith believes, it does not dispute. But this man, apparently holding God suspect, will not believe anything until he has first examined it with his reason. When the Prophet says, "Unless you believe, you shall not understand," this man decries willing faith as levity, misusing that testimony of Solomon: "He that is hasty to believe is light of head." Let him therefore blame the Blessed Virgin Mary for quickly believing the angel when he announced to her that she should conceive and bring forth a son. Let him also blame him who, while on the verge of death, believed those words of One who was also dying: "This day thou shalt be with me in Paradise."

Source 10 from Cecil Headlam, The Story of Oxford *(London: Dent, 1907), pp. 234–235.*

10. Anonymous Account of a Student Riot at Oxford, 13th century

They [the townsmen] seized and imprisoned all scholars on whom they could lay hands, invaded their inns, made havoc of their goods and trampled their books under foot. In the face of such provocation the Proctors[13] sent their bedels[14] about the town, forbidding the students to leave their inns. But all commands and exhortations were in vain. By nine o'clock next morning, bands of scholars were parading the streets in martial array. If the Proctors failed to restrain them, the mayor was equally powerless to restrain his townsmen. The great bell of S. Martin's rang out an alarm; oxhorns were sounded in the streets; messengers were sent into the country to collect rustic allies. The clerks,[15] who numbered three thousand in all, began their attack simultaneously in various quarters. They broke open warehouses in the Spicery, the Cutlery and elsewhere. Armed with bows and arrows, swords and bucklers, slings and stones, they fell upon their opponents. Three they slew, and wounded fifty or more. One band, led by Fulk de Neyrmit, Rector of Piglesthorne, and his brother, took up a position in High Street between the Churches of S. Mary and All Saints', and attacked the house of a certain Edward Hales. This Hales was a longstanding enemy of the clerks. There were no half measures with him. He seized his crossbow, and from an upper chamber sent an unerring shaft into the eye of the pugnacious rector. The death of their valiant leader caused the clerks to lose heart. They fled, closely pursued by the townsmen and country-folk. Some were struck down in the streets, and others who had taken refuge in the churches were dragged out and driven mercilessly to prison, lashed with thongs and goaded with iron spikes.

Complaints of murder, violence and robbery were lodged straight-way with the King by both parties. The townsmen claimed three thousand pounds' damage. The commissioners, however, appointed to decide the matter, condemned them to pay two hundred marks, removed the bailiffs, and banished twelve of the most turbulent citizens from Oxford. Then the terms of peace were formally ratified.

13. **proctor:** university official who maintained order and supervised examinations.
14. **bedel:** assistant to the proctor.
15. **clerks:** here, students and teachers.

Source 11 *from Dana Carleton Munro, editor and translator,* Translations and Reprints from the Original Sources of European History, *vol. 2, no. 3 (Philadelphia: University of Pennsylvania Press, no date), pp. 19–21.*

11. Jacques de Vitry's Description of Student Life at Paris, ca 1225

Almost all the students at Paris, foreigners and natives, did absolutely nothing except learn or hear something new. Some studied merely to acquire knowledge, which is curiosity; others to acquire fame, which is vanity; others still for the sake of gain, which is cupidity and the vice of simony. Very few studied for their own edification, or that of others. They wrangled and disputed not merely about the various sects or about some discussions; but the differences between the countries also caused dissensions, hatreds and virulent animosities among them, and they impudently uttered all kinds of affronts and insults against one another.

They affirmed that the English were drunkards and had tails; the sons of France proud, effeminate and carefully adorned like women. They said that the Germans were furious and obscene at their feasts; the Normans, vain and boastful; the Poitevins, traitors and always adventurers. The Burgundians they considered vulgar and stupid. The Bretons were reputed to be fickle and changeable and were often reproached for the death of Arthur. The Lombards were called avaricious, vicious and cowardly; the Romans, seditious, turbulent and slanderous; the Sicilians, tyrannical and cruel; the inhabitants of Brabant, men of blood, incendiaries, brigands and ravishers; those of Flanders, fickle, prodigal, gluttonous, yielding as butter, and slothful. After such insults, from words they often came to blows.

I will not speak of those logicians, before whose eyes flitted constantly "the lice of Egypt," that is to say, all the sophistical subtleties, so that no one could comprehend their eloquent discourses in which, as says Isaiah, "there is no wisdom." As to the doctors of theology, "seated in Moses' seat," they were swollen with learning, but their charity was not edifying. Teaching and not practicing, they have "become as sounding brass or a tinkling cymbal," or like a canal of stone, always dry, which ought to carry water to "the bed of spices." They not only hated one another, but by their flatteries they enticed away the students of others; each one seeking his own glory, but caring not a whit about the welfare of souls.

Having listened intently to these words of the Apostle, "If a man desire the office of a bishop, he desireth a good work," they kept multiplying the prebends,[16] and seeking after the offices; and yet they sought the work

---

16. **prebends:** that part of church revenues paid as a clergyman's salary.

[169]

decidedly less than the preëminence, and they desired above all to have "the uppermost rooms at feasts and the chief seats in the synagogue, and greetings in the market." Although the Apostle James said, "My brethren, be not many masters," they on the contrary were in such haste to become masters, that most of them were not able to have any students, except by entreaties and payments. Now it is safer to listen than to teach, and a humble listener is better than an ignorant and presumptuous doctor. In short, the Lord had reserved for Himself among them all, only a few honorable and timorous men, who had not stood "in the way of sinners," nor sat down with the others in the envenomed seat.

Sources 12 and 13 from Charles Homer Haskins, The Rise of Universities *(Ithaca, N.Y.: Cornell University Press, 1957), pp. 77–80; pp. 85–87.*

12. **Two Letters, 13th century**

B. to his venerable master A., greeting. This is to inform you that I am studying at Oxford with the greatest diligence, but the matter of money stands greatly in the way of my promotion,[17] as it is now two months since I spent the last of what you sent me. The city is expensive and makes many demands; I have to rent lodgings, buy necessaries, and provide for many other things which I cannot now specify. Wherefore I respectfully beg your paternity that by the promptings of divine pity you may assist me, so that I may be able to complete what I have well begun. For you must know that without Ceres and Bacchus Apollo[18] grows cold.

To his son G. residing at Orleans P. of Besançon sends greetings with paternal zeal. It is written, "He also that is slothful in his work is brother to him that is a great waster." I have recently discovered that you live dissolutely and slothfully, preferring license to restraint and play to work and strumming a guitar while the others are at their studies, whence it happens that you have read but one volume of law while your more industrious companions have read several. Wherefore I have decided to exhort you herewith to repent utterly of your dissolute and careless ways, that you may no longer be called a waster and your shame may be turned to good repute.

17. **promotion:** that is, attaining his degree.
18. **Ceres:** Roman god of grain. **Bacchus:** god of wine. **Apollo:** god of wisdom.

13. Three Anonymous Student Poems, 12th century

I, a wandering scholar lad,
   Born for toil and sadness,
Oftentimes am driven by
   Poverty to madness.

Literature and knowledge I
   Fain would still be earning,
Were it not that want of pelf[19]
   Makes me cease from learning.

These torn clothes that cover me
   Are too thin and rotten;
Oft I have to suffer cold,
   By the warmth forgotten.

Scarce I can attend at church,
   Sing God's praises duly;
Mass and vespers both I miss,
   Though I love them truly.

Oh, thou pride of N——,
   By thy worth I pray thee
Give the suppliant help in need,
   Heaven will sure repay thee.

Take a mind unto thee now
   Like unto St. Martin;
Clothe the pilgrim's nakedness,
   Wish him well at parting.

So may God translate your soul
   Into peace eternal,
And the bliss of saints be yours
   In His realm supernal.

We in our wandering,
Blithesome and squandering,
   Tara, tantara, teino!

Eat to satiety,
Drink with propriety;
   Tara, tantara, teino!

Laugh till our sides we split,
Rags on our hides we fit;
   Tara, tantara, teino!

Jesting eternally,
Quaffing infernally:
   Tara, tantara, teino!
         etc.

Some are gaming, some are drinking,
Some are living without thinking;
And of those who make the racket,
Some are stripped of coat and jacket;
Some get clothes of finer feather,
Some are cleaned out altogether;
No one there dreads death's invasion,
But all drink in emulation.

19. **pelf:** a contemptuous term for money.

QUESTIONS TO CONSIDER

You have now examined medieval universities and colleges from four points of view—those of the authorities who established them, the teachers who taught in them, the church officials who criticized them, and the students who attended them. In refining your description of university life, think first about points on which a number of sources agree. What role did religious and secular authorities play in the universities, both in their founding and in day-to-day operations? What privileges were extended to teachers and students, and how did these benefits affect their relationship with townspeople? Given these privileges along with student attitudes and actions, what opinion would you expect townspeople to have of students? Which of Sorbon's rules would you expect to have been frequently broken? What qualities did authorities and teachers alike see as vital to effective teaching? What qualities did both try to encourage in students? Would students have agreed about any of these? What problems did the authorities, teachers, and students all agree were most pressing for students?

Now turn to points on which you have contradictory information. How would you compare Abelard's beliefs about the role of logic in education with those of Bernard and de Vitry? How might Bernard and de Vitry have viewed Anselm's attempt to prove the existence of God through reason? Would Abelard have be-

lieved that the rules for students set out in Sources 1 through 4 helped or hindered the learning process? What suggestions for educational improvements might a philosopher like Abelard have made? A churchman like Bernard? Would Anselm and Odofredus have agreed about the proper methods and aims of education?

De Vitry's critique and the student poetry have pointed out that the rules for student life set out in Sources 1 through 4 were not always followed. The consequences of St. Bernard's criticism similarly demonstrate that Abelard's assertion of the need for free discussion of all topics was an ideal and not always the reality in medieval universities. In 1140, St. Bernard convinced the church leadership at the Council of Sens to condemn Abelard's teachings. Abelard appealed to the pope, who upheld the council's decision, and Abelard retired to a monastery, never to teach again. What does this incident indicate about where the ultimate authority in the university lay? Does this assertion of papal authority contradict any of the ideas expressed in other sources for this chapter besides Abelard's writings?

Some of the contradictions you have discovered are inherent in the highly different points of view of the four groups and are irreconcilable. You must, however, make some effort to resolve those contradictions that involve conflicting points of *fact* rather than simply conflicting *opinions*. Historians resolve contradictions in their sources by a variety of methods: by assessing the authors' intent and possible biases, giving weight to evidence that is likely to be most objective; by judging each source as partially valid, speculating on how each author's point of view might have affected his or her description; by trying to find additional information confirming one side or the other. At this point you can use the first two methods in your own thinking: Which observers do you judge to be most objective? Why did the students, teachers, and officials have different viewpoints in the first place? (You can also think about the third method historians use to resolve contradictions in their evidence: What other types of sources would you examine to confirm what you have discovered here?) Once you have made these judgments, you can complete your description of medieval university life.

Now move on to the second part of your task in this chapter, which is to compare medieval and modern university life. Some of the more striking contrasts have probably already occurred to you, but the best way to proceed is to think first about your evidence. What types of sources would give you the information for modern universities that you have unearthed for medieval ones? What are the modern equivalents of the medieval rules and ordinances? Of descriptions of student actions? Of student poetry? Of course announcements? Of philosophical treatises? Besides such parallel sources, where else can you find information about modern universities? What types of sources generated from modern universities,

or from their students and teachers, have no medieval equivalent?

After considering these points of similarity and difference in sources, we are ready to make a specific comparison of university life in medieval and modern times. Because higher education in the United States is so diverse—some colleges and universities are public and some private, some religious and some nonsectarian, some residential and some commuter—it would be best if you compared your own institution with the more generalized description of medieval universities that you have developed. Do you see any modern equivalents to the privileges granted students by popes and kings? To the frequent clashes between universities and their surrounding communities? To the pope's restriction of "academic freedom" in the case of Abelard? How would you compare the relationship between religious and political authorities in medieval universities and in your own institution? The concern of authorities for the methods and content of higher education? How would you compare student residential life? Student problems? The students themselves? Relations between students and their parents? How would you compare the subjects taught? The method of teaching? The status of the faculty? Relations between students and teachers? Teachers' and students' views of the ultimate aims of education?

Once you have drawn up your comparison, you will need to perform what is often the most difficult task of any historical inquiry, which is to suggest reasons for what you have discovered. In doing this, you need to speculate not only about why some things have changed, but also about why others have remained the same. In your view, what is the most important difference between medieval and modern universities, and why?

EPILOGUE

The pattern set by Paris and Bologna was a popular one; by 1500, more than eighty universities were in existence throughout Europe. Often a dispute at one university, particularly among the faculty of theology, would lead a group of teachers and students to move elsewhere to form their own university. Sometimes they left one city because they felt the townspeople were overcharging them for food and lodging. Students often traveled from university to university in search of the best teachers or most amenable surroundings; because there were no admission forms or credits required for graduation, transferring from school to school was much easier in the Middle Ages than it is today.

As you have deduced from the sources, medieval students and teachers were criticized for all the seven deadly sins: greed, sloth, pride, lust, gluttony, envy, and anger. Toward the end of the Middle Ages, the university system itself came under increasing attack for being too remote from worldly concerns, providing students only with useless philosophical information that would never help them in the real world of politics and business. Especially in Italy, independent teachers of speech and writing began

to offer young men who wanted an education an alternative to universities, setting up academies to teach practical rhetorical and literary skills for those who planned to engage in commerce, banking, or politics. This new program of study, called *humanism*, emphasized language and literature rather than theology and philosophy.

Though the universities initially opposed the humanist curriculum, by the sixteenth century a considerable number, especially the newer ones, began to change their offerings. They established endowed chairs for teachers of Latin, Greek, and Hebrew, particularly because students who had trained at humanist secondary schools demanded further language training. Some of the oldest universities, such as Paris, were the slowest to change, but eventually they modified their program to keep students from going elsewhere.

The gradual introduction of humanism set a pattern that universities were to follow when any new body of knowledge or subject matter emerged. Innovative subjects and courses were at first generally taught outside the universities in separate academies or institutes, then slowly integrated into the university curriculum. In the seventeenth and eighteenth centuries, natural science was added in this way; in the nineteenth century, the social sciences and modern languages; and in the twentieth, a whole range of subjects, such as agriculture, engineering, and the fine arts. (The University of Paris continued to be the slowest to change well into the twentieth century; for example, it did not add sociology as a discipline until the 1960s. Modernization of the curriculum was one of the demands of the 1968 student revolt in Paris.) Thus, even though the university has survived since the Middle Ages, Peter Abelard or Robert de Sorbon might have difficulty recognizing the institution in its present-day form.

CHAPTER EIGHT

CAPITALISM AND CONFLICT

IN THE MEDIEVAL CLOTH TRADE

During the early Middle Ages, western Europe was largely a rural society. Most of the cities of the Roman Empire had shrunk to villages, and the roads the Romans had built were allowed to fall into disrepair. Manors and villages were relatively self-sufficient in basic commodities such as grain and cloth, and even in times of famine they could not import the food they needed because the cost of transportation was too high. Much local trade was carried out by barter, and any long-distance trade that existed was handled by Jews, Greeks, and Syrians, who imported luxury goods like spices, silks, and perfumes from the Near East. These extremely expensive commodities were purchased only by nobles and high-ranking churchmen. The lack of much regional trade is reflected in the almost complete absence of sources about trade before the tenth century. Commercial documents are extremely rare, and both public and private records

testify to the agrarian nature of early medieval society.

This situation began to change in the tenth century, when Vikings in the north and Italians in the south revived long-distance European commerce. The Vikings initially raided and plundered along the coasts of northern Europe, but they soon turned to trading with the very people whose lands they had threatened. At the same time, merchants from the cities of Genoa, Pisa, and Florence were taking over former Muslim trade routes in the western Mediterranean. These Italian merchants began to keep increasingly elaborate records of their transactions and devised new methods of bookkeeping to keep track of their ventures. They developed new types of partnerships to share the risks and found ways to get around the medieval Christian church's prohibition of the lending of money at interest (termed *usury*). These changes, combined with the growth in trade, led to a transformation of the European economy often called the *Commercial Revolution*.

Once western European merchants began to trade more extensively with the East, particularly after the Crusades in the twelfth century, it became clear that the balance of trade favored the East; Eastern luxuries such as spices and silks were paid for primarily in gold. Gradually, however, western European merchants began to add high- and medium-quality woolen cloth, with Italian merchants trading cloth made in Flanders (modern-day Belgium and northeast France) to Asia and Africa, carrying it all the way to the court of Genghis Khan. They also shipped increasing quantities of cloth to other locations in Europe, eventually importing raw wool from England to supply the Flemish clothmakers and handling both long-distance and regional trade.

The reinvigoration of trade in the Commercial Revolution came with, and was one of the causes of, a rebirth of town life. Especially in Italy and the Low Countries, but in many other parts of Europe as well, towns began to spring up around cathedrals, monasteries, and castles or at locations favorable for trade, such as ports or major crossroads. Many of these became cloth-producing centers, as weavers and other artisans involved in the many stages of cloth production gathered together to manufacture goods for regional and long-distance traders. Cloth merchants in these towns—sometimes in combination with the merchants of other types of products—joined together to form a merchants' guild that prohibited nonmembers from trading in the town. These same merchants often made up the earliest town government, serving as mayors and members of the city council, so that a town's economic policies were determined by its merchants' self-interest. Acting through the city council, the merchants' guilds determined the hours that markets would be open, decided which coins would be accepted as currency, and set prices on imported and local goods. Foreign affairs were also guided by the merchants, and cities formed alliances, termed *hanses*, with other cities to gain trading benefits.

From its beginnings, the trade in fine cloth was organized as a capitalist enterprise. Cloth merchants, called *drapers*, purchased raw materials, hired workers for all stages of production, and then sold the finished cloth; they rarely did any production themselves, and in some parts of Europe they were actually forbidden to do so. Some stages of production might be carried out in drapers' homes or in buildings that they owned, but more often production was carried out in the houses of those that they hired, who were paid by the piece rather than by the hour or day; these workers, especially those who wove cloth, might in turn hire several people to weave alongside them.

Cloth went through many stages from sheep to finished cloth. Once the sheep were sheared, the wool was sorted, beaten, and washed; it was then carded and spun by women using either hand spindles or, after the thirteenth century, spinning wheels. Next, the thread was prepared for weaving by *warpers*, who wound the long threads for the warp (warp threads are those that run lengthwise on a piece of cloth), and by *spoolers,* who wound woof threads (woof threads are those that run crosswise). The prepared thread went to the weavers, who used horizontal treadle looms. After the cloth was woven, it went to *fullers,* who stamped the cloth with their feet in troughs full of water, alkaline earth, and urine to soften it and fill in the spaces between the threads. (In the thirteenth century in some parts of Europe, fulling began to take place in water-powered fulling mills.) The cloth was then cleaned, hung to dry on wooden frames called *tenters,* and stretched to the correct width. The cloth was finished by repeatedly brushing it with thistle-like plants called *teasles* set in rows on a frame and then shearing the resulting fuzz off with large shears. It could be dyed at any stage in this process, as wool, thread, or whole cloth.

Some of these processes, such as dyeing, weaving, and shearing, required great skill and were usually reserved for men; others, such as spinning, sorting, and stretching on the tenter, called for less skill and were often carried out by women or young people. Once the cloth had been sheared for the final time, it went to the drapers, who monopolized all cutting of bolts of cloth and, thus, all retail sales. In areas where merchants organized production on a huge scale, such as Florence, there was a distinction between merchants and drapers, with the major merchants doing no actual cloth cutting themselves but simply hiring drapers; in most parts of Europe, however, merchants cut as well as sold, and were often called merchant-drapers.

Especially in Flanders and Florence, the merchants who controlled the cloth trade attempted to regulate everything down to the smallest detail. They set up precise standards of quality with severe penalties for those who did not meet them, regulated the length of the workday and the wages of all workers, and sent out inspectors regularly to enforce the ordinances and handle disputes. At first there was little opposition, but, beginning in the twelfth and thirteenth centuries in many areas, cloth workers challenged the merchants' control through strikes and revolts, and attempted to form their own organizations, called *craft guilds.* (At the same time, those who produced or handled many other sorts of products, such as shoemakers, butchers, and blacksmiths, were also forming separate craft guilds.) In some areas, such as Florence, the cloth merchants were successful at stopping all organizing and suppressing all rebellions, but in others, such as many cities in Flanders, the merchants lost, and the wool workers were able to form their own guilds and even become part of the city government for at least a short period of time. In some places, those artisans who were highly skilled and who owned some of their own equipment, such as weavers, fullers, dyers, and shearers, were able to form guilds, whereas the less-skilled spinners and sorters were not.

In periods during which they were able to form independently, the craft guilds took over the regulation of production from the merchant guilds. They set quality standards for their particular product and regulated the size of workshops, the training period, and the conduct of members. In most cities, individual guilds, such as those of weavers or dyers, achieved a monopoly in the production of one particular product, forbidding non-members to work. The craft guild then chose some of its members to act as inspectors and set up a court to hear disputes between members, although the city court remained the final arbiter, particularly in cases involving conflict between merchants and artisans or between members of craft guilds and those who were not members.

Each guild set the pattern by which members were trained. If one wanted to become a dyer, for instance, one spent four to seven years as an apprentice and then at least that long as a journeyman, working in the shop of a master dyer, after which one could theoretically make one's masterpiece. If the masterpiece was approved by the other master dyers and if they thought the market in their town was large enough to allow for another dyer, one could then become a master and start a shop. Though the amount of time a candidate had to spend as an apprentice and a journeyman varied slightly from guild to guild, all guilds—both those in the cloth industry and those in other sorts of production—followed this same three-stage process. The apprentices and journeymen generally lived with the master and his family, and were often forbidden to marry. Conversely, many

guilds required that masters be married, as they believed a wife was absolutely essential to the running of the shop and the household, and also felt that married men were likely to be more stable and dependable.

The master's wife assisted in running the shop, often selling the goods her husband had produced. Their children, both male and female, also worked alongside the apprentices and journeymen; the sons were sometimes formally apprenticed, but the daughters generally were not, since many guilds limited formal membership to males. Most guilds did allow a master's widow to continue operating a shop for a set period of time after her husband's death, for they recognized that she had the necessary skills and experience. Such widows paid all guild dues, but did not vote or hold office in the guilds because they were not considered full members. The fact that women were not formally guild members did not mean that they did not work in guild shops, however, for alongside the master's wife and daughters, female domestic servants often performed the less-skilled tasks. In addition, there were a few all-female guilds in several European cities, particularly Cologne and Paris, in which girls were formally apprenticed in the same way boys were in regular craft guilds.

Both craft and merchants' guilds were not only economic organizations, but also systems of social support. Though they were harsh against outsiders, they were protective and supportive of their members. They took care of elderly masters who could no longer work, and often supported masters' widows and orphans. They maintained an altar at a city church, and provided for the funerals of members and baptisms of their children. Guild members marched together in city parades, and reinforced their feelings of solidarity with one another by special ceremonies and distinctive dress.

Whether workers were able to form separate craft guilds or not, conflicts between merchants and workers over the cloth trade were a common feature of medieval town life in the major centers of cloth production. These conflicts often disrupted cloth production from a certain area, allowing other areas to expand their trade. In the late fourteenth century, for example, mass rebellions in Florence and Flanders benefited English weavers, who began to turn a greater percentage of English wool into cloth rather than exporting it as raw wool to the Continent. Government policy in England also helped the English weavers, as the crown in 1347 imposed a 33 percent tariff on the export of raw wool, while setting only a 2 percent tariff on the export of finished cloth. The crown also ordered people to wear English cloth (a provision that was very difficult to enforce) and en-

couraged Flemish cloth-makers displaced by unrest in their own towns to settle in England. Flemish cloth-makers also migrated to many towns in Germany, and by the sixteenth century the production of wool cloth was more dispersed throughout Europe than it had been several centuries earlier.

Often the change from the medieval to the modern economy is described as "the rise of capitalism," a change accompanied by "the rise of the middle class." Though specialists in the period disagree about many aspects of the development of capitalism, they agree that cloth production and trade was the earliest and most important capitalist enterprise in medieval Europe. Thus we can see in the cloth trade many of the issues that would emerge later in other parts of the economy, and that are still issues facing business and governments today. Your task in this chapter will be to use a variety of sources regarding cloth production from several parts of Europe to answer these questions: What were the key economic and social goals of governments, merchant-capitalists, and artisans regarding the cloth trade, and how did they seek to achieve these aims? What economic and social conflicts emerged as the cloth trade grew and changed?

SOURCES AND METHOD

In analyzing the development of the cloth trade, historians have a wide variety of documents at their disposal. Because cloth was regarded by

city and national governments as so important, their records include many laws that refer to the cloth trade, and often describe royal or municipal actions that encouraged cloth production. Some of the earliest attempts by governments to gather statistical information also refer to wool and cloth. The merchants' and later craft guilds themselves kept records—both regulations and ordinances, and records of judgments against those who broke these ordinances. Private business documents and personal documents such as contracts also often refer to aspects of the cloth trade.

In general, these sources can be divided into two basic types, a division that holds equally for sources from many other historical periods. The first type is *prescriptive*—laws, regulations, and ordinances that describe how the cloth trade was supposed to operate and how the guild or government officials who wrote the ordinances hoped things would be. These documents do not simply describe an ideal, however; they were generally written in response to events already taking place, so they can tell us about real problems and the attitudes of guilds and officials toward these problems. It is sources such as these that will allow us to answer the first of our questions, for they tell us specifically about goals and efforts to achieve them. What they cannot tell us is if any of these efforts worked, or what problems these efforts might have caused. For this we need to turn to a second type of primary evidence, *descriptive* documents such as court records and statistical information. Through these records we can observe how regulations were actually enforced, and assess—to a limited degree, because medieval statistics must always be used very carefully— the results of government and guild efforts to build up the cloth trade. As you are reading the sources, then, the first question you have to ask yourself is whether the record is prescriptive or descriptive, for confusing the two can give a very skewed view of medieval economic and social issues. (This kind of discrimination must be applied to any historical source, of course, and is not always an easy task. Sometimes even prominent historians have built a whole pyramid of erroneous theories about the past by assuming prescriptive sources accurately described reality. We investigated one example of this in Chapter 2 on classical Athens.)

The first three selections are all laws regarding the wool trade issued by territorial rulers. Source 1 comes from what are termed the laws of King Edward the Confessor of England (though they were written after his reign, sometime after 1115), setting out what were termed the "Liberties of London," or what we would term the rights accorded the citizens of London by the king. Source 2 is a similar law of the Count of Holland regarding the city of Dortrecht. Read each of these carefully. What special privileges were granted to the citizens of these towns by their rulers? Source 3 is a proclamation of the Countess of Flanders in 1224. What extra inducement did she offer to encourage wool production in the town of Courtrai? At this point you may want to begin a three-column list or chart, one column for the goals stated either explicitly or implicitly in the sources, a second for the actions taken to achieve those goals, and a third for the conflicts alluded to or discussed.

The next three sources are regulations regarding those who worked in cloth production issued by merchants' guilds or by the city councils, which were usually dominated by the merchants. Source 4 is from the English town of Winchester, Source 5 from the German town of Stendal, and Source 6 from the Flemish town of Arras. Read each of these sources carefully and add the information there to your three-column list. What were the most important aims of the merchants? What punishments did they set for those who broke the regulations, and how did they otherwise enforce their rules? Do the kinds of distinctions they make between groups—citizens and foreigners; those who make cloth and those who cut and sell it; members of artisans' families and non-members; masters, journeymen, and apprentices in a shop—suggest or perhaps contribute to social conflicts? What other types of conflicts are mentioned explicitly? (In all of these sources, the word *guest* or *foreigner* is used for someone who comes from a different town or village, and not necessarily from a different country.)

Though in many cities we do not have complete records of how well the provisions set forth in the ordinances were actually carried out, we can get glimpses from court records and similar sources from some cities. Through these we can see some instances of the enforcement of regulations and of the conflicts that this could cause. Sources 7 through 11 are examples of actual cases involving disputes in the cloth trade; Sources 7 and 8 are from fourteenth-century Flanders, and Sources 9 through 11 from sixteenth-century Germany. In Source 7, what is Jacquemars des

Mares' aim? That of the cloth inspectors and the city council? How well do the actions of the city councils in Sources 7, 8, and 9 reinforce the aims of the merchants as set out in Sources 4, 5, and 6? Though the ultimate decision of the city councils in Sources 10 and 11 is not known, from the supplications themselves we can get a good idea of actions taken by members of the weavers' guild. Do these fit with the aims of the merchants, or are the aims of these artisans somewhat different? Why might the women have appealed to the city council, made up largely of merchants, to rectify actions taken against them by artisans?

Along with government records, private records can give us additional information about the cloth trade. Most private business documents are primarily descriptive in nature, although they can also contain information about the aims of those who drew them up. Source 12 contains two apprenticeship contracts from the thirteenth century. What were the aims of the parents involved and of the master weavers? Can we get any hints of potential conflicts that arose in apprenticeships? Source 13 contains several insurance contracts for wool and cloth shipments from a fourteenth-century Italian merchant. Why would wool traders have wanted to enlist his services? How does their using an insurer fit with others of their actions?

The final sources for this chapter are statistical and rely on both official and private records. Source 14 consists of two charts of the total number of cloths produced in Florence and

Ypres in Flanders, based on guild records. Source 15 consists of two charts of the export of raw wool and wool cloth from England, based on customs records that began after customs duties were imposed in 1347. These records do not include cloth made for use in England and report *only* exports that went through the customs office (there was a great deal of smuggling, so they may significantly underreport the total amounts exported), but we can use them in conjunction with the charts of Source 14 to ascertain general trends. How would you compare the trends in cloth production for the three areas? How would you assess the success of English government policies that encouraged weaving? How might the decline in the amount of raw wool exported from England have affected weaving in Florence, Ypres, and other areas, despite the efforts there of governments or merchants?

Source 1 from Benjamin Thorpe, Ancient Laws and Institutes of England *(London: Eyre and Spottiswoode, 1840), p. 462.*

1. Laws Regarding Foreign Merchants Under King Edward the Confessor of England, after 1115

And after he has entered the city, let a foreign merchant be lodged wherever it please him. But if he bring dyed cloth, let him see to it that he does not sell his merchandise at retail, but that he sell not less than a dozen pieces at a time. And if he bring pepper, or cumin, or ginger, or alum, or brasil wood, or resin, or incense, let him sell not less than fifteen pounds at a time. But if he bring belts, let him sell not less than a thousand at a time. And if he bring cloths of silk, or wool or linen, let him see that he cut them not, but sell them whole.

Also a foreign merchant may not buy dyed cloth, nor make the dye in the city, nor do any work which belongs by right to the citizens.

Source 2 from C. Gross, The Gild Merchant *(Oxford: Clarendon, 1890), vol. I, p. 293.*

2. Law Regarding Cloth Cutting Under the Count of Holland, 1200

I, Theodore, by the grace of God, Count of Holland, and Adelaide, Countess of Holland, my wife, wish it to be known to all, both present and future, that we decree that our townsmen of Dortrecht may enjoy in their own right the following freedom in the said town, namely, that it is permitted to no one in Dortrecht to cut cloth for retail sale except to those who are designated by this trade, being called cutters of cloth, and except they be in the hanse[1] and fraternity of the townsmen belonging to Dortrecht. And that this charter, instituted by us, may forever be secure and intact, we corroborate it by affixing our seals thereto, and the signatures of witnesses.

These are the witnesses. . . .

Source 3 from Roy C. Cave and Herbert H. Coulson, A Source Book for Medieval Economic History *(New York: Biblo and Tannen, 1965), p. 374.*

3. Proclamation Regarding Taxes by the Countess of Flanders, 1224

I, Joan, Countess of Flanders and Hainault, wish it to be known to all both now and in the future, that I and my successors cannot and ought not to take any tax or payment from the fifty men who shall come to live at Courtrai, for as long as they remain here, to work in the woolen industry from this day on. But their heirs, after the decease of their parents, shall serve me just as my other burgesses do. Given at Courtrai, in the year of the Lord 1224, on the feast of St. Cecilia.

---

1. **hanse:** in this instance, the merchants' guild.

Source 4 from Beverley Town Documents, *edited by A. F. Leach, Publications of the Selden Society, vol. XIV (London: Selden Society, 1900), appendix II, pp. 134–135.*

4. City Ordinances Regarding Weavers in Winchester, England, ca 1209

This is the law of the Fullers and Weavers of Winchester: Be it known that no weaver or fuller may dry or dye cloth nor go outside the city to sell it. They may sell their cloth to no foreigner, but only to merchants of the city. And if it happens that, in order to enrich himself, one of the weavers or fullers wishes to go outside the city to sell his merchandise, he may be very sure that the honest men of the city will take all his cloth and bring it back to the city, and that he will forfeit it in the presence of the aldermen and honest men of the city. And if any weaver or fuller sell his cloth to a foreigner, the foreigner shall lose his cloth, and the other shall remain at the mercy of the city for as much as he has. Neither the weaver nor the fuller may buy anything except for his trade but by making an agreement with the mayor. No free man[2] can be accused by a weaver or a fuller, nor can a weaver or a fuller bear testimony against a free man. If any of them become rich, and wish to give up his trade, he may forswear it and turn his tools out of the house, and then do as much for the city as he is able in his freedom.

Sources 5 and 6 from Roy C. Cave and Herbert H. Coulson, A Source Book for Medieval Economic History *(New York: Biblo and Tannen, 1965), pp. 246–248; pp. 250–252.*

5. City Ordinances Regarding Guilds in Stendal, Germany, 1231 and 1233

We make known ... that we, ... desiring to provide properly for our city of Stendal, have changed, and do change, for the better, the laws of the gild [*sic*] brethren, and of those who are called cloth-cutters, so that they might have the same laws in this craft as their gild brethren the garment-cutters in Magdeburg have been accustomed to observe in the past.

These are the laws:

1. No one shall presume to cut cloth, except he be of our craft; those who break this rule will amend to the gild with three talents.[3]

2. **free man:** a citizen of Winchester. The weavers and fullers were not fully citizens at this point, but probably came from outside Winchester.

3. **talents, denarii, solidi:** different coins in circulation in Stendal. A mark was worth about 160 denarii; a solidus was worth about 25 denarii. The value of a talent varied widely.

2. Thrice a year there ought to be a meeting of the brethren, and whoever does not come to it will amend according to justice.

3. Whoever wishes to enter the fraternity whose father was a brother and cut cloth will come with his friends to the meeting of the brethren, and if he conduct himself honestly, he will be able to join the gild at the first request on payment of five solidi, and he will give six denarii to the master. And if he be dishonest and should not conduct himself well, he should be put off until the second or third meeting. But any of our citizens who wish to enter the gild, if he be an honest man, and worthy, will give a talent to the brethren on entry into the gild, and will present a solidus to the master. But if a guest who is an honest man should decide to join our fraternity, he will give thirty solidi to the gild on his entry, and eighteen denarii to the master. . . . But if any brother should make cloth against the institutions of the brethren, and of their decrees, which he ought on the advice of the consuls to observe, he will present to the consuls by way of emendation one talent for each offense or he will lose his craft for a year.

4. But if any one be caught with false cloth, his cloth will be burned publicly, and verily, the author of the crime will amend according to justice. . . .

9. If any one should marry a widow whose husband was of the craft, he will enter the fraternity with three solidi.

6. Shearers' Charter from Arras, Flanders, 1236

Here is the Shearers' Charter, on which they were first founded.

This is the first ordinance of the shearers, who were founded in the name of the Fraternity of God and St. Julien, with the agreement and consent of those who were at the time mayor and aldermen.

1. Whoever would engage in the trade of a shearer shall be in the Confraternity of St. Julien, and shall pay all the dues, and observe the decrees made by the brethren.

2. That is to say: first, that whoever is a master shearer shall pay 14 solidi to the Fraternity. And there may not be more than one master shearer working in a house. And he shall be a master shearer all the year, and have arms for the need of the town.

3. And a journeyman shall pay 5 solidi to the Fraternity.

4. And whoever wishes to learn the trade shall be the son of a burgess or he shall live in the town for a year and a day; and he shall serve three years to learn this trade.

5. And he shall give to his master 3 *muids*[4] for his bed and board; and he ought to bring the first *muid* to his master at the beginning of his apprenticeship, and another *muid* a year from that day, and a third *muid* at the beginning of the third year.

---

4. **muid:** a silver coin in circulation in Arras.

6. And no one may be a master of this trade of shearer if he has not lived a year and a day in the town, in order that it may be known whether or not he comes from a good place. . . .

9. And whoever does work on Saturday afternoon, or on the Eve of the Feast of Our Lady, or after Vespers on the Eve of the Feast of St. Julien, and completes the day by working, shall pay, if he be a master, 12 denarii, and if he be a journeyman, 6 denarii. And whoever works in the four days of Christmas, or in the eight days of Easter, or in the eight days of Pentecost, owes 5 solidi. . . .

11. And an apprentice owes to the Fraternity for his apprenticeship 5 solidi. . . .

13. And whoever does work in defiance of the mayor and aldermen shall pay 5 solidi. . . .

16. And those who are fed at the expense of the city shall be put to work first. And he who slights them for strangers owes 5 solidi: but if the stranger be put to work he cannot be removed as long as the master wishes to keep him. . . . And when a master does not work hard he pays 5 solidi, and a journeyman 2 solidi. . . .

18. And after the half year the mayor and aldermen shall fix such wages as he ought to have. . . .

20. And whoever maligns the mayor and aldermen, that is while on the business of the Fraternity, shall pay 5 solidi. . . .

23. And if a draper or a merchant has work to do in his house, he may take such workmen as he wishes into his house, so long as the work be done in his house. And he who infringes this shall give 5 solidi to the Fraternity. . . .

25. And each master ought to have his arms when he is summoned. And if he has not he should pay 20 solidi. . . .

32. And if a master does not give a journeyman such wage as is his due, then he shall pay 5 solidi.

33. And he who overlooks the forfeits of this Fraternity, if he does not wish to pay them when the mayor and aldermen summon him either for the army or the district, then he owes 10 solidi, and he shall not work at the trade until he has paid. Every forfeit of 5 solidi, and the fines which the mayor and aldermen command, shall be written down. All the fines of the Fraternity ought to go for the purchase of arms and for the needs of the Fraternity.

34. And whatever brother of this Fraternity shall betray his confrère for others shall not work at the trade for a year and a day. . . .

36. And should a master of this Fraternity die and leave a male heir he may learn the trade anywhere where there is no apprentice.

37. And no apprentice shall cut to the selvage[5] for half a year, and this is to obtain good work. And no master or journeyman may cut by himself because

---

5. **selvage:** very edge of the cloth.

no one can measure cloth well alone. And whoever infringes this rule shall pay 5 solidi to the Fraternity for each offense.

38. Any brother whatsoever who lays hands on, or does wrong to, the mayor and aldermen of this Fraternity, as long as they work for the city and the Fraternity, shall not work at his trade in the city for a year and a day.

And if he should do so, let him be banished from the town for a year and a day, saving the appeal to Monseigneur the King and his Castellan. . . .

Sources 7 and 8 from Carolly Erickson, The Records of Medieval Europe *(Garden City, New York: Anchor, 1971), p. 238. Translated by Carolly Erickson.*

7. Judgment Against a Draper in Flanders, mid-14th century

When Jacquemars des Mares, a draper, brought one of his cloths to the great cloth hall of Arras and sold it, the aforesaid cloth was examined by the *espincheurs*[6] as is customary, and at the time they had it weighed, it was half a pound over the legal weight. Then, because of certain suspicions which arose, they had the cloth dried, and when it was dry, it weighed a half pound less than the legal weight. The *espincheur* brought the misdeed to the attention of the Twenty;[7] Jacquemars was fined 100 shillings.

8. Dispute Between Master Fullers and Their Apprentices in Flanders, 1345

A point of discussion was mooted between the apprentice fullers on the one hand, and the master fullers on the other. The apprentices held that, as they laid out in a letter, no one could have work done in his house without taking apprentices. . . . For they complained of fulling masters who had their children work in their houses, without standing [for jobs] in the public square like the other apprentices, and they begged that their letter be answered. The fulling masters stated certain arguments to the contrary. The aldermen sent for both parties and for the Twenty also and asked the masters if indeed they kept their children as apprentices; each master said he did. It was declared by the aldermen that every apprentice must remain in the public square, as reason demanded.

Done in the year of 1344 [1345], in the month of February, and through a full sitting of the aldermen.

6. **espincheur:** cloth inspector.

7. **Twenty:** court of twenty men, made up of members of the city council.

Source 9 from Merry E. Wiesner, translator, unpublished decisions in Nuremberg Stadtarchiv, Quellen zur Nürnbergische Geschichte, Rep. F5, no. 68/I, fol. 58 (1577).

9. Decision by the
Nuremberg City Council, 1577

The honorable city council has decided to deny the request of Barbara Hansmesser that she be allowed to dye wool because the blanketweavers' guild has so adamantly opposed it. Because her husband is not a citizen, they are both ordered to get out of the city and find work in some other place, with the warning that if they are found in the vicinity of this city, and are doing any work here, work will be taken from them and the yarn cut to pieces. They can count on this.

Sources 10 and 11 from Merry E. Wiesner, translator, unpublished supplications in Frankfurt Stadtarchiv, Zünfte, Ugb. C-50, Ss, no. 4; Ugb. C-32, R, no. 1.

10. Widow's Supplication to
the Frankfurt City Council,
late 16th century

Distinguished and honorable sirs, I, a poor and distressed widow, wish to respectfully report in what manner earlier this year I spun some pounds of yarn, 57 to be exact, for the use of my own household. I wanted to take the yarn to be woven into cloth, but didn't know whom I should give it to so that I could get it worked into cloth the quickest and earliest.

Therefore I was talking to some farm women from Bornheim, who were selling their produce in front of the shoemakers' guild house, and they told me about a weaver that they had in Bornheim who made good cloth and could also make it quickly. I let him know—through the farmers' wives—that I wanted him to make my cloth. I got the yarn together and sent my children to carry it to him; as they were on their way, the weavers here grabbed the yarn forcefully from my children, and took it to their guild house. They said they had ordinances which forbade taking yarn to foreigners to weave, and told me they would not return it unless I paid a fine.

I then went to the lord mayors, asking them about this ordinance that would let people confiscate things without warning from the public streets. They said they didn't known about any such ordinance, and that my yarn should have long been returned to me. I then went to the overseer of the guild, master Adlaff Zimmermann who lives by the Eschenheimer tower, who answered me with rough, harsh words that they would in no way return my yarn to me, and that the guild did have such an ordinance.

Therefore I respectfully request, if they do have such an ordinance, I didn't know anything about it, and so ask you humbly and in God's name to tell the weavers to return my yarn. If, according to this ordinance, I am supposed to pay a fine, they should take it from the yarn, and give the rest back. I ask this of your honorable sirs, as the protectors of widows and orphans, and pray that you will help me.

Your humble servant, Agatha, the widow of the late Conrad Gaingen.

11. Widow's Supplication to the Frankfurt City Council, late 16th century

Most honorable and merciful gentlemen, you certainly know what a heavy and hard cross God has laid on me, and in what a miserable situation I find myself, after the much too early death of my late husband, with my young children, all of them still minors and some still nursing. This unfortunate situation is well known everywhere.

Although in consideration of my misfortune most Christian hearts would have gladly let me continue in my craft and occupation, and allowed me to earn a little piece of bread, instead the overseers of the woolweavers' guild came to me as soon as my husband had died, in my sorrow and even in my own house. Against all Christian charity, they began to order changes in my workshop with very harsh and menacing words. They specifically ordered that my apprentice, whom I had raised and trained at great cost and who had just come to be of use to me in the craft, leave me and go to them, which would be to their great advantage but my greater disadvantage. They ordered this on the pretense that there was no longer a master here so he could not finish his training.

Honorable sirs, I then humbly put myself under the protection of the lord mayors here, and asked that the two journeymen and the apprentice be allowed to continue on in their work as they had before unimpeded until a final judgment was reached in the matter. Despite this, one of the weavers began to shout at my journeymen whenever he saw them, especially if there were other people on the street. In his unhindered and unwarranted boldness, he yelled that my workshop was not honorable, and all journeymen who worked there were thieves and rascals. After doing this for several days, he and several others came into my workshop on a Saturday, and, bitter and jealous, pushed my journeymen out. They began to write to all places where this craft is practiced to tell other masters not to accept anyone who had worked in my workshop.

I now humbly beg you, my honorable and gracious sirs, protect me and my hungry children from such abuse, shame, and insult. Help my journeymen, who were so undeservedly insulted, to regain their honor. I beg you, as the protector of humble widows, to let my apprentice stay with me, as apprentices are allowed to stay in the workshops of widows throughout the entire Holy Roman Empire, as long as there are journeymen, whether or not there is a master present. Protect me from any further insults of the woolweavers' guild, which does nothing to increase the honor of our city, which you, honorable sirs, are charged to uphold. I plead with you to grant me my request, and allow me to continue my workshop.

Source 12 from Roy C. Cave and Herbert H. Coulson, A Source Book for Medieval Economic History *(New York: Biblo and Tannen, 1965), pp. 256–257.*

12. Two Apprenticeship Contracts, 13th century

Be it known to present and future aldermen that Ouede Ferconne apprentices Michael, her son, to Matthew Haimart on security of her house, her person, and her chattels,[8] and the share that Michael ought to have in them, so that Matthew Haimart will teach him to weave in four years, and that he (Michael) will have shelter, and learn his trade there without board. And if there should be reason within two years for Michael to default she will return him, and Ouede Ferconne, his mother, guarantees this on the security of her person and goods. And if she should wish to purchase his freedom for the last two years she may do so for thirty-three solidi, and will pledge for that all that has been stated. And if he should not free himself of the last two years let him return, and Ouede Ferconne, his mother, pledges this with her person and her goods. And the said Ouede pledges that if Matthew Haimart suffers either loss or damage through Michael, her son, she will restore the loss and damage on the security of herself and all her goods, should Michael do wrong.

April the ninth. I, Peter Borre, in good faith and without guile, place with you, Peter Feissac, weaver, my son Stephen, for the purpose of learning the trade or craft of weaving, to live at your house, and to do work for you from the feast of Easter next for four continuous years, promising you by this agreement to take care that my son does the said work, and that he will be faithful and trustworthy in all that he does, and that he will neither steal nor take anything away from you, nor flee nor depart from you for any reason, until he has completed his apprenticeship. And I promise you by this agreement that I will reimburse you for all damages or losses that you incur or sustain on my behalf, pledging all my goods, etc.; renouncing the benefit of all

8. **chattels:** personal property.

laws, etc. And I, the said Peter Feissac, promise you, Peter Borre, that I will teach your son faithfully and will provide food and clothing for him.

Done at Marseilles, near the tables of the money-changers. Witnesses, etc.

Source 13 from Robert S. Lopez and Irving W. Raymond, editors and translators, Medieval Trade in the Mediterranean World *(New York: Columbia University Press, 1955), pp. 263–265, no. 138.*

13. Insurance Contracts from Pisa, 1384

This is a book of Francesco of Prato and partners, residing in Pisa, and we shall write in it all insurances we shall make in behalf of others. May God grant us profit from these and protect us from dangers.

[*Seal of Francesco son of Marco*]

A memorandum that on September 7, 1384, in behalf of Baldo Ridolfi and partners we insured for 100 gold florins wool in the ship of Guilhem Sale, Catalan, [in transit] from Peñiscola to Porto Pisano. And from the said 100 florins we received 3 gold florins in cash, and we insured against all risks, as is evident by a record by the hand of Gherardo d'Ormanno which is undersigned by our hand.

Said ship arrived safely in Porto Pisano and unloaded on . . . October, 1384, and we are free from the insurance.

A memorandum that on September 10 in behalf of Ambrogio, son of Bino Bini, we insured for 200 gold florins Milanese cloth in the ship of Bartolomeo Vitale, [in transit] from Porto Pisano to Palermo. And from the said 200 florins we received 8 gold florins, charged to the debit account of Ambrogio on *c.* 174, and no other record appears [written] by the hand of any broker.

Arrived in Palermo safely.

First graph in Source 14 from R. S. Lopez, "Hard Times and Investment in Culture," The Renaissance: Medieval or Modern *(Boston: D.C. Heath, 1959); second graph from H. van Werveke, "De omgang van de Ieperse lakenproductie in de veertiende eeuw," Medelelingen, K. Vlaamse Acad. voor Wetensch., Letteren en schone Kunsten van Belgie (1947). Both reprinted in* Harry A. Miskimin, The Economy of Early Renaissance Europe, 1300–1460 *(Englewood Cliffs, N.J.: Prentice-Hall, 1969), p. 94.*

14. Trends in the Cloth Trade in Florence and Ypres

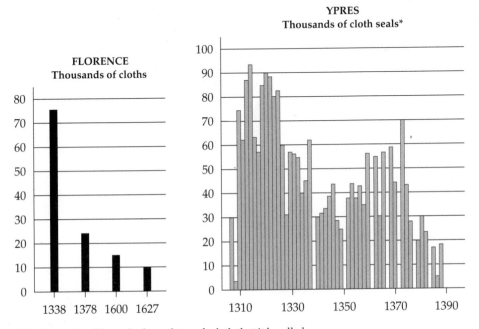

*The drapers' guild attached a seal to each cloth that it handled.

Table in Source 15 from A. R. Bridbury, Economic Growth: England in the Later Middle Ages *(London: G. Allen and Unwin, 1962), p. 32. Used by permission of the author; graphs adapted from H. C. Darby, editor,* A New Historical Geography of England *(Cambridge, England: Cambridge University Press, 1973), p. 219. Reprinted with permission of Cambridge University Press.*

15. English Exports of Raw Wool and Cloth, Based on Customs Records, ca 1350–1550

Years	Raw wool (sacks)	Woollen cloths (as equivalent to sacks of raw wool)
1361–70	28,302	3,024
1371–80	23,241	3,432
1381–90	17,988	5,521
1391–1400	17,679	8,967
1401–10	13,922	7,651
1411–20	13,487	6,364
1421–30	13,696	9,309
1431–40	7,377	10,051
1441–50	9,398	11,803
1471–80	9,299	10,125
1481–90	8,858	12,230
1491–1500	8,149	13,891

1 Raw Wool Exports

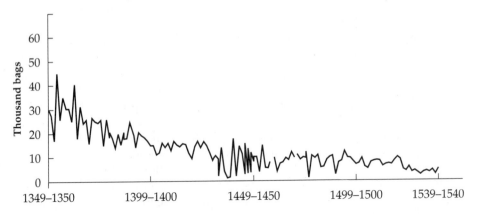

2 Cloth Exports

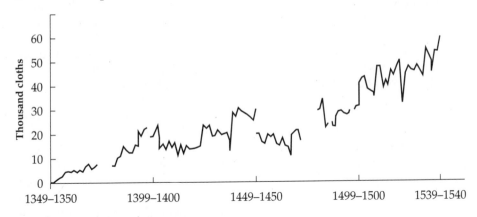

The records you have read shed some light on a wide variety of issues in the medieval cloth trade, as well as providing information on other social and economic matters. To draw some general conclusions and answer the questions for this chapter, you will need to go back to your list of goals, actions, and conflicts, and put together the information from the various sources. Because our focus here is on cloth production and sales, you will also need to leave aside what you have learned about other issues, though this may be very interesting to you. Investigating social and economic questions often involves not only uncovering sources that deal with your problem directly, but also extracting small bits of information from sources that cover a great many other areas, such as the city council records of Sources 9 through 11. Being a social historian requires that you discipline yourself to stick to the topic; though it may be fascinating to read every entry about every issue, this will not help with the completion of your research project.

Going back, then, to your list: How would you describe the key aims of territorial rulers regarding the cloth trade? Of local ruling bodies such as city councils? Do the sources you have read here lead you to support the thesis that city ordinances generally reflect the aims of cloth merchants? How might the aims of territorial rulers and merchants come into conflict? (For one example, how might cloth merchants or artisans already working in cloth production in Courtrai feel about the tax breaks that the Countess of Flanders gave to immigrants into the city in Source 3? What might cloth merchants do in response to this to maintain their monopoly on the cloth trade? For another, how might merchants in raw wool have regarded the changing nature of English exports as traced in Source 15 and the government tariff policies that were responsible for this?) In addition to shaping government policies, what private actions do you find merchants engaging in to achieve their goals?

Turning to the relationship of the merchants—or the city councils, usually dominated by merchants—to the artisans: What actions by artisans are explicitly prohibited in city ordinances or guild charters? (See Sources 4, 5, and 6.) How do these prohibitions reflect merchant aims? How would you describe the attitudes of merchants toward artisans—suspicious, friendly, hostile, paternalistic, fraternal? How did groups or individuals use the conflicts between these two to their own advantage? (The best examples here are the supplications quoted in Sources 10 and 11 and the dispute recorded in Source 8. To whom did the women and the apprentices turn to for help, and about which groups were they complaining? In the women's supplications, what sort of language do they use to persuade authorities to help them?)

Turning to the workplace itself: How would you characterize the atmosphere in the houses of most woolworkers—collegial and friendly, or divided and somewhat hostile? As you have no doubt noticed, ordinances regulated not simply individual workers, but their families as well. What special privileges were given to members of the master's family? Who objected to these privileges, and why? How did the guilds treat widows of their members? Do you see any discrepancy in the discussion of widows in the ordinances and in the actual treatment of a member's widow in Source 11? How do the guilds react to women working who were not the wives or widows of guild members? Would you regard the guilds as generally helpful to families or helpful to only certain types of families? Along with the privileges accorded to the master's family members, what other sources of dispute between masters and journeymen, and between masters and apprentices, are mentioned in the sources? How might the goals of the craft guild masters and those of the merchants come into conflict in the handling of these disputes?

You are now ready to answer the questions posed by this chapter: What were the key economic and social goals of governments, merchant-capitalists, and artisans regarding the cloth trade, and how did they seek to achieve these aims? What economic and social conflicts emerged as the cloth trade grew and changed?

EPILOGUE

Because of its capitalist organization and complex division of labor, the medieval cloth trade is often seen as a harbinger of modern economic developments. As you have read the sources for this chapter, you have probably discovered other areas in which there are parallels between the medieval cloth trade and the modern economy. Many of the goals of governments, merchants, and artisans that we have seen expressed in the medieval sources are shared by modern governments, corporations, and unions: the expansion of domestic production, the maintenance of order in the workplace, the limitation of risk, the highest level of profit, steady wages and job security, protection from foreign competition, the replacement of exports of raw materials with exports of manufactured products. As they were in the Middle Ages, these goals are often contradictory, if not mutually exclusive.

Many of the actions taken by medieval authorities and individuals continue to appear on the evening news as it reports economic developments: protectionist legislation, tax breaks to promote the development of industry and job creation, preferential treatment for certain groups, the transfer of jobs to places where wages are lower or workers are less likely to strike, immigration policies that promote the immigration of workers with specific skills, fraud and falsification of merchandise in an attempt to increase profits.

Many of the conflicts we have seen here still beset workplaces in the twentieth century: disputes over wage levels and the right to work; disagreements between labor and management over who controls certain aspects of the workplace; conflicts between older and younger workers, now often expressed as issues of seniority; and demands that employers pay more attention to the family responsibilities of their employees and make the workplace more "family friendly." Methods of enforcing aims and resolving conflicts that were tried in the Middle Ages are still often tried today, such as turning to outside authorities or arbitrators, revolts and strikes, and blacklisting and fines.

Though in the contemporary economy production of many types of goods often faces conflicts—automobiles, electronic and computer equipment, and agricultural products usually gain the most headlines—cloth

[197]

and clothing production is still an important issue for many nations, corporations, and unions. Many of the commercials promoting the retail giant Wal-Mart's policy of buying products made in the United States highlight cloth and clothing manufacturers. The attempts by U.S. immigration authorities to make employers responsible for making sure their foreign-born employees have the necessary work permits have targeted sportswear makers in New York and California who hire undocumented aliens. Lawsuits by U.S. companies charging copyright infringement are often brought against foreign manufacturers of such items as T-shirts and beach towels. Just as cloth production in the Middle Ages was a harbinger of trends and conflicts in the modern economy, cloth production at the end of the twentieth century may also be a harbinger of the future. The internationalization of the marketplace and work force that it points to perhaps would not seem so strange to the Countess of Flanders or Francesco of Prato, nor would the difficulties that can result from this seem so strange to the woolworkers of Florence or Ypres.

CHAPTER NINE

LAY PIETY AND

HERESY IN

THE LATE MIDDLE AGES

THE PROBLEM

During the late Middle Ages, the Christian church went through a period of turmoil and disunity, with corruption and abuse evident at all levels of its hierarchy. Though the Church was officially an independent institution, many of its officials, such as bishops and archbishops, were actually chosen by secular nobles and rulers, who picked their own relatives or others who would do as they were told. Officials who were elected or appointed from within the Church itself were often selected for their administrative and legal skills, not for their piety, high moral standards, or religious devotion. These problems extended all the way to the papacy, which for much of the fourteenth century was located not in Rome but in Avignon in southern France, where it was dominated by the French monarchy. During this time

the papacy lost its stature as an international power and had difficulty raising revenue from many parts of Europe, especially from the English, who rightly suspected that money sent to the pope might end up in the coffers of the French king, with whom they were at war. The Avignon popes had ever-increasing needs for revenue because they had to hire mercenaries to keep the Papal States in Italy under control, build palaces and churches in Avignon that reflected the power and prestige of the papacy, and pay the salaries of a growing corps of lawyers and bureaucrats who administered the papal empire.

The papacy devised a number of ways to meet its increasing need for money. Though the outright selling of Church offices, termed *simony*, was strictly forbidden, the popes required all candidates to pay for the privilege of taking over a vacant office, then hand over a large share of their first year's revenues directly to the papacy. Official prohibitions, such as those against priests having concubines or giving Church land to family members, could be ignored if the cleric paid the pope for a special dispensation. The papacy also collected money directly from laypeople, charging fees for clerical services such as marriage or baptism and for dispensations that legitimized children born out of wedlock.

The most lucrative source of income for the papacy proved to be the granting of *indulgences*. Indulgences were based on three doctrines developed by the medieval Church—the sacrament of penance, the concept of Purgatory, and the Treasury of Merit. To partake of the sacrament of penance, a believer was to confess all sins to a priest and be truly sorry, or contrite, for them, after which the priest absolved the believer, often requiring him or her to carry out certain acts as penance for these sins, such as saying prayers or going on pilgrimages. According to Church doctrine, penance did not end with death but might be extended into Purgatory, where Christians spent time atoning for the sins for which they had not done earthly penance. Only after a set time in Purgatory could most Christians be admitted to heaven. (Those who were going to hell, on the other hand, went directly there.)

Along with the doctrines of penance and Purgatory, the Church also developed the idea of the Treasury of Merit. This treasury was seen as a collection of all the superlative good deeds and meritorious acts that the apostles, saints, and other good people had done during their lives, which the pope as head of the Church could dispense as he wished through the granting of indulgences. The recipient of an indulgence received a share in the Treasury of Merit that took the place of having to do individual penance. Originally granted to people who performed special services for the Church, such as participating in crusades, indulgences gradually came to be exchanged for cash contributions. Though official theology taught that priestly absolution and true contrition were still necessary, unscrupulous indulgence peddlers often sold indulgences outright as easy substitutes for penance. Indulgences also began to be granted to relieve people of time in Purgatory and even to allow believers to shorten deceased relatives' time in Purgatory. To many people, it seemed that the Church was teaching that one could buy one's way into heaven, though this was not actually so.

Because Church officials at all levels were often chosen for their family connections or their legal and financial skills, they also bent official doctrines and saw their posts primarily in terms of income rather than spiritual duties. Bishops spent much of their time at the papal court trying to win the pope's favor and squeezed all possible revenues out of their dioceses in order to pay for their offices. These absentee officials, who left the affairs of the diocese in the hands of substitutes, often had very little idea about the needs or problems of their territory. Those who were successful in gaining papal backing might be appointed to many different offices simultaneously; they collected the income from all their posts, appointed badly paid proxies to carry out their duties, and might actually never even visit the diocese over which they were bishop.

With so little supervision, parish priests and monks were sometimes lax in their standards of morality and spiritual observance. Frequently parish priests were poor and badly educated, for most of the Church's wealth stayed in the hands of higher officials, who provided no opportunity for priests to gain an education; some priests did not even know Latin, but simply recited the Mass by rote without understanding what they were saying. During the week they farmed just as their parishioners did, for the income from tithes was not sufficient to support them. Some of the monasteries and convents maintained high standards, but others, caught in the squeeze for revenue, admitted any applicant who would pay the entrance fee, without determining if the person was fit for the monastic life.

With the Church embroiled in these problems, we might expect that people would turn away from religion to concentrate on other aspects of life, but this was not the case. Religion continued to dominate the lives of people in the late Middle Ages, which was in fact perhaps the most religious period in all of European history. What did change, however, was how people expressed and experienced their Christian faith. Not surprisingly, they turned away somewhat from the institutional Church and sought more direct paths to God through individual actions.

Much of this lay piety was supported by the Church hierarchy because it did not question basic theological doctrines such as life after death; the importance of the sacraments of baptism, communion, and penance; the honor owed to saints and their relics; and the right of the pope to grant indulgences, collect taxes, and determine correct doctrine. Pious laypeople also made frequent donations, which swelled the Church's revenue. Some individuals and groups went beyond personal piety, however, to question the Church's wealth and many of its central doctrines. The Church declared such people heretics and set up inquisitorial courts to investigate, try, and condemn them.

Your task in this chapter will be to examine late medieval lay piety and religious practices, both those approved by the institutional Church and those condemned as heresy. How did common people in the Middle Ages experience and express their religious faith? How did the Church as an institution respond to laypeople's ideas and actions?

SOURCES AND METHOD

Medieval Christianity, multifaceted in nature, may be explored from a number of angles. Christianity was a faith shared by most people living in Europe, whether they were highly educated or uneducated, wealthy or poor. We can find information about how educated men understood and interpreted Christianity fairly easily by reading theological treatises and official Church decisions, but these may not accurately reflect the religious views of the majority. For this perspective, we must turn to a much smaller group of sources that throw light on the religious beliefs of the common people.

Learning about and reconstructing the ideas of common people in the premodern period is extremely difficult, for such people were by and large illiterate. The surviving written records of their thoughts and actions thus all come through the filter of literate observers, whose perspective and understanding of events might differ radically from the participants'. This is especially a problem when we are examining religious ideas, for most people who could read and write in the Middle Ages were clerics and thus part of the institutional Church. It was often hard for such observers to be objective about criticism directed against the Church, or even to comprehend how uneducated people interpreted and understood theological concepts.

Because of these problems, we must ask several questions before turning to any written source about popular religious belief. Who actually wrote the document? Was the writer recording the words of an illiterate person or simply describing actions he or she had observed? Why was this piece written? If the writer is recording the words of someone else, did he or she clearly understand the language being spoken, or might there be some problems because of dialect? Is the writer translating a vernacular language such as English or French into Latin, and so possibly mistranslating religious ideas? Why were this person's thoughts recorded—did that person wish it or did the authorities, as was the case with trial records?

Artistic evidence might seem more direct, for people who could not read or write sculpted, painted, and made stained-glass windows. They did not always choose their own subject matter or sign their works, however, so medieval art does not directly express the individual personality and concerns of the artist in the way that modern art does. What it does reveal, however, is how common people learned about religion from windows and statues depicting biblical and other Christian scenes. We can also use frequently recurring images as a rough guide to popular religious sentiments, for individuals and groups commissioned art that reflected their own concerns. The dominance of certain images shifted throughout the Middle Ages as people's attitudes toward the Church and the right way to approach God changed.

Using artistic evidence as a source of information about popular belief requires a different set of initial questions from those needed for written evidence. Where and when was the piece probably made? Can we learn anything about the artist or patron, such as his or her identity? Where was the piece originally displayed? Are the materials simple enough that the piece could have been ordered or purchased by someone who was not wealthy? Is the image common or unusual?

Keeping in mind the limitations we have noted, turn now to the written sources. The first two are *sermon stories*, tales of miracles that learned preachers used in their public sermons; later they were collected by many different preachers and used widely in sermons all over Europe. These stories are consequently not written *by* laypeople but *for* them and reflect official Church doctrines. They do not present sophisticated theology, however, but show us how common people learned about Christianity. As you read, note the kinds of people who appear as main characters. Why would preachers use characters like these?

In the first sermon, to whom does the woman turn for assistance? When her prayers are not answered immediately, what does she do? Why would the preacher condone such a dramatic action? (To answer this question, think about the impact this story would have on the female members of the audience; Mary may not have responded instantly to prayer, but, like most mothers, she did so immediately once her child was taken from her.) What qualities of Mary does this story emphasize?

The second sermon discusses an important element in lay piety, the belief in saints and relics. Does the author support or condemn these beliefs? Is it the relics themselves or faith in them that is important? Why would the author, himself a priest, describe the priest in the story as "wily" and "wicked"? (Again, keep in mind the audience. Given the problems most people recognized in the Church, how would a lay audience respond to a story in which the hero is also a layperson?)

Though most laypeople in the Middle Ages could not read, some of them could, and one of the most popular types of reading material was stories about the lives of saints, termed *hagiography*. Like sermon stories, hagiography often presented quite ordinary people whose lives were touched by God and who could serve as an inspiration. Source 3 comes from the best-known collection of saints' lives, *The Golden Legend*, first composed in the late thirteenth century by an Italian bishop, and then translated and recopied throughout Europe during the late Middle Ages. It describes events from the life of St. Nicholas (the original Santa Claus) and miracles attributed to him after his death, and would have been familiar even to those who could not read because they would have heard this story from those who could. What type of people does Nicholas assist? What sort of problems does he solve for them?

[203]

Taking these three sources together, what types of actions do you think preachers and writers of hagiography were trying to encourage in people? What traits of lay piety did they praise?

The remaining written sources directly record the thoughts and actions of laypeople, some of whom the Church supported and some of whom it condemned. None could read or write Latin, and so they qualified as unlearned by medieval standards, though some could read their own vernacular language. Source 4 is taken from the *Revelations* of Bridget of Sweden, a noblewoman who lived from 1303 to 1373. After her husband's death, Bridget traveled to Rome, where she began to see visions and give advice based on these visions to both laypeople and Church officials. Because she could not speak Latin, she wrote or dictated her visions in Swedish; these were later translated by her confessors and eventually were published in Latin. At the end of her life, Bridget made a pilgrimage to Jerusalem, where she had the visions reprinted here. How would you describe these visions? How did the fact that she was a woman shape her religious experience?

Source 5 is drawn from the first autobiography ever written in English, that of Margery Kempe, who was probably born in 1373, the same year Bridget died. Kempe, a middle-class woman from the town of King's Lynn, was illiterate in English as well as Latin. Although she was married and had fourteen children, she began to see visions in which Christ demanded that she set herself apart from most women. At the end of her most unusual life, she dictated her autobiography to several male scribes, who wrote it down in English. As you read, note how Kempe describes her actions and behavior. What made her most open to criticism? How does she defend her actions? She refers to herself, always in the third person, as "this creature." What does this practice indicate about her self-consciousness? Do her actions reflect this self-image? What aspects of Christianity most inspire or disturb her? How was the official reaction to her influenced by the fact that she was a woman?

The last two written sources come from trial records. Source 6 contains six testimonies from the Inquisition carried out between 1318 and 1325 by Jacques Fournier, Bishop of Pamiers in southern France. All six accused were illiterate peasants who spoke Occitan, a regional dialect; their words were translated by scribes into Latin. Fournier launched the Inquisition because he suspected large numbers of people in his district to be *Albigensians* (also called Cathars), followers of a heretical movement that rejected many basic Church doctrines. Albigensians regarded the material world as evil and not made by God and did not believe in the possibility of eternal life. They denied the power of many Church ceremonies and rituals and urged that any Church leader, including the pope, should not be obeyed if he did not live up to rigorous moral standards.

As you read the testimonies, note which specific Christian beliefs were being challenged. Given their statements, would you call the peasants who were being questioned Christians? How might problems of translation have affected the records? How might the fact that this was a trial have affected what the individuals said?

Source 7 comes from a heresy trial of sixty people suspected of Lollard beliefs, conducted in the diocese of Norwich, England, between 1428 and 1431. Lollards followed the ideas of John Wyclif, an English scholar who lived in the fourteenth century; the selection itself presents all of the basic Lollard beliefs. Most of the trial record is in Latin because it was conducted by ecclesiastical authorities and recorded by clerics, but a few of the confessions were written down in English. The selection here is one of those, with the spelling modernized. What does the accused admit to having believed? The list of unacceptable beliefs in many heresy trials reflects not only the ideas of the person confessing but also those the inquisitors thought were especially dangerous and in need of suppression. What did the inquisitors in this case appear particularly concerned about? How would this emphasis have shaped the confession? How was the accused to prove he had given up his heresy? Given his beliefs, would you call the person under questioning a Christian?

Now examine the two visual sources. Both are wooden statues carved in the fourteenth or fifteenth centuries by unknown artists and originally placed in churches in southern Germany. They are examples of the two most common religious images of the late Middle Ages. What aspects of popular belief that you have identified from the written sources do they reflect? Mary is shown wearing a crown and holding an orb, a sphere representing the world that normally was carried by monarchs. What qualities are emphasized through this depiction? Christ is shown in a dramatic pose of suffering. What does this attitude emphasize about his nature? Given what you now know about how common people understood Christianity, why would these two subjects be the most popular? Why do you think there is no depiction of God the Father?

THE EVIDENCE

Source 1 from C. C. S. Bland, editor and translator, Miracles of the Blessed Virgin Mary *(London: Routledge, 1928), p. 118.*

1. A Sermon Story About the Virgin Mary, 13th century

A certain woman of simple and upright life used to worship the Holy Mary, Mother of God, often strewing flowers and herbs before her image.

Now it chanced that the woman's only son was taken prisoner. And the mother weeping for him would not be comforted, and prayed with all her heart to the Blessed Virgin Mary for her son's deliverance. But seeing it was all in vain, she entered the church and thus addressed the image of the Blessed Virgin, "O Blessed Virgin Mary, often have I asked thee for the deliverance of my son and thou hast not heard me. Therefore, as my son was taken from me, so will I take away thine and will put him in durance as hostage for mine."

And taking the image of the Child from the bosom of Mary, she went home, wrapped him up in a clean cloth, and shut him up carefully in a chest. And, behold, the following night the Blessed Mary appeared to the captive youth bidding him to go forth and said to him: "Tell your mother to give me my Son." And he coming to his mother, described how he had been set free. But she with great rejoicing carried back the image of Jesus to Mary and gave her thanks.

Source 2 from Dana Carleton Munro, editor and translator, Translations and Reprints from the Original Sources of European History, *vol. 2, no. 4 (Philadephia: University of Pennsylvania Press, no date), p. 14.*

2. A Sermon Story About Relics, 13th century

A certain knight loved most ardently the above-mentioned martyr, St. Thomas of Canterbury,[1] and sought everywhere to obtain some relic of him. When a certain wily priest, in whose house he was staying, heard of this he said to him, "I have by me a bridle which St. Thomas used for a long time,

---

1. **Thomas Becket:** the Archbishop of Canterbury who was murdered on the steps of the cathedral on the orders of Henry II for opposing the king's wishes. He was quickly made a saint, and Canterbury became the most popular pilgrimage site in England.

and I have often experienced its virtues." When the knight heard this, and believed it, he joyfully paid the priest the money which the latter demanded and received the bridle with great devotion.

God truly, to whom nothing is impossible, wishing to reward the faith of the knight and for the honor of his martyr, deigned to work many miracles through the same bridle. The knight seeing this founded a church in honor of the martyr and in it he placed as a relic the bridle of that most wicked priest.

Source 3 from Iacobus de Voragine, The Golden Legend, *included in* Lives of the Saints, *translated by William Caxton and selected and edited by George V. O'Neill, S.J. (Cambridge: Cambridge University Press, 1914), pp. 62–71.*

3. Extracts from the Life of St. Nicholas, *The Golden Legend*, ca 1270

Nicholas, citizen of the city of Patras, was born of rich and holy kin, and his father was Epiphanes and his mother Johane. In his young age he eschewed the plays and japes[2] of other young children. He used and haunted gladly holy Church; and all that he might understand of holy Scripture he executed it in deed and work after his power. And when his father and mother were departed out of this life, he began to think how he might distribute his riches, and not to the praising of the world but to the honor and glory of God. And it was so that one, his neighbor, had then three daughters, virgins, and he was a nobleman: but for the poverty of them together, they were constrained and in very purpose to abandon them to sin. And when the holy man Nicholas knew hereof he had great horror of this, and threw by night secretly into the house of the man a mass of gold wrapped in a cloth. And when the man arose in the morning, he found this mass of gold, and rendered to God therefor great thankings, and therewith he married his oldest daughter. And a little while after this holy servant of God threw in another mass of gold; which the man found, and thanked God, and purposed to wake for to know him that so had aided him in his poverty. And after a few days Nicholas doubled the mass of gold, and cast it into the house of this man. He awoke by the sound of the gold, and followed Nicholas, which fled from him, and he said to him: "Sir, flee not away so but that I may see and know thee." Then he ran after him more hastily, and knew that it was Nicholas; and anon he kneeled down, and would have kissed his feet, but the holy man would not, but required him not to tell nor discover this thing as long as he lived.

2. **japes:** toys.

It is read in a chronicle that the blessed Nicholas was at the Council of Nice; and on a day, as a ship with mariners were in perishing on the sea, they prayed and required devoutly Nicholas, servant of God, saying: "If those things that we have heard of thee said to be true, prove them now." And anon a man appeared in his likeness, and said: "Lo! see ye me not? ye called me"; and then he began to help them in their exploit of the sea, and anon the tempest ceased. And when they were come to his church, they knew him without any man to show him to them, and yet they had never seen him. And then they thanked God and him of their deliverance. And he bade them to attribute it to the mercy of God and to their belief, and nothing to his merits.

It was so on a time that all the province of S. Nicholas suffered great famine, in such wise that vitaille[3] failed. And then this holy man heard say that certain ships laden with wheat were arrived in the haven. And anon he went thither and prayed the mariners that they would succor the perished at least with an hundred muyes of wheat of every ship. And they said: "Father, we dare not, for it is meted and measured, and we must give reckoning thereof in the garners[4] of the emperor in Alexandria." And the holy man said to them: "Do this that I have said to you, and I promise, in the truth of God, that it shall not be lessed or minished when ye shall come to the garners." And when they had delivered so much out of every ship, they came into Alexandria and delivered the measure that they had received. And then they recounted the miracle to the ministers of the emperor, and worshipped and praised strongly God and his servant Nicholas. Then this holy man distributed the wheat to every man after that he had need, in such wise that it sufficed for two years, not only for to sell but also to sow. . . .

And when it pleased Our Lord to have him depart out this world, he prayed Our Lord that he would send him his angels; and inclining his head he saw the angels come to him, whereby he knew well that he should depart, and began this holy Psalm: "In te domine speravi," unto "in manus tuas," and so saying: "Lord, into thine hands I commend my spirit," he rendered up his soul and died, the year of Our Lord three hundred and forty-three. . . .

There was a Jew that saw the virtuous miracles of S. Nicholas, and did do make an image of the saint, and set it in his house, and commanded him that he should keep well his house when he went out, and that he should keep well all his goods, saying to him: "Nicholas, lo! here be all my goods, I charge thee to keep them, and if thou keep them not well, I shall avenge me on thee in beating and tormenting thee." And on a time, when the Jew was out, thieves came and robbed all his goods, and left unborne away only the image. And when the Jew came home he found him robbed of all his goods. He areasoned the image, saying these words: "Sir Nicholas, I had set you in my house for to keep my goods from thieves, wherefore have ye not kept them? Ye shall receive sorrow and torments, and shall have pain for the thieves. I shall

3. **vitaille:** food.

4. **garners:** storehouses for grain.

avenge my loss and refrain my woodness in beating thee." And then took the Jew the image, and beat it, and tormented it cruelly. Then happed a great marvel, for when the thieves departed the goods, the holy saint, like as he had been in his array, appeared to the thieves, and said to them: "Wherefore have I been beaten so cruelly for you and have so many torments? See how my body is hewed and broken; see how that the red blood runneth down by my body; go ye fast and restore it again, or else the ire of God Almighty shall make you as to be one out of his wit, and that all men shall know your felony, and that each of you shall be hanged." And they said: "Who art thou that sayest to us such things?" And he said to them: "I am Nicholas the servant of Jesu Christ, whom the Jew hath so cruelly beaten for his goods that ye bare away." Then they were afeared, and came to the Jew, and heard what he had done to the image, and they told him the miracle, and delivered to him again all his goods. And thus came the thieves to the way of truth, and the Jew to the way of Jesu Christ.

A man, for the love of his son, that went to school for to learn, hallowed,[5] every year, the feast of S. Nicholas much solemnly. On a time it happed that the father had to make ready the dinner, and called many clerks to this dinner. And the devil came to the gate in the habit of a pilgrim for to demand alms; and the father anon commanded his son that he should give alms to the pilgrim. He followed him as he went for to give to him alms, and when he came to the quarfox[6] the devil caught the child and strangled him. And when the father heard this he sorrowed much strongly and wept, and bare the body into his chamber, and began to cry for sorrow, and say: "Bright sweet son, how is it with thee? S. Nicholas, is this the guerdon[7] that ye have done to me because I have so long served you?" And as he said these words, and other semblable,[8] the child opened his eyes, and awoke like as he had been asleep, and arose up tofore all, and was raised from death to life.

Source 4 from Katharina M. Wilson, editor, Medieval Women Writers *(Athens: University of Georgia Press, 1984), p. 245. Selection translated by Barbara Obrist.*

4. Two Visions of Bridget of Sweden, 1370s

After this the Virgin Mary appeared again to me, in the same place, and said: it has been a long time since in Rome I promised you that I would show you here in Bethlehem how my offspring had been born. And although in Naples I showed you something of it, that is to say the way I was standing when I gave

5. **hallowed:** honored.
6. **quarfox:** crossroads.
7. **guerdon:** reward.
8. **semblable:** similar ones.

birth to my son, you still should know for sure that I stood and gave birth such as you have seen it now—my knees were bent and I was alone in the stable, praying; I gave birth to him with such exultation and joy of my soul that I had no difficulties when he got out of my body or any pain. Then I wrapped him in swaddling clothes that I had prepared long ago. When Joseph saw this he was astonished and full of joy and happiness, because I had given birth without any help.

At the same place where the Virgin Mary and Joseph were adoring the boy in the cradle, I also saw the shepherds, who had been watching their flocks, coming so that they could look at the child and adore it. When they saw the child, they first wanted to find out whether it was a male or a female, for angels had announced to them that the savior of the world had been born, and they had not said that it was a savioress. Then the Virgin Mary showed to them the nature and the male sex of the child. At once they adored him with great awe and joy. Afterward they returned, praising and glorifying God for all they had heard and seen.

Source 5 from W. Butler-Bowdon, editor, The Book of Margery Kempe *(London: Oxford University Press, 1936), pp. 41–42, 86–88, 161–165, 167–168. Reprinted by permission of Oxford University Press.*

5. From the Autobiography of Margery Kempe, ca 1430

This creature, when Our Lord had forgiven her her sin, as has been written before, had a desire to see those places where He was born, and where He suffered His Passion,[9] and where He died, with other holy places where He was in His life, and also after His resurrection.

As she was in these desires, Our Lord bade her, in her mind, two years ere she went, that she should go to Rome, to Jerusalem and to Saint James,[10] and she would fain have gone but she had no money.

And then she said to Our Lord:—"Where shall I get money to go with to these Holy Places?"

Our Lord answered to her:—"I shall send thee friends enough in divers countries of England to help thee. And, daughter, I shall go with thee in every country and provide for thee, I shall lead thee thither, and bring thee back again in safety. And no Englishman shall die in the ship that thou art in. I shall

9. **Passion:** the crucifixion.
10. **St. James of Compostella:** a cathedral in northwestern Spain.

keep thee from all wicked men's power. And, daughter, I say to thee that I will that thou wearest clothes of white and no other colour, for thou shalt be arrayed after My will."

"Ah! Dear Lord, if I go arrayed in other manner than other chaste women do, I dread the people will slander me. They will say I am a hypocrite and wonder at me."

"Yea, daughter, the more ridicule that thou hast for My love, the more thou pleasest Me."

Then this creature durst not otherwise do than she was commanded in her soul. . . .

So they went forth into the Holy Land till they could see Jerusalem. And when this creature saw Jerusalem, riding on an ass, she thanked God with all her heart, praying Him for His mercy that, as He had brought her to see His earthly city of Jerusalem, He would grant her grace to see the blissful city of Jerusalem above, the city of Heaven. Our Lord Jesus Christ, answering her thought, granted her to have her desire.

Then for the joy she had, and the sweetness she felt in the dalliance with Our Lord, she was on the point of falling off her ass, for she could not bear the sweetness and grace that God wrought in her soul. Then two pilgrims, Duchemen, went to her, and kept her from falling; one of whom was a priest, and he put spices in her mouth to comfort her, thinking she had been sick. And so they helped her on to Jerusalem, and when she came there, she said:—

"Sirs, I pray you be not displeased though I weep sore in this holy place where Our Lord Jesus Christ was quick and dead."

Then went they to the temple in Jerusalem and they were let in on the same day at evensong time, and abode there till the next day at evensong time. Then the friars lifted up a cross and led the pilgrims about from one place to another where Our Lord suffered His[11]. . . and His Passion, every man and woman bearing a wax candle in one hand. And the friars always, as they went about, told them what Our Lord suffered in every place. The aforesaid creature wept and sobbed as plenteously as though she had seen Our Lord with her bodily eye, suffering His Passion at that time. Before her in her soul she saw Him verily by contemplation, and that caused her to have compassion. And when they came up on to the Mount of Calvary,[12] she fell down because she could not stand or kneel, and rolled and wrested with her body, spreading her arms abroad, and cried with a loud voice as though her heart would have burst asunder; for, in the city of her soul, she saw verily and clearly how Our Lord was crucified. Before her face, she heard and saw, in her ghostly sight, the mourning of Our Lady, of Saint John, and Mary Magdalene and of many others that loved Our Lord.

11. Word missing in manuscript.

12. **Calvary:** where Jesus is believed to have been crucified.

And she had such great compassion and such great pain, at seeing Our Lord's pain that she could not keep herself from crying and roaring though she should have died for it. And this was the first cry[13] that ever she cried in any contemplation. And this manner of crying endured many years after this time, for aught any man might do, and therefore, suffered she much despite and much reproof. The crying was so loud and so wonderful that it made the people astounded unless they had heard it before, or unless they knew the cause of the crying. And she had them so often that they made her right weak in her bodily might, and especially if she heard of Our Lord's Passion. . . .

> [*She returned to England, where her crying upset many people and she was called to appear before the Archbishop of York.*]

On the next day she was brought into the Archbishop's Chapel, and there came many of the Archbishop's retinue, despising her, calling her "Lollard" and "heretic" and swearing many a horrible oath that she should be burnt.

And she, through the strength of Jesus, spoke back to them:—

"Sirs, I dread ye shall be burnt in Hell without end, unless ye amend in your swearing of oaths, for ye keep not the Commandments of God. I would not swear as ye do for all the money in this world."

Then they went away, as if they had been shamed. She then, making her prayer in her mind, asked grace so to be demeaned that day as was most pleasure to God, and profit to her own soul, and good example to her fellow Christians.

Our Lord, answering her, said it should be right well. At the last, the said Archbishop came into the chapel with his clerks, and sharply he said to her:—

"Why goest thou in white? Art thou a maiden?"

She kneeling on her knees before him, said:—

"Nay, sir, I am no maiden. I am a wife."

He commanded his retinue to fetch a pair of fetters and said she should be fettered, for she was a false heretic.

Then she said:—"I am no heretic, nor shall ye prove me one."

The Archbishop went away and left her standing alone. Then she made her prayers to Our Lord God Almighty to help her and succour her against all her enemies, ghostly and bodily, a long while, and her flesh trembled and quaked wonderfully, so that she was fain to put her hands under her clothes, so that it should not be espied.

Afterwards the Archbishop came again into the Chapel with many clerks, amongst whom was the same doctor who had examined her before, and the monk that had preached against her a little time before in York. Some of the

---

13. **cry:** outcry, scream.

people asked whether she were a Christian woman or a Jew; some said she was a good woman; some said "Nay."

Then the Archbishop took his seat and his clerks also, each of them in his degree, many people being present.

And during the time while the people were gathering together and the Archbishop taking his seat, the said creature stood all behind, making her prayers for help and succour against her enemies with high devotion, so long that she melted all into tears.

And at the last she cried aloud therewith, so that the Archbishop and his clerks and many people had great wonder of her, for they had not heard such crying before. When her crying was passed, she came before the Archbishop and fell down on her knees, the Archbishop saying full boisterously unto her:—

"Why weepest thou, woman?"

She, answering, said:—"Sir, ye shall wish some day that ye had wept as sore as I."

Then anon, the Archbishop put to her the Articles of our Faith,[14] to which God gave her grace to answer well and truly and readily without any great study, so that he might not blame her. Then he said to the clerks:—

"She knoweth her Faith well enough. What shall I do with her?"

The clerks said:—"We know well that she can say the Articles of Faith, but we will not suffer her to dwell amongst us, for the people hath great faith in her dalliance, and, peradventure, she might pervert some of them.". . .

Then said the Archbishop to her:—"Thou shalt swear that thou wilt neither teach nor challenge the people in my diocese."

"Nay, sir, I shall not swear," she said, "for I shall speak of God, and rebuke those that swear great oaths wheresoever I go, unto the time that the Pope and Holy Church hath ordained that no man shall be so bold as to speak of God, for God Almighty forbiddeth not, sir, that we shall speak of Him. And also the Gospel maketh mention that, when the woman had heard Our Lord preach, she came before Him with a loud voice and said:—'Blessed be the womb that bore Thee, and the teats that gave Thee suck.' Then Our Lord again said to her, 'Forsooth, so are they blessed that hear the word of God and keep it.' And therefore, sir, methinketh that the Gospel giveth me leave to speak of God."

"Ah! Sir," said the clerks, "here wot we well that she hath a devil within her, for she speaketh of the Gospel."

As quickly as possible, a great clerk brought forth a book and laid Saint Paul, for his part, against her, that no woman should preach.[15]

---

14. **Articles of Faith:** a standard series of questions, in which a person suspected of heresy was asked if he or she believed in the central doctrines of Christianity—the Trinity, the Virgin Birth, the efficacy of the sacraments, heaven and hell, the power of the Pope.

15. The first letter to Timothy in the New Testament, which until recently was believed to have been written by the apostle Paul, orders women to keep silent in church.

She answering thereto said:—"I preach not, sir; I come into no pulpit, I use but communication and good words, and that I will do while I live." . . .

She, kneeling down on her knees, asked his blessing. He, praying her to pray for him, blessed her and let her go.

Then she, going again to York, was received by many people and full worthy clerks, who rejoiced in Our Lord, Who had given her, unlettered, wit and wisdom to answer so many learned men without disgrace or blame, thanks be to God.

Source 6 from Edward Peters, editor, Heresy and Authority in Medieval Europe: Documents in Translation *(Philadelphia: University of Pennsylvania Press, 1980), pp. 259–261. Selection translated by Steven Sargent. Reprinted by permission.*

6. Testimony from the Inquisition Led by Jacques Fournier, Bishop of Pamiers, 1318–1325

Testimony of Arnaud de Savinhan

"He said that as long as he could remember, which might be about thirty years since he was then about forty-five years old, he had believed completely that God had not made the world, namely heaven, earth, and the elements, but that it had always been existing in and of itself, and was not made by God nor by anyone else. Nevertheless he always had believed that Adam was the first man and that God had made him, and thereafter there had been human generation. But before God had made Adam, the world had lasted infinitely into the past; and he [the witness] did not believe that the world had had a beginning.

"He also said that he had believed for all that time up to the beginning of May in the present year that the world had never had a beginning, and thus that it would never end, and that the world would go on in the same way in the future as it did now; and that just as men were generated now and as they had been generated from Adam onward, there would always be in the future the generation of men, and of vines, and of the other plants, and of all animals; nor would that generation ever end. He believed that there was no other world except the present one."

Testimony of Raimond de l'Aire, of Tignac

An older man told him that a mule has a soul as good as a man's "and from this belief he had by himself deduced that his own soul and those of other men are nothing but blood, because when a person's blood is taken away, he dies. He also believed that a dead person's soul and body both die, and that after death nothing human remains, because he didn't see anything leave the mouth of a person when he dies. From this he believed that the human soul after death has neither good nor evil, and that there is no hell or paradise in another world where human souls are rewarded or punished."

Testimony of Guillemette Benet

"Asked if, since she believed that human souls died with the bodies, she also believed that men would be resurrected and would live again after death, she answered that she did not believe that the resurrecting of the human body would happen, since she believed that as the dead body was buried, the soul was buried with the body; and since she saw that the body putrefied, she believed that it would never be resurrected. . . .

"Asked if she believed that the soul of Jesus Christ, who died on the cross, had died with his body, she answered yes, because although God is not able to die, nevertheless Jesus Christ died and therefore, even though she believed that God always existed, nevertheless she did not believe that Christ's soul lived and existed. . . .

"Asked if she believed that Christ was resurrected, she said yes and that God had done this."

Testimony of Arnaud Gelis, of Pamiers

Arnaud's beliefs	*Roman Catholic orthodoxy*
1. The souls of dead people do not do any other penance except to wander from church to church, some faster, some slower according to their sinfulness.	1. All souls of dead people go to purgatory, where they do the penance they had not completed on earth. And when this is done they go to the heavenly paradise where Christ, Mary, the angels, and the saints reside.
2. After they are finished going around to churches through the streets, the souls go to the place of rest, which is on this earth. They stay there until the judgment day.	2. When their penance is done, the souls of the dead go to the joy of the celestial paradise, which is no place of rest on earth, but rather in heaven.
3. No soul of any man except the most saintly goes directly to heaven or the heavenly kingdom. Souls do this on the day of judgment.	3. All souls of the dead, when their penance is done in purgatory (if they had need of it), enter the heavenly kingdom.

[215]

4. Souls of children who died before baptism go to an obscure place until the judgment day. There they feel neither pain nor pleasure. After the judgment day they enter paradise.

5. No soul of a dead person, no matter how evil, has entered or will enter hell.

6. At the last judgment God will have mercy on all who held the Christian faith and no one will be damned, no matter how evil he was.

7. Christ will have mercy on the souls of all heretics, Jews, and pagans; therefore none of them will be damned.

8. Human souls, both before the body's death and after, have their own bodily form just like their external body. And the souls have distinct members like hands, eyes, feet, and the rest.

9. Hell is a place only for demons.

4. The souls of unbaptized children will never be saved or enter the kingdom of heaven.

5. The souls of all evil persons— i.e., those who perpetrate great crimes that they do not confess or do penance for—go immediately after death to hell, where they stay and are punished for their sins.

6. All souls that held the Christian faith and accepted its sacraments and obeyed its commandments will be saved; but those who, even though holding the faith and accepting the sacraments, did not live according to the commandments will be damned.

7. All souls of heretics, pagans, and Jews, who did not want to believe in Christ, will be damned. They will be punished eternally in hell.

8. Human souls, both while in the body and after its death, because they are spirits, are not corporeal, nor do they have corporeal members, nor do they eat or drink, nor do they suffer such corporeal necessities.

9. Hell is a place for demons and for wicked people, where each is punished eternally as he deserves.

Disbelief in Indulgences: Testimony of Guillelme Cornelhano

"He also said that about two years before around the feast of Pentecost . . . a seller of indulgences passed by [him and Guillelma Vilara, wife of Arnald Cuculli] who had with him many indulgences. And after he had left them, Guillelma said, "Do you believe that any man is able to indulge or absolve anyone of his sins? Don't believe it, because no one can absolve anyone except God." And when he himself said that the pope and all priests could absolve man from sins, Guillelma answered that it was not so, only God could [do that]."

Testimony of Peter Sabatier

"When questioned, Peter said and confessed willingly that about three years ago on a certain day in the village of Varillis . . . when he returned from the church [to his house], he said that whatever things the priests and clerics were chanting and singing in the church were lies and tricks; but he never doubted, rather always believed, that the sacraments of the church and its articles of faith were true."

He persisted in this belief "for about a year, and believed out of silliness that priests and clerics, in singing and chanting those things in the church while performing the divine offices, sang and chanted in order to have the contributions, and that there was no good effect wrought by those divine offices."

Source 7 from Norman P. Tanner, editor, Heresy Trials in the Diocese of Norwich, 1428–1431, *Camden Fourth Series, vol. 20 (London: Royal Historical Society, 1977), pp. 111–113. Selection translated by Merry E. Wiesner.*

7. A Norwich Heresy Trial, 1428–1431

In the name of God, before you, the worshipful father in Christ, William, by the grace of God bishop of Norwich, I, John Reve, a glover from Beccles in your diocese, your subject, feeling and understanding that I have held, believed, and affirmed errors and heresies which be counted in this confession, that is to say:

That I have held, believed, and affirmed that the sacrament of baptism done in water in the form customary to the church is of no avail and not to be demanded if the father and mother of the child are christened and of Christian beliefs.

Also that the sacrament of confirmation done by a bishop is not profitable or necessary to man's salvation.

Also that confession ought not to be made to any priest, but only to God, for no priest has the power to forgive a man of sin.

Also that I have held, believed and affirmed that no priest has the power to make God's body in the sacrament of the altar, and that after the sacramental words said by a priest at mass nothing remains except a loaf of material bread.

Also that only consent of love in Jesus Christ between a man and woman of Christian beliefs is sufficient for the sacrament of matrimony, without any contract of words or solemnizing in church.

Also that I have held, believed and affirmed that only God has power to make the sacraments, and no other creature.

Also that I have held, believed and affirmed that no creature of Christian belief is required to fast in Lent, on the Umber Days, Fridays, vigils of saints nor any other times which the Church commands should be fasted, but it is lawful for people of Christian beliefs to eat meat at all such times and days. And in affirming this opinion I have eaten meat on Fridays and the other aforementioned days.

Also I have held, believed and affirmed that it is lawful for all Christ's people to do all bodily work on Sundays and all other days which the Church has commanded to be held holy, if people keep themselves from other sins at such days and times.

Also I have held, believed and affirmed that every man may lawfully and without sin withhold and withdraw his tithes and offerings from churches and curates, if it is done prudently.

Also I have held, believed and affirmed that it is lawful for God's people to act contrary to the precepts of the Church.

Also that censures of the Church and sentences of cursing whether from bishops, prelates, or other ordinaries are not to be taken into account or dreaded, for as soon as such bishops or ordinaries curse any man, Christ himself assails him.

Also that I have believed, held, and affirmed that no manner of worship ought to be done to any images of the crucifix, of Our Lady or of any other saints.

Also that no manner of pilgrimages ought to be done to any places of saints, but only to poor people.

Also that I have held and believed that it is not lawful to swear in any case.

Also that I have held, believed, and affirmed that the pope of Rome is the Antichrist and has no power in the Holy Church as St. Peter had unless he follows in the steps of Peter in his manner of living.

Also that all bishops, prelates and priests of the Church are the Antichrist's disciples.

Also that I have held, believed and affirmed that it is as meritorious and as profitable to all Christ's people to be buried in meadows or in wild fields as it is to be buried in churches or churchyards.

Because of which and many other errors and heresies which I have held, believed, and affirmed within your diocese, I am called before you, worshipful father, who has the cure of my soul. And you are fully informed that the said my holding, believing, and affirming are judged errors and heresies and contrary to the Church of Rome, wherefore I willingly follow the doctrine of holy Church and depart from all manner of heresy and error and turn with good heart and will to the unity of the Church. Considering that holy Church will not spare her bosom to him that will return nor God will the death of a sinner but rather that he be returned and live, with a pure heart I confess, detest and despise my said errors and heresies, and the said opinions I confess as heretical and erroneous and repugnant to the faith of the Church at Rome and all universal holy Church. And for as much as I showed myself corrupt and unfaithful through the said things that I so held, believed, and affirmed, from henceforth I will show myself uncorrupt and faithful, and I promise to keep the faith and doctrine of the holy Church truly. And I abjure and forswear all manner of error and heresy, doctrine and opinion against the holy Church and the determination of the Church of Rome—namely the opinions listed before—and swear by these holy gospels which I am bodily touching that from henceforth I shall never hold error nor heresy nor false doctrine against the faith of holy Church and the determination of the Church of Rome. No such things shall I obstinately defend. I shall defend no person holding or teaching such things openly or privately. I shall never after this time be an assistor, counselor, or defender of heretics or of any person suspected of heresy. I shall never ally myself with them. I shall not wittingly show fellowship to them, nor give them counsel, gifts, succor, favor, or comfort. If I know any heretics or any persons suspected of heresy, or people who counsel, assist or defend them, or any persons holding private conventicles or meetings, or holding any singular opinions different from the common doctrine of the Church, I shall let you, worshipful father, or your vicar general in your absence or the diocesans of such persons know soon and immediately. So help me God at holy doom and these holy gospels.

In witness of which things I subscribe here with my own hand a cross—X. And to this part intended to remain in your register I set my sign. And that other part I receive with your seal to keep with me until my life's end. Given at Norwich in the chapel of your palace, xviii day of the month of April in the year of our Lord one thousand four hundred and thirty.

Source 8 from Bavarian National Museum, Munich.

8. Madonna, Germany, ca 1430

Source 9 from Cathedral of St. Vitus, Prague (Foto Marburg/Art Resource, NY).

9. Crucifix, Germany, 14th century

QUESTIONS TO CONSIDER

The written sources and the religious statues have provided you with evidence for the two central questions of this chapter. Looking again at those questions, you can see that the first concerns the religious beliefs and practices of laypeople, and the second the official Church reaction to those beliefs and practices. You now need to sort through the sources to separate the information you have gained about each question.

Look first at lay piety itself. Which Christian beliefs were numbers of people attracted to? Why were these beliefs especially appealing? Why might it have been difficult for most people to respond to more esoteric points of theology such as the Trinity? Many of the sources have described or depicted the extremely important role of the Virgin Mary in lay piety. Why do you think people turned to her, rather than to God the Father, in their prayers and devotions? In official Christian theology, Mary is not a goddess but completely human, and believers were urged to honor but not to worship her. From the sources, do you think most laypeople understood this distinction? Looking at the first sermon story, which relates beliefs and practices approved of by the Church, was this distinction always made clear to laypeople?

You have seen that religion was not simply a matter of belief for most people but also of real-world practices and acts. What practices were most popular? How did people see

these as contributing to their spiritual lives? One of the sermon stories, the life of St. Nicholas, and the works of Bridget and Margery Kempe refer matter-of-factly to visions and miracles. What does this imply about the divisions between the natural and supernatural in most people's minds?

The two heresy trials record beliefs that deviated from those officially accepted. Do you find evidence of similar beliefs, though perhaps not carried so far, in any of the other sources? For example, what religious beliefs and practices of Margery Kempe opened her to the accusation of heresy? How would you compare the two heresies from the sources reprinted here? Does either appear to deviate further from official Church teachings than the other? Which teachings do both dispute? Can you make any generalizations about late medieval heresy from these examples, or are the differences between them more striking than the similarities?

Now turn to the second question. Official Church reaction to lay piety was both positive and negative. Positive reactions included attempts by preachers and priests to shape popular belief and to encourage certain actions that they felt strengthened the Church. Judging by the sermon stories and the life of St. Nicholas, what beliefs and practices were preachers and hagiographers trying to encourage? Did the religious statuary encourage similar ideas? How did the archbishop try to influence Margery Kempe? Negative reactions included the Church's attempts to eradicate unacceptable beliefs and behavior, with sanctions ranging from mild scoldings to execution for heresy. Judging from the heresy trials and Margery Kempe's autobiography, what kinds of beliefs were Church officials especially worried about? Did they appear to be more concerned with beliefs or with behavior?

Many of those charged with heresy or with suspect beliefs in the late Middle Ages were women, and the Church hierarchy was of course totally male. Thinking particularly of the experience of Margery Kempe, do you find evidence of gender differences in official attitudes toward lay piety? Even women whose ideas were initially accepted could later be judged heretical. For example, Bridget of Sweden was made a saint less than twenty years after her death, but only forty years later the authenticity of her visions was questioned and she was dismissed by some Church officials as a chatterbox deluded by the devil. Do you find anything in the visions printed here that might have been disturbing to the all-male clerical establishment?

Both lay piety and official reaction to it were shaped by political and economic factors as well as by theology and doctrine. From your sources, which beliefs and practices encouraged or condemned by the Church would have had economic repercussions? Especially in the Norwich heresy trial, which ideas did the Church view as a political threat? Why would the ideas expressed in that trial have been seen as more dangerous than those of Margery Kempe? Reread the discussion in your text of the political and economic changes that late medieval Europe experienced. How was the Church involved in these changes? Do your sources provide evidence for any of the developments described in your text?

You are now ready to answer the two central questions of this chapter: How did common people in the Middle Ages experience and express their religious faith? How did the Church as an institution respond to laypeople's beliefs and practices? Are your answers more complex or less complex than you expected?

EPILOGUE

Most of the strong lay piety in the late Middle Ages remained inside the boundaries judged acceptable by the Church. Groups branded as heretics were usually small, and they were quite successfully wiped out by intensive inquisitions and campaigns of persecution such as those carried out against the Albigensians and Lollards.

Persecution did not put an end to dissatisfaction with the institutional Church, however, nor were preachers and priests ever able to exert total control over the beliefs or activities of common people. Indeed, the more historians study the beliefs of "unlearned" people, the more they discover that people do not passively absorb what they are told but add to it their own ideas. Illiteracy does not preclude imagination or intelligence, and influence between the learned elite and the common people runs in both directions.

Though lay dissatisfaction persisted, it did not cause the institutional Church to change or initiate reforms during the late Middle Ages. In 1377, the papacy returned to Rome, and when the pope died the following year the Roman people forced the college of cardinals, the body of church officials who chose the popes, to elect an Italian pope. This pope, Urban VI, tried to reform some of the Church's problems but did so in such a belligerent way that he set most of the college of cardinals against him. They responded by declaring that the pope's election was invalid because they had been put under duress and, calling for his resignation, elected another pope. Urban did not step down, however, and a forty-year power split began in which two and later three popes simultaneously excommunicated the others, collected taxes, made appointments, and granted indulgences. The Great Schism, as this period is called, was probably the low point in the history of organized Christianity in the West, but the eventual reunification of the Church in 1417 did not resolve all problems. For the next century, the popes con-

centrated their energies on artistic patronage and expansion of their political power in Italy. Despite several major attempts at reform and increasing recognition of internal problems by many Church officials and scholars throughout Europe, low standards of discipline and morality, and high levels of corruption, persisted.

Martin Luther's break with the Catholic church in the early sixteenth century began as yet another attempt at reform but quickly grew into a revolution that split Western Christianity from that time on. The swift and widespread acceptance of Luther's ideas gave vivid testimony to the depth of popular dissatisfaction with the Church. At the very beginning, at least, common people in many parts of Germany saw the Protestant Reformation as the change they had been looking for, a movement that emphasized personal piety and played down the priest's role in the individual's salvation. Supporting Luther initially, they quickly realized that he was not the leader they had hoped for and that he attacked many of the practices, such as pilgrimages or the veneration of Mary, that were dearest to them. Thus the strong lay piety movement of the late Middle Ages is an important factor in understanding not just medieval Christianity in all its complexity but the roots of the Reformation as well.

CHAPTER TEN

THE RENAISSANCE

MAN AND WOMAN

The age we know as the Renaissance had its beginnings in the fourteenth century as a literary movement among educated, mostly upper-class men in northern Italian cities, notably Florence. Such writers as Petrarch attempted to emulate as closely as possible the literary figures of ancient Rome, believing that these men, especially Cicero, had attained a level of style and a command of the Latin language that had never since been duplicated. Petrarch's fascination with antiquity did not stop with language, however, but also included an interest in classical architecture and art; he spent long hours wandering around the large numbers of Roman ruins remaining in Italy. His obsession with the classical past also led him to reject the thousand-year period between his own time and that of Rome, viewing this as a "dark," "gothic," or at best "middle" age—a deep trough between two peaks of civilization. Though Petrarch himself did not call his own period the *Renaissance*—a word that means "rebirth"—he clearly believed he was witnessing the dawning of a new age.

Writers and artists intending to recapture the glory that was Rome would have to study Roman models, and Petrarch proposed an appropriate course of study or curriculum termed the *studia humanitates*, or simply "liberal studies" or the "liberal arts." Like all curricula, it contained an implicit philosophy, a philosophy that came to be known as *humanism*. Humanism was not a rigorous philosophical system like Aristotelianism, nor an all-encompassing belief system like Christianity, but what we might better call an attitude toward learning and toward life.

This new attitude had a slow diffusion out of Italy, with the result that the Renaissance "happened" at very different times in different parts of Europe. Because it was not a single historical event in the same sense as the French Revolution or the

Peloponnesian War, the Renaissance is difficult to date. Roughly, we can say it began in Italy in the fourteenth century; spread to France, Germany, and Spain by the end of the fifteenth century; to England by the early part of the sixteenth century; and not until the seventeenth century to Scandinavia. Thus the Renaissance preceded the Reformation—which *was* an event—in most of Europe, took place at the same time as the Reformation in England, and came after the Reformation in Scandinavia. Shakespeare, for example, is considered a "Renaissance" writer even though he lived 250 years after Petrarch.

Though the chronology may be somewhat confusing, there are certain recurring features of humanism through the centuries. One of these is a veneration of the classical past. Petrarch concentrated primarily on Latin and ancient Rome, but during the mid-fifteenth century humanists also began to emphasize Greek language, art, architecture, philosophy, and literature. Though they disagreed about the relative merits of the classical philosophers and writers, all agreed that classical philosophy and literature were of paramount importance to their own culture.

Another feature of humanism is its emphasis on individualism. Medieval society was corporate—that is, oriented toward, and organized around, people acting in groups. Medieval political philosophy dictated that the smallest component of society was not the individual but the family. An individual ruler stood at the top of medieval society, but this ruler was regarded as tightly bound to the other nobles by feudal alliances and, in some ways, as simply the greatest of the nobles. Workers banded together in guilds; pious people formed religious confraternities; citizens swore an oath of allegiance to their own city. Even art was thought to be a group effort, with the individual artist feeling no more need to sign a work than a baker did to sign each loaf of bread. (We know the names of some medieval artists from sources such as contracts, bills of sale, and financial records, but rarely from the paintings or sculptures themselves.)

Christianity encouraged this sense of community as well. Though Christians were baptized and participated in most other sacraments as individuals, the priest represented the whole community when he alone drank wine at communion, and Christ was believed to have embodied all of Christianity when he died. Christians were encouraged to think of themselves as part of one great "Christendom" and to follow the example of Christ by showing humility and meekness rather than the self-assurance that draws attention to the individual.

These attitudes began to shift during the Renaissance. The family, the guild, and other corporate groups remained important social forces, but some individuals increasingly viewed the group as simply a springboard to far greater individual achievement that could be obtained through talent or hard work. Rather than defining themselves primarily within the context of the group, some prized their own sense of uniqueness and individuality, hiring artists to paint or sculpt their portraits and writers to produce verbal likenesses. Caught up in this new individualism, artists and writers themselves began to paint their own self-portraits and write autobiographies. Visual artists, believing that their skill at painting or sculpture was a result not simply of good training but of individual genius, began to sign their works. Rather than the vices they were to medieval Christians, self-confidence and individualism became virtues for many people. Humanists wrote not only biographies of prominent individuals but also treatises that described the attributes of the ideal person. In their opinion, that person should be well rounded and should also exhibit the quality of *virtù*—a word that does not mean virtue but rather the ability to make an impact in one's chosen field of endeavor.

The notion of individualism includes a belief that the people and objects of this world are important, at least important enough to warrant a picture or a verbal description. This belief, usually called *secularism*, is also a part of humanism. Secularism is a highly charged word in modern American political jargon—even more so when expanded to *secular humanism*—and may be too strong a term to apply to Renaissance thinkers. No one in the Renaissance denied the existence of God or the central importance of religion in human life. What they did reject was the idea that it was necessary to forsake the material world and retire to a life of contemplation in order to worship

God. God had created this world full of beauty, including the human body, to be appreciated. The talents of each person should be developed to their fullest through education and then displayed to the world because those talents came from God. Studying pre-Christian philosophers such as Plato or Aristotle could enhance an understanding of Christianity because God could certainly have endowed these thinkers with great wisdom even though they were not Christian.

The basis for all these features of humanism—classicism, individualism, secularism—was learning, and humanists all agreed on the importance of education, not just for the individual but also for society as a whole. During the mid-fifteenth century many humanists, such as Leonardo Bruni, began to stress that a proper liberal education was based on training for service to society as well as on classical models. Medieval education had been primarily an organ of the Church, oriented to its needs. Church and cathedral schools trained students to read and write so that they could copy manuscripts, serve as church lawyers, and write correspondence. Monks, priests, and nuns also used their education to honor the glory of God by reciting prayers, studying the Bible and other religious works, composing and singing hymns, or simply speculating on the nature of God. In the Middle Ages the ultimate aim of human life was to *know*, and particularly to know God, so medieval education was often both inwardly directed and otherworldy, helping individuals to come to a better understanding of God. The Renaissance humanists, on the other hand, believed the ultimate aim of human life was to *act,* so humanist education was resoundingly outwardly directed and this-worldly, emphasizing practical skills such as public speaking and writing that would benefit any politician, diplomat, military leader, or businessman. This education was not to be used in a monastery where only God could see it, but in the newly expanding cities and towns of northern Italy, cities that were growing steadily richer thanks to the development of trade we examined in Chapter 8. The primarily classical humanism of the fourteenth century was gradually transformed into civic humanism as humanists took employment as city secretaries and historians and as merchants and bankers sent their sons to humanist schools.

Humanism underwent a further transformation in the sixteenth century, when the governing of the cities of northern Italy was taken over by powerful noblemen. These rulers hired humanists as secretaries, tutors, diplomats, and advisers, and they established humanist academies in their capital cities. Unlike medieval rulers, who saw themselves primarily as military leaders, Renaissance rulers saw themselves as the leaders of all facets of life in their territories. Thus they supported poets and musicians as well as generals, learned several languages, and established their court as the cultural as well as political center of the territory.

Reflecting this new courtly milieu, humanists began to write biographies of rulers and to reflect on the qualities that were important in the ideal ruler and courtier. The trait of *virtù,* so vital in an individual, was even more critical in a ruler. For a ruler, *virtù* meant the ability to shape society as a whole and leave an indelible mark on history. Humanists held up as models worthy of emulation such classical rulers as Alexander the Great and Julius Caesar.

In many ways, then, Renaissance thinkers broke with the immediate medieval past in developing new ideals for human behavior. For one group, however, this break was not so complete. When humanists described the ideal woman, she turned out to be much more like her medieval counterpart than the "Renaissance man" was. The problem of female education was particularly perplexing for humanists. Medieval women, like medieval men, had been educated to serve and know God. Renaissance men were educated to serve the city or the state, which no humanist felt was a proper role for women. If women were not to engage in the type of public activities felt to be the proper arena for displaying talent and education, why should they be educated at all? Should the new virtues of self-confidence and individualism be extended to include women? Or should women be the link with the older Christian virtues of modesty and humility? How could women properly show *virtù*—a word whose roots lie in the word *vir,* which meant "man"—when to do so required public actions? Should women, perhaps, be even more encouraged to remain within the private sphere of home and family, given the opinions of classical philosophers such as Aristotle (which we saw in Chapter 2) about the proper role of women? In their consideration of the proper "Renaissance woman," humanists often exhibited both the tension between, and their attempts to fuse, the pagan classical and medieval Christian traditions.

In this chapter, you will examine the writings of several humanists describing the ideal educational pro-gram for boys and girls, the ideal male and female courtier, and the ideal ruler. In addition, you will read one short section from the autobiography of a humanist and another from the biography of a ruler written by a humanist; you will also look at several portraits. How do these authors describe the ideal man, woman, and ruler? How were these ideals expressed in written descriptions and visual portraits of actual Renaissance people?

SOURCES AND METHOD

The written sources in this chapter are primarily prescriptive; in other words, they present ideals that their humanist authors hoped people would emulate. In Chapter 2 we used prescriptive literature to compare ideals and reality in classical Athens, but here we will explore only the ideals themselves. Our questions and methodology are those of intellectual historians, who are interested in the development of ideas as well as in how those ideas relate to other types of changes. Intellectual history is an especially important dimension of the Renaissance, which was primarily an intellectual rather than a political or social movement. The questions you need to keep most in mind, then, relate to the ideas set forth here: What qualities was the ideal man, woman, or ruler supposed to possess? How were these qualities to be inculcated in young people? On the basis of these qualities, what did humanists think was most important in human existence? How did authors and artists portraying real people—in biographies, autobiographies, or portraits—express similar ideas?

Whenever we use prescriptive literature as our historical source, we must first inquire into the author's motives. Why did our Renaissance writers believe that people had to be instructed in matters of behavior? Were they behaving badly, or were they confronting new situations in which they would not know how to act? The intentions of these humanist authors were fairly straightforward because they believed themselves to be living in a new age, a rebirth of classical culture. In their minds, people needed to be informed about the values of this new age and instructed in the means for putting these values into practice. The humanist authors were thus attempting to mold new types of people to fit a new world, not simply correcting attitudes and behavior they felt were wrong or misguided. Consequently, humanist prescriptive literature concentrates on the positive, telling people what to do rather than what not to do (unlike much other prescriptive literature, such as the Ten Commandments).

Before you read the written selections, look at the three portraits. The first is a self-portrait by the German artist Albrecht Dürer; the second a portrait of an Italian woman known simply as Simonetta, by the Italian artist Sandro Botticelli or a member of his workshop; the third a sculpture of the Venetian general Bartolommeo Colleoni by Andrea del Verrocchio. How would you describe the expressions of the subjects in each of these portraits? Do any of them exhibit the qualities prized by the humanists—individualism, *virtù*, self-confidence? What other traits did the artist choose to emphasize? What differences do you see in the portrait of the woman compared with those of the two men? Now proceed to the written evidence.

Sources 4 and 5 are letters from humanists to members of the nobility. The first, discussing the proper education for men, is from Peter Paul Vergerius to Ubertinus, the son of the ruler of Padua, Italy; the second, discussing the proper education for women, is from Leonardo Bruni to Lady Baptista Malatesta, the daughter of the Duke of Urbino. As you read them, note both the similarities and the differences in the two courses of study. What factors might account for this? What is the ultimate purpose of the two educational programs?

Sources 6 and 7 are taken from one of the most popular advice manuals

ever written, Baldassare Castiglione's *The Courtier*. Castiglione was himself a courtier in Urbino, Mantua, and Milan, and he wrote this discussion of the perfect courtier and court lady in the form of a dialogue between noblemen. As you did for Sources 4 and 5, compare the qualities prescribed for men and women, respectively. How do these relate to the educational program discussed in Sources 4 and 5?

Source 8 comes from one of the most widely read pieces of political advice ever written, Machiavelli's *The Prince*. Like Castiglione, Niccolo Machiavelli had served various governments and had watched rulers and states rise and fall in late-fifteenth- and early-sixteenth-century Italy. What does he believe is the most critical factor or factors in the training of a prince? What qualities should a ruler possess to be effective and display *virtù*?

The first five documents are all straightforward prescriptive literature, as the authors' frequent use of such words as "ought" and "should" indicates. This was not the only way humanists communicated their ideals, however; biographies of real people also expressed these ideals. To use biographies as a source of ideas, we must take a slightly more subtle approach, identifying those personal characteristics the author chose to emphasize, those that might have been omitted, and the way in which each biographer manipulated the true personality of his subject to fit the humanist ideal. These are points to consider as you read the next two documents. Source 9 is from the autobiography of Leon Battista Alberti, which you will note is written in the third person. How does Alberti describe himself? How did his life reflect the new humanist ideals? Why might he have chosen to write in the third person instead of saying "I"? Source 10 is Polydore Vergil's description of Henry VII of England, who ruled from 1485 to 1509. What does it tell us about Renaissance monarchs and also about the author?

Once you have read the written selections, return to the portraits. Do you find anything there that you did not see before?

Source 1 from German Information Center.

1. Albrecht Dürer, *Self-Portrait in a Fur Coat*, 1500

Source 2 from Staatliche Museen zu Berlin—Preussischer Kulturbesitz Gemaldegalerie. Photograph: Jorg P. Anders.

2. Workshop of Botticelli (ca 1444–1510), so-called *Simonetta*

Source 3 from Venice (Alinari/Art Resource, NY).

3. Andrea del Verrocchio (ca 1435–1488), Sculpture of General Bartolommeo Colleoni

Sources 4 and 5 from W. H. Woodward, editor and translator, Vittorino da Feltre and Other Humanist Educators *(London: Cambridge University Press, 1897), pp. 102, 106–107, 109, 110; pp. 126–129, 132, 133.*

4. Peter Paul Vergerius, Letter to Ubertinus of Padua, 1392

3. We call those studies *liberal* which are worthy of a free man; those studies by which we attain and practice virtue and wisdom; that education which calls forth, trains, and develops those highest gifts of body and of mind which ennoble men, and which are rightly judged to rank next in dignity to virtue only. For to a vulgar temper gain and pleasure are the one aim of existence, to a lofty nature, moral worth and fame. It is, then, of the highest importance that even from infancy this aim, this effort, should constantly be kept alive in growing minds. . . .

We come now to the consideration of the various subjects which may rightly be included under the name of "Liberal Studies." Amongst these I accord the first place to History, on grounds both of its attractiveness and of its utility, qualities which appeal equally to the scholar and to the statesman. Next in importance ranks Moral Philosophy, which indeed is, in a peculiar sense, a "Liberal Art," in that its purpose is to teach men the secret of true freedom. History, then, gives us the concrete examples of the precepts inculcated by Philosophy. The one shows what men should do, the other what men have said and done in the past, and what practical lessons we may draw therefrom for the present day. I would indicate as the third main branch of study, Eloquence, which indeed holds a place of distinction amongst the refined arts. By philosophy we learn the essential truth of things, which by eloquence we so exhibit in orderly adornment as to bring conviction to differing minds. And history provides the light of experience—a cumulative wisdom fit to supplement the force of reason and the persuasion of eloquence. For we allow that soundness of judgment, wisdom of speech, integrity of conduct are the marks of a truly liberal temper. . . .

4. The principal "Disciplines" have now been reviewed. It must not be supposed that a liberal education requires acquaintance with them all: for a thorough mastery of even one of them might fairly be the achievement of a lifetime. Most of us, too, must learn to be content with modest capacity as with modest fortune. Perhaps we do wisely to pursue that study which we find most suited to our intelligence and our tastes, though it is true that we cannot rightly understand one subject unless we can perceive its relation to the rest. The choice of studies will depend to some extent upon the character of individual minds. . . .

Respecting the general place of liberal studies, we remember that Aristotle would not have them absorb the entire interests of life: for he kept steadily in view the nature of man as a citizen, an active member of the State. For the man who has surrendered himself absolutely to the attractions of Letters or of speculative thought follows, perhaps, a self-regarding end and is useless as a citizen or as prince.

5. Leonardo Bruni, Letter to Lady Baptista Malatesta, ca 1405

There are certain subjects in which, whilst a modest proficiency is on all accounts to be desired, a minute knowledge and excessive devotion seem to be a vain display. For instance, subtleties of Arithmetic and Geometry are not worthy to absorb a cultivated mind, and the same must be said of Astrology. You will be surprised to find me suggesting (though with much more hesitation) that the great and complex art of Rhetoric should be placed in the same category. My chief reason is the obvious one, that I have in view the cultivation most fitting to a woman. To her neither the intricacies of debate nor the oratorical artifices of action and delivery are of the least practical use, if indeed they are not positively unbecoming. Rhetoric in all its forms—public discussion, forensic argument, logical fence, and the like—lies absolutely outside the province of women.

What Disciplines then are properly open to her? In the first place she has before her, as a subject peculiarly her own, the whole field of religion and morals. The literature of the Church will thus claim her earnest study. Such a writer, for instance, as St. Augustine affords her the fullest scope for reverent yet learned inquiry. Her devotional instinct may lead her to value the help and consolation of holy men now living; but in this case let her not for an instant yield to the impulse to look into their writings, which, compared with those of Augustine, are utterly destitute of sound and melodious style, and seem to me to have no attraction whatever.

Moreover, the cultivated Christian lady has no need in the study of this weighty subject to confine herself to ecclesiastical writers. Morals, indeed, have been treated of by the noblest intellects of Greece and Rome. What they have left to us upon Continence, Temperance, Modesty, Justice, Courage, Greatness of Soul, demands your sincere respect. . . .

But we must not forget that true distinction is to be gained by a wide and varied range of such studies as conduce to the profitable enjoyment of life, in which, however, we must observe due proportion in the attention and time we devote to them.

First amongst such studies I place History: a subject which must not on any account be neglected by one who aspires to true cultivation. For it is our duty to understand the origins of our own history and its development; and the achievements of Peoples and of Kings.

For the careful study of the past enlarges our foresight in contemporary affairs and affords to citizens and to monarchs lessons of incitement or warning in the ordering of public policy. From History, also, we draw our store of examples of moral precepts. . . .

The great Orators of antiquity must by all means be included. Nowhere do we find the virtues more warmly extolled, the vices so fiercely decried. From them we may learn, also, how to express consolation, encouragement, dissuasion or advice. . . .

I come now to Poetry and the Poets—a subject with which every educated lady must shew herself thoroughly familiar. For we cannot point to any great mind of the past for whom the Poets had not a powerful attraction. . . . Hence my view that familiarity with the great poets of antiquity is essential to any claim to true education. For in their writings we find deep speculations upon Nature, and upon the Causes and Origins of things, which must carry weight with us both from their antiquity and from their authorship. Besides these, many important truths upon matters of daily life are suggested or illustrated. All this is expressed with such grace and dignity as demands our admiration.

But I am ready to admit that there are two types of poet: the aristocracy, so to call them, of their craft, and the vulgar, and that the latter may be put aside in ordering a woman's reading. A comic dramatist may season his wit too highly: a satirist describe too bluntly the moral corruption which he scourges: let her pass them by. . . .

But my last word must be this. . . . All sources of profitable learning will in due proportion claim your study. None have more urgent claim than the subjects and authors which treat of Religion and of our duties in the world; and it is because they assist and illustrate these supreme studies that I press upon your attention the works of the most approved poets, historians and orators of the past.

Sources 6 and 7 from Baldassare Castiglione, The Book of the Courtier, *trans. Charles S. Singleton, ed. Edgar Mayhew (Garden City, New York: Doubleday, 1959), pp. 32, 34, 70–71; pp. 206–208, 211–212. Copyright © 1959 by Charles S. Singleton and Edgar de N. Mayhew. Used by permission of Doubleday, a division of Random House, Inc.*

6. From Baldassare Castiglione, *The Courtier,* 1508–1516

"I hold that the principal and true profession of the Courtier must be that of arms which I wish him to exercise with vigor; and let him be known among the others as bold, energetic, and faithful to whomever he serves. And the repute of these good qualities will be earned by exercising them in every time and place, inasmuch as one may not ever fail therein without great blame.

And, just as among women the name of purity, once stained, is never restored, so the reputation of a gentleman whose profession is arms, if ever in the least way he sullies himself through cowardice or other disgrace, always remains defiled before the world and covered with ignominy. Therefore, the more our Courtier excels in this art, the more will he merit praise." . . .

Then signor Gasparo replied: "As for me, I have known few men excellent in anything whatsoever who did not praise themselves; and it seems to me that this can well be permitted them, because he who feels himself to be of some worth, and sees that his works are ignored, is indignant that his own worth should lie buried; and he must make it known to someone, in order not to be cheated of the honor that is the true reward of all virtuous toil. Thus, among the ancients, seldom does anyone of any worth refrain from praising himself. To be sure, those persons who are of no merit, and yet praise themselves, are insufferable; but we do not assume that our Courtier will be of that sort."

Then the Count said: "If you took notice, I blamed impudent and indiscriminate praise of one's self: and truly, as you say, one must not conceive a bad opinion of a worthy man who praises himself modestly; nay, one must take that as surer evidence than if it came from another's mouth. I do say that whoever does not fall into error in praising himself and does not cause annoyance or envy in the person who listens to him is indeed a discreet man and, besides the praises he gives himself, deserves praises from others; for that is a very difficult thing." . . .

"I would have him more than passably learned in letters, at least in those studies which we call the humanities. Let him be conversant not only with the Latin language, but with Greek as well, because of the abundance and variety of things that are so divinely written therein. Let him be versed in the poets, as well as in the orators and historians, and let him be practiced also in writing verse and prose, especially in our own vernacular; for, beside the personal satisfaction he will take in this, in this way he will never want for pleasant entertainment with the ladies, who are usually fond of such things. And if, because of other occupations or lack of study, he does not attain to such a perfection that his writings should merit great praise, let him take care to keep them under cover so that others will not laugh at him, and let him show them only to a friend who can be trusted; because at least they will be of profit to him in that, through such exercise, he will be capable of judging the writing of others. For it very rarely happens that a man who is unpracticed in writing, however learned he may be, can ever wholly understand the toils and industry of writers, or taste the sweetness and excellence of styles, and those intrinsic niceties that are often found in the ancients.

"These studies, moreover, will make him fluent, and (as Aristippus said to the tyrant) bold and self-confident in speaking with everyone. However, I would have our Courtier keep one precept firmly in mind, namely, in this as in everything else, to be cautious and reserved rather than forward, and take care not to get the mistaken notion that he knows something he does not know."

7. From Baldassare Castiglione, *The Courtier*, 1508–1516

I think that in her ways, manners, words, gestures, and bearing, a woman ought to be very unlike a man; for just as he must show a certain solid and sturdy manliness, so it is seemly for a woman to have a soft and delicate tenderness, with an air of womanly sweetness in her every movement. . . .

[Again] . . . many virtues of the mind are as necessary to a woman as to a man; also, gentle birth; to avoid affectation, to be naturally graceful in all her actions, to be mannerly, clever, prudent, not arrogant, not envious, not slanderous, not vain, not contentious, not inept, to know how to gain and hold the favor of her mistress [queen or presiding lady at court] and of all others, to perform well and gracefully the exercises that are suitable for women. And I do think that beauty is more necessary to her than to the Courtier, for truly that woman lacks much who lacks beauty. . . . I say that, in my opinion, in a Lady who lives at court a certain pleasing affability is becoming above all else, whereby she will be able to entertain graciously every kind of man with agreeable and comely conversation suited to the time and place and to the station of the person with whom she speaks, joining to serene and modest manners, and to that comeliness that ought to inform all her actions, a quick vivacity of spirit whereby she will show herself a stranger to all boorishness; but with such a kind manner as to cause her to be thought no less chaste, prudent, and gentle than she is agreeable, witty, and discreet: thus, she must observe a certain mean (difficult to achieve and, as it were, composed of contraries) and must strictly observe certain limits and not exceed them.

Now, in her wish to be thought good and pure, this Lady must not be so coy, or appear so to abhor gay company or any talk that is a little loose, as to withdraw as soon as she finds herself involved, for it might easily be thought that she was pretending to be so austere in order to hide something about herself which she feared others might discover; for manners so unbending are always odious. Yet, on the other hand, for the sake of appearing free and amiable she must not utter unseemly words or enter into any immodest and unbridled familiarity or into ways such as might cause others to believe about her what is perhaps not true; but when she finds herself present at such talk, she ought to listen with a light blush of shame. . . .

And to repeat briefly a part of what has already been said. I wish this Lady to have knowledge of letters, of music, of painting, and know how to dance and how to be festive, adding a discreet modesty and the giving of a good impression of herself to those other things that have been required of the

Courtier. And so, in her talk, her laughter, her play, her jesting, in short in everything, she will be most graceful and will converse appropriately with every person in whose company she may happen to be, using witticisms and pleasantries that are becoming to her.

Source 8 from Niccolo Machiavelli, The Prince and the Discourses, *translated by Luigi Ricci, revised by E. R. P. Vincent (New York: Random House, 1950), pp. 4, 53, 55, 56, 61–62. Reprinted by permission of Oxford University Press.*

8. From Niccolo Machiavelli, *The Prince*, 1513

I desire no honour for my work but such as the novelty and gravity of its subject may justly deserve. Nor will it, I trust, be deemed presumptuous on the part of a man of humble and obscure condition to attempt to discuss and direct the government of princes; for in the same way that landscape painters station themselves in the valleys in order to draw mountains or high ground, and ascend an eminence in order to get a good view of the plains, so it is necessary to be a prince to know thoroughly the nature of the people, and one of the populace to know the nature of princes. . . .

A prince should therefore have no other aim or thought, nor take up any other thing for his study, but war and its organisation and discipline, for that is the only art that is necessary to one who commands, and it is of such virtue that it not only maintains those who are born princes, but often enables men of private fortune to attain to that rank. And one sees, on the other hand, that when princes think more of luxury than of arms, they lose their state. The chief cause of the loss of states, is the contempt of this art, and the way to acquire them is to be well versed in the same. . . .

But as to exercise for the mind, the prince ought to read history and study the actions of eminent men, see how they acted in warfare, examine the causes of their victories and defeats in order to imitate the former and avoid the latter, and above all, do as some men have done in the past, who have imitated some one, who has been much praised and glorified, and have always kept his deeds and actions before them. . . .

It now remains to be seen what are the methods and rules for a prince as regards his subjects and friends. . . .

From this arises the question whether it is better to be loved more than feared, or feared more than loved. The reply is, that one ought to be both feared and loved, but as it is difficult for the two to go together, it is much safer to be feared than loved, if one of the two has to be wanting. For it may be said of men in general that they are ungrateful, voluble, dissemblers, anxious to avoid danger, and covetous of gain; as long as you benefit them, they are entirely yours; they offer you their blood, their goods, their life, and their children, as I have before said, when the necessity is remote; but when it approaches, they revolt. And the prince who has relied solely on their words, without making other preparations, is ruined; for the friendship which is gained by purchase and not through grandeur and nobility of spirit is bought but not secured, and at a pinch is not to be expended in your service. And men have less scruple in offending one who makes himself loved than one who makes himself feared; for love is held by a chain of obligation which, men being selfish, is broken whenever it serves their purpose; but fear is maintained by a dread of punishment which never fails.

Still, a prince should make himself feared in such a way that if he does not gain love, he at any rate avoids hatred; for fear and the absence of hatred may well go together, and will be always attained by one who abstains from interfering with the property of his citizens and subjects or with their women. And when he is obliged to take the life of any one, let him do so when there is a proper justification and manifest reason for it; but above all he must abstain from taking the property of others, for men forget more easily the death of their father than the loss of their patrimony. Then also pretexts for seizing property are never wanting, and one who begins to live by rapine will always find some reason for taking the goods of others, whereas causes for taking life are rarer and more fleeting.

But when the prince is with his army and has a large number of soldiers under his control, then it is extremely necessary that he should not mind being thought cruel; for without this reputation he could not keep an army united or disposed to any duty.

Source 9 from James Bruce Ross and Mary Martin McLaughlin, editors, The Portable Renaissance Reader *(New York: Viking, 1953), pp. 480–485, 490–492. Selection translated by James Bruce Ross. Copyright 1953, renewed 1981 by Viking Penguin Inc. Used by permission of Viking Penguin, a division of Penguin Books USA Inc.*

9. From Leon Battista Alberti, *Autobiography,* after 1460(?)

In everything suitable to one born free and educated liberally, he was so trained from boyhood that among the leading young men of his age he was considered by no means the last. For, assiduous in the science and skill of dealing with arms and horses and musical instruments, as well as in the pursuit of letters[1] and the fine arts, he was devoted to the knowledge of the most strange and difficult things. And finally he embraced with zeal and forethought everything which pertained to fame. To omit the rest, he strove so hard to attain a name in modelling and painting that he wished to neglect

1. **letters:** Alberti means the humanist program of study, primarily the study of languages and literature.

nothing by which he might gain the approbation of good men. His genius was so versatile that you might almost judge all the fine arts to be his. Neither ease nor sloth held him back, nor was he ever seized by satiety in carrying out what was to be done.

He often said that not even in letters had he noticed what is called the satiety of all things among mortals; for to him letters, in which he delighted so greatly, seemed sometimes like flowering and richly fragrant buds, so that hunger or sleep could scarcely distract him from his books. At other times, however, those very letters swarmed together like scorpions before his eyes, so that he could see nothing at all but books. Therefore, when letters began to be displeasing to him, he turned to music and painting and exercise.

He played ball, hurled the javelin, ran, leaped, wrestled, and above all delighted in the steep ascent of mountains; he applied himself to all these things for the sake of health rather than sport or pleasure. . . .

At length, on the orders of his doctors, he desisted from those studies which were most fatiguing to the memory, just when they were about to flourish. But in truth, because he could not live without letters, at the age of twenty-four he turned to physics and the mathematical arts. He did not despair of being able to cultivate them sufficiently, because he perceived that in them talent rather than memory must be employed. At this time he wrote for his brother *On the Advantages and Disadvantages of Letters,* in which booklet, taught by experience, he discussed whatever could be thought about letters. And he wrote at this time for the sake of his soul several little works: *Ephebia, On Religion, Deiphira,* and more of this sort in prose; then in verse, *Elegies* and *Eclogues,* and *Discourses,* and works on love of such a kind as to inculcate good habits in those who studied them and to foster the quiet of the soul. . . .

Although he was affable, gentle, and harmful to no one, nevertheless he felt the animosity of many evil men, and hidden enmities, both annoying and very burdensome; in particular the harsh injuries and intolerable insults from his own relatives. He lived among the envious and malevolent with such modesty and equanimity that none of his detractors or rivals, although very hostile towards him, dared to utter a word about him in the presence of good and worthy men unless it was full of praise and admiration. Even by these envious ones he was received with honour face to face. But, in truth, when he was absent, those who had pretended to love him most slandered him with every sort of calumny, wherever the ears of the fickle and their like lay open. For they took it ill to be exceeded in ability and fame by him who, far inferior to them in fortune, had striven with such zeal and industry. There were even some among his kinsmen (not to mention others) who, having experienced his humanity, beneficence, and liberality, conspired against him most ungratefully and cruelly in an evil domestic plot, and those barbarians aroused the boldness of servants to strike him with a knife, blameless as he was.

He bore injuries of this kind from his kinsmen with equanimity, more in silence than by indignantly resorting to vengeance or permitting the shame and ignominy of his relatives to be made public. . . .

He could endure pain and cold and heat. When, not yet fifteen, he received a serious wound in the foot, and the physician, according to his custom and skill, drew together the broken parts of the foot and sewed them through the skin with a needle, he scarcely uttered a sound of pain. With his own hands, though in such great pain, he even aided the ministering doctor and treated his own wound though he was burning with fever. And when on account of a pain in his side he was continually in an icy sweat, he called in musicians, and for about two hours he strove by singing to overcome the force of the malady and the agony of the pain. His head was by nature unable to endure either cold or wind; but by persistence he learned to bear them, gradually getting used to riding bareheaded in summer, then in winter, and even in raging wind. By some defect in his nature he loathed garlic and also honey, and the mere sight of them, if by chance they were offered to him, brought on vomiting. But he conquered himself by force of looking at and handling the disagreeable objects, so that they came to offend him less, thus showing by example that men can do anything with themselves if they will. . . .

When his favourite dog died he wrote a funeral oration for him.

Source 10 from Denys Hay, editor and translator, The Anglia Historia of Polydore Vergil, *AD 1485–1537, book 74 (London: Camden Society, 1950), p. 147.*

10. From Polydore Vergil, *Anglia Historia*, ca 1540

Henry reigned twenty-three years and seven months. He lived for fifty-two years. By his wife Elizabeth he was the father of eight children, four boys and as many girls. He left three surviving children, an only son Henry prince of Wales, and two daughters, Margaret married to James king of Scotland, and Mary betrothed to Charles prince of Castile. His body was slender but well built and strong; his height above the average. His appearance was remarkably attractive and his face was cheerful, especially when speaking; his eyes were small and blue, his teeth few, poor and blackish; his hair was thin and white; his complexion sallow. His spirit was distinguished, wise and prudent; his mind was brave and resolute and never, even at moments of the greatest danger, deserted him. He had a most pertinacious memory. Withal he was not devoid of scholarship. In government he was shrewd and prudent, so that no one dared to get the better of him through deceit or guile. He was gracious and kind and was as attentive to his visitors as he was easy of access. His hospitality was splendidly generous; he was fond of having foreigners at his court and he freely conferred favours on them. But those of his subjects who were indebted to him and who did not pay him due honour or who were generous only with promises, he treated with harsh severity. He well knew how to maintain his royal majesty and all which appertains to kingship at every time and in every place. He was most fortunate in war, although he was constitutionally more inclined to peace than to war. He cherished justice above all things; as a result he vigorously punished violence, manslaughter and every other kind of wickedness whatsoever. Consequently he was greatly regretted[2] on that account by all his subjects, who had been able to conduct their lives peaceably, far removed from the assaults and evil doing of scoundrels. He was the most ardent supporter of our faith, and daily participated with great piety in religious services. To those whom he considered to be worthy priests, he often secretly gave alms so that they should pray for his salvation. He was particularly fond of those Franciscan friars whom they call Observants, for whom he founded many convents, so that with his help their rule should continually flourish in his kingdom. But all these virtues were obscured latterly only by avarice, from which (as we showed above) he suffered. This avarice is surely a bad enough vice in a private individual, whom it forever torments; in a monarch indeed it may be considered the worst vice, since it is harmful to everyone, and distorts those qualities of trustfulness, justice and integrity by which the state must be governed.

QUESTIONS TO CONSIDER

The first step in exploring the history of ideas is to focus on and define the ideas themselves. Once you have done that by reading the selections and thinking about the questions proposed in Sources and Method, you need to take the next step, which is to compare the ideas of various thinkers. In this way you can trace the development of ideas, how they originate and mature and change in the mind of one thinker after another. First, ask specific questions, such as: What would Bruni think of Castiglione's court lady? How would Leon Battista Alberti be judged by Castiglione's standards? Did Polydore Vergil and Machiavelli have the same ideas about the personal qualities of a ruler? Would a man educated according to the ideas of Vergerius have fitted into Castiglione's ideal court? Would a ruler have wanted him? Would Bruni's learned lady have made a good member of Castiglione's court? Would Botticelli's Simonetta? Does Machiavelli's prince display the qualities Vergerius envisioned in a liberally educated man? How do the main qualities of Machiavelli's prince compare with those of Castiglione's courtier? Why might they be quite different? From the portrait, how might Dürer have been judged by each of the writers? Could we think of Verrocchio's sculpture of Colleoni as a portrait of a Machiavellian ruler? How did the artists' ideals for men, women, and rulers differ from the writers'?

Once you have made these specific comparisons, you can move on to broader comparisons of the basic assumptions of the authors and artists: What was the underlying view of

2. **regretted:** missed after he died.

human nature for these writers? Was this the same for men and women? You have probably noticed that all the writers and artists presented here are male. Given what you have now learned about ideals for men and women, would you have expected most Renaissance writers to be male?

Many intellectual historians are interested not only in the history of ideas themselves but also in their social and political origins. These historians want to know what people thought and why they thought the way they did. This type of intellectual history is called the *sociology of knowledge* because it explores the societal context of ideas in the same way that sociology examines past and present social groups. The sociology of knowledge is a more speculative field than the history of ideas alone because it attempts to discover the underlying reasons that cause people to develop different ways of thinking in different historial periods—a process that can be quite difficult to discern. Nevertheless, from the information your text provides about the social and political changes occurring during the Renaissance, you can also consider some sociology of knowledge questions: Why did humanism first arise in northern Italy and not elsewhere in Italy? Why was religion regarded as especially important for women? How did Castiglione's career affect his view of poli-

tics? How did Machiavelli's? What transformation of the status of artists during the Renaissance allowed both Alberti and Dürer to depict themselves in the ways they did? Given that the documents range from 1392 to 1540, what political changes might have accounted for the varying ideals proposed for the individual? How did the ideals proposed for rulers reflect the actual growth of centralized political power? How might the growth of that power have shaped the ideals set forth by Machiavelli and Polydore Vergil? Questions such as these take us somewhat beyond the scope of our original enquiry, but they are important to ask in looking at any ideological change, particularly a sensibility as far-reaching as the Renaissance. Humanism did not spring up in a vacuum but at a very specific time and place.

We must also be careful, however, not to overemphasize social and political background in tracing the development of ideas. Intellectual historians prefer to speak of "necessary conditions" or "background factors" rather than "causes." A movement as diffuse and long lasting as humanism necessarily stemmed from a wide variety of factors, so do not feel concerned if you find yourself qualifying your answers to the questions in the last paragraph with such words as "might," "perhaps," and "possibly."

EPILOGUE

Scholars and writers throughout Western history have attempted to revive the classical past, but none of these efforts before or after were to produce the long-lasting effects of the Italian Renaissance. In many ways Petrarch was right: It was the dawn of a new age. As the ideas and ideals of humanism spread, writers all over Europe felt that they had definitely broken with the centuries-long tradition that directly preceded them. It was at this point that historians began the three-part division of Western history that we still use today: antiquity, the Middle Ages or medieval period, and the modern period. (If you pause to reflect on what "middle" implies, you will see that no one living in the tenth century would have described him- or herself as living in the "Middle Ages.")

The effects of the Renaissance were eventually felt far beyond the realms of literature and art. Humanist schools and academies opened throughout Europe, and eventually the older universities changed their curricula to add courses in Latin, Greek, and Hebrew language and literature. In northern Europe, humanists became interested in reforming the Church, bringing it back to the standards of piety and morality they believed had been present in the early Church, in the same way that Petrarch had tried to return the Latin language to its ancient standards. This movement, termed *Christian humanism,* would be one of the background factors behind the Protestant Reformation, as learned people began to realize from their studies that the Church was now far removed from the ideas and standards of the early Christians. The intense Renaissance interest in the physical world, combined with monetary greed and missionary impulses, led to the exploration and eventual colonization of much of the non-European world. This secular spirit was also important in setting the stage for the Scientific Revolution of the seventeenth century.

Humanist ideas about the perfect man, woman, and ruler were originally directed at the upper classes but would eventually find a much larger audience. Castiglione's *The Courtier* was translated into every European language, and the personal characteristics he outlined for the ideal courtier became those expected of the middle-class gentleman. Echoes of the Renaissance ideal for women are still with us; a glance at women's magazines or at contemporary advice manuals for girls will show you that physical beauty, morality, femininity, and religion are often still seen to be the most important personal qualities a woman can possess. Machiavelli's *The Prince* has more dramatic echoes, as many modern dictators clearly would agree that it is more important to be feared than loved.

We should not overemphasize the effects of the intellectual changes of the Renaissance on people living during that period, however. Only a very small share of the population, primarily wealthy, urban, and, as we have seen, male, participated at all in cultural life, whether as consumers

[246]

or as producers. Most people's lives were shaped much more during this period by economic changes and by religious practices than by the cultural changes we looked at in this chapter. In fact, in their efforts to stress the elitism of Renaissance culture, some historians have questioned whether the term *Renaissance* itself is a valid one, and prefer simply to use the more neutral phrase "late medieval and early modern period."

Even among the elites, many aspects of the Middle Ages continued during the Renaissance. Despite the emergence of individualism, family background remained the most important determinant of a person's so-cial and economic standing. Despite an emphasis on the material, secular world, religion remained central to the lives of the elite as well as the common people. Though some artists were recognized as geniuses, they were still expected to be dependable, tax-paying members of society—that is, members of the community like everybody else. The fact that so many humanists felt it necessary to set standards and describe ideal behavior gives us a clue that not everyone understood or accepted that they were living in a new age: People have no need to be convinced of what they already believe is true.

CHAPTER ELEVEN

PAGANS, MUSLIMS, AND CHRISTIANS IN THE

MENTAL WORLD OF COLUMBUS

THE PROBLEM

Along with inspiring a number of television specials, parades, scholarly conferences, and exhibitions, the 500th anniversary of the first voyage of Columbus has recently sparked a great debate about the man himself and the impact of his actions. Was he an intrepid explorer, one of the few Europeans not afraid to sail out of sight of land? Was he a religious zealot and mystic, convinced that God had called him to fight the power of Islam and convert people to Christianity by force if necessary? Was he an ethnocentric racist, unable to appreciate the cultures of the people with whom he came into contact? Did his voyages usher in a period of global interchange, bringing new crops across the Atlantic in both directions? Or did they instead bring demographic devastation to the New World, with European diseases killing the vast majority of the population of Central America? How did they set the stage for the African slave trade, which became the largest

forced movement of people in human history?

The debate surrounding these questions has perhaps become more polemical than it should, but one of its positive results has been a greater interest in seeing Columbus within his historical context. Earlier celebrations of Columbus, such as that in 1892, tended to present him as a lonely hero, a man who stuck to his dreams despite the ridicule and scorn of most of his contemporaries, and prevailed, proving that earth was round when most people thought that it was flat. Columbus was often described as the first "modern man," in the sense that he was interested in venturing into the unknown simply to find what was there. This heroic view can still be found in the popular press, with Columbus portrayed as the direct ancestor to modern astronauts and praised as one of the few people who was able to throw off the shackles of medieval ideas.

By contrast, during the last several decades, many historians of the European explorations have downplayed the personal role of Columbus and

[248]

other early explorers, and focused instead on technological, economic, political, and religious factors, arguing that without these, Columbus's voyages would not have happened. This is part of a more general rejection of what is often termed the "Great Man" school of history, with scholars examining factors other than individual personalities that contributed to major historical changes. In the case of the explorations, historians point to technological changes in the fifteenth and sixteenth centuries, such as improvements in shipbuilding, navigational instruments, and weaponry, that allowed Europeans to carry out the voyages they wished. In Portugal and Spain, the monarchies were gradually building up their authority, taking power away from the feudal nobility. They were developing new tax bases, which brought in steady revenue, and looking for ways to further expand both their wealth and their political power. The Portuguese hoped to reach gold mines in the African interior and find an alternative route for Eastern spices and luxury products, ending the monopoly of Italian merchants, who made enormous profits when they transported Eastern goods across the Mediterranean. In the late fifteenth century, Spain was in the final stages of the *reconquista*, the reconquering of Spain from the Muslims, which had begun centuries earlier. In 1492, under the leadership of King Ferdinand of Aragon and Queen Isabella of Castile, Aragonese and Castilian armies conquered Granada, a small territory in southern Spain that was the last Muslim holding, and Spanish

soldiers no longer had a mission on the Spanish mainland.

Historians have concluded that all of these developments set the stage for Portugal and Spain, and religion provided additional motivation. Making contact with the East for spices would not only break the monopoly of Italian merchants, but also allow western Europeans to challenge the Muslims who controlled the spice trade before it reached the Mediterranean. Asia and Africa offered the prospect of millions of people who could be converted to Christianity, and then enlisted to oppose the Muslims. The Ottoman Turks were slowly advancing into Europe, taking Constantinople in 1453 and besieging Vienna half a century later, so that finding allies against Muslim power was becoming even more important in European eyes.

Looking at these factors in hindsight, it does appear that the voyages of Columbus were almost inevitable, and some of the scholarship from the Columbus quincentennial celebrations pays very little attention to Columbus himself. Other scholars, however, have turned their attention back to Columbus as an individual, arguing that seeing him in context does not mean losing him in that context. These investigations have explored not only the economic, religious, and political setting of Columbus's voyages, but also his own intellectual background. As they have delved deeper into his motivations and ideas, they have discovered that he was influenced not only by his Christian faith and a desire for riches, but also by the works of earlier

Chapter 11

Pagans,

Muslims, and

Christians in the

Mental World

of Columbus

geographers and travelers, including classical-era pagans and medieval Muslims and Christians. Columbus spent his youth and young manhood in the port cities of Italy and the Iberian peninsula, where he read works of theoretical and practical geography and travel, and talked with sailors, scholars, and ship captains from a wide variety of backgrounds, all of whom had notions of what was to be found beyond the western horizon. Thus, when Columbus left Spain in 1492, he may have sailed off on waters that were unknown to European sailors, but he carried with him a clear idea of what he expected to find, as did other early explorers and the rulers who sent them. His preconceptions, and those of other early explorers, shaped his reactions to the Americas, Africa, and Asia, and the initial reactions of these early explor-

ers in many ways set the patterns for racial and ethnic relations for centuries to come. Therefore, to understand why European exploration and colonization proceeded the way it did, we need to understand not only technological and political factors, but also the mental world of the earliest explorers.

Columbus provides an especially good entry into this, not only because he was regarded as the New World's "discoverer" for so long, but also because he left records of what he was reading and to whom he was talking. Your task in this chapter will be to read Columbus's own writings along with some of the works Columbus read or heard about to answer the following question: How did earlier works of geography and travel shape the mental world of Columbus, and thus influence the "Age of Discovery"?

SOURCES AND METHOD

This chapter focuses on the intellectual history of one individual, a topic that has been prominent in the writing of history for centuries. If you wander through the history, philosophy, and biography sections of any library or bookstore, you will find countless books devoted to "So-and-so's Thought About This" or "The Ideas of So-and-so" or "The Influence of So-and-so on This" (or "on Them"). The authors of these books have generally used the same method you will use this chapter: careful reading of the writings of their subject. If they are especially in-

terested in exploring the roots of their subject's ideas, intellectual historians and biographers generally start with the person's writings to identify key ideas, then work backwards to try to determine the sources of these notions. They turn to works that the individual is known to have read or possessed, searching through them for ideas that come out later in the writings or actions of the individual. This is exactly what we will be doing in this chapter: Starting with Columbus's own words, and then turning to works he identifies as the sources of his ideas or is known to have possessed. Our task will be made easier by the fact in some cases the actual books that he owned, complete with his own marginal notes, still survive. As many intellectual historians do, we will return to his words again at the end, and test our conclusions about his intellectual inheritance.

Source 1 is a letter written by Columbus to the king and queen of Spain in 1492, which serves as the prologue to his journal from his first voyage. The journal was not published during Columbus's lifetime, and the original has disappeared, although we do have an early-sixteenth-century copy by Bartolomé de las Casas, whose father and uncle had sailed with Columbus. Las Casas was one of the first missionaries to the natives of the New World and opposed their treatment at the hands of the Spanish, so there is some question as to whether he might have changed parts of the journal. Source 2 is another letter from Columbus to Ferdinand and Isabella, apparently written in 1501, and also contained in a different document, this time the biography of Columbus written by his son Ferdinand. As with las Casas's copy of Columbus's journal, there is also controversy about this biography, for Ferdinand's original Spanish manuscript has been lost and the first printed version is an Italian translation published in 1571. Most scholars accept that it was actually written by Ferdinand sometime in the 1530s and was based on his father's papers; Ferdinand was a scholar and book collector, and it is his library—now located in Seville—that contained his father's own books. Ferdinand was devoted to his father and also involved in litigation with the Spanish

Crown about grants of property promised to his father, so the work highlights Columbus's heroism, but many things that it relates are supported by other sources. Thus, although there are disagreements about certain aspects of the works from which Sources 1 and 2 are taken, most scholars see these letters as authentic.

Read these two sources carefully. In Source 1, what does Columbus say motivated him to sail west? What did he (and Ferdinand and Isabella) expect to find? Why did he go in 1492, as opposed to some other year? In Source 2, who does Columbus say he spoke with about his interests? What sorts of things did he learn in preparation for his voyage?

Source 3 is a further selection from Ferdinand's biography that describes in greater detail what Columbus was reading and hearing. What were the main ideas Columbus gained from the ancient Greek geographers Ptolemy and Marinus and the medieval Muslim geographer al-Farghani? How are these ideas supported by the other authors he has read, such as Marco Polo and Pierre d'Ally? What did he learn from talking with Portuguese pilots and other acquaintances? From reading these first three sources, you now have some ideas about what Columbus expected, and where his expectations came from.

One of the first actions we as modern historians take in studying any development is weeding out obviously fictitious or mythical material. Though we recognize that views of "the facts" vary greatly from

Chapter 11

Pagans,

Muslims, and

Christians in the

Mental World

of Columbus

observer to observer, we still attempt to exclude information that is clearly fictitious or impossible, or that sounds suspiciously like a myth created after the events. Modern scholarly biographies of George Washington, for example, do not include the story about him chopping down the cherry tree unless they are discussing the myths that have grown up around Washington. The distinction between fact and fiction is not a particularly useful one as we investigate Columbus's mental world, however, for Columbus and other sixteenth-century explorers read what we now recognize as the reports of mythological travelers just as carefully as they read the reports of real ones. Earlier real travelers were also steeped in the same myths, so that their reports repeat stories that had been told for centuries, often blending these seamlessly with descriptions of events and people that they actually saw. In answering the central question for this chapter, then, we need to take into account all the works that Columbus read or heard about, whether we now regard them as fiction, fact, or a combination of the two. (The dividing line between fact and fiction is often still not clear today, particularly for events for which there is no additional corroboration.) Thus you will need to read the next nine sources carefully, as you flesh out Columbus's mental world.

As is clear from the selections you have read, scholars from classical antiquity were very important to Columbus. Source 4 is a portion of Ptolemy's *Geography*, which was written in Greek in the second century A.D.

Ptolemy's work was unknown in western Europe in the Middle Ages, but this changed in the early fifteenth century when it was translated from Greek into Latin, quickly recopied many times, and by 1465 printed, using the newly developed printing press with movable metal type. Given the respect that Renaissance scholars had for the ancient world, Ptolemy's work quickly acquired the status of a classic, and his text and maps continued to be reprinted even after the Portuguese and Spanish voyages had proved them wrong. On his first voyage, Columbus had a copy of the Rome 1478 edition of Ptolemy's *Geography* in his sea chest. Source 5 is a brief selection from the *Natural History* of the first-century Roman official Pliny, the most popular Roman writer on natural phenomena. His work was frequently recopied throughout the Middle Ages and was printed in the fifteenth century; Columbus owned an Italian translation that had been printed in Venice in 1489. Read these selections carefully. How much of the globe in terms of longitude does Ptolemy propose is contained in the "known world," that is, Eurasia? What is the estimation of Marinus? What assurances does Ptolemy give his readers that his work is accurate? Conversely, how does he explain observations that might not match his? The selections from Pliny describe various peoples he has heard about in Asia. What physical and behavioral traits does he report?

As we saw in Sources 1 and 3, Columbus also studied the work of Muslim scholars and geographers, either in Latin translations or by talking with people who read and spoke Arabic. He took individuals who spoke Arabic on both his first and fourth voyages, assuming that they would have more luck communicating with the residents of the Indies and the great khan than those who spoke only European languages. Sources 6 and 7 are selections from medieval Muslim scholars: Source 6 is from the *Geography* of Abu Abdallah Mohammed Idrisi (1100–1166), who worked for many years as a geographer and cartographer at the court of King Roger II of Sicily, and Source 7 is from the enormous work of the scholar Ibn Fadl Allah al'Umari (d. 1358), the *Masalik al-Absar.* In Source 6, Idrisi describes several islands in the Atlantic off the coasts of Portugal and north Africa, and reports what some sailors who had set out sailing west from Lisbon said they had found. In Source 7, al'Umari reports what he was told the fourteenth-century Berber sultan of Mali, Mansa Musa, reported when talking with Egyptian officials while on his way to Mecca. Read these accounts carefully. What does Idrisi relate about the inhabitants of various Atlantic islands? What do the Maghrourins in Source 6 and the ship captain in Source 7 report that they have found? How might these accounts have contributed to Columbus's desire to sail westward, as well as shaping his expectations?

During the thirteenth century, the Mongols under Genghis and then Kublai Khan controlled an enormous empire stretching from eastern Europe to the Pacific. They welcomed

trade and established enough order so that travelers could generally proceed safely, and large numbers of merchants, missionaries, and ambassadors crossed the Mongol Empire regularly. The next three sources all stem from this period of *Pax Mongolica* (Mongol Peace). Source 8 is an extract from a letter from John of Monte Corvino (1247–1328), a Western Christian friar sent by the pope to the Mongols. John stayed for a long time as a missionary, and wrote three letters back to members of his religious order, the Franciscans, asking for their support. Source 9 is a short part of *The Travels of Marco Polo* (ca 1253–1324). Polo was a Venetian merchant who apparently spent twenty years in Asia and often acted as a representative for Kublai Khan. His work was written, with the help of a writer of romance stories, shortly after he returned to Europe, and was widely translated, copied, and then published. Source 10 is from a work entitled *The Travels of Sir John Mandeville,* purportedly written by an English knight who traveled from Europe to Asia in the mid-fourteenth century. Mandeville claimed to have served the sultan of Egypt and the Mongol khan, but it is now believed that the work was largely fictional, based on Polo's reports, stories that dated back to Alexander the Great's eastern conquests, and Pliny's *Natural History.* Though its veracity is now questioned, in the fourteenth century it was not, and it was translated from the French in which it was originally written into every European language. Of these three, Columbus would have known about

Chapter 11

Pagans,

Muslims, and

Christians in the

Mental World

of Columbus

John of Monte Corvino indirectly, and about Polo and Mandeville by reading their works: Columbus's own copy of Polo's book survives, with extensive notes in the margins in his own hand. Read these selections, which describe societies in central and southeast Asia. How does John of Monte Corvino describe his efforts at converting the residents of China? What else does he report about the realm of the khan? What do Polo and Mandeville both think is most important to report? How does their reaction to the people they describe differ from their reaction to the natural products of these areas?

Columbus was not the only person in fifteenth-century Europe who was speculating about traveling west and reading widely in geography and travel literature. Pierre d'Ailly, the bishop of Cambrai and chancellor at the university of Paris, relied on the works of ancient authors as well as medieval Muslims and Christians when writing his *Imago Mundi* in 1410, an encyclopedic account of the inhabitants of the world, of which Source 11 is a brief extract. Columbus made over 900 annotations in his copy, which was a Latin version printed in 1485. Paolo del Pazzo Toscanelli was a physician, astronomer, and humanist who in 1474 sent a letter and world map to a cleric friend in Lisbon, and in 1481 sent a copy of these to Columbus. The map has been lost, but the letter survives, and is reprinted here as Source 12. Read both of these sources carefully. What geographical information do they contain? What do they report about the inhabitants of the western (or eastern) islands?

About the natural products of these places? What authorities do the authors rely on for their information?

Columbus's mental world was shaped not only by words, but also by visual images, particularly those contained on maps; as you read in Source 1, one of his goals was to "make a new chart for navigation . . . and show everything by means of drawing." None of Columbus's actual maps survive, but we have a good idea of what they were, as maps were often included with the books he read, and other contemporary maps have survived. Sources 13 and 14 are two maps from the fifteenth century. Source 13 is a world map from the edition of Ptolemy's *Geography* that Columbus owned—with Ptolemy's calculation of 177 degrees of longitude in the "known earth"; Source 14 is a sailor's chart of the islands of the Atlantic drawn in 1455 in Genoa, Columbus's home town. On these maps you can see many of the islands referred to in the written sources—the Fortunate Isles (labeled on Source 14 as the "Insulle Fortunate Sanct Brandanus" after the sixth-century Irish monk St. Brendan, who according to legend first discovered them), the Canaries (on the bottom of Source 14), the Madeira group (in the middle of Source 14 with each island named, including Porto Santo), the Azores (labeled "Insulla de ventura" on Source 14), and Taprobane near India on Source 13. (The Portuguese had reached Madeira and the Canaries in the fourteenth century, and the Azores in the early fifteenth; these island groups appear on medieval Muslim maps as well.)

Source 14 also shows the large (and nonexistent) island of Antillia past the Azores, for which a Portuguese expedition set out in 1487. How would these maps have reinforced the ideas that Columbus gained through reading and conversation?

For the final reading in this chapter, we return to Columbus himself. Source 15 is a letter describing Columbus's first voyage, written while he was stopping near the Azores on his return from this voyage, and sent from Lisbon so that it would arrive at the court of Ferdinand and Isabella right before he got there. It was published in Spanish, the language in which he wrote, in 1493, translated into Latin and published in many editions in that language, and then translated into other European languages, including a rhymed version in Italian. It thus became very widely known, and formed the basis of many people's first impressions of the "New World."[1] What does Columbus say he expected to find, in terms of both natural products and human culture? Based on your reading of the previous sources, where do these preconceptions come from? How do Columbus's expectations fit with the people he actually met? How does he treat the people he meets, and how does he explain or justify this treatment? What natural products does he describe, and what does he promise Ferdinand and Isabella in terms of natural resources?

---

1. Columbus himself did not use the phrase *New World* until his discovery of the coast of South America on his third voyage in 1498. At that point, he noted that he had found a "very great continent . . . until today unknown," and wrote that God had made him "the messenger of the new world." He still thought this new continent was off the coast of Asia, however, and on his fourth voyage, along the coast of Central America, he assumed that he was in Indochina and close to India. The phrase *New World* began to show up on world maps around 1505. Shortly after that, the word *America* also appeared, based on the name of Amerigo Vespucci, an Italian explorer-navigator whom the German mapmaker Martin Waldseemüller mistakenly thought had discovered America. Waldseemüller commented that it was especially appropriate that America be named after a man, as both Europe and Asia had been named after demigoddesses. By 1513 Waldseemüller knew that he had been wrong and wanted to omit "America" from future maps, but the name had already stuck.

Chapter 11
Pagans,
Muslims, and
Christians in the
Mental World
of Columbus

THE EVIDENCE

Source 1 from John Boyd Thacher, Christopher Columbus: His Life, His Work, His Remains (New York: Kraus Reprints, 1967), vol. I, pp. 513–515. Reprinted by permission.

1. Prologue to the Journal of Christopher Columbus (1493)

PROLOGUE

Because, most Christian and very exalted and very excellent and very powerful Princes, King and Queen of the Spains and of the Islands of the Sea, our Lords, in this present year of 1492 after your Highnesses had made an end to the war of the Moors, who were reigning in Europe, and having finished the war in the very great city of Granada, where in this present year on the 2nd day of the month of January, I saw the Royal banners of your Highnesses placed by force of arms on the towers of the Alhambra, which is the fortress of the said City: and I saw the Moorish King come out to the gates of the City and kiss the Royal hands of your Highnesses, and the hands of the Prince, my Lord: and then in that present month, because of the information which I had given your Highnesses about the lands of India, and about a Price who is called Great Khan, which means in our Romance language, King of Kings,—how he and his predecessors had many times sent to Rome to beg for men learned in our Holy Faith that they might be instructed therein, and that the Holy Father had never furnished them, and so, many peoples believing in idolatries and receiving among themselves sects of perdition, were lost:—your Highnesses, as Catholic Christians and Princes, loving the Holy Christian faith and the spreading of it, and enemies of the sect of Mahomet and of all idolatries and heresies, decided to send me, Christopher columbus, to the said regions of India, to see the said Princes and the peoples and lands, and learn of their disposition, and of everything, and the measures which could be taken for their conversion of our Holy Faith: and you ordered that I should not go to the east by land, by which it is customary to go, but by way of the west, whence until to-day we do not know certainly that any one has gone. So that, after having banished all the Jews from all your Kingdoms and realms,[2] in the same month of January, your Highnesses ordered me to go with a sufficient fleet to the said regions of India: and for that purpose granted me great favours and ennobled me, that from then henceforward I might entitle myself *Don* and should be High Admiral of the Ocean-Sea [*Atlantic*—Ed.] and Viceroy and perpetual Governor of all the is-

---

2. In January 1492, Ferdinand and Isabella issued a royal edict expelling all practicing Jews from Spain in their attempts to achieve total religious orthodoxy.

lands and continental land which I might discover and acquire, and which from now henceforward might be discovered and acquired in the Ocean-Sea, and that my eldest son should succeed in the same manner, and thus from generation to generation for ever after. . . . Also, Lords and Princes, besides describing each night what takes place during the day, and during the day, the sailings of the night, I propose to make a new chart for navigation, on which I will locate all the sea and the lands of the Ocean-Sea, in their proper places, under their winds; and further, to compose a book and show everything by means of drawing, by the latitude from the equator and by longitude from the west, and above all, it is fitting that I forget sleep, and study the navigation diligently, in order to thus fulfil these duties, which will be a great labour.

Sources 2 and 3 from The Life of the Admiral Christopher Columbus by His Son Ferdinand, *translated and annotated by Benjamin Keen (New Brunswick, N.J.: Rutgers University Press, 1958), p. 10; pp. 15–18, 23, 24. Copyright © 1959, 1992 by Rutgers, The State University. Reprinted by permission of Rutgers University Press.*

2. Letter from Christopher Columbus to Ferdinand and Isabella (1500)

Very High Kings:[3]

From a very young age I began to follow the sea and have continued to do so to this day. This art of navigation incites those who pursue it to inquire into the secrets of this world. I have passed more than forty years in this business and have traveled to every place where there is navigation up to the present time. I have had dealings and conversation with learned men, priests, and laymen, Latins and Greeks, Jews and Moors, and many others of other sects. I found Our Lord very favorable to this my desire, and to further it He granted me the gift of knowledge. He made me skilled in seamanship, equipped me abundantly with the sciences of astronomy, geometry, and arithmetic, and taught my mind and hand to draw this sphere and upon it the cities, rivers, mountains, islands, and ports, each in its proper place. During this time I have made it my business to read all that has been written on geography, history, philosophy, and other sciences. Thus Our Lord revealed to me that it was feasible to sail from here to the Indies, and placed in me a burning desire to carry out this plan. Filled with this fire, I came to Your Highnesses. All who knew of my enterprise rejected it with laughter and mockery. They would not heed the arguments I set forth or the authorities I cited. Only Your Highnesses had faith and confidence in me.

3. Beth Isabella and Ferdinand were rulers in their own right, Isabella of Castile and Ferdinand of Aragon, so that Columbus refers to them both here as "kings."

Chapter 11

Pagans,

Muslims, and

Christians in the

Mental World

of Columbus

3. From *The Life of the Admiral Christopher Columbus by His Son Ferdinand*

Turning to the reasons which persuaded the Admiral to undertake the discovery of the Indies, I say there were three, namely, natural reasons, the authority of writers, and the testimony of sailors. With respect to the first—the natural reasons—he believed that since all the water and land in the world form a sphere, it would be possible to go around it from east to west until men stood feet to feet, one against the other, at opposite ends of the earth. In the second place, he assumed and knew on the authority of approved writers that a large part of this sphere had already been navigated and that there remained to be discovered only the space which extended from the eastern end of India, known to Ptolemy and Marinus,[4] eastward to the Cape Verde and Azore Islands, the westernmost land discovered up to that time. Thirdly, he believed that this space between the eastern end, known to Marinus, and the said Cape Verde Islands could not be more than the third part of the great circle of the sphere, because Marinus had already described in the East fifteen of the twenty-four [astronomical] hours or parts into which the world is divided; therefore, to reach the Cape Verdes barely required eight more hours, since even Marinus did not begin his description very far to the West. . . .

The fifth argument, which gave the greatest support to the view that this space was small, was the opinion of Alfragan,[5] and his followers, who assign a much smaller size to the earth than all the other writers and geographers, calculating a degree to be only $56\frac{2}{3}$ miles;[6] whence the Admiral inferred that since the whole sphere was small, of necessity that space of the third part which Marinus left as unknown had to be small and therefore could be navigated in less time. From this he also inferred that since the eastern end of India was not yet known, that end must be the one which is close to us in the West; therefore any lands that he should discover might be called the Indies. . . .

The second reason that inspired the Admiral to launch his enterprise and helped justify his giving the name "Indies" to the lands which he discovered was the authority of many learned men who said that one could sail westward from the western end of Africa and Spain to the eastern end of India,

---

4. For Ptolemy, see Source 4. Marinus of Tyre was a Greek geographer of the second century A.D.

5. Alfragan (al-Farghani) was a Muslim astronomer and geographer from the end of the eighth century.

6. Alfragan was reckoning in Arabic miles of 2164 meters; this works out to 66 nautical miles per degree.

and that no great sea lay between. . . . Pliny, in the second book of his *Natural History*, Chapter 3, also says that the ocean surrounds the whole earth and that its length from east to west is that from India to Cádiz. . . .

Marco Polo, a Venetian, and John Mandeville tell in their travel accounts that they journeyed far beyond the eastern lands described by Ptolemy and Marinus; they do not speak of the Western Sea, but from their description of the East it could be argued that India neighbors on Africa and Spain. Pierre d'Ailly, in Chapter 8 "Concerning the Size of the Habitable Earth," of his treatise *Concerning the Form of the World*, and Julius Capitolinus,[7] in *Concerning the Habitable Places* and many other treatises, say that India and Spain are near each other in the West.

The Admiral's third and last motive for seeking the Indies was his hope of finding before he arrived there some island or land of great importance whence he might the better pursue his main design. He found support for this hope in the authority of many learned men and philosophers who were certain that the land area of the globe was greater than that of the water. This being so, he argued that between the end of Spain and the known end of India there must be many other islands and lands, as experience has since shown to be true.

He believed this all the more because he was impressed by the many fables and stories which he heard from various persons and sailors who traded to the western islands and seas of the Azores and Madeira. Since these stories served his design, he was careful to file them away in his memory. I shall tell them here in order to satisfy those who take delight in such curiosities.

A pilot of the Portuguese King, Martín Vicente by name, told him that on one occasion, finding himself four hundred and fifty leagues[8] west of Cape St. Vincent,[9] he fished out of the sea a piece of wood ingeniously carved, but not with iron. For this reason and because for many days the winds had blown from the west, he concluded this wood came from some islands to the west.

Pedro Correa, who was married to a sister of the Admiral's wife, told him that on the island of Pôrto Santo[10] he had seen another piece of wood brought by the same wind, carved as well as the aforementioned one, and that canes had also drifted in, so thick that one joint held nine decanters of wine. He said that in conversation with the Portuguese King he had told him the same thing and had shown him the canes. Since such canes do not grow anywhere in our lands, he was sure that the wind had blown them from some neighboring

7. For Pliny, see Source 5; for Marco Polo, Source 9; for John Mandeville, Source 10; and for Pierre d'Ailly, Source 11. Julius Capitolinus was a Roman writer of about A.D. 300.

8. **league:** usually around 3 nautical miles, though its exact distance has varied.

9. Cape St. Vincent is the southwest corner of Portugal.

10. Pôrto Santo is one of the islands of Madeira.

Chapter 11

Pagans,

Muslims, and

Christians in the

Mental World

of Columbus

islands or perhaps from India. Ptolemy in the first book of his *Geography*, Chapter 17, writes that such canes are found in the eastern parts of the Indies.

Source 4 from Geography of Claudius Ptolemy, *translated and edited by Edward Luther Stevenson (New York: New York Public Library, 1932), extracts from chapters 3, 5, 6, 12. Courtesy of The New York Public Library, Astor, Lenox and Tilden Foundations.*

4. From Ptolemy's *Geography*

Those geographers who lived before us sought to fix correct distance on the earth, not only that they might determine the length of the greatest circle, but also that they might determine the extent which a region occupied in one plane on one and the same meridian. After observing therefore, by means of the instruments of which I have spoken, the points which were directly over each terminus of the given distance, they calculated from the intercepted part of the circumference of the meridian, distances on the earth.

[Ptolemy then describes various instruments for measuring shadows, and notes how one uses measurements of the shadows at different points on the earth's surface to calculate the circumference of the earth. This method was first devised by Eratosthenes (ca 275–195 B.C.), librarian of the Museum of Alexandria and the first in the West to write a book titled "Geography."]

After these preliminary remarks we are able to make a beginning of our work. Since, however, all regions cannot be known fully on account of their great size, or because they are not always of the same shape or because not yet satisfactorily explored, and a greater length of time makes our knowledge of them more certain, we think we should say something to the readers of our geography on the subject of varying traditions at various times, viz., of some portions of our continents, on account of their great size, we have as yet no knowledge; with regard to other parts we do not know what is their real nature, because of the negligence of those who have explored them in failing to give us carefully prepared reports; other parts of the earth are different to-day from what they were, either on account of revolution or from transformation, in which processes they are known to have partially passed into ruin.

We consider it necessary therefore for us to pay more attention to the newer records of our own time, weighing, however, in our description these new records and those of former times and deciding what is credible and what is incredible.

Marinus the Tyrian, the latest of the geographers of our time, seems to us to have thrown himself with the utmost zeal into this matter.

He is known to have found out many things that were not known before. He has searched most diligently the works of almost all the historians who preceded him. He has not only corrected their errors, but the reader can clearly see that he has undertaken to correct those parts of the work which he himself had done badly in the earlier editions of his geographical maps. . . .

[However,] He considers that our earth[11] extends a greater distance in longitude eastward, and to a greater distance in latitude southward than is right and true.

[Marinus had proposed that the Eurasian land mass extended 225°, but Ptolemy arrives at a different figure.]

. . . Hence, the length of the known earth, that is, from the meridian drawn through or terminated by the Fortunate Islands[12] in the extreme west, to Sera[13] in the extreme east is 177°15′.

Source 5 from Pliny, Natural History, *translated by H. Rackham. Loeb Classical Library (Cambridge, Mass.: Harvard University Press, 1938), vol. 2, pp. 377, 521.*

5. From Pliny, *Natural History*

After leaving the Caspian Sea and the Scythian Ocean our course takes a bend towards the Eastern Sea as the coast turns to face eastward. The first part of the coast after the Scythian promontory is uninhabitable on account of snow, and the neighbouring region is uncultivated because of the savagery of the tribes that inhabit it. This is the country of the Cannibal Scythians who eat human bodies; consequently the adjacent districts are waste deserts thronging with wild beasts lying in wait for human beings as savage as themselves. . . . Megasthenes[14] states that on the mountain named Nulus there are people with their feet turned backwards and with eight toes on each foot, while on many of the mountains there is a tribe of human beings with dogs' heads, who wear a covering of wild beasts' skins, whose speech is a bark and who live on the produce of hunting and fowling, for which they use their nails as weapons; he says that they numbered more than 120,000 when he published his work. Ctesias[15] writes that also among a certain race of India the women bear children only once in their life-time, and the children begin to turn grey directly after birth; he also describes a tribe of men called the

11. By "our earth" Ptolemy means the land mass of the world known to him, that is, Eurasia and Africa.
12. **Fortunate Islands:** the name given to various Atlantic Island groups. Here, probably the Canaries.
13. **Sera:** probably Seram (Ceram), an island in Indonesia.
14. Megasthenes was sent as an envoy to an Indian ruler by the ruler of Syria in about 300 B.C. His report survived, in fragments, to Pliny's time.
15. Ctesias was a Greek physician and historian of Persia and India who lived about 400 B.C.

Chapter 11

Pagans,

Muslims, and

Christians in the

Mental World

of Columbus

Monocoli who have only one leg, and who move in jumps with surprising speed; the same are called the Umbrella-foot tribe, because in the hotter weather they lie on their backs on the ground and protect themselves with the shadow of their feet; and that they are not far away from the Cave-dwellers; and again westward from these there are some people without necks, having their eyes in their shoulders.

Source 6 from Pierre-Amédée Jaubert, La Géographie d'Édrisi, *translated from Arabic (Amsterdam: Philo Press, 1975), 3rd climate, 1st section, pp. 200–201; 4th climate, 1st section, pp. 26–29. English translation by Julius Ruff.*

6. From Abu Abdallah Mohammed Idrisi, *Geography*

In the same sea there is the Island of Calhan, the inhabitants of which are human in form but bear animal heads. They plunge into the sea, draw out of its depths the animals that they were able to catch, and then feed on them. Another island of the same sea is named the Island of the Two Magician Brothers. . . . It lies opposite the port of Asafi[16] and at such a distance that, when the atmosphere is free of mist over the sea, it is said that from the continent one can catch sight of the smoke that rises from the island. . . . "Curious details relative to this island were gathered from the words of the Maghrourins,[17] travelers from the town of Achbouna (Lisbon) in Spain when the port of Asafi received this name because of them. The account of this adventure is rather long, and we will have the opportunity to return to it when Lisbon is our subject."

In this sea there also lies an island of vast extent covered with thick darkness. It is named the Island of Sheep because there are indeed many of them there. But the flesh of these animals is so bitter that it is impossible to eat it, if we give credit to the account of the Maghrourins. Near the island that we have just mentioned there is Raca, the island of the birds[18]. . . .

It was from Lisbon that the Maghrourins' expedition departed "having the objective to know what comprises the ocean and what its limits are." As we said above, there still exists a street bearing the name Maghrourin Street (or Road) in Lisbon near the hot baths.

Here is how the thing came about. Eight close relatives got together and built a transport ship into which they loaded water and provisions sufficient for a voyage of several months. They set forth on the sea at the first east

16. **Asafi:** the town of Safi, on the west coast of present-day Morocco.
17. **Maghrourins:** the word means "adventurers."
18. Perhaps one of the Canary Islands.

breeze. After having sailed for about eleven days, they reached a poorly-illuminated sea in which heavy waves emitted a rank odor and concealed numerous reefs. Fearing destruction, they changed the direction of their sails and hastened south for twelve days and reached the Island of Sheep, thus named because numerous flocks of sheep graze there without shepherds or anyone to guard them.

Having landed on this island, they found there a spring of flowing water and wild fig-trees. They caught and killed some sheep, but the flesh of them was so bitter that it was impossible to feed on it. They only kept the skins, sailed again twelve days, and finally caught sight of an island that seemed inhabited and cultivated. They approached it in order to learn what it was but were soon surrounded by boats, made prisoners, and led to a town situated on the seashore. They entered a house where they saw men of great height, swarthy, and of reddish color, wearing long hair, and women who were of a rare beauty. They remained three days in this house. On the fourth day they saw a man arrive who spoke the Arab language and who asked them who they were, why they had come, and what was their country. They told him all of their adventures; the latter gave them good hope and told them he was an interpreter. Two days later they were presented to the king of the land who asked them the same questions, to which they replied, as they had already replied to the interpreter, that they had ventured forth on the sea in order to learn what was strange and curious in it and to ascertain its extreme limits.

When the king heard them thus speak, he began to laugh and said to the interpreter: Explain to these people that once upon a time my father ordered some of his slaves to embark on this sea and that they traversed its breadth for a month until, the sky's light having entirely failed them, they were forced to give up this vain undertaking. The king, moreover, ordered the interpreter to assure the Maghrourins of his goodwill so that they might hold a good opinion of him, which was done. They then returned to their prison and remained there until a west wind arose and their captors blindfolded them, made them board a boat, and had them row for some time on the sea. We sailed, they said, for nearly three days and three nights and we reached a shore where they landed us, with our hands bound behind our backs, and where we were abandoned. We remained there until sunrise in the most dejected state because of the bonds which strongly tied us and which much troubled us. Finally, having heard bursts of laughter and human voices, we began to utter cries. Then some inhabitants of the country came to us and, finding us in such a miserable situation, talked with us and posed various questions to which we replied with the tale of our adventure. They were Berbers. One of them said to us: Do you know how far you are from your own county? Upon our negative reply, he added: It is a two-month journey from the spot where you find yourselves to your native land. Those among these individuals who seemed the most eminent said unceasingly: Wasafi (Alas!). This is why the name of the place is

Chapter 11

Pagans,

Muslims, and

Christians in the

Mental World

of Columbus

today still Asafi. It is the port that we have already described as being at the end of the west.

Source 7 from Ibn Fadl Allah al'Umari, Masalik al-Absar, *manuscript in Cairo MS. English translation in Abbas Hamdani, "An Islamic Background to the Voyages of Discovery," in Salma Khadra Jayyusi,* The Legacy of Muslim Spain *(Leiden: E.J. Brill, 1992), p. 276. Reprinted by permission of Abbas Hamdani.*

7. From Ibn Fadl Allah al-Umari, *Masalik al-Absar*

The ruler who preceded me did not believe it was impossible to reach the extremity of the ocean that encircles the earth [here meaning the Atlantic]; he wanted to reach that [end], and was determined to pursue his plan. So he equipped two hundred boats full of men, and many others with water, gold and provisions, sufficient for several years. He ordered the captain not to return until he had reached the other end of the ocean, or until he had exhausted the provisions and water. So they set out on their journey. They were absent for a long period, and at last just one boat returned. When questioned, the captain replied: "O Prince, we navigated for a long period, until we saw in the midst of the ocean a great river which flowed massively. My boat was the last one; others were ahead of me, and they were drowned in the great whirlpool and never came out again. I sailed back to escape this current."[19] But the Sultan would not believe him. He ordered two thousand boats to be equipped for him and for his men, and one thousand more for water and provisions. Then he conferred the regency on me for the term of his absence and departed with his men, never to return or show any sign of life. In this manner I became the sole ruler of the empire.

Source 8 from Henry Yule, editor and translator, H. Cordier, reviser of 2d ed., Cathay and the Way Thither *(London: Hakluyt Society, 1913–1916), vol. III, pp. 45–51. Notes from A. Andrea and J. Overfield,* The Human Record *(Boston: Houghton Mifflin, 1990), pp. 350–352. Copyright ©1990 by Houghton Mifflin Company. Used by permission.*

8. Letter of John of Monte Corvino

I, Friar John of Monte Corvino, of the order of Minor Friars,[20] departed from Tauris, a city of the Persians,[21] in the year of the Lord 1291, and proceeded to

---

19. A number of historians have concluded that this river was the Amazon in Brazil, as ocean currents in this region can carry ships across the Atlantic.

20. **Minor Friars:** the "lesser brethren," the official name of the Franciscans.

21. Tauris (modern Tabriz, Iran) was the capital city of the il-khan of Persia.

India. And I remained in the country of India, wherein stands the church of St. Thomas the Apostle, for thirteen months, and in that region baptized in different places about one hundred persons. The companion of my journey was Friar Nicholas of Pistoia, of the order of Preachers[22] who died there, and was buried in the church aforesaid.

I proceeded on my further journey and made my way to Cathay, the realm of the Emperor of the Tatars[23] who is called the Grand Cham.[24] To him I presented the letter of our Lord the Pope, and invited him to adopt the Catholic Faith of our Lord Jesus Christ, but he had grown too old in idolatry. However he bestows many kindnesses upon the Christians, and these two years past I am abiding with him. . . .

I have built a church in the city of Cambaliech,[25] in which the king has his chief residence. This I completed six years ago; and I have built a belltower to it, and put three bells in it. I have baptized there, as well as I can estimate, up to this time some 6,000 persons; and if those charges against me of which I have spoken had not been made, I should have baptized more than 30,000. And I am often still engaged in baptizing.

Also I have gradually bought one hundred and fifty boys, the children of pagan parents, and of ages varying from seven to eleven, who had never learned any religion. These boys I have baptized, and I have taught them Greek and Latin after our manner. Also I have written out Psalters for them, with thirty Hymnaries and two Breviaries.[26] By help of these, eleven of the boys already know our service, and form a choir and take thier weekly turn of duty as they do in convents, whether I am there or not. Many of the boys are also employed in writing out Psalters and other things suitable. His Majesty the Emperor moreover delights much to hear them chanting. I have the bells rung at all the canonical hours, and with my congregation of babes and sucklings I perform divine service, and the chanting we do by ear because I have no service book with the notes.

A certain king of this part of the world, by name George, belonging to the sect of Nestorian Christians,[27] and of the illustrious family of that great king

---

22. Also known as the Dominicans.

23. **Emperor of the Tatars:** Timur (1294–1307). Although Western visitors used the names Tatar (or, incorrectly, Tartar) and Mongol interchangeably, the Tatars, who spoke a Turkic language, were not Mongols. There was, however, some intermarriage among these various steppe nomads. For example, the Turkish warlord Timur the Lame (1336–1405) had some Mongol ancestry.

24. More often spelled "khan."

25. **Cambaliech:** Khanbalik.

26. Various prayer books.

27. **Nestorian Christians:** followers of Nestorius, a fifth-century Christian leader who held ideas about the relationship between the divine and human natures of Jesus Christ that differed from those held by a majority of Church leaders. Nestorius's ideas were declared to be heresy, but they were accepted by many Christians in Iraq, Iran, and India. Nestorian Christians today number around 100,000, many of whom are in the United States.

Chapter 11

Pagans,

Muslims, and

Christians in the

Mental World

of Columbus

who was called Prester John[28] of India, in the first year of my arrival here attached himself to me, and being converted by me to the truth of the Catholic faith, took the lesser orders,[29] and when I celebrated mass he used to attend me wearing his royal robes. Certain others of the Nestorians on this account accused him of apostasy, but he brought over a great part of his people with him to the true Catholic faith, and built a church on a scale of royal magnificence in honor of our God, of the Holy Trinity, and of our lord the Pope, giving it the name of the *Roman Church.*

This King George six years ago departed to the Lord a true Christian, leaving as his heir a son scarcely out of the cradle, and who is now nine years old. And after King George's death his brothers, perfidious followers of the errors of Nestorius, perverted again all those whom he had brought over to the church, and carried them back to their original schismatical creed. And being all alone, and not able to leave his Majesty the Cham, I could not go to visit the church above-mentioned, which is twenty days' journey distant.

Yet, if I could but get some good fellow-workers to help me, I trust in God that all this might be retrieved, for I still possess the grant which was made in our favor by the late King George before mentioned. So I say again that if it had not been for the slanderous charges which I have spoken of, the harvest reaped by this time would have been great!

Indeed if I had had but two or three comrades to aid me 'tis possible that the Emperor Cham would have been baptized by this time! I ask then for such brethren to come, if any are willing to come, such I mean as will make it their great business to lead exemplary lives. . . .

I have myself grown old and grey, more with toil and trouble than with years; for I am not more than fifty-eight. I have got a competent knowledge of the language and character which is most generally used by the Tatars. And I have already translated into that language and character the New Testament and the Psalter, and have caused them to be written out in the fairest penmanship they have; and so by writing, reading, and preaching, I bear open and public testimony to the Law of Christ. And I had been in treaty with the late King George, if he had lived, to translate the whole Latin ritual, that it might be sung throughout the whole extent of his territory; and whilst he was alive I used to celebrate mass in his church, according to the Latin ritual, reading in the before-mentioned language and character the words of both the preface and the Canon.[30]

And the son of the king before-mentioned is called after my name, John; and I hope in God that he will walk in his father's steps.

28. **Prester John:** a mythic Christian king of the East, who supposedly sought reunion with the West. His kingdom was variously located in Ethiopia, India, and Central Asia, all of which had Christian communities long separated from the West.

29. He was admitted to the four lesser clerical offices below those of priest, deacon, and sub deacon.

30. **preface and canon:** two parts of the Mass.

As far as I ever saw or heard tell, I do not believe that any king or prince in the world can be compared to his majesty the Cham in respect to the extent of his dominions, the vastness of their population, or the amount of his wealth. Here I stop.

Dated at the city of Cambalec in the kingdom of Cathay, in the year of the Lord 1305, and on the 8th day of January.

Source 9 from Manuel Komroff, The Travels of Marco Polo *(New York: The Modern Library, 1953), pp. 259–260, 263, 267, 274, 280, 281–282, 289–290, 303–304. Copyright 1926 by Boni & Liveright, Inc., renewed 1953 by Manuel Komroff. Reprinted by permission of Liveright Publishing Corporation.*

9. From *The Travels of Marco Polo*

Zipangu [Japan] is an island in the eastern ocean, situated at the distance of about fifteen hundred miles from the main-land, or coast of Manji.

It is of considerable size; its inhabitants have fair complexions, are well made, and are civilized in their manners. Their religion is the worship of idols. They are independent of every foreign power, and governed only by their own kings. They have gold in the greatest abundance, its sources being inexhaustible, but as the king does not allow it being exported, few merchants visit the country. Nor is it frequented by much shipping from other parts.

The extraordinary richness of the sovereign's palace, according to what we are told by those who have access to the place, is a wonderful sight. The entire roof is covered with a plating of gold, in the same manner as we cover houses, or more properly churches, with lead. The ceilings of the halls are of the same precious metal; many of the apartments have small tables of pure gold, of considerable thickness; and the windows also have golden ornaments. So vast, indeed, are the riches of the palace, that it is impossible to convey an idea of them.

In this island there are pearls also, in large quantities, of a pink colour, round in shape, and of great size equal in value to, or even exceeding that of the white pearls. . . .

In this island of Zipangu and the others in its vicinity, their idols are fashioned in a variety of shapes, some of them having the heads of oxen, some of swine, of dogs, goats, and many other animals. . . .

The various ceremonies practiced before these idols are so wicked and diabolical that it would be nothing less than an abomination to give an account of them in this book. The reader should, however, be informed that the idolatrous inhabitants of these islands, when they seize the person of an enemy who has not the means of effecting his ransom for money, invite to their house

Chapter 11

Pagans,

Muslims, and

Christians in the

Mental World

of Columbus

all their relations and friends. Putting their prisoner to death they cook and eat the body, in a convivial manner, asserting that human flesh surpasses every other in the excellence of its flavour. . . .

Departing from Ziamba, and steering between south and south-east, fifteen hundred miles, you reach an island of very great size, named Java. According to the reports of some well-informed navigators, it is the greatest in the world, and has a compass above three thousand miles. It is under the dominion of one king only, nor do the inhabitants pay tribute to any other power. They are worshippers of idols.

The country abounds with rich commodities. Pepper, nutmegs, spikenard, galangal, cubebs, cloves and all the other valuable spices and drugs, are the produce of the island; which occasion it to be visited by many ships laden with merchandise, that yields to the owners considerable profit.

The quantity of gold collected there exceeds all calculation and belief. . . .

In this kingdom are found men with tails, a span[31] in length, like those of the dog, but not covered with hair. The greater number of them are formed in this manner, but they dwell in the mountains, and do not inhabit towns. . . .

Leaving the island of Zeilan,[32] and sailing in a westerly direction sixty miles, you reach the great province of Maabar, which is not an island, but a part of the continent of the greater India, as it is termed, being the noblest and richest country in the world.

The natives of this part of the country always go naked, excepting that they cover with a piece of cloth those parts of the body which modesty dictates.

The king is no more clothed than the rest, except that he has a piece of richer cloth, and is honourably distinguished by various kinds of ornaments, such as a collar set with jewels, sapphires, emeralds, and rubies, of immense value. . . .

Distant from Kesmacoran about five hundred miles toward the south, in the ocean, there are two islands within about thirty miles from each other. One of these is inhabited by men, without the company of women, and is called Island of Males; and the other by women, without men, which is called the Island of Females.

The inhabitants of both are of the same race, and are baptized Christians, but hold the law of the Old Testament. The men visit the Island of Females, and remain with them for three successive months, namely, March, April, and May, each man occupying a separate habitation along with his wife. They then return to the male island, where they live the rest of the year, without the society of any female.

The wives retain their sons with them until they are of the age of twelve years, when they are sent to join their fathers. The daughters they keep at

31. **span:** nine inches.
32. **Zeilan:** Ceylon.

home until they become marriageable, and then they bestow them upon some of the men of the other island.

Source 10 from The Travels of Sir John Mandeville *(London: Macmillan, 1905), pp. 103–104, 125–130.*

10. From *The Travels of Sir John Mandeville*

Beside that isle that I have spoken of, there is another isle that is clept[33] Sumobor. That is a great isle, and the king thereof is right mighty. The folk of that isle make them always to be marked in the visage[34] with an hot iron, both men and women, for great noblesse, for to be known from other folk; for they hold themselves most noble and most worthy of all the world. And they have war always with the folk that go all naked.

And fast beside is another isle, that is clept Betemga, that is a good isle and a plenteous. And many other isles be thereabout, where there be many of diverse folk, of the which it were too long to speak of all.

But fast beside that isle, for to pass by sea, is a great isle and a great country that men clepe Java. And it is nigh two thousand mile in circuit. And the king of that country is a full great lord and a rich and a mighty, and hath under him seven other kings of seven other isles about him. This isle is full well inhabited and full well manned. There grow all manner of spicery, more plenteously than in any other country, as of ginger, cloves-gilofre, canell, seedwall, nutmegs and maces. . . .

Many other spices and many other goods grow in that isle. For of all things is there plenty, save only of wine. But there is gold and silver, great plenty.

And the king of that country hath a palace full noble and full marvellous, and more rich than any in the world. . . .

In that isle is a dead sea, that is a lake that hath no ground; and if anything fall into that lake it shall never come up again. In that lake grow reeds, that be canes, that they clepe Thaby[35] that be thirty fathoms[35] long. . . . Of those canes they make houses and ships and other things, as we have here, making houses and ships of oak or of any other trees. And deem no man that I say it but for a trifle, for I have seen of the canes with mine own eyes, full many times, lying upon the river of that lake, of the which twenty of our fellows ne might not lift up ne bear one to the earth. . . .

33. **clept:** called.
34. **visage:** face.
35. **fathom:** six feet.

Chapter 11

Pagans,

Muslims, and

Christians in the

Mental World

of Columbus

Afterward men go by many isles by sea unto an isle that men clepe Milke. And there is a full cursed people For they delight in nothing more than for to fight and to slay men. And they drink gladliest man's blood, the which they clepe Dieu. And the more men that a man may slay, the more worship he hath amongst them. And if two persons be at debate and, peradventure, be accorded[36] by their friends of by some of their alliance, it behoveth[37] that every of them shall be accorded drink of other's blood: and else the accord ne the alliance is nought worth: ne it shall not be no reproof to him to break the alliance and the accord, but if every of them drink of others' blood. . . .

Beside the land of Chaldea is the land of Amazonia, that is the land of Feminye. And in that realm is all women and no man; not, as some men say, that men may not live there, but for because that the women will not suffer no men amongst them to be their sovereigns.

For sometime there was a king in that country. And men married, as in other countries. And so befell that the king had war with them of Scythia, the which king hight[38] Colopeus, that was slain in battle, and all the good blood of his realm. And when the queen and all the other noble ladies saw that they were all widows, and that all the royal blood was lost, they armed them and, as creatures out of wit, they slew all the men of the country that were left; for they would that all the women were widows as the queen and they were. And from that time hitherwards they never would suffer men to dwell amongst them longer than seven days and seven nights; ne that no child that were male should dwell amongst them longer than he were nourished; and then sent to his father. And when they will have any company of man then they draw them towards the lands marching next to them. And then they have loves that use them; and they dwell with them an eight days or ten, and then go home again. And if they have any knave child they keep it a certain time, and then send it to the father when he can go alone and eat by himself; or else they slay it. And if it be a female they do away that one pap with an hot iron. And if it be a woman of great lineage they do away the left pap that they may the better bear a shield. And if it be a woman on foot they do away the right pap, for to shoot with bow turkeys: for they shoot well with bows.

36. **accorded:** reconciled.
37. **behoveth:** is necessary.
38. **hight:** was called.

Source 11 from Pierre d'Ailly, Imago Mundi, *translated by Edwin F. Keever (Wilmington, N.C.: privately published, 1948), extracts from chapters 41, 42, 49.*

11. From Pierre d'Ailly, *Imago Mundi*

We also discuss other islands of the ocean which Isidore has in mind. . . .

The Fortunate Isles signify by their name that all things are usually propitious: fortunate because of the abundance of fruitage. The forests yield precious fruit trees; the slopes of the hills are clothed with promising grape vines. Hence it is an error of the gentiles to regard the islands as Paradise because of the fecundity of the soil. The first of them is called Nembriona, the second Juniona, the third Theode, the fourth Capraria, another Minaria, which is in a dense and vaporous cloud. Then Caninaria, abounding in dogs of immense size. All of the isles have many birds, good pastures, a great number of palms, nut trees and pines; rich in honey, and plentiful in animals, forests and fish. These islands are situated in the ocean opposite the left side of the Mauretania, between the south and the west, closest to the west, and scattered about over intervals of the sea.

The Gorgodes Islands of the ocean are in the direction of a promontory called 'Esperacerus'. They are inhabited by the Gorgodes, women of destructiveness, with coarse and hairy bodies. The islands were named for them. They are distant from the continent by a two-day sail. . . .

On account of its marvels special notice must be taken of Taprobane the island of India which, according to Oresius[39] contains ten cities. It lies in the east where the Indian Ocean begins, extending 875,000 paces in length, and 225,000 stadia in breadth. It is totally cut off by an interflowing stream. It is full of pearls and precious stones. Part of it abounds in beasts and elephants, and part is inhabited by the people, who are powerful in body beyond all measurements; with red hair, blue eyes and harsh voices. They hold no intercourse by speech with any other tribe. They offer their commodities with other merchants on the river-bank, and exchange amenities reluctantly. With them life is prolonged beyond human infirmity, so that one who dies a centenarian comes to his end immaturely. They take no sleep during the day. Annual harvests are never interrupted. Houses are small and humble; of cities they know nothing. Fruits are plentiful. They enjoy husbandry and hunting; indeed they take pleasure in pursuing tigers and elephants. Quite oddly they cover the capacious houses of their families with the backs of turtles. . . .

After having discussed the heavens and the earth and their respective parts it seems fitting to say something about water. . . .

---

39. **Orosius:** Paulus Orosius (fl. 390–417), a cleric and author of a popular geographic and historical treatise, *Historia adversum paganos.*

Chapter 11

Pagans,

Muslims, and

Christians in the

Mental World

of Columbus

. . . The water runs down from one pole toward the other into the body of the sea and spreads out between the confines of Spain and the beginning of India, of no great width, in such a way that the beginning of India can be beyond the middle of the equinoctial circle and approach beneath the earth quite close to the coast of Spain. Likewise Aristotle and his commentator in the 'Libro Coeli et Mundi' came to the same conclusion because there are so many elephants in those regions. Says Pliny: 'Around Mt. Atlas elephants abound.' So also in India and even in ulterior Spain there are great herds of elephants. But, reasons Aristotle, the elephants in both those places ought to show similar characteristics; if widely separated they would not have the same characteristics. Therefore he concludes those countries are close neighbors and that a small sea intervenes; and moreover that the sea covers three-quarters of the earth; that the beginnings of the east and the west are near by, since a small sea separates them.

Source 12 from The Life of the Admiral Christopher Columbus by His Son Ferdinand, trans. and annotated by Benjamin Keen (New Brunswick, NJ: Rutgers University Press, 1958), pp. 19–22. Copyright © 1959, 1992 by Rutgers, The State University. Reprinted by permission of Rutgers University Press.

12. Letter to Columbus from Paolo del Pozzo Toscanelli

Paolo the physician, to Christopher Columbus, Greetings.

I perceive your noble and grand desire to go to the places where the spices grow; and in reply to your letter I send you a copy of another letter which some time since I sent to a friend of mine, a gentleman of the household of the most serene King of Portugal, before the wars of Castile,[40] in reply to another which by command of His Highness he wrote me on this subject; and I send you another sea-chart like the one I sent him, that your demands may be satisfied. A copy of that letter of mine follows:

Paolo the physician, to Fernão Martins, canon of Lisbon, Greetings.

I was glad to hear of your intimacy and friendship with your most serene and magnificent King. I have often before spoken of a sea route from here to the Indies, where the spices grow, a route shorter than the one which you are pursuing by way of Guinea. You tell me that His Highness desires from me some statement or demonstration that would make it easier to understand and take that route. I could do this by using a sphere shaped like the earth, but I decided that it would be easier and make the point clearer if I showed that

40. Wars between Portugal and Castile 1475–1479, which ended in Castilian victory.

route by means of a sea-chart. I therefore send His Majesty a chart drawn by my own hand, upon which is laid out the western coast from Ireland on the north to the end of Guinea, and the islands which lie on that route, in front of which, directly to the west, is shown the beginning of the Indies, with the islands and places at which you are bound to arrive, and how far from the Arctic Pole or the Equator you ought to keep away, and how much space or how many leagues intervene before you reach those places most fertile in all sorts of spices, jewels, and precious stones. And do not marvel at my calling "west" the regions where the spices grow, although they are commonly called "east"; because whoever sails westward will always find those lands in the west, while one who goes overland to the east will always find the same lands in the east.

The straight lines drawn lengthwise on this map show the distance from east to west; the transverse lines indicate distance from north to south. I have also drawn on the map various places in India to which one could go in case of a storm or contrary winds, or some other mishap.

And that you may be as well informed about all those regions as you desire to be, you must know that none but merchants live and trade in all those islands. There is as great a number of ships and mariners with their merchandise here as in all the rest of the world, especially in a very noble port called Zaiton,[41] where every year they load and unload a hundred large ships laden with pepper, besides many other ships loaded with other spices. This country is very populous, with a multitude of provinces and kingdoms and cities without number, under the rule of a prince who is called the Great Khan, which name in our speech signifies King of Kings, who resides most of the time in the province of Cathay. His predecessors greatly desired to have friendship and dealings with the Christians, and about two hundred years ago they sent ambassadors to the Pope, asking for many learned men and teachers to instruct them in our faith; but these ambassadors, encountering obstacles on the way, turned back without reaching Rome. In the time of Pope Eugenius[42] there came to him an ambassador who told of their great feeling of friendship for the Christians, and I had a long talk with him about many things: about the great size of their royal palaces and the marvelous length and breadth of their rivers, and the multitude of cities in their lands, so that no one river alone there are two hundred cities, with marble bridges very long and wide, adorned with many columns. This country is as rich as any that has ever been found; not only could it yield great gain and many costly things,

41. **Zaiton:** modern Tsinkiang, on the inlet of Formosa Strait.

42. Pope Eugenius IV (1431–1447), who convened a church council in Florence, attempting to unite the various branches of the Christian church. Representatives of eastern Christian churches attended this council, and the envoy Toscanelli reports speaking with probably was a Nestorian Christian sent by a Mongol ruler.

Chapter 11

Pagans,

Muslims, and

Christians in the

Mental World

of Columbus

but from it may also be had gold and silver and precious stones and all sorts of spices in great quantity, which at present are not carried to our countries. And it is true that many learned men, philosophers and astronomers, and many other men skilled in all the arts, govern this great province and conduct its wars.

From the city of Lisbon due west there are twenty-six spaces marked on the map, each of which contains two hundred and fifty miles, as far as the very great and noble city of Quinsay.[43] This city is about one hundred miles in circumference, which is equal to thirty-five leagues, and has ten marble bridges. Marvelous things are told about its great buildings, its arts, and its revenues. That city lies in the province of Mangi, near the province of Cathay,[44] in which the king resides the greater part of the time. And from the island of Antillia,[45] which you call the Island of the Seven Cities, to the very noble island of Cipango,[46] there are ten spaces, which make 2,500 miles, that is two hundred and twenty-five leagues. This land is most rich in gold, pearls, and precious stones, and the temples and royal palaces are covered with solid gold. But because the way is not known, all these things are hidden and covered, though one can travel thither with all security.

Many other things could I say, but since I have already told them to you by word of mouth, and you are a man of good judgment, I know there remains nothing for me to explain. I have tried to satisfy your demands as well as the pressure of time and my work has permitted, and I remain ready to serve His Highness and answer his questions at greater length if he should order me to do so.

Done in the city of Florence, June 25, 1474.

43. **Quinsay:** modern Hangchow.

44. Drawing on Marco Polo, Toscanelli uses the term *Mangi* for southern China, and *Cathay* for northern China.

45. **Antilla:** a mythical island in the Atlantic. See Source 14.

46. **Cipango:** Japan.

Source 13 from Tony Campbell, The Earliest Printed Maps 1472–1500 (London: British Library, 1987), plate 36. Photo: British Library.

13. Map of the World from Ptolemy's Geography

Chapter 11

Pagans,

Muslims, and

Christians in the

Mental World

of Columbus

Source 14 from R. A. Skelton, Explorers' Maps: Chapters in the Cartographic Record of Geographical Discovery *(London: Routledge and Kegan Paul, 1958), fig. 29. Photo: Biblioteca Nazionale di Roma.*

14. Sailor's chart (detail) of the Atlantic Islands drawn by Bartolomeo Pareto in Genoa (1455)

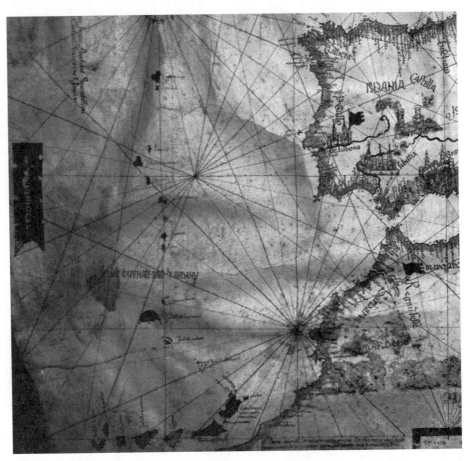

Source 15 from R. H. Major, editor and translator, Select Letters of Christopher Columbus *(London: Hakluyt Society, 1847), pp. 1–15.*

15. Letter from Christopher Columbus (1493)

A letter addressed to the noble Lord Raphael Sanchez, Treasurer to their most invincible Majesties, Ferdinand and Isabella, King and Queen of Spain, by Christopher Columbus, to whom our age is greatly indebted, treating of the islands of India recently discovered beyond the Ganges, to explore which he had been sent eight months before under the auspices and at the expense of their said Majesties.

Knowing that it will afford you pleasure to learn that I have brought my undertaking to a successful termination, I have decided upon writing you this letter to acquaint you with all the events which have occurred in my voyage, and the discoveries which have resulted from it. Thirty-three days after my departure from Cadiz I reached the Indian sea, where I discovered many islands, thickly peopled, of which I took possession without resistance in the name of our most illustrious Monarch, by public proclamation and with unfurled banners. To the first of these islands, which is called by the Indians Guanahani, I gave the name of the blessed Saviour (San Salvador), relying upon whose protection I had reached this as well as the other islands; to each of these I also gave a name, ordering that one should be called Santa Maria de la Concepcion,[47] another Fernandina,[48] the third Isabella,[49] the fourth Juana,[50] and so with all the rest respectively. As soon as we arrived at that, which as I have said was named Juana, I proceeded along its coast a short distance westward, and found it to be so large and apparently without termination, that I could not suppose it to be an island, but the continental province of Cathay.[51] Seeing, however, no towns or populous places on the sea coast, but only a few detached houses and cottages, with whose inhabitants I was unable to communicate, because they fled as soon as they saw us, I went further on, thinking that in my progress I should certainly find some city or village. At length, after proceeding a great way and finding that nothing new presented itself, and that the line of coast was leading us northwards (which I wished to avoid, because it was winter, and it was my intention to move southwards; and because moreover the winds were contrary), I resolved not to attempt any further progress, but rather to turn back and retrace my course to a certain bay that I had observed, and from which I afterwards dispatched two of our men

47. **Santa Maria de la Concepcion:** North Caico.
48. **Fernandina:** Little Inagua.
49. **Isabella:** Great Inagua.
50. **Juana:** Cuba.
51. **Cathay:** China.

Chapter 11

Pagans,

Muslims, and

Christians in the

Mental World

of Columbus

to ascertain whether there were a king or any cities in that province. These men reconnoitred the country for three days, and found a most numerous population, and great numbers of houses, though small, and built without any regard to order: with which information they returned to us. In the mean time I had learned from some Indians whom I had seized, that the country was certainly an island: and therefore I sailed towards the east, coasting to the distance of three hundred and twenty-two miles, which brought us to the extremity of it; from this point I saw lying eastwards another island, fifty-four miles distant from Juana, to which I gave the name of Española.[52] I went thither, and steered my course eastward as I had done at Juana, even to the distance of five hundred and sixty-four miles along the north coast. This said island of Juana is exceedingly fertile, as indeed are all the others; it is surrounded with many bays, spacious, very secure, and surpassing any that I have ever seen; numerous large and healthful rivers intersect it, and it also contains many very lofty mountains. All these islands are very beautiful, and distinguished by a diversity of scenery; they are filled with a great variety of trees of immense height, and which I believe to retain their foliage in all seasons; for when I saw them they were as verdant and luxuriant as they usually are in Spain in the month of May—some of them were blossoming, some bearing fruit, and all flourishing in the greatest perfection, according to their respective stages of growth, and the nature and quality of each: yet the islands are not so thickly wooded as to be impassable. The nightingale and various birds were singing in countless numbers, and that in November, the month in which I arrived there. There are besides in the same island of Juana seven or eight kinds of palm trees, which, like all other trees, herbs, and fruits, considerably surpass ours in height and beauty. The pines also are very handsome, and there are very extensive fields and meadows, a variety of birds, different kinds of honey, and many sorts of metals, but no iron. In that island also which I have before said we named Española, there are mountains of very great size and beauty, vast plains, groves, and very fruitful fields, admirably adapted for tillage, pasture, and habitation. The convenience and excellence of the harbours in this island, and the abundance of the rivers, so indispensable to the health of man, surpass anything that would be believed by one who had not seen it. The trees, herbage, and fruits of Española are very different from those of Juana, and moreover it abounds in various kinds of spices, gold, and other metals. The inhabitants of both sexes in this island, and in all the others which I have seen, or of which I have received information, go always naked as they were born, with the exception of some of the women, who use the covering of a leaf, or small bough, or an apron of cotton which they prepare for that purpose. None of them, as I have already said, are possessed of any iron, neither have they weapons, being unacquainted with, and indeed

52. **Española:** Hispaniola, or San Domingo.

incompetent to use them, not from any deformity of body (for they are well-formed), but because they are timid and full of fear. They carry however in lieu of arms, canes dried in the sun, on the ends of which they fix heads of dried wood sharpened to a point, and even these they dare not use habitually; for it has often occurred when I have sent two or three of my men to any of the villages to speak with the natives, that they have come out in a disorderly troop, and have fled in such haste at the approach of our men, that the fathers forsook their children and the children their fathers. This timidity did not arise from any loss or injury that they had received from us; for, on the contrary, I gave to all I approached whatever articles I had about me, such as cloth and many other things, taking nothing of theirs in return: but they are naturally timid and fearful. As soon however as they see that they are safe, and have laid aside all fear, they are very simple and honest, and exceedingly liberal with all they have; none of them refusing any thing he may possess when he is asked for it, but on the contrary inviting us to ask them. They exhibit great love towards all others in preference to themselves: they also give objects of great value for trifles, and content themselves with very little or nothing in return. I however forbad that these trifles and articles of no value (such as pieces of dishes, plates, and glass, keys, and leather straps) should be given to them, although if they could obtain them, they imagined themselves to be possessed of the most beautiful trinkets in the world. It even happened that a sailor received for a leather strap as much gold as was worth three golden nobles, and for things of more trifling value offered by our men, especially newly coined blancas, or any gold coins, the Indians would give whatever the seller required; as, for instance, an ounce and a half or two ounces of gold, or thirty or forty pounds of cotton, with which commodity they were already acquainted. Thus they bartered, like idiots, cotton and gold for fragments of bows, glasses, bottles, and jars; which I forbad as being unjust, and myself gave them many beautiful and acceptable articles which I had brought with me, taking nothing from them in return; I did this in order that I might the more easily conciliate them, that they might be led to become Christians, and be inclined to entertain a regard for the King and Queen, our Princes and all Spaniards, and that I might induce them to take an interest in seeking out, and collecting, and delivering to us such things as they possessed in abundance, but which we greatly needed. They practise no kind of idolatry, but have a firm belief that all strength and power, and indeed all good things, are in heaven, and that I had descended from thence with these ships and sailors, and under this impression was I received after they had thrown aside their fears. Nor are they slow or stupid, but of very clear understanding; and those men who have crossed to the neighbouring islands give an admirable description of everything they observed; but they never saw any people clothed, nor any ships like ours. On my arrival at that sea, I had taken some Indians by force from the first island that I came to, in order that they might learn our language, and communicate to us what they knew respecting the country;

Chapter 11

Pagans,

Muslims, and

Christians in the

Mental World

of Columbus

which plan succeeded excellently, and was a great advantage to us, for in a short time, either by gestures and signs, or by words, we were enabled to understand each other. These men are still travelling with me, and although they have been with us now a long time, they continue to entertain the idea that I have descended from heaven; and on our arrival at any new place they published this, crying out immediately with a loud voice to the other Indians, "Come, come and look upon beings of a celestial race": upon which both women and men, children and adults, young men and old, when they got rid of the fear they at first entertained, would come out in throngs, crowding the roads to see us, some bringing food, others drink, with astonishing affection and kindness. Each of these islands has a great number of canoes, built of solid wood, narrow and not unlike our double-banked boats in length and shape, but swifter in their motion: they steer them only by the oar. These canoes are of various sizes, but the greater number are constructed with eighteen banks of oars, and with these they cross to the other islands, which are of countless number, to carry on traffic with the people. I saw some of these canoes that held as many as seventy-eight rowers. In all these islands there is no difference of physiognomy, of manners, or of language, but they all clearly understand each other, a circumstance very propitious for the realization of what I conceive to be the principal wish of our most serene King, namely, the conversion of these people to the holy faith of Christ, to which indeed, as far as I can judge, they are very favourable and well-disposed. I said before, that I went three hundred and twenty-two miles in a direct line from west to east, along the coast of the island of Juana; judging by which voyage, and the length of the passage, I can assert that it is larger than England and Scotland united; for independent of the said three hundred and twenty-two miles, there are in the western part of the island two provinces which I did not visit; one of these is called by the Indians Anam, and its inhabitants are born with tails. These provinces extend to a hundred and fifty-three miles in length, as I have learnt from the Indians whom I brought with me, and who are well acquainted with the country. But the extent of Española is greater than all Spain from Catalonia to Fontarabia, which is easily proved, because one of its four sides which I myself coasted in a direct line, from west to east, measures five hundred and forty miles. This island is to be regarded with especial interest, and not to be slighted; for although as I have said I took possession of all these islands in the name of our invincible King, and the government of them is unreservedly committed to his said Majesty, yet there was one large town in Española of which especially I took possession, situated in a remarkably favourable spot, and in every way convenient for the purposes of gain and commerce. To this town I gave the name of Navidad del Señor, and ordered a fortress to be built there, which must by this time be completed, in which I left as many men as I thought necessary, with all sorts of arms, and enough provisions for more than a year. I also left them one caravel, and skilful workmen both in ship-building and other arts, and engaged the favor and friendship of the King of the island in their behalf, to a degree that would not be believed, for these people are so amiable and friendly that even the King took a pride in calling me his brother. But supposing their feelings should become changed, and they should wish to injure those who have remained in the fortress, they could not do so, for they have no arms, they go naked, and are moreover too cowardly; so that those who hold the said fortress, can easily keep the whole island in check, without any pressing danger to themselves, provided they do not transgress the directions and regulations which I have given them. As far as I have learned, every man throughout these islands is united to but one wife, with the exception of the kings and princes, who are allowed to have twenty: the women seem to work more than the men. I could not clearly understand whether the people possess any private property, for I observed that one man had the charge of distributing various things to the rest, but especially meat and provisions and the like. I did not find, as some of us had expected, any cannibals amongst them, but on the contrary men of great deference and kindness. Neither are they black, like the Ethiopians: their hair is smooth and straight: for they do not dwell where the rays of the sun strike most vividly,—and the sun has intense power there, the distance from the equinoctial line being, it appears, but six-and-twenty degrees. On the tops of the mountains the cold is very great, but the effect of this upon the Indians is lessened by their being accustomed to the climate, and by their frequently indulging in the use of very hot meats and drinks. Thus, as I have already said, I saw no cannibals, nor did I hear of any, except in a certain island called Charis,[53] which is the second from Española on the side towards India, where dwell a people who are considered by the neighbouring islanders as most ferocious: and these feed upon human flesh. The same people have many kinds of canoes, in which they cross to all the surrounding islands and rob and plunder wherever they can; they are not different from the other islanders, except that they wear their hair long, like women, and make use of the bows and javelins of cane, with sharpened spear-points fixed on the thickest end, which I have before described, and therefore they are looked upon as ferocious, and regarded by the other Indians with unbounded fear; but I think no more of them than of the rest. These are the men who form union with certain women, who dwell alone in the island Matenin,[54] which lies next to Española on the side towards India; these latter employ themselves in no labour suitable to their own sex, for they use bows and javelins as I have already described their paramours as doing, and for defensive armour have plates of brass, of which metal they possess great abundance. They assure me that there is another island larger than Española, whose inhabitants have no hair, and which abounds in gold more than any of the rest. I bring with me individuals of this

53. **Charis:** Query Carib, the Indian name of Puerto Rico.
54. **Matenin:** one of the Virgin Islands—which, is uncertain.

Chapter 11

Pagans,

Muslims, and

Christians in the

Mental World

of Columbus

island and of the others that I have seen, who are proofs of the facts which I state. Finally, to compress into few words the entire summary of my voyage and speedy return, and of the advantages derivable therefrom, I promise, that with a little assistance afforded me by our most invincible sovereigns, I will procure them as much gold as they need, as great a quantity of spices, of cotton, and of mastic[55] (which is only found in Chios), and as many men for the service of the navy as their Majesties may require.

55. **mastic:** a resin used as an astringent and in varnish.

QUESTIONS TO CONSIDER

Columbus was not simply a sponge soaking up ideas he had read or heard about, but selectively chose those that supported his goals. From what you have read, you can probably guess which estimate of the size of the known world he adopted, Marinus's view of 225 degrees of longitude or Ptolemy's smaller version of 177 degrees.[56] Can you see how the maps printed in Ptolemy's *Geography*, such as that in Source 13, might have actually reinforced this larger estimate? (A hint here: Do the maps show an east coast for Asia?) As his son notes in Source 3, Columbus's estimates were also based on his calculations of the size of a longitudinal degree, which he took from the Arabic geographer al-Farghani as about 45 miles, not realizing (or not choosing to realize) that al-Farghani had reckoned in Arabic miles, which were

longer than the Roman miles Columbus used.[57]

As you have seen, along with ideas about the size of the globe and the distance from Europe to Asia, Columbus also developed clear preconceptions about the natural world and human cultures to be found in "the Indies." You have now read reports about both the islands of the Atlantic (Source 6) and the Eastern regions of Asia (Sources 8 through 10). Do you see any common features in these? Do these features emerge in Columbus's own writings? How might these commonalities have affected Columbus's assessment of his location?

The letters of John of Monte Corvino (Source 8) and Paolo Toscanelli (Source 12) both discuss the conversion of people in China to Christianity, a goal that looms especially large in Columbus's discussion of his and his sovereigns' motivations in Source 1. What comments

56. The actual size of the world known to Ptolemy and Marinus, which probably stretched from eastern Vietnam to the Canaries, is 127 degrees.

57. When the relative length of Arabic miles are taken into account, al-Farghani's estimates set the degree at 66 nautical miles, much closer to the actual distance of 60 nautical miles than Columbus's estimate of 45 miles.

does he make about this in his actual description of the New World (Source 15)? How do these comments fit with the actual experiences of John of Monte Corvino and with Toscanelli's report of his discussion with the ambassador from Cathay?

When evaluating Columbus's preconceptions, we must realize that he not only discussed these with many people in Europe, but also shared them, as best he could, with the Native Americans he met. You can see from Columbus's letter that the people he met did not initially oppose him and (if we choose to believe him on this point) were interested in pleasing him. How might they have responded to his questions about cannibals, tailed humans, and Amazon women? To his questions about the availability of gold and spices? What do they apparently tell him about people and natural products found on nearby islands? Would

such interchanges have worked to lodge Columbus's ideas more firmly or less firmly in his mind?

This chapter has asked you to focus on the mental world of Columbus, but you have probably noticed that most of the authors cite the same authorities that he does, that Aristotle, Ptolemy, Pliny, al-Farghani, and Marco Polo crop up everywhere. This reverence for standard authorities is often described as a hallmark of medieval European culture, with Columbus described as one of the first "modern men" who broke with this pattern. Based on your reading in this chapter, would you agree with this assessment? Does it surprise you that Columbus named the group of West Indian islands he discovered the Antilles (Antillia)? Would you say that Columbus regarded his voyages as extending earlier works of geography and travel, or as breaking with them?

EPILOGUE

As we have seen in this chapter, Columbus was eclectic in his reading and conversation, drawing information from wherever he could find it without regard for the culture or religion of the author or speaker. This breadth was accompanied, however, by a bitter opposition to Islam, a sense of European cultural superiority, and a view of himself as destined by God to spread Christianity. (He frequently signed his first name as *Christo-fero*—"Christ carrier" in

Latin—using the Greek letters for Christ as the first part of his name.) These tendencies did not come primarily from his readings, however, for earlier travelers, especially those to China during the Mongol Peace, show little evidence of racial prejudice; Columbus's contemporary Piero Toscanelli also describes with respect the "learned men ... skilled in all the arts" who govern China.

The New World was not China, however, and the respect accorded Chinese culture by medieval Europeans did not transfer to the cultures of the New World. In part, this was

Chapter 11

Pagans,

Muslims, and

Christians in the

Mental World

of Columbus

because they were *new;* that is, they were unknown to ancient authorities. Not only were there no Amazons, cannibals, or people with tails, but these were people who were completely outside a world-view derived from the Greeks and the Bible. (We would probably be less surprised to find intelligent life somewhere else in the universe than fifteenth-century Europeans were at finding the Americas and their residents.) This came at the time of the "rebirth" of classical culture in Europe, as we saw in Chapter 10, when educated Europeans prized, studied, and attempted to emulate the art, architecture, literature, and philosophy of the ancient Greeks and Romans. The peoples and cultures of the New World were so foreign to this enterprise, so far outside the newly developed story of highs and lows in European culture, that Europeans were unable—or unwilling—to accept them or learn about them on their own terms. Europeans in the sixteenth and seventeenth centuries did read travelers' accounts, as Columbus had, and these now included some from the New World, but these were often mixed together with stories from Pliny and John Mandeville. Thus, accounts from the New World became variations on those accounts of cannibals, dog-headed people, and hairy women that had been told for centuries by ancient, Muslim, and Christian authors.

Once New World cultures were fitted into existing traditions of the exotic and bizarre, they could also be regarded as inferior, a tendency exacerbated by the ease of the initial Spanish conquests. This combined with assessments of African inferiority bolstered by the expansion of the African slave trade to create a greater sense of European cultural superiority than had been evident earlier. The contacts between ethnic groups that became more common in the sixteenth century led not to a breakdown of preconceptions or increased toleration, but to a sharpened awareness of difference and heightened racism. It is interesting to speculate about what the history of race relations in the modern world might have been had Columbus's willingness to absorb ideas from many cultures, rather than his ethnocentrism, prevailed.

CHAPTER TWELVE

THE SPREAD

OF THE REFORMATION

In 1517, an Augustinian monk in the German province of Saxony named Martin Luther (1483–1546) began preaching and writing against papal *indulgences,* those letters from the pope that substituted for earthly penance or time in Purgatory for Christians who earned or purchased them. Luther called for an end to the sale of indulgences because this practice encouraged people to believe that sins did not have to be taken seriously but could be atoned for simply by buying a piece of paper. In taking this position, he was repeating the ideas expressed more than one hundred years earlier by John Hus (1369?–1415), a Czech theologian and preacher. Many of Luther's other ideas had also been previously expressed by Hus, and even earlier by John Wyclif (1328–1384), an English philosopher and theologian. All three objected to the wealth of the Church and to the pope's claims to earthly power; called for an end to pilgrimages and the veneration of saints;

said that priests were no better than other people, and that in fact all believers were priests; and believed that the Bible should be available for all people to read for themselves in their own language.

Though Luther's beliefs were quite similar to those of Wyclif and Hus, their impact was not. Wyclif had gained a large following and died peacefully in his bed; less than twenty years after his death, however, English rulers ordered anyone espousing his beliefs to be burned at the stake as a heretic, and so the movement he started was more or less wiped out. Hus himself was burned at the stake in 1415 at the Council of Constance, which ordered the bones of Wyclif to be dug up and burned as well. Hus's followers were not as easily steered back to the fold or stamped out as Wyclif's had been, but his ideas never spread beyond Bohemia (modern-day Czech Republic). Martin Luther's actions, on the other hand, led to a permanent split in Western Christianity, dividing an institution that had existed as a unified body for almost 1,500 years.

Within only a few years, Luther gained a huge number of followers in Germany and other countries, inspiring other religious reformers to break with the Catholic church in developing their own ideas. This movement has come to be known collectively as the "Protestant Reformation," though perhaps *Revolution* might be a more accurate term.

To understand why Luther's impact was so much greater than that of his predecessors, we need to examine a number of factors besides his basic set of beliefs. As with any revolution, social and economic grievances also played a role. Many different groups in early-sixteenth-century German society were disturbed by the changes they saw around them. Peasants wanted the right to hunt and fish as they had in earlier times and objected to new taxes that their landlords imposed on them. Bitter at the wealth of the Church, they believed that the clergy were more interested in collecting money from them than in providing spiritual leadership. Landlords, watching the price of manufactured goods rise even faster than they could raise taxes or rents, blamed urban merchants and bankers, calling them greedy and avaricious. Those with only small landholdings were especially caught in an inflationary squeeze and often had to sell off their lands. This was particularly the case for the free imperial knights, a group of about 3,000 individuals in Germany who owed allegiance directly to the emperor but whose landholdings were often less than one square mile. The knights were also losing their reason for exis-

tence because military campaigns increasingly relied on infantry and artillery forces rather than mounted cavalry. All these groups were becoming nationalistic and objected to their church taxes and tithes going to the pope, whom they regarded as primarily an Italian prince rather than an international religious leader.

Political factors were also important in the Protestant Revolution. Germany was not a centralized monarchy like France, Spain, and England, but a collection of hundreds of semi-independent territories loosely combined into a political unit called the Holy Roman Empire, under the leadership of an elected emperor. Some of these territories were ruled by nobles such as princes, dukes, or counts; some were independent cities; some were ecclesiastical principalities ruled by archbishops or bishops; and some were ruled by free imperial knights. Each territory was jealous of the power of its neighbors and was equally unwilling to allow the emperor any strong centralized authority. This effect usually worked to the benefit of the individual territories, but it could also work to their detriment. For example, the emperor's weakness prevented him from enforcing such laws against alleged heretics as the one the English king had used against Wyclif's followers, with the result that each territory was relatively independent in matters of religion. On the other hand, he was unable to place limits on papal legal authority or tax collection in the way the stronger kings of western Europe could, with the result that Germany supported many more indulgence peddlers than England or Spain.

The decentralization of the Holy Roman Empire also left each territory more vulnerable than before to external military threats, the most significant of which in the early sixteenth century was the Ottoman Turks. Originating in central Asia, the Turks had adopted the Muslim religion and begun a campaign of conquest westward. In 1453 they took Constantinople, and by 1500 they were nearing Vienna, arousing fear in many German rulers. The Turkish threat combined with social and economic grievances among many sectors of society to make western Europeans feel that the end of the world was near or look for a charismatic leader who would solve their problems.

Technological factors also played a role in the Protestant Revolution. The printing press was developed in Germany around 1450, and by Luther's time there were printers in most of the major cities in Europe. The spread of printing was accompanied by a rise in literacy, so that many more people were able to read than in the time of Wyclif or Hus. They were also more able to buy books and pamphlets, for the rag paper used by printers was much cheaper than the parchment or vellum used by copyists in earlier centuries. Owning a Bible or part of a Bible to read in one's own language was now a realistic possibility.

In many ways, then, the early sixteenth century was a favorable time for a major religious change in western Europe. Your task in this chapter will be to assess how that change occurred. How were the ideas of Luther disseminated so widely and so quickly? How were they made attractive to various groups within German society?

SOURCES AND METHOD

Before you look at the evidence in this chapter, think about how ideas are spread in modern American society. What would be the best ways to reach the greatest number of people if you wanted to discuss a new issue or present a new concept? You might want to use health issues as an example, for these often involve totally new ideas and information on one hand and are regarded as vitally important on the other. Think, for example, about the means by which the dangers of cigarette smoking or information about the spread of AIDS are communicated. To answer the first question, we will need to examine the sixteenth-century equivalents of these forms of communication. Health is an appropriate parallel because the most important such issue for many people in the sixteenth century was the health of their souls, a problem directly addressed by Luther and the other reformers.

The spread of the Reformation was perhaps the first example of a successful multimedia campaign; in consequence, as you might imagine, we will be using a wide variety of sources. As you read the written sources and look at the visual evidence, keep in mind that people were seeing, hearing, and reading all these materials at once. As in any successful advertising or propaganda campaign, certain ideas were reinforced over and over again to make sure the message was thoroughly communicated. You will need to pay particular attention, then, to those points that come up in more than one type of source.

Though they were seeing, hearing, or reading the same message, different groups within German society interpreted Protestant ideas differently. They latched on to certain concepts that had relevance for their own situations and often attached Protestant ideas to existing social, political, or economic grievances. Artists and authors spreading the Protestant message often conveyed their ideas in ways they knew would be attractive to various social groups. In answering the second question, it is important to note the portrayal of various social groups and pay attention to the frequency with which these portrayals appear. Thus, as you look at the visual sources and read the written ones, jot down one list of the ideas expressed and another of the ways in which various types of people are depicted. In this way, you will begin to see which ideas are central and perceived as popular, and which might be interpreted differently by different people.

Source 1 is a sermon delivered in 1521 by Martin Luther in Erfurt on his way to the Diet of Worms, a meeting of the leaders of the territories in the Holy Roman Empire. It is not based on Luther's own notes but was written down by a person in the audience, who then gave the transcript to a local printer. This sermon is thus a record of both how the Reformation message was spread orally—so many people wanted to hear him that the church where Luther preached could not hold them all—and how it was spread in written form, for seven editions of the sermon appeared in 1521 alone. What teachings of the Catholic church did Luther criticize, and what ideas of his own did he emphasize? In assessing how ideas are spread, we have to pay attention not only to the content of the message but also to the form. In what sorts of words and images did Luther convey his ideas to his large audience?

The next sources—three hymns—also serve as both oral and written evidence. Martin Luther believed that congregational hymn singing was an important part of a church service and an effective way to teach people about theology. In this tactic he anticipated modern advertisers, who recognize the power of a song or jingle in influencing people's choices. The first two hymns were written by Luther and the third by Paul Speratus, an early follower. As you read them, pay attention to both their content and their images. What ideas from Luther's sermon are reinforced in the hymns? What sorts of mental pictures do the words produce? (Keep in mind that you are reading these simply as poetry, whereas sixteenth-century people sang them. You may know the tune of "A Mighty Fortress," which is still sung in many Protestant congregations today; if so, you can use your knowledge of its musical setting to help you assess the impact of the hymn and its message.)

The Lutheran message would certainly not have spread as widely as it did if church services were its only forum. The remaining sources are those that people might have encountered anywhere. The woodcuts all come from Protestant pamphlets—small, inexpensive paperbound booklets written in German that were readily available in any city with a printer—or *broadsheets*—single-sheet posters that were often sold alone or as a series. These documents are extremely complex visually and need to be examined with great care. Most of the images used would have been familiar to any sixteenth-century person, but they may not be to you. Here, then, are some clues to help guide your analysis.

In Source 5, the person on the right wearing the triple crown with money on the table in front of him is the pope. The devils in front of the table are wearing the flat hats worn by cardinals; the pieces of paper with seals attached that they are handing out are indulgences. At the bottom are the flames of hell; at the top, heaven with a preacher and people participating in the two Church sacraments that the Protestants retained, baptism and communion.

Source 6, another heaven and hell image, shows Christ at the top deciding who will stay in heaven and two linked devils at the bottom dragging various people to hell. The right-hand devil wears the triple-crowned papal tiara, the left-hand one, the rolled turban worn by Turks. Included in the hell-bound group on the right are men wearing the flat cardinal's hat, the pointed hat of bishops, and the distinctive haircut of monks.

Source 7 comes from a series of woodcut contrasts. The left pictures show biblical scenes and the right the contemporary Church. The top left picture shows Christ with his disciples; the top right, the pope. From their hats and haircuts you can recognize some of the people gathered in front of the pope; those kneeling are wearing crowns, which in the sixteenth century were worn only by rulers. The bottom left picture shows Christ and the moneychangers at the temple at Jerusalem; the bottom right, the pope and indulgences.

Source 8 is the cover of a pamphlet called "The Wolf's Song." By now you recognize the hats and haircuts of the wolves at the top and sides; some of the geese wear crowns, and many carry jeweled necklaces. The choice of animals is intentional. Wolves were still a threat to livestock in sixteenth-century Europe, and geese were regarded as foolish, silly creatures willing to follow their leader blindly into dangerous situations.

Source 9 is a woodcut by the well-known German artist Lucas Cranach, whom Luther commissioned to illustrate his pamphlet "Against the Papacy at Rome, Founded by the Devil" (1545). It shows two men defecating into the papal triple crown.

Taking all of the images into account, what message do the woodcuts convey about the pope and other Catholic clergy? About the Protestant clergy?

Which images and ideas are frequently repeated? How do these fit in with what was preached or sung in church?

The last source is a pamphlet by an unknown author printed in 1523. It is written in the form of a dialogue, a very common form for these Reformation printed materials. Read it, as you did the sermon and the hymns, for both content and tone. Why do you think the author chose these two characters to convey his message? What do they criticize about Catholic practices? How do the ideas expressed here compare with those in Luther's sermon? Which of the woodcuts might have served as an illustration for this pamphlet?

THE EVIDENCE

Source 1 from John W. Doberstein, editor, Luther's Works, *vol. 51 (Philadelphia: Fortress, 1959), pp. 61–66. Reprinted by permission.*

1. Sermon Preached by Martin Luther in Erfurt (Germany), 1521

Dear friends, I shall pass over the story of St. Thomas this time and leave it for another occasion, and instead consider the brief words uttered by Christ: "Peace be with you" [John 20:19] and "Behold my hands and my side" [John 20:27], and "as the Father has sent me, even so I send you" [John 20:21]. Now, it is clear and manifest that every person likes to think that he will be saved and attain to eternal salvation. This is what I propose to discuss now.

You also know that all philosophers, doctors and writers have studiously endeavored to teach and write what attitude man should take to piety. They have gone to great trouble, but, as is evident, to little avail. Now genuine and true piety consists of two kinds of works: those done for others, which are the right kind, and those done for ourselves, which are unimportant. In order to find a foundation, one man builds churches; another goes on a pilgrimage to St. James'[1] or St. Peter's[2]; a third fasts or prays, wears a cowl, goes barefoot, or does something else of the kind. Such works are nothing whatever and must be completely destroyed. Mark these words: none of our works have any power whatsoever. For God has chosen a man, the Lord Christ Jesus, to crush death, destroy sin, and shatter hell, since there was no one before he came who did not inevitably belong to the devil. The devil therefore thought he would get a hold upon the Lord when he hung between the two thieves and

1. St. James of Compostella, a cathedral in northern Spain.
2. A cathedral in Rome.

was suffering the most contemptible and disgraceful of deaths, which was cursed both by God and by men [cf. Deut. 21:23; Gal. 3:13]. But the Godhead was so strong that death, sin, and even hell were destroyed.

Therefore you should note well the words which Paul writes to the Romans [Rom. 5:12–21]. Our sins have their source in Adam, and because Adam ate the apple, we have inherited sin from him. But Christ has shattered death for our sake, in order that we might be saved by his works, which are alien to us, and not by our works.

But the papal dominion treats us altogether differently. It makes rules about fasting, praying, and butter-eating, so that whoever keeps the commandments of the pope will be saved and whoever does not keep them belongs to the devil. It thus seduces the people with the delusion that goodness and salvation lies in their own works. But I say that none of the saints, no matter how holy they were, attained salvation by their works. Even the holy mother of God did not become good, was not saved, by her virginity or her motherhood, but rather by the will of faith and the works of God, and not by her purity, or her own works. Therefore, mark me well: this is the reason why salvation does not lie in our own works, no matter what they are; it cannot and will not be effected without faith.

Now, someone may say: Look, my friend, you are saying a lot about faith, and claiming that our salvation depends solely upon it; now, I ask you, how does one come to faith? I will tell you. Our Lord Christ said, "Peace be with you. Behold my hands, etc." [John 20:26–27]. [In other words, he is saying:] Look, man, I am the only one who has taken away your sins and redeemed you, etc.; now be at peace. Just as you inherited sin from Adam—not that you committed it, for I did not eat the apple, any more than you did, and yet this is how we came to be in sin—so we have not suffered [as Christ did], and therefore we were made free from death and sin by God's work, not by our works. Therefore God says: Behold, man, I am your redemption [cf. Isa. 43:3], just as Paul said to the Corinthians: Christ is our justification and redemption, etc. [I Cor 1:30]. Christ is our justification and redemption, as Paul says in this passage. And here our [Roman] masters say: Yes, *Redemptor*, Redeemer; this is true, but it is not enough.

Therefore, I say again: Alien works, these make us good! Our Lord Christ says: I am your justification. I have destroyed the sins you have upon you. Therefore only believe in me; believe that I am he who has done this; then you will be justified. For it is written, *Justicia est fides*, righteousness is identical with faith and comes through faith. Therefore, if we want to have faith, we should believe the gospel, Paul, etc., and not the papal breves,[3] or the decretals,[4] but rather guard ourselves against them as against fire. For everything that comes from the pope cries out: Give, give; and if you refuse, you are of

3. **breve:** letter of authority.
4. **decretal:** decree on matters of doctrine.

the devil. It would be a small matter if they were only exploiting the people. But, unfortunately, it is the greatest evil in the world to lead the people to believe that outward works can save or make a man good.

At this time the world is so full of wickedness that it is overflowing, and is therefore now under a terrible judgment and punishment, which God has inflicted, so that the people are perverting and deceiving themselves in their own minds. For to build churches, and to fast and pray and so on has the appearance of good works, but in our heads we are deluding ourselves. We should not give way to greed, desire for temporal honor, and other vices and rather be helpful to our poor neighbor. Then God will arise in us and we in him, and this means a new birth. What does it matter if we commit a fresh sin? If we do not immediately despair, but rather say within ourselves, "O God, thou livest still! Christ my Lord is the destroyer of sin," then at once the sin is gone. And also the wise man says: *Septies in die cadit iustus et resurgit.*" "A righteous man falls seven times, and rises again" [Prov. 24:16].

The reason why the world is so utterly perverted and in error is that for a long time there have been no genuine preachers. There are perhaps three thousand priests, among whom one cannot find four good ones—God have mercy on us in this crying shame! And when you do get a good preacher, he runs through the gospel superficially and then follows it up with a fable . . . or he mixes in something of the pagan teachers, Aristotle, Plato, Socrates, and others, who are all quite contrary to the gospel, and also contrary to God, for they did not have the knowledge of the light which we possess. Aye, if you come to me and say: The Philosopher says: Do many good works, then you will acquire the habit, and finally you will become godly; then I say to you: Do not perform good works in order to become godly; but if you are already godly, then do good works, though without affectation and with faith. There you see how contrary these two points of view are.

In former times the devil made great attacks upon the people and from these attacks they took refuge in faith and clung to the Head, which is Christ; and so he was unable to accomplish anything. So now he has invented another device; he whispers into the ears of our Junkers[5] that they should make exactions from people and give them laws. This way it looks well on the outside; but inside it is full of poison. So the young children grow up in a delusion; they go to church thinking that salvation consists in praying, fasting, and attending mass. Thus it is the preacher's fault. But still there would be no need, if only we had right preachers.

The Lord said three times to St. Peter: *"Petre, amas me? etc.; pasce oves meas"* [John 21:15–17]. "Peter, feed, feed, feed my sheep." What is the meaning of *pascere*? It means to feed. How should one feed the sheep? Only by preaching the Word of God, only by preaching faith. Then our Junkers come along and

---

5. **junker:** member of the landowning nobility.

say: *Pascere* means *leges dare,* to enact laws, but with deception. Yes, they are well fed! They feed the sheep as the butchers do on Easter eve. Whereas one should speak the Word of God plainly to guide the poor and weak in faith, they mix in their beloved Aristotle, who is contrary to God, despite the fact that Paul says in Col. [2:8]: Beware of laws and philosophy. What does "philosophy" mean? If we knew Greek, Latin, and German, we would see clearly what the Apostle is saying.

Is not this the truth? I know very well that you don't like to hear this and that I am annoying many of you; nevertheless, I shall say it. I will also advise you, no matter who you are: If you have preaching in mind or are able to help it along, then do not become a priest or a monk, for there is a passage in the thirty-third and thirty-fourth chapters of the prophet Ezekiel, unfortunately a terrifying passage, which reads: If you forsake your neighbor, see him going astray, and do not help him, do not preach to him, I will call you to account for his soul [Ezek. 33:8; 34:10]. This is a passage which is not often read. But I say, you become a priest or a monk in order to pray your seven canonical hours and say mass, and you think you want to be godly. Alas, you're a fine fellow! It [i.e., being a priest or monk] will fail you. You say the Psalter, you pray the rosary, you pray all kinds of other prayers, and say a lot of words; you say mass, you kneel before the altar, you read confession, you go on mumbling and maundering; and all the while you think you are free from sin. And yet in your heart you have such great envy that, if you could choke your neighbor and get away with it creditably, you would do it; and that's the way you say mass. It would be no wonder if a thunderbolt struck you to the ground. But if you have eaten three grains of sugar or some other seasoning, no one could drag you to the altar with red-hot tongs.[6] You have scruples! And that means to go to heaven with the devil. I know very well that you don't like to hear this. Nevertheless, I will tell the truth, I must tell the truth, even though it cost me my neck twenty times over, that the verdict may not be pronounced against me [i.e., at the last judgment].

Yes, you say, there were learned people a hundred or fifty years ago too. That is true; but I am not concerned with the length of time or the number of persons. For even though they knew something of it then, the devil has always been a mixer, who preferred the pagan writers to the holy gospel. I will tell the truth and must tell the truth; that's why I'm standing here, and not taking any money for it either. Therefore, we should not build upon human law or works, but rather have true faith in the One who is the destroyer of sin; then we shall find ourselves growing in Him. Then everything that was bitter before is sweet. Then our hearts will recognize God. And when that happens we shall be despised, and we shall pay no regard to human law, and then the pope will come and excommunicate us. But then we shall be so

6. Because of the rule that the priest must say Mass fasting.

united with God that we shall pay no heed whatsoever to any hardship, ban, or law.

Then someone may go on and ask: Should we not keep the man-made laws at all? Or, can we not continue to pray, fast, and so on, as long as the right way is present? My answer is that if there is present a right Christian love and faith, then everything a man does is meritorious; and each may do what he wills [cf. Rom. 14:22], so long as he has no regard for works, since they cannot save him.

In conclusion, then, every single person should reflect and remember that we cannot help ourselves, but only God, and also that our works are utterly worthless. So shall we have the peace of God. And every person should so perform his work that it benefits not only himself alone, but also another, his neighbor. If he is rich, his wealth should benefit the poor. If he is poor, his service should benefit the rich. When persons are servants or maidservants, their work should benefit their master. Thus no one's work should benefit him alone; for when you note that you are serving only your own advantage, then your service is false. I am not troubled; I know very well what man-made laws are. Let the pope issue as many laws as he likes, I will keep them all so far as I please.

Therefore, dear friends, remember that God has risen up for our sakes. Therefore let us also arise to be helpful to the weak in faith, and so direct our work that God may be pleased with it. So shall we receive the peace he has given to us today. May God grant us this every day. Amen.

Source 2 from Ulrich Leupold, editor, Luther's Works, *vol. 53 (Philadelphia: Fortress, 1965), p. 305. Copyright © 1965 Fortress Press. Used by permission of Augsburg Fortress.*

2. Luther, *Lord, Keep Us Steadfast in Thy Word*, hymn, 1541–1542

1.   Lord, keep us steadfast in thy Word,
And curb the pope's and Turk's vile sword,
Who seek to topple from the throne
Jesus Christ, thine only Son.

2.   Proof of thy might, Lord Christ, afford,
For thou of all the lords art Lord;
Thine own poor Christendom defend,
That it may praise thee without end.

3.   God Holy Ghost, who comfort art,
Give to thy folk on earth one heart;

Stand by us breathing our last breath,
Lead us to life straight out of death.

Sources 3 and 4 from Lutheran Book of Worship *(Minneapolis: Augsburg, 1978), hymn 229; hymn 297. Source 3: Copyright © 1978. Used by permission of Augsburg Publishing House. Source 4: Copyright © 1941 Concordia Publishing House. Used by permission.*

3. Luther, *A Mighty Fortress Is Our God*, hymn, 1527–1528

1. A mighty fortress is our God,
A sword and shield victorious;
He breaks the cruel oppressor's rod
And wins salvation glorious.
The old satanic foe
Has sworn to work us woe!
With craft and dreadful might
He arms himself to fight.
On earth he has no equal.

2. No strength of ours can match his might!
We would be lost, rejected.
But now a champion comes to fight,
Whom God himself elected.
You ask who this may be?
The Lord of hosts is he!
Christ Jesus, mighty Lord,
God's only Son, adored.
He holds the field victorious.

3. Though hordes of devils fill the land
All threat'ning to devour us,
We tremble not, unmoved we stand;
They cannot overpow'r us,
Let this world's tyrant rage;
In battle we'll engage!
His might is doomed to fail;
God's judgment must prevail!
One little word subdues him.

4. God's Word forever shall abide,
No thanks to foes, who fear it;
For God himself fights by our side
With weapons of the Spirit.

Were they to take our house,
Goods, honor, child, or spouse,
Though life be wrenched away,
They cannot win the day.
The Kingdom's ours forever!

4. Paul Speratus, *Salvation unto Us Has Come*, hymn, 1524

1.   Salvation unto us has come
By God's free grace and favor;
Good works cannot avert our doom,
They help and save us never.
Faith looks to Jesus Christ alone,
Who did for all the world atone;
He is our mediator.

2.   Theirs was a false, misleading dream
Who thought God's law was given
That sinners might themselves redeem
And by their works gain heaven.
The Law is but a mirror bright
To bring the inbred sin to light
That lurks within our nature.

3.   And yet the Law fulfilled must be,
Or we were lost forever;
Therefore God sent his Son that he
Might us from death deliver.
He all the Law for us fulfilled,
And thus his Father's anger stilled
Which over us impended.

4.   Faith clings to Jesus' cross alone
And rests in him unceasing;
And by its fruits true faith is known,
With love and hope unceasing.
For faith alone can justify;
Works serve our neighbor and supply
The proof that faith is living.

5.   All blessing, honor, thanks, and praise
To Father, Son, and Spirit,
The God who saved us by his grace;
All glory to his merit.
O triune God in heav'n above,
You have revealed your saving love;
Your blessed name we hallow.

Source 5 from Kupferstichkabinett Staatliche Museen zu Berlin, Preussischer Kulturbesitz, Berlin. Photograph by Jorg P. Anders.

5. Matthias Gerung, Broadsheet, Lauingen (Germany), 1546

Source 6 from the Mitchell Collection, London.

6. Matthias Gerung, Broadsheet, Lauingen, 1546

7. Lucas Cranach, Pamphlet, Wittenberg (Germany), 1521

9. Lucas Cranach, Pamphlet, Wittenberg, 1545[7]

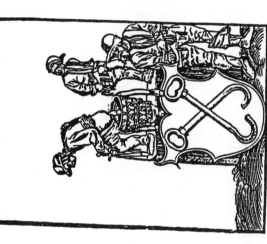

Bapft hat dem reich Chrifti gethon
Wie man hie handelt feine Cron.
Machts je zweifeltig: fpricht der geift
Schenckt getroft ein: Gott ifts ders heist.
Mart. Luth. ☙

7. The lines below the woodcut read, "The pope has done to the kingdom of Christ/What is here being done to his own crown.

8. Unknown Artist, Pamphlet, Augsburg
(Germany), 1522

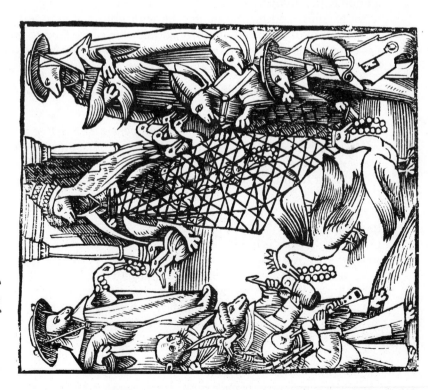

Source 10 from Oskar Schade, Satiren und Pasquille aus der Reformationszeit, *vol. 2, no. 15 (Hannover: 1863). Selection translated by Merry E. Wiesner.*

10. Anonymous German Pamphlet, 1523

A dialogue between two good friends named Hans Tholl and Claus Lamp, talking about the Antichrist[8] and his followers.

They are in a good mood while drinking wine and sit and discuss some ideas from the letters of Paul.

PREFACE

Dear Christians and brothers, if we want to recognize and know the Antichrist, we have to go to the brothers who can read, so that they will read us the second chapter of the second letter of Paul to the Thessalonians. There we will clearly find him, with his gestures and manners, how he acted and still acts, how he is now revealed so that we do not have to wait any longer but can know him despite his masks. How the devil sends his followers to knock us down, and how the old women and bath maids see him. We have long been blind to the lies and deceits of Satan, the devil. Because we have not paid attention to the divine warnings from Daniel, Paul, Christ, Peter, and the apocalypse of John, God has tormented us with ghosts and apparitions who will take us all with them to hell. Why should this cause God to suffer when He has offered you His holy word? If you don't want it, then go to the devil, for he is here now. He sees, finds, and possesses.

It happened that Hans Tholl and Claus Lamp were looking for each other and finally found each other in the evening.

CLAUS: My friend Hans, where have you been all day? I've been looking for you. The innkeeper has a good wine for two cents, and I wanted to drink a glass of wine with you.
HANS: Dear friend, I've been in a place that I wouldn't take six glasses of wine for.
CLAUS: So tell me where you have been.
HANS: I've got exciting news.
CLAUS: Well, what is it then? Tell me!
HANS: I was in a place where a friend read to four of us from the Bible. He read in the second chapter of the second letter of Paul to the Thessalonians about the Antichrist and how one is to recognize him.
CLAUS: Oh I would have given a penny to have been there.

8. **Antichrist:** the devil.

HANS: I want you to believe that I haven't heard anything like this in my whole life; I wouldn't have given three pennies to miss it.

CLAUS: Can't you remember anything, Hans? Can you tell me something about it?

HANS: I think I can tell you about almost the whole chapter, and only leave a little out.

CLAUS: So tell me! But let's get some wine first. I'll pay for yours.

HANS: Here's to your money!

CLAUS: Innkeeper, bring some wine.

HANS: What does he get for it?

CLAUS: He gets two cents. Now, tell me! I really want to hear what you will say about the Antichrist.

HANS: I'll tell you, but it will seem strange to you.

CLAUS: Why?

HANS: It seemed strange and odd to me, too, that people or states are the Antichrist.

CLAUS: Go ahead, then, you're boring me.

HANS: Stop that. All right, here's what the chapter says: "Dear brothers," Paul writes to the Thessalonians, "We ask you in the name of the coming of Christ and our coming together for the same, that you not be moved in your senses (or from your senses), or frightened by the spirit or the word or by letters supposedly coming from us, saying that the day of the Lord has come or will be coming soon. Let no one deceive you in any way, it will come only when there is disagreement and disunity (even though they all say they are preaching and believing nothing but the Gospel and Christianity) and the man of lawlessness will be disclosed, the son of damnation, who is against the gospel. Then he will be raised up (here Claus Lamp began to understand) above everything that is called a god (or is worshipped as a god) until he sits in the temple of God and lets himself be prayed to as if he were God." Claus, what are you thinking about? Do you know this man of lawlessness?

CLAUS: Now all the devils will come for you! He is no other beast than the Pope and his realm. I would never in my whole life have realized that if you hadn't been there [to hear it]. I'll buy you a second glass of wine!

HANS: Be quiet! I want to tell you more.

CLAUS: My dear friend, still more?

HANS: Of course. First I'll tell you the reason why I was talked to for so long.

CLAUS: My friend, for God's sake keep talking!

HANS: So listen! Here is the text: Paul says: "Don't you remember the things that I told you when I was with you? And now you know what is holding him (or what you should pay attention to), and that he will be revealed in his time. I tell you, that now he is doing so many evil and underhanded things, that only those who stop it now will stop it when his time comes fully. And then he will be revealed, the lawless one"—listen here, Claus—"who the lord Jesus Christ will slay with the breath of His mouth and will totally destroy with the light of His coming. But the coming of the Antichrist is through the activity of Satan, the devil, with great power and supposed signs and wonders, and with misguided celebration of the evil of those who will be destroyed. Because they would not accept the love of truth" (this clearly refers to the Gospel) "and be saved, God sends them the results of their errors, a great delusion, so that they believe the lies and are all condemned who did not believe the truth but agreed to the evil (and took it on themselves)." See that, Claus! Now you have heard why God has allowed error. Even though we have long wanted not to do wrong, we still hard-headedly keep doing it.

CLAUS: That says a lot. I would set my life on it, if it were only half as important. Now I hear and see that God allows very little understanding.

HANS: Yes, and why? People don't want to know very much and don't go to the Bible. God has hardened them and we are so godless. God will make us suffer because we don't ask about the truth. If we only had half as much concern about the health of our souls as we have about material goods, we wouldn't have come so far from the right path. As you have just heard, it isn't God who sent the so-called preachers [to lead us astray]. Here, I'll say it to you straight: Paul goes on to say: "Dear brothers, we should give thanks to God at all times because he chose you from the beginning, and he called you through the Gospel" (and not through other fairy-stories, as people are now saying).

CLAUS: Unfortunately you are right. Right now I hear strange things about the beast of the Antichrist from priests and monks. God help us!

HANS: Yes, we need to pray earnestly to God to send us good preachers, that preach the pure Gospel and leave the fairy-stories at home.

CLAUS: My friend, I am still thinking about the Antichrist, that he has begun so many devilish things and made the whole world to be his fool.

HANS: That astonishes me, too. But you have now heard from Paul, when he says: "God has allowed them to be deluded because they have not accepted the truth." We haven't noticed this, and the priests have hidden it from us.

CLAUS: I believe that the devil has possessed them all so that they haven't preached to us about these things.

HANS: They are afraid that people would recognize that their God, the Pope, is the Antichrist. People are supposed to honor and pray to him, just like Paul says about the Antichrist. So they are afraid.

CLAUS: That's really true. They've thought: If we tell the lay people this, they will notice and think about how they have to kiss the Pope's foot and call him "most holy." And some know-it-alls even say: The Pope can't do any wrong; he can't sin.

HANS: It's amazing that God has allowed this to happen for so long, that it hasn't been made clear that we have been so blind. What really matters is that we have deserted the truth, my dear Claus. Let's ask God for the true faith! I see clearly that everything will soon be over, that the Last Judgment stands right before the door!

CLAUS: My dear brother Hans, I've thought that for a long time. Shall we go home?

HANS: Yes, let's drink up and go.

CLAUS: I don't want to drink any more, because I have been so seized by pity and compassion. I see that things will end soon. My dear Hans, I want to take this thing to its end with you, so I have to ask: what do you think about the fact that there is such a commotion now about Luther and his writings?

HANS: I think it's because he has discovered the Antichrist. He can't stand it, and I believe he will make many martyrs. I've heard that it has already started in some places; in Antwerp three people have been burnt because of his teachings. And I've heard that in some places they are imprisoning people and hunting them down.

CLAUS: If that's true, that's what's supposed to happen. I have always heard that the Antichrist will make martyrs and will pay money so that people will kill those who do not believe in him but instead preach the word of God.

HANS: I've heard that, too. Now to the next thing: when I want to hear more things read, I'll tell you.

CLAUS: My dear friend, I'll let everything be open to you, because I see clearly what will come out of it. I see clearly, if I want to be saved, I have to come back to the true faith, from which without a doubt the Antichrist and his horde have led us. God give you a good night!

HANS: Same to you! See that you don't forget what I've said.

CLAUS: I won't for the rest of my life. God be praised.

QUESTIONS TO CONSIDER

In exploring how the Reformation movement grew and took root throughout Europe, many scholars point to the printing press as the key factor in explaining why Luther's reforms had a much greater impact than those of Wyclif and Hus. After examining the sources, would you agree? What difference did it make that Luther's sermons were not only delivered but also printed? That hymns were taught not simply to choirs of monks or clergymen but to congregations of laypeople, out of hymnals that were printed and might be purchased by any fairly well-to-do member? That small pamphlets such as the one reproduced here were written in German and appeared in paperback?

Several historians have also pointed to the opposite effect, that the Protestant emphasis on individual reading of the Bible dramatically increased the demand for books. Judging by the language, what sort of person might have bought Luther's sermon or the pamphlet? What effects would you expect the Protestant Reformation to have had on literacy? The religious conflict itself was also a spur to book production and book buying, and religious works were the best sellers of the sixteenth century. What techniques did the pamphlet writer use to make his work more appealing to a buyer? How might including some of the woodcuts have affected sales?

Of course, the great majority of people in the sixteenth century could not read, so it may be wrong to overemphasize written sources of communication. As you noticed in the dialogue, however, people who could not read often turned to their neighbors who could, and so printed pamphlets were often heard by many who could not read them themselves. This dialogue itself was probably read out loud and may even have been acted out, which we know was the case with more elaborate dialogues containing stage directions and a whole cast of characters. Do you think this dialogue would have been effective read aloud rather than silently? The printing press also increased the circulation of visual images; woodcuts such as those reproduced here often became best sellers. Why did so many people purchase these woodcuts? If a person's only contact with Protestant thinking were images such as these, how would his or her beliefs have differed from those of a person who could read Luther's words as well?

To answer the second question— how the Protestant message was made attractive to people—look at your list of frequently repeated ideas and images. Which seem directed to all Christians? For example, what do the sources say about the role of good works in helping a person achieve salvation? The role of faith? Why might these ideas have been appealing? What was wrong with the Catholic clergy? In contrast, what did "good preachers" do and emphasize? Why might the contrast have made Luther's ideas attractive?

Though ideas and images were often repeated, not everyone understood them in the same way or was attracted to them for the same reasons. Different groups within German society responded to different parts of the Protestant message and must be examined separately. Begin with the peasants. How are they depicted in the various sources? Why did the pamphlet writer and the artist of Source 9 choose to make their characters peasants? In the heaven and hell woodcuts, where are peasants and poor people? Why would peasants have been particularly attracted to the criticism of indulgences? Why would Luther's ideas about the value of good works have appealed to them? Source 5 shows nobles in fancy feathered hats near hell, and Source 8 depicts rulers as geese; how would peasants have responded to these images? In the dialogue, Claus and Hans both agree that the Last Judgment is near. Why might sixteenth-century peasants have accepted this idea of the imminence of the end of the world?

Now consider the nobles and rulers. We have already noted that several of the woodcuts portray them negatively. How did Luther portray them in his sermon? Though hostility to nobles and rulers is evident in the Protestant message, many of the movement's ideas and images appealed to this class. Look, for example, at the upper right picture in Source 7. How does this scene reflect the hostility of rulers to the papacy? The noble class was primarily responsible for military actions in sixteenth-century Germany. How would they have responded to the language of the hymns? What effect might linking the Turks and the pope in the hymn in Source 2 and the woodcut of Source 6 have had? Sources 1, 3, 6, and 10 all include devils attacking people or dragging them to hell at the Last Judgment. Why might nobles have been attracted to such imagery? What message would they have gotten from imagery linking such devils with the pope? In what ways did the reasons why Luther's ideas appealed to nobles contradict the reasons they appealed to peasants?

Other groups in German society appear only rarely in the sources given here, so you will not be able to discover as much about the ways in which the Protestant message attracted them as you can in the case of peasants and nobles. You may, however, want to review the sources for evidence relating to the middle class, which you can find most easily in the woodcuts. Which of your answers about the reasons certain ideas were appealing to peasants or nobles would also apply to middle-class people?

You are now ready to answer both questions posed in this chapter. How were the basic concepts of the Reformation communicated to a wide range of the population? How were these concepts made attractive to different groups?

EPILOGUE

Though Luther's initial message was one of religious reform, people quickly saw its social, economic, and political implications. The free imperial knights used Luther's attack on the wealth of the Church and his ideas about the spiritual equality of all Christians to justify their rebellion in 1521. Quickly suppressed, this uprising was followed by a more serious rebellion by peasants in 1525. Peasants in south Germany added religious demands, such as a call for "good pastors" and an end to church taxes, to their long-standing economic grievances and took up arms. The Peasants' War spread eastward and northward but was never unified militarily, and it was brutally put down by imperial and noble armies later in the same year.

Given some of Luther's remarks about rulers and human laws (as you read in the sermon), the peasants expected him to support them. He did not, but urged them instead to obey their rulers, for in his opinion religion was not a valid justification for political revolution or social upheaval. When the peasants did not listen and continued their rebellion, Luther turned against them, calling them "murdering and thieving hordes." He supported the rulers in their slaughter of peasant armies, and his later writings became much more conservative than the sermon you read here.

The nobles and rulers who accepted Luther's message continued to receive his support, however. Many of the German states abolished the Catholic church and established their own Protestant churches under their individual ruler's control. This expulsion led to a series of religious wars between Protestants and Catholics that were finally ended by the Peace of Augsburg in 1555. The terms of the peace treaty allowed rulers to choose between Catholicism and Lutheran Protestantism; they were further given the right to enforce religious uniformity within their territories. By the middle of the sixteenth century, then, the only people who could respond as they chose to the Protestant message were rulers.

Achieving religious uniformity was not as simple a task as it had been earlier, however. Though rulers attempted to ban materials they did not agree with and prevent their subjects from reading or printing forbidden materials, religious literature was regularly smuggled from city to city. Because printing presses could produce thousands of copies of anything fairly quickly, ideas of all types spread much more quickly than they had earlier. Once people can read, it is much more difficult to control the information they take in; though

rulers could control their subjects' outward religious activities, they could not control their thoughts.

Rulers were not the only ones who could not control thinking and the exchange of ideas during the sixteenth century. As Luther discovered to his dismay, once ideas are printed and widely disseminated, they take on a life of their own; no matter how much one might wish, they cannot be called back or be made to conform to their original meaning. Not only did German knights and peasants interpret Luther's message in their own way, but other religious reformers, building on what he had written, developed their own interpretations of the Christian message. They used the same variety of methods that had been so successful in spreading Luther's ideas to communicate their own, and the Protestant Reformation became a multifaceted movement with many different leaders and numerous plans for action.

The Catholic church, learning from Protestant successes, began to publish its own illustrated pamphlets with negative images of Luther and other Protestant leaders along with explanations of its theology in easy-to-understand language. In this chapter we have looked exclusively at Lutheran propaganda, but the oral, written, and visual techniques of communication presented here were employed by all sides in the sixteenth-century religious conflict. Later they would be adapted for other political and intellectual debates.

CHAPTER THIRTEEN

PEASANT VIOLENCE: REBELLION AND RIOT IN

EARLY MODERN EUROPE, 1500–1789

THE PROBLEM

Most of us, being all too familiar with the problems of late-twentieth-century urban America, probably tend to have an idealized view of traditional rural societies as somehow more peaceful than our own. Yet historians are finding that the opposite was the case: Many traditional rural societies experienced quite high levels of violence.

In early modern Europe, violence was a commonplace of rural life. Historians of criminal justice have found that levels of individual acts of violence, in the form of assaults and murders, were quite high and that even social elites, such as the nobility, engaged in such behavior. Common, too, were collective acts of violence by European peasants. These were the people who tilled the soil and who owed a part of their produce, and sometimes their labor, to noble landowners, often called *seigniors*, in a society that was still widely feudalized.

Peasant collective violence assumed two chief forms, rebellions and riots. Rebellions were widespread expressions of collective violence that extended beyond the confines of individual villages and that endured for more than a few days. Rebels aimed at changing their government, its policies, or the society in which they lived. The occasions on which peasants took up arms were numerous. Indeed, one of the twentieth century's most insightful historians, noting the possibilities for conflict in a landholding system in which peasants owed rents and other dues to their seigniors, wrote:

> To the historian, whose task is merely to observe and explain, agrarian revolt is as natural to the seigniorial regime as strikes, let us say, are to large scale capitalism.[1]

1. Marc Bloch, *French Rural History: An Essay on its Basic Characteristics,* translated by Janet Sondheimer (Berkeley: University of California Press, 1966), p. 170.

Chapter 13

Peasant Violence:

Rebellion and

Riot in Early

Modern Europe,

1500–1789

Riots probably were more common than outright rebellions and differed from them in several ways. They were generally localized outbursts of group violence that were rather spontaneous and thus lacked planning and organization. Riots also generally were of short duration, rarely lasting more than one or two days, and they commonly represented an expression of local anger at some very tangible problem, rather than an attempt to effect sweeping change.

The origins and nature of these acts of peasant collective violence must be sought first in the outlook of the peasants. Early modern peasants had a distinct view of government. Their society retained memories of the individual's right to petition the monarch directly for solutions to problems. Many peasants saw their taking up of arms to protest government policy as a simple extension of their right to petition. In doing this, they believed that they were in no way being disloyal to the king; rather, they believed that their good king had been misled by evil or corrupt advisers into bad policies. "If the king only knew!" was a sentiment that was widely expressed by peasant rebels in this period to justify their uprisings to seek changes of officials or policies.

Popular religion also sometimes justified rebellion in the minds of peasants. Problems of late medieval and early modern Europe, including the bubonic plague, schisms in the Church, and the advance of the Turks, convinced some that the end of the world was approaching, and that a coming day of judgment would be followed by a new millennium, or period of peace and perfection. In preparation for the latter event, the world had to be purged of its evil, and some peasant revolts had this millenarian aspect to them.

Cultural historians also find a unique concept of time among early modern European peasants. While for us time is essentially a linear concept, marked, in human development, by progress, for peasants five centuries ago time could be circular. That is, human development could include the return of past conditions; in particular, the peasant mentality retained an idealized vision of an earlier "golden age" when conditions had been much better. The desire to recover those better times is often found as a goal of peasant violence.

The primitive agricultural methods of the age also were at the root of some peasant violence. Working the land with simple wooden plows that rarely broke the soil deeply enough and farming without modern techniques of fertilization and crop rotation, peasant cultivators lived a subsistence existence in which they barely met their families' needs, their obligations to Church and state, and their dues to their seigniors in years of good harvest. As a result, they were prone to panics and riots in the face of threats to their food supplies. Indeed, mere rumors of such threats would prompt local rioting.

Peasant revolts and riots erupted within the institution that was the essential focus of peasant existence: the village or parish community. Peasant social and economic life took place within this community, and it was within the village that peasants rallied to counter any real or perceived threat to their existence.

Two chief threats to that traditional existence arose during the period from 1500 to 1789 and were the main causes of rural violence in this period. The first of these threats was economic in nature. The economy of the West was beginning its slow evolution from a subsistence agricultural economy to an economy driven by exchange on international markets and nascent industrial capitalism. Our sources will reveal the effects of such changes on early modern peasants. They could be wrenching at times, manifesting themselves in such varied forms as increased seigniorial dues, innovative and disruptive ways of administering agricultural land, and higher food prices driven by market forces that were beyond the control or even the understanding of peasants. Such developments provoked considerable resistance to changes in traditional peasant ways.

The second cause of peasant unrest was the growing power of the state. This was felt in a variety of ways, including military conscription of peasant boys, but chiefly in the rising tax burden that governments imposed on their subjects. The sixteenth, seventeenth, and eighteenth centuries were periods of extensive warfare, and every state sought to increase its tax revenues to sustain the costs of war. To raise war taxes, expensive,

centralized bureaucracies also had to be created, further increasing revenue demands on the peasants who formed the mass of the state's subjects and often intruding deeply into their rural worlds. The new government officials often tried to supplant traditional rural administrative practices in order to raise revenues more efficiently, and these governmental and fiscal innovations also encountered peasant resistance.

Peasants responded to these developments with violence that may appear rather bizarre to twentieth-century students of history, who are accustomed to defining revolutions as movements aimed at creating new governmental or social orders. Many historians have noted that early modern peasant rebellions and riots aimed not at creating a new order, but, instead, at protecting the status quo or restoring an older social or governmental order.

In this chapter we will assess the origins and nature of European peasant rebellions and riots over three centuries. In the sources that constitute the core of this chapter, you should seek answers to several fundamental questions, understanding, of course, that the sources are describing just a few of thousands of such acts of violence. What were the causes of these acts of collective violence by European peasants? Were these actions revolutionary in that they sought a new social, political, or economic order? What do these events tell you about traditional rural society in Europe? Who participated in such violence, and who led it?

Chapter 13

Peasant Violence:

Rebellion and

Riot in Early

Modern Europe,

1500–1789

SOURCES AND METHOD

We have assembled a number of different kinds of sources to assist you in answering the basic questions posed in this chapter. Nonetheless, you quickly will perceive that this evidence has two basic origins. One part of the evidence is the work of nonpeasants, usually various people in authority who were concerned with the reestablishment of order after collective violence. Some of the authors of such sources, as you will see, had little concern with the peasants' point of view and assumed that rebellions and riots were the work of the very lowest, and materially the most dispossessed, elements of society. Persons in authority also tended to believe that outsiders often stirred up peasant revolts and riots, and that peasants themselves were incapable of mobilizing and directing a movement. Since for centuries historians chiefly consulted the works of such authority figures, their writings long reflected the opinions evident in these sources.

The second origin of our evidence is sources written by the peasants themselves, or their representatives. Until recently, these sources frequently were more difficult for historians to consult because they generally were buried in police and administrative archives. In such sources, we can come closer to ascertaining the causes of peasant unrest, but we often find that their authors lack a complete understanding of the problems that led them to revolt.

The sources are drawn from a number of different rebellions and riots from 1525 to 1789. The events recounted in these sources occurred all over Europe (in England, France, Germany, the Habsburg monarchy, Piedmont-Sardinia, and Russia) and were selected to illustrate several different manifestations of collective violence. Sources 1 and 2 originated in German peasant revolts in the late fifteenth and early sixteenth centuries. Germany was the scene of widespread, powerful peasant rebellions in this period; indeed, some observers estimate that as many as 300,000 peasants took up arms in the German Peasants' Revolt of 1525. A number of problems produced these disturbances, including the continuing effects of a late medieval economic crisis that was in part the result of the devastation of Europe's population by the bubonic plague.

By the second half of the fifteenth century, Germany's population, recovering from the plague's effects, was growing, and that growth dramatically affected the status of peasants. The increased labor supply drove wages downward, while the sheer growth in population increased demand for food, and therefore its price. Seigniors, seeking to profit from this situation, caused growing discontent among their peasants as they pursued several different strategies to maximize the income from their estates. The lords increasingly appropriated for their own use common lands that traditionally had been open to all for the grazing of livestock and other purposes. They also shortened the peasants' leases on lands in order to raise rents at each renewal to keep up with inflation and to collect the fees that peasants paid their lord at renewal. And seigniors increased labor services and other dues collected from their peasants, so that the latter sensed a real worsening of their conditions. Clerical institutions, to which the peasants owed the tithe, which was usually paid in agricultural goods, also sought to maximize their incomes, and peasant resentment of an increasingly rigorous collection of the tithe also rose.

Policies pursued by German rulers also dismayed peasants. Germany in this period was a collection of more than 300 independent principalities, loosely governed by the Holy Roman Emperor. The rulers of many of these German states in this period sought to strengthen and modernize their realms, at a rising cost to the peasant. New bureaucracies, increasingly costly in terms of taxes, eroded traditional regional or communal political autonomy and imposed, in place of old customary laws, new law codes based on Roman law principles.

Other factors affected peasant response to these developments. Early modern agriculture was extremely vulnerable to weather conditions, blights, and pests, and German peasants in this period endured a great deal of suffering from failed harvests; as an example, in one part of the Holy Roman Empire, Alsace, harvests failed fifteen times in the period from 1475 to 1525. Such failures, amid their other problems, led many

peasants to a belief that divine intervention might dramatically improve their lot. Indeed, astrological prediction, particularly attractive to the less educated, foretold dramatic events for the year 1525 and encouraged peasant action at that time.

One final element that also contributed to peasant unrest, at least after 1517, was the Protestant Reformation, whose main German leader was Martin Luther. Certainly Luther condemned peasant rebellion when it broke out, but his message defying the authority of Rome must have caused already restive peasants to question the established authority of their seigniors, and of at least local officials of Church and state.

The convergence of these developments produced widespread peasant rebellion in German lands, beginning with the Bundschuh Rebellion in Alsace as early as the 1439–1444 period. The name of this rebellion was derived from the symbol that the peasants displayed on their banners, the peasants' heavy work shoe (*schuh* is "shoe" in German), which was bound by a thong (*bund* in German; the word has a double meaning, "thong" or "tie" but also "association"). The shoe on rebel peasant banners often supported symbols of the papacy and the Holy Roman Emperor, representing the peasants' rejection of all authority save that of the pope and the emperor. German peasants also raised such banners in 1493, 1502, 1513, 1517, and 1525.

Source 1 is a wood block engraving of peasants with a *bundschuh* banner. The work of a sixteenth-century

Chapter 13

Peasant Violence:
Rebellion and
Riot in Early
Modern Europe,
1500–1789

engraver, the picture portrays the revolt of German peasants in 1525. What symbol rests on the shoe on the banner? What is the response to the banner of the peasants at the right of the picture? What do you conclude from this about peasant loyalties? Why does this picture suggest peasant millenarianism to you? In the background of the picture, among portrayals of peasant labor, you will notice a picture of the Old Testament prophet Abraham sacrificing his son Isaac. Why do you think the artist included this scene?

Source 2 also comes from the German Peasants' Revolt of 1525, the last and greatest of the early modern rebellions in Germany. It began in southwest Germany in the summer of 1524 and engulfed most of the southern and central parts of the country in 1525. The rebellion started as a strike rather than a rebellion, with peasant communities refusing to work until they negotiated better conditions from their lords. But soon peasants selected leaders, marched around their regions to rally support, and turned to violence. German peasant rebels chose the same targets in 1525 as they had in earlier uprisings: the authority represented by castles and monasteries. These places were plundered and sometimes their occupants were killed as the peasants forged themselves into military forces to oppose the armies of the German princes.

German peasants frequently asked literate members of their communities, such as priests or craftsmen, to draft lists of their demands for change. Since many peasant commu-

nities drafted such lists of the local problems that prompted them to revolt, historians have a good record of the rebellion's causes. Probably the most concise of these is the Twelve Articles of the Upper Swabian Peasants (Upper Swabia was a region in southwestern Germany), which represents a distillation of over three hundred peasant grievances drafted by a Protestant pastor, Christoph Schappeler, and a Protestant layman, Sebastien Lutzer. Because the authors drew on actual peasant grievances in writing their document, the Twelve Articles, presented in Source 2, offer an authentic expression of peasant desires. This document also became a call to action for other peasants because the new printing presses of the early sixteenth century allowed the Twelve Articles to be reproduced in quantity and circulated widely. Moreover, there is evidence that they were read aloud to rally illiterate audiences to the cause of revolt, and even though the peasant rebels proved unable to unify their forces and, thus, were defeated and brutally punished by the armies of German rulers, the Twelve Articles had an enduring significance. Peasants in about one-third of the rebel areas, despite their defeat, succeeded in reaching agreements with their lords that met at least some of the desires stated in articles.

What role in their revolt did the authors of the Twelve Articles ascribe to the new religious teaching of the Reformation? What are the peasants' demands in the area of religion? What view do the authors express on serfdom? What were peasant complaints with regard to noble rights to land use and feudal dues? How did the peasants justify their position? What effect do you think the Twelve Articles would have had on peasant audiences hearing them for the first time?

English peasants experienced some of the same problems as their German contemporaries. The growth of England's post-plague population in the fifteenth and sixteenth centuries held down wages and drove up prices for necessities, while currency debasement to finance an ambitious foreign policy only added to inflation. Exacerbating the rural economic difficulties engendered by inflation was a substantial change in English agriculture. Landowners sought to benefit from rising prices for agricultural goods by increasing their production. This could be done in several ways. One way was to clear forest land and to bring wastelands under the plow, but the amount of such land was limited. Another way for landowners to increase output was through enclosure.

This practice, which had been occurring in England from as early as the thirteenth century, proceeded in two ways. Some nobles and gentry encroached on the common lands of their estates, chiefly pastures traditionally set aside for their tenants' livestock, enclosing these areas with fences or hedges for their own use. Other estate owners simply evicted tenants who could not prove their rights to small farms on large estates and consolidated these lands, again enclosing them with fences or hedges.

Landowners particularly engaged in enclosure to undertake large-scale sheep raising. The general population growth of the West in the fifteenth and sixteenth centuries led to demand for increasing quantities of wool cloth for clothing, and England long had been the source for much of Europe's raw wool. Thus, much of the newly enclosed land was used to pasture sheep. But this process of enclosure was not without cost for those who were not substantial landowners. Loss of common rights reduced the incomes of many peasants, while enclosure entirely displaced others from the land. Indeed, sixteenth-century officials charged with maintaining public order had to deal with large numbers of wandering poor, the victims of this structural change in agriculture. Such officials also faced rising peasant opposition to enclosure.

Anti-enclosure riots, in which crowds knocked down fences and leveled hedges, were the most common form of rural protest in the early sixteenth century. But in the late 1540s the number of such riots against agricultural innovation increased, and, as we will see in one case, some of them grew into outright rebellion. Several political developments seen to have contributed to this growing peasant militancy. King Henry VIII died on January 28, 1547, and the crown passed to his son, Edward VI, a boy of nine years of age, who lacked the authority of his father. Administrative authority in the late 1540s was in the hands of the monarch's uncle, Edward Seymour, Duke of Somerset and Lord Protector. Somerset had

Chapter 13

Peasant Violence:

Rebellion and

Riot in Early

Modern Europe,

1500–1789

considerable sympathy for the peasantry affected by enclosure. He issued two proclamations ordering the cessation of the practice and, over the opposition of landowners, sent out royal commissions to investigate enclosure abuses. The apparent support of the Protector encouraged many in their opposition to enclosure and hastened open rebellion in the county of Norfolk, an area of extensive wool and cloth production.

Events in that county moved toward violence in the summer of 1549, culminating at Wymondham on the feast of the Translation of St. Thomas Becket, a traditional gathering for peasants in the area. Much more than religious ceremony marked the observance of this day on Sunday, July 7, 1549. Peasants also seem to have heatedly discussed their grievances over enclosure, for the next day, crowds returning from Wymondham began to demolish fences and hedges in the area. Soon these violent crowds coalesced into a major force of perhaps 16,000 men under the leadership of Robert Kett (1492–1549), a local landowner. Kett led his followers to capture the county seat, Norwich, then England's second largest city. There Kett presided over a very conservative resistance to enclosure. He and his followers did not question royal authority and the law; rather, they set up law courts to try landowners for their abuses.

As much as he might have sympathized with the demands of Kett and his followers, Somerset could not ignore the threat to public order posed by such events. Thus, he dispatched an army that recaptured Norwich,

crushed the rebellion, and captured its leaders. The authorities executed Kett in December 1549.

Kett and his followers, like the German peasants of 1525, left a statement of their objectives, the Twenty-Nine Demands addressed to the king, which are excerpted in Source 3. This document reveals the causes of Kett's rebellion, but shows signs of having been hastily drafted: The demands represent a diverse list of grievances, presented in no systematic order. Indeed, although the rebels accepted the religious reforms of Henry VIII that had taken England out of the Roman Catholic Church, they also offered a number of demands for clerical reform (which are not included in Source 3). As you read these demands, you also will note that local concerns often intruded into the rebels' list. Thus, in the first demand that "no man shall enclose any more," drafters sought an exemption from this requirement for the large number of Norfolk residents who raised saffron for use as a textile dye.

Against what practices and which social group are these demands directed? In what tone do the drafters of these demands address the monarch? Why would you consider this an essentially conservative document rather than a revolutionary one? Given the great concern about property rights in the demands, what do you think was the social and economic status of their authors?

Numerous peasant rebellions erupted in France in the sixteenth and seventeenth centuries, particularly in the southwestern quarter of the kingdom. The cause of these rebellions was the rising royal tax burden imposed on the peasants and the way in which it was collected. Taxes were increasing during the sixteenth and seventeenth centuries because France frequently was at war and royal revenues had to rise to meet military costs. But often taxes went up far more than the government's expenses. This was because the monarchy, lacking a sufficient bureaucratic structure to collect all its taxes, "farmed out" most of its indirect taxes. Under this system, syndicates of investors bid for the right to collect a royal tax; in order to make a profit, they had to collect the amount the crown expected from the tax plus additional sums to defer the cost of collection and to provide a profit margin.

Peasant taxpayers were well aware of this system and scorned the collectors, whom they called *gabelleurs* after the *gabelle,* a tax-farmed fee on salt sales. Peasants also detested the new royal tax officials, the *élus,* charged with assessing the main royal tax, the *taille.* The taille, paid only by commoners, was levied on a parish, and then taxes were assessed on parish residents, in principle in proportion to their worth. But because this tax was a parish obligation and not an individual obligation, a taxpayer might have to pay more than his proportionate share if his neighbors were delinquent in paying or if wealthy and influential parishioners secured tax exemptions for themselves.

In 1636, amid a period of military emergency in which France was invaded by her enemies in the Thirty Years' War, taxes increased dramatically. So, too, did the local costs for garrisoning royal troops. The result was the revolt of the Croquants[2] of the Angoumois and Saintonge regions of southwestern France when officials tried to collect taxes in April 1636. Armed peasants assembled at the sound of their local parish alarm bells, selected leaders, and killed or drove off tax collectors, burned their homes, and besieged towns where they sought refuge. They were led by the wealthier peasants, parish priests, or local nobles forced by the crowd to take leadership roles because of their military experience.

With much of its military strength committed in the Thirty Years' War, the royal government at first met the Croquants' rebellion with a mixture of force and temporary concessions on tax issues, and the rebellion spread to the neighboring province of Périgord in 1637. Even though by the end of 1637 royal forces had defeated the peasants and captured and executed their leaders, extensive violence against tax officials continued until 1643.

The Angoumois rebels, in particular, left an excellent record of their objectives, as peasant leaders had assembled in June 1636 to draft lists of these goals. Seldom did peasants protest the power of local noblemen or the basic principle of royal taxation.

2. **Croquants:** the origin of this name, used as a term of derision for peasant rebels in several regions of southwestern France in the early modern period, is uncertain. Perhaps it is from the town of Crocq, or perhaps from croc, which is the name of the cudgel many peasants carried.

Chapter 13

Peasant Violence:

Rebellion and

Riot in Early

Modern Europe,

1500–1789

Rather, they argued against new royal taxes in the belief that these taxes were the work of corrupt royal officials and that the king would grant peasants tax relief if he only knew of his subordinates' dishonesty. In advancing their protest, peasants looked back nostalgically to an earlier age of lower taxes and demanded the return of those times.

While Angoumois Croquants stated their demands particularly well, their manifestos repeat themes that were common in the numerous French peasant rebellions from 1548 to 1675. Thus Source 4, a manifesto drafted by the peasants of Angoumois in 1636, typifies the demands of many early modern French peasant rebellions. What evidence do you find here of peasant concern for local problems and an effort on the part of peasants to exercise powers of government? What enemies in their own midst did the peasants single out? What abuses in taxation did the peasants protest? What response to their protest do you think they expected from the king? What role did peasants demand of the local nobility?

Seventeenth-century peasant revolts also challenged the authority of the tsar of Russia. As in France, we may find the roots of the greatest of these, that of Stepan Razin (1630?–1671), in the development of the early modern state. As we have seen in France, warfare placed extraordinary demands on the resources of the seventeenth-century monarchy, and the wars of Tsar Michael (r. 1613–1645) and Tsar Alexis (r. 1645–1676) with Sweden, Poland, Turkey, and the warlike Tartar tribes

along Russia's southern borders required great increases in taxation.

To collect new taxes, the government had to create an efficient bureaucratic apparatus, and the seventeenth century witnessed a growing centralization of the Russian state. New officials from the capital, Moscow, assumed most of the authority formerly exercised by local officials, including those at the village level, who traditionally had been elected. Thus, many Russians perceived the new officals as usurpers. In addition, because Tsar Michael and Tsar Alexis both took the throne as adolescents and were weak rulers who often let avaricious groups of advisers run the state apparatus for them, these officials were also seen by many as rapaciously dishonest.

New taxes, however, would produce no revenue if there were no taxpayers, and many Russian peasants fled to the frontiers of the country, to the steppes and the fertile Volga River valley in the south or to Siberia in the east, to escape taxes and military service. Indeed, on Russia's frontier in the southern valleys of the Don and Volga Rivers, a virtually independent society, that of the Cossacks, flourished and attracted many refugees fleeing from state authority.

Cossacks were descended from fugitives from the tsar's rule who recognized no authority but their own. They had their own general assembly, a *Krug;* elected their own chief, or *ataman;* and refused to pay taxes. They also forbade extensive agriculture in their lands, fearing the encroachment of Russian serfdom, and lived as hunters, fishermen, herders, and occasionally bandits and pirates. In return for their freedom and occasional payments from the treasury in Moscow, Cossacks performed services for the tsar, such as patrolling the frontier and providing defense against warlike tribes including the Crimean Tartars.

In response to the erosion of its tax base by the flight of taxpayers, the tsar's government produced the Sobornoye Ulozhenie, or Law Code of 1649, which sought to lock Russia's people into their existing condition in order to tax them efficiently. It required townsmen never to change their hometowns and to follow their fathers' occupations. Serfs lost any possibility of ever escaping their bondage to their lords.

In the years after 1649, the country experienced conditions that produced a great deal of unrest. Peasants continued to flee to the frontiers, and the numbers doing so grew greatly when Russia resumed its wars with Poland and Sweden after 1654. In response, the government for the first time sent agents to areas of the Volga Valley to recapture these fugitives. The financial demands of war also prompted the government to attempt to replace silver currency with copper, and the resulting inflation led to a revolt in Moscow in 1662. All the while, the country's losses mounted in the war with Poland, which lasted until 1667. And disease swept the country in the 1660s, killing perhaps 700,000 to 800,000 persons.

Out of these problems grew the Razin revolt. Razin was a Cossack leader who first achieved prominence in 1667 by leading a Cossack plundering expedition in the Volga Valley and the Caspian Sea. By 1670, his band of pirates had become a rebel army, and he announced his intention to march on Moscow to free the country from the tsar's evil advisers. His followers spread leaflets throughout the countryside as they advanced, proclaiming his loyalty to the tsar and his intent to "establish the Cossack way . . . so that all men will be equal."[3]

Razin amassed a great following, who often called him "Father." Escaped serfs, fearing recapture, joined his Cossack force, as did members of the lower clergy drawn from the peasantry, and even whole army units that also were of peasant origin. Everywhere Razin appeared, peasants burned local manor houses and the records of their obligations to their seigniors, and sometimes killed their lords. While Razin's force ultimately numbered perhaps 20,000 men, it was a poorly disciplined and ill-equipped force that was defeated in October 1670 when it encountered tsarist forces that were well equipped and well led.

Razin, wounded, retreated but was captured by Cossack leaders, who feared that his rebellion would lead to an increase in the tsar's authority in their region. They turned him over to the government, and he was executed in June 1671. The rebellion he had started dragged on for a while longer, but the army brutally crushed the revolt in the end; some

3. Quoted by Paul Avrich, *Russian Rebels, 1600–1800* (New York: Schocken Books, 1972), p. 89.

Chapter 13

Peasant Violence:

Rebellion and

Riot in Early

Modern Europe,

1500–1789

seventeenth-century observers estimated rebel losses in battle and in the ensuing repression at 100,000.

Source 5 recounts an incident in Razin's rebellion. It is part of a rather large literature written by foreign visitors to seventeenth-century Russia, a country then only poorly known in western Europe. Such accounts are not always reliable as sources because their value depends on their authors' knowledge of the country. The author of Source 5, Ludwig Fabritius, however, knew Russia well. A Dutch soldier employed with his stepfather, Paul Rudolph Breem, to serve as an expert on western European military methods in the Russian army, Fabritius lived in Russia from 1660 to 1677. He then served in the Swedish diplomatic corps, and died in Stockholm in 1729. While we must understand when we read Fabritius's account that his loyalties were with the tsar, he does provide a reliable account of events. Against whom does he say Razin directed his revolt? Who joined Razin's cause? Why might you think that Razin had not completely given up his earlier, plundering ways? What military effect do you think the decision, recounted here, to postpone the advance on Moscow in favor of an attack on Astrakhan had on Razin's campaign?

In the polyglot central European monarchy of the Habsburgs, such large-scale peasant rebellions also were a real concern to authorities, especially in the Bohemian lands that today form a large part of the Czech Republic. These lands had been the center of the religious reform movement of John Hus (1369–1415), which

had separated many residents of this area from the Roman Catholic Church. The Habsburgs, however, reimposed Catholicism in the wake of the Bohemian revolt that opened the Thirty Years' War, and the Habsburg defeat of Bohemian Protestants at the Battle of White Mountain (1620) permitted the monarchy to dispossess defeated Protestant noblemen of their lands and replace them with non-Bohemian lords who were loyal to the dynasty and its faith. These new, foreign seigniors imposed a harsh regime on peasants who, in the past, had achieved considerable freedom by converting their seigniorial obligations into cash payments; even the *robot* (*robota* is Slavonic for "work"), a requirement for peasant labor on the lord's behalf, had been convertible. The post-1620 settlement, however, confirmed the principle of *nexus subditelae*, which held that peasants on noble manors were subjects not of the monarch but of their seigniors, who thus had the power to administer justice on their lands, collect the peasants' taxes to the crown, and exact payments and labor from the peasants as their landlords. The new lords rigorously exacted their due, including the *robot*, which commonly came to represent a peasant obligation to the seignoir of three days' labor per week. From the peasants' standpoint, this obligation was made worse by the fact that it took precedence over all their other responsibilities; thus, at harvest time, the peasants' own crops might remain uncut and susceptible to weather damage while they harvested the fields of the seignior. Peasants did not passively accept such changes, and a large peasant rebellion erupted in Bohemia in 1680.

By the mid-eighteenth century, however, change in these conditions seemed imminent. The government of Maria Theresa (Archduchess of Austria and Queen of Bohemia and Hungary, 1740–1780) recognized that a modern state required tax revenues, which could be raised only from free and prosperous farmers. The monarch therefore ordered government inquiries into peasant conditions as a basis for their reform. Source 6 is an excerpt from a report resulting from such an inquiry in 1769. This is part of a large body of investigatory material produced by most eighteenth-century governments, representing the pioneering efforts of early modern states to generate hard data on which to base policy decisions. Such reports provide twentieth-century historians with essential information for understanding the society and economy of an earlier age. Source 6 is the work of an observant official of the Habsburg monarchy, who argues strongly for reform of the conditions of Bohemian peasants. Even with such evidence at hand, however, Maria Theresa was unable to achieve timely change in Bohemia as a result of the local nobility's opposition to reform. The monarch recognized that delay might prove costly. Indeed, in a letter in early 1775, she predicted that failure to achieve change in Bohemia might lead to revolt because desperate men could be dangerous. Her fears proved well founded. In January 1775, a revolt bred of discontent with

both the peasants' obligations to their seigniors and the reimposition of Catholicism broke out in eastern and northern Bohemia. Peasant leaders formed a government that declared its loyalty to Maria Theresa and proclaimed, mistakenly, that she actually had abolished the *robot* but that the nobility had suppressed her orders. Moreover, they led a large force against the capital, Prague, that required more than 40,000 troops to defeat. The monarchy's actions in the wake of its victory were conciliatory: Its officials executed only seven peasant leaders, and, more importantly, they renewed their efforts at reform in Bohemia.

Consider the conditions described in Source 6. What powers did Bohemian seigniors have over their peasants? What effect on the peasants did the report's author ascribe to the *robot?* How do you think peasants felt about such a significant decline in their condition over the previous several generations?

Rebellion in France is the subject of Source 7. In 1789, King Louis XVI (r. 1774–1792) called a meeting of the Estates General, a legislative body that had not met in 175 years, in an to attempt to secure sufficient taxes to prevent his government's impending bankruptcy. Economic difficulties were the lot of the king's subjects, too; the harvest of 1788 had been a meager one because of late summer storms, and in 1789 food prices were extremely high and the wandering poor filled the roads in search of jobs and food.

Election of the Estates General had raised peasants' hopes for some

Chapter 13

Peasant Violence:

Rebellion and

Riot in Early

Modern Europe,

1500–1789

improvement in their lot, especially when the representatives of the Third Estate of the Estates General declared that they would write a constitution for the country in defiance of the king's wishes. Indeed, when the king began to move troops to Versailles, where the Estates met, to disband the body, Parisians rose in rebellion and seized control of the capital on July 14, 1789; in provincial cities, similar municipal revolutions occurred. Although the king abandoned his military coup, news of these events reached the countryside. There the numerous wandering poor seem to have been the root of wild rumors that bands of brigands or foreign troops were coming to punish the peasants for their support of reform by burning their ripening crops. Through much of rural France, parish alarm bells rang in late July and early August, calling peasants to arm themselves for defense.

Of course the "brigands" never appeared, but armed peasants vented their anger against the property of their local seigniors in the rebellion known as the Great Fear. The particular targets of peasant violence were the archives of local manor houses containing records of their obligations, and many of these were burned. Source 7 is an account of the peasant attack on the Château of Cuireau, in the province of Dauphiné, drafted in October 1789 by an investigatory commission established by the provincial legislature. Written soon after the Great Fear, the account probably presents events accurately. What sorts of fears excited the peasants of Dauphiné? With what

did the peasants arm themselves? How many peasant bands stormed the Château of Cuireau? What was their objective? What role did rumor and tales of plots play in this uprising? Why might you conclude that what it is important for us to understand is what the peasants *thought* was happening rather than what we as historians know actually was happening?

Riots also disturbed the peace of early modern Europe, and many of them originated in the same problems that produced rural rebellion, often aristocratic attempts to modify the terms of peasant land tenure. But since early modern governments maintained none of the criminal justice data-gathering apparatus of the modern state, historians must carefully peruse sources like court records, the rather mundane administrative paperwork of government, and private correspondence for evidence of armed resistance. Indeed, Sources 8 and 9 come from the mass of petitions routinely received by every early modern ruler and from the voluminous private correspondence often carried on by educated early modern Europeans.

Source 8 includes two petitions originating in a series of large riots on the manor controlled by the Rottenbuch Abbey in Bavaria during the economic hard times of the Thirty Years' War. Beginning in the second decade of the seventeenth century, the abbey's prior sought to expel a number of peasant families from the manor in a dispute over land tenure. Peasants resisted these efforts over the period from 1619 to 1628 in a series of riots that required the ruler of Bavaria, Duke Maximilian I, to dispatch troops to the area to keep order and to arrest peasant leaders. One of these seemed to have been George Vend, whose personal property and home the authorities confiscated when they ordered Vend to leave his farm in Rottenbuch. Vend, however, defied this order, returning to his farm at least four times. Each defiance resulted in his arrest and expulsion from Rottenbuch.

In fact, Vend seems not to have left the area, for he participated in a mass two-day march of Rottenbuch peasants to Bavaria's capital, Munich, in August 1628 to petition the duke for redress of their grievances against the abbey and its prior. Vend was again arrested, and the authorities punished him by cutting off his ear and banishing him from Bavaria for life, a penalty that rendered him dead for purposes of civil law, as we will see in Source 8. Nevertheless, Vend ignored his banishment and returned to Rottenbuch with his family to plow his land. Again the authorities arrested him and expelled him from Bavaria, and the prior ordered that any local peasant feeding or sheltering Vend's wife, Christina, and his children would be fined. Christina then petitioned the duke to undo all of these penalties. The low rate of literacy among early modern peasant women suggests that Christina Vend must have used the services of a notary or attorney to draft the petitions reproduced in Source 8. She presented two petitions to the duke, the first one in February 1629 and the second the following month. The duke rejected the first and granted the requests in the second.

What role do you think George Vend played in the events at Rottenbuch? What difference in tone may have accounted for the failure of the first petition and the success of the second? What does this suggest to you that Bavaria's ruler sought in the country's peasantry? What elements of the settlement proposed in the second petition might suggest to you that the whole dispute might have originated in the prior's attempt to increase the abbey's revenues at Rottenbuch?

Peasant riots also occurred in Savoy, a province in an emerging state whose eighteenth-century territories are now part of southern France and northern Italy. The territories of the dukes of Savoy experienced several problems in the early eighteenth century that contributed to peasant unrest. The duke chose to fight neighboring France in the War of the Spanish Succession (1701–1714), and enemy forces occupied part of his territories, at considerable cost to their inhabitants. The ducal foreign policy was costly to them, too, as it required tax increases. Taxes remained high after the war, when the duke, Victor Amadeus II (r. 1675–1730), added the island of Sardinia to his territories in Savoy and Piedmont (northern Italy) and acquired a royal title, king of Piedmont-Sardinia.

While war and taxes reduced peasant resources, the duke sought to enhance his own revenues by selling titles of nobility, often to middle-class persons who could ill afford the investment. These new nobles often

Chapter 13

Peasant Violence:

Rebellion and

Riot in Early

Modern Europe,

1500–1789

attempted to recoup their investments quickly by redrafting surveys of their estate lands in their own favor and generally increasing peasants' seigniorial dues. This process of innovation encountered widespread resistance, as a nobleman named Vuy found in 1717.

Vuy had acquired the administration of a domain in Gets, Savoy, that was the possession of the chapter of Barnabite monks at Thonon, Savoy. On Sunday, March 14, 1717, Vuy, with an armload of papers supporting his right to the revenues of Gets, assembled the local peasants after Mass in a customary meeting place, the village cemetery, to advise them of his newly acquired authority. The crowd of several hundred was armed with sticks and clubs, and their reaction to their new seignior was recounted by Vuy himself in the letter that is excerpted in Source 9. It is an eyewitness account of events, although, since Vuy survived, we should probably assume that he embellished his account of the ferocity of the crowd.

What action did the crowd take against Vuy? Why do you think the crowd was so angry? Why would you not be surprised to learn that a careful study of Savoyard police and judicial records produced evidence of many other such violent incidents during this period?

Another frequent cause of early modern riots was the scarcity of food or its high price. The development of modern capitalism was fundamentally reshaping the provision of foodstuffs in the early modern period. Governments abandoned traditional controls on the trade and price of bread and other staples, and food supplies flowed not so much to where they were needed as to the markets, often in large and wealthy cities, that offered the highest prices to sellers. The result in many cases was higher prices for basic foods or a sudden shortage in supply. People responded violently to such developments. Indeed, food riots posed such an important threat to peace in this period that most governments carefully observed oscillations in food prices that might cause trouble, and some rulers attempted to restore regulations on the distribution of flour and the price of bread to keep that staple affordable.

Food riots could take several forms. Market riots generally occurred in urban areas when city residents, suspecting that speculators were driving food prices higher by hoarding flour or bread, stormed granaries and bakeries in search of those goods. Another form of crowd action, generally known by its French name, *entrave*, was driven by fear of hunger. In this action, peasant mobs stopped grain shipments to markets outside of their regions. A third form of collective action, a variety of food riot that the French call *taxation populaire*, expressed what one historian has called the "moral economy" of the crowd. In this form of riot, crowd members seized control of bread or grain in a period of shortage and high price and sold the foodstuffs at what they deemed a "just price." The "just price" always was far below market prices in times of shortage, but its uniformity throughout whole regions suggests widespread consensus among people as to the price that the poor could afford. Interestingly, the crowd turned the proceeds of such sales over to the merchants or bakers from whom it had seized the food.

A period of widespread food rioting, called the Flour War, erupted in the countryside around Paris in April 1775, as a result of the convergence of two developments. First, the grain harvest of 1774 was a poor one, and in 1775 bread prices rose as a consequence. Second, at almost the same time, the royal government announced complete freedom of the grain trade as a step toward implementing the economic thought of eighteenth-century Enlightenment thinkers, which called for free trade. From the peasants' perspective, rising food prices and the movement of grain to new markets outside their regions portended disaster and starvation, and they responded forcefully. Peasants stopped barges and wagons loaded with grain and brought *taxation populaire* to many a village, in some cases doubtlessly encouraged by unfounded rumors of royal orders to sell grain at a certain price. Violence abated only when the government moved two armies into the region in May 1775.

Source 10 presents a record of one riot in the Flour War. It is a record of an interrogation of a rioter by the Maréchaussée, or rural police, of eighteenth-century France. Such records can be very useful to the historian because they often provide researchers with almost verbatim accounts of the conflicts and actions of persons who normally leave historians no written records of their activities. The accused rioter, Louis Marais, did not deny being in the thick of the crowd action of May 3, 1775, but he did deny leading the riot. What evidence do you find that the peasants had an idea of a "just price" for wheat? Reflecting on the causes of the Flour War, why might you find the peasants' actions a political statement? How were these peasants simply responding to changes in government policy? How were the peasants attempting to restore earlier conditions?

Using this background on peasant violence, turn now to the evidence. As you read it, seek to formulate answers to the central questions of this chapter. What were the causes of these acts of collective violence by European peasants? Were these actions revolutionary in that they sought a new social, political, or economic order? What do these events tell you about traditional rural society in Europe? Who participated in such violence, and who led it?

Chapter 13

Peasant Violence:

Rebellion and

Riot in Early

Modern Europe,

1500–1789

THE EVIDENCE

Source 1 from Otto Brandt, Der deutsche Bauernkrieg *(1929), p. 25. Reprinted in Roland H. Bainton,* Here I Stand: A Life of Martin Luther *(New York: New American Library, 1963), p. 210.*

1. The German Peasants' Revolt of 1525: The *Bundschuh* Banner.

Source 2 from James Harvey Robinson and Merrick Whitcomb, editors, Translations and Reprints from the Original Sources, vol. II, no. 6: The Period of the Early Reformation in Germany *(Philadelphia: University of Pennsylvania Press, 1902).*

2. The German Peasants' Revolt of 1525: The Twelve Articles of the Peasants

Peace to the Christian reader, and the Grace of God through Christ.

There are many evil writings put forth of late which take occasion on account of the assembling of the peasants, to cast scorn upon the Gospel, saying: Is this the fruit of the new teaching, that no one should obey but all should everywhere rise in revolt, and rush together to reform, or perhaps destroy entirely, the authorities, both ecclesiastical and lay? The articles below shall answer these godless and criminal fault-finders, and serve in the first place to remove the reproach from the word of God and, in the second place, to give a Christian excuse for the disobedience or even the revolt of the entire Peasantry. In the first place the Gospel is not the cause of revolt and disorder, since it is the message of Christ, the promised Messiah, the Word of Life, teaching only love, peace, patience and concord. Thus, all who believe in Christ should learn to be loving, peaceful, long-suffering and harmonious. This is the foundation of all the articles of the peasants (as will be seen) who accept the gospel and live according to it. . . . In the second place, it is clear that the peasants demand that this Gospel be taught them as a guide in life, and they ought not to be called disobedient or disorderly. . . . Therefore, Christian reader, read the following articles with care and then judge. Here follow the articles:

The First Article: First, it is our humble petition and desire, as also our will and resolution, that in the future we should have power and authority so that each community should choose and appoint a pastor, and that we should have the right to depose him should he conduct himself improperly. The pastor thus chosen should teach us the Gospel pure and simple, without any addition, doctrine or ordinance of man. For to teach us continually the true faith will lead us to pray God that through his grace this faith may increase within us and become a part of us. For if his grace work not within us we remain flesh and blood, which availeth nothing; since the Scripture clearly teaches that only through true faith can we come to God. . . .

The Second Article: According as the just tithe is established by the Old Testament and fulfilled in the New, we are ready and willing to pay the fair tithe of grain. The word of God plainly provides that in giving according to right to God and distributing to his people the services of a pastor are required. We will that for the future our church provost, whomsoever the community may appoint, shall gather and receive this tithe. From this he shall give to the pastor, elected by the whole community, a decent and sufficient maintenance for

Chapter 13

Peasant Violence:

Rebellion and

Riot in Early

Modern Europe,

1500–1789

him and his . . . , as shall seem right to the whole community (or, with the knowledge of the community). What remains over shall be given to the poor of the place, as the circumstances and the general opinion demand. Should anything farther remain, let it be kept, lest anyone should have to leave the country from poverty. Provision should also be made from this surplus to avoid laying any land tax on the poor. . . .

. . . The small tithes,[4] whether ecclesiastical or lay, we will not pay at all, for the Lord God created cattle for the free use of man. We will not, therefore, pay farther an unseemly tithe which is of man's invention.

The Third Article: It has been the custom hitherto for men to hold us as their own property, which is pitiable enough, considering that Christ has delivered and redeemed us all, without exception by the shedding of his precious blood, the lowly as well as the great. Accordingly, it is consistent with Scripture that we should be free and wish to be so. Not that we would wish to be absolutely free and under no authority. God does not teach us that we should lead a disorderly life in the lusts of the flesh, but that we should love the Lord our God and our neighbor. We would gladly observe all this as God has commanded us in the celebration of the communion. He has not commanded us not to obey the authorities, but rather that we should be humble, not only towards those in authority, but towards everyone. We are thus ready to yield obedience according to God's law to our elected and regular authorities in all proper things becoming to a Christian. We, therefore, take it for granted that you will release us from serfdom, as true Christians, unless it should be shown us from the Gospel that we are serfs.

The Fourth Article: In the fourth place it has been the custom heretofore, that no poor man should be allowed to touch venison or wild fowl, or fish in flowing water, which seems to us quite unseemly and unbrotherly, as well as selfish and not agreeable to the word of God. In some places the authorities preserve the game to our great annoyance and loss, recklessly permitting the unreasoning animals to destroy to no purpose our crops, which God suffers to grow for the use of man, and yet we must remain quiet. This is neither godly nor neighborly. For when God created man he gave him dominion over all the animals, over the birds of the air and over the fish in the water. Accordingly it is our desire if a man holds possession of waters that he should prove from satisfactory documents that his right has been unwittingly acquired by purchase. We do not wish to take it from him by force, but his rights should be exercised in a Christian and brotherly fashion. But whosoever cannot produce such evidence should surrender his claim with good grace.

---

4. **small tithe:** peasants owed tithes to support the Church, although the right to collect these could be owned by laymen. The small tithe was payable on the value of livestock in much of Germany and also as a percentage of the crop of fruits or vegetables. The great tithe was payable on grains.

The Fifth Article: In the fifth place we are aggrieved in the matter of wood-cutting, for the noble folk have appropriated all the woods to themselves alone. If a poor man requires wood he must pay double for it. . . . It is our opinion in regard to a wood, which has fallen into the hands of a lord, whether spiritual or temporal, that unless it was duly purchased it should revert again to the community. . . .

The Sixth Article: Our sixth complaint is in regard to the excessive services demanded of us, which are increased from day to day. We ask that this matter be properly looked into so that we shall not continue to be oppressed in this way, and that some gracious consideration be given us, since our forefathers were required only to serve according to the word of God.

The Seventh Article: Seventh, we will not hereafter allow ourselves to be farther oppressed by our lords, but will let them demand only what is just and proper according to the word of the agreement between the lord and the peasant. . . .

The Eighth Article: In the eighth place, we are greatly burdened by holdings which cannot support the rent exacted from them. The peasants suffer loss in this way and are ruined; and we ask that the lords may appoint persons of honor to inspect these holdings, and fix a rent in accordance with justice, so that the peasant shall not work for nothing, since the laborer is worthy of his hire.

The Ninth Article: In the ninth place, we are burdened with a great evil in the constant making of new laws. We are not judged according to the offence, but sometimes with great ill will, and sometimes much too leniently. In our opinion we should be judged according to the old written law, so that the case shall be decided according to its merits, and not with partiality.

The Tenth Article: In the tenth place, we are aggrieved by the appropriation by individuals of meadows and fields which at one time belonged to a community. These we will take again into our own hands. . . .

The Eleventh Article: In the eleventh place we will entirely abolish the due called *Todfall*[5] . . . , and will no longer endure it, nor allow widows and orphans to be thus shamefully robbed against God's will, and in violation of justice and right, as has been done in many places, and by those who should shield and protect them. . . .

Conclusion: In the twelfth place it is our conclusion and final resolution, that if one or more of the articles here set forth should not be in agreement with the word of God, as we think they are, such article we will willingly recede from, when it is proved really to be against the word of God by a clear

---

5. **todfall:** death tax. This was a sort of transfer fee, payable to the peasants' seignior, when the peasant proprietor died and his property passed to his heir. Its traditional form in Germany required a male heir to give up his best horse and best garment and a female heir to render her best cow and best garment.

Chapter 13

Peasant Violence:

Rebellion and

Riot in Early

Modern Europe,

1500–1789

explanation of the Scripture. . . . Likewise, if more complaints should be discovered which are based upon truth and the Scriptures, and relate to offences against God and our neighbor, we have determined to reserve the right to present these also, and to exercise ourselves in all Christian teaching. For this we shall pray God, since he can grant this, and he alone. The peace of Christ abide with us all.

Source 3 from Stephen K. Land, Kett's Rebellion: The Norfolk Rising of 1549 *(Ipswich: The Boydell Press; Totowa, N.J.: Rowman and Littlefield, 1977), pp. 63–66. Reprinted by permission of Boydell & Brewer Ltd.*

3. The Twenty-Nine Demands of Kett's Rebellion, 1549

1. We pray your grace that where it is enacted for inclosing that it be not hurtfull to such as have enclosed saffron grounds for they be greatly chargeable to them, and that from henceforth no man shall enclose any more.

2. We certifie your grace that whereas the lords of the manors have been charged with certain free rent, the same lords have sought means to charge the freeholders to pay the same rent, contrary to right.

3. We pray your grace that no lord of no manor shall common[6] upon the commons.

4. We pray that priests from henceforth shall purchase no lands neither free nor bond, and the lands that they have in possession may be letten to temporal men,[7] as they were in the first year of the reign of King Henry VII.[8]

5. We pray that reedground and meadowground[9] may be at such price as they were in the first year of King Henry VII.

6. We pray that all the marshes that are held of the King's majesty by free rent or of any other, may be again at the price that they were in the first year of King Henry VII. . . .

9. We pray that the payments of castleward rent,[10] and blanch farm,[11] and office lands,[12] which hath been accustomed to be gathered of the tenaments, whereas we suppose the lords ought to pay the same to their bailiffs for their rents gathering, and not the tenants.

6. **common:** to pasture one's herds.

7. **letten to temporal men:** leased to nonclergy.

8. King Henry VII, the first monarch of the governing Tudor family, ruled from 1485 to 1509.

9. **reedground and meadowground:** marshy areas and pasture land.

10. **castleward rent:** a levy on buildings in the proximity of a royal castle to pay for its upkeep.

11. **blanch farm:** sometimes also called "white rents," these were the fixed rents of tenants on manors and were so named because they were paid in silver, or "white" money.

12. **office lands:** crown lands. This article protests lords shifting their obligations to the crown to their tenants.

10. We pray that no man under the degree of a knight of esquire keep a dove house,[13] except it hath been of an old ancient custom.

11. We pray that all freeholders and copyholders may take the profits of all commons, and there to common, and the lords not to common nor take profits of the same. . . .

13. We pray your grace to take all liberty of leet[14] into your own hands whereby all men may quietly enjoy their commons with all profits.

14. We pray that copyhold[15] land that is unreasonable rented may go as it did in the first year of King Henry VII and that at the death of a tenant or of a sale the same lands to be charged with an easy fine as a capon[16] or a reasonable sum of money for a remembrance. . . .

16. We pray that all bond men[17] may be made free for God made all free with his precious blood shedding.

17. We pray that rivers may be free and common to all men for fishing and passage. . . .

21. We pray that it be not lawful to the lords of any manor to purchase lands freely and to let them out again by copy of court roll to their great advantage and to the undoing of your poor subjects. . . .

27. We pray your grace to give license and authority by your gracious commission under your great seal to such commissioners as your poor commons hath chosen, or to as many of them as your majesty and your council shall appoint and think meet, for to redress and reform all such good laws, statutes, proclamations, and all other your proceedings, which hath been bidden by your Justices of your peace, Sheriffs, Escheators,[18] and others your officers, from your poor commons, since the first year of the reign of your noble grandfather King Henry the seventh.[19] . . .

29. We pray that no lord, knight, esquire, nor gentleman do graze nor feed any bullocks or sheep if he may spend forty pounds a year by his lands but only for the provision of his house.[20]

---

13. **dove house:** a structure used as a nesting place for pigeons. English and European noblemen often maintained such structures for the pigeons that they hunted for sport. The pigeons often fed on the crops of neighboring peasants.

14. **leet:** a court meeting annually or semiannually in which certain manor lords judged local disputes.

15. **copyhold:** landholding rights proven by record in the rolls of a manorial court.

16. **capon:** a rooster castrated to improve its flesh when cooked.

17. **bond men:** literally, feudal serfs. Such persons were extremely rare in sixteenth-century England.

18. **Escheator:** a royal official appointed for each county to oversee escheats, that is, the property that reverted to the crown when its deceased owners had no legal heirs.

19. This demand calls for the election of delegates, or commissioners, from Norfolk to reform laws made since 1485.

20. **provision of his house:** those animals necessary to feed the households. This demand intends to limit the grazing of livestock by gentry to such a number, thus limiting their pursuit of large-scale stock raising.

Chapter 13

Peasant Violence:

Rebellion and

Riot in Early

Modern Europe,

1500–1789

Source 4 from Archives Nationales de France, U793, f⁰ˢ 88–89 v⁰; reprinted in Yves-Marie Bercé, Histoire des Croquants: Étude des soulèvements populaires au XVIIᵉ siècle dans le Sud-Ouest de la France (Geneva: Librairie Droz, 1974), vol. II, p. 738. Translated by Julius R. Ruff.

4. Manifesto of the Peasants of the Angoumois, 1636

The assembly of the common people, having deliberated, ordered the following in a few words.

All inhabitants of each parish are directed to gather all payments due the priest of each parish and place them in the safekeeping of the two richest parishioners who will give the inhabitants an exact count of them. The priest will receive 300 *livres*[21] of this free and clear in estimated value of goods or in money. The remainer will be used to repair the church and to care for the parish poor.

We also direct all inhabitants of each parish to arm themselves according to their means and to be well supplied with lead and powder under the threat of a 20 *livres* fine for lacking powder and lead and being rebels.

We also direct each parish in the future, when they have received their assessments, to tax only three-quarters of the principal of the *taille*, because His Majesty will have lowered it for us, and also to tax only one-half of the increase in garrison costs because this has gone up by one-half in six years.

We direct each parish, when it wishes to apportion the *taille* among its citizens, to call upon the parish priest to undertake the process conscientiously and to assess the tax obligations among those with sufficient property to pay them. This is to be done without regard for personal connections and without fear of the power of the rich in order to relieve the poor of God.

We direct each parish to make the nobility provide arms and march in our cause under threat of having their manor houses burned and being denied payment of rents and *agriers*[22] due them.

We direct each parish to pass on a copy of this decree under penalty of being destroyed by our movement.

Sirs, we warn you that the real *gabelleurs* are the *élus* . . . , the richest of each parish who pay practically nothing. It has been confirmed in Paris that the *élus* of Saintes and Fontenay gather impositions of 60,000 *livres* over and above the sums authorized by His Majesty. All things considered, we have or-

---

21. *livres:* the main unit of Old Regime French currency, containing 20 *sous*. *Livres* means "pounds," but it is not translated as such because the French *livre* and British pound sterling were not equal in value.

22. *agriers:* a payment in kind, about 12 percent of the crop, which peasants owed their lords.

dered without appeal that the *élus* will be arrested by the commune in order to render justice . . . and make them restore with interest the notorious sums that they have stolen.

And as for the rich of each parish who completed the people's ruin, they must be excluded from the apportioning of the *taille* in the future and assessed their correct portion.

Source 5 from Ludwig Fabritius, Account of the Razin Rebellion, Oxford Slavonic Papers, *vol. 10 (1955), reprinted in Anthony Cross, editor,* Russia Under Western Eyes, 1517–1825 *(London: Elek Books, 1971), pp. 120–123.*

5. Ludwig Fabritius's Account of the Stepan Razin Revolt, 1670

Then Stenka[23] with his company started off upstream, rowing as far as Tsaritsyn, whence it took him only one day's journey to Panshin, a small town situated on the Don. Here he began straightaway quietly gathering the common people around him, giving them money, and promises of great riches if they would be loyal to him and help to exterminate the treacherous boyars.[24]

This lasted the whole winter, until by about spring he had assembled 4,000 to 5,000 men. With these he came to Tsaritsyn and demanded the immediate surrender of the fortress; the rabble soon achieved their purpose, and although the governor tried to take refuge in a tower, he soon had to give himself up as he was deserted by one and all. Stenka immediately had the wretched governor hanged; and all the goods they found belonging to the Tsar and his officers as well as to the merchants were confiscated and distributed among the rabble.

Stenka now began once more to make preparations. Since the plains are not cultivated, the people have to bring their [grain] from Nizhniy-Novgorod and Kazan down the Volga in big boats known as *nasady,* and everything destined for Astrakhan has first to pass Tsaritsyn. Stenka Razin duly noted this, and occupied the whole of the Volga, so that nothing could get through to Astrakhan. Here he captured a few hundred merchants with their valuable goods, taking possession of all kinds of fine linen, silks, striped silk material, sables, soft leather, ducats, talers, and many thousands of rubles in Russian money, and merchandise of every description—these men used to do much trade with the Persians, the Bokharans, the Uzbeks, and the Tartars.

23. **Stenka:** the diminutive of "Stepan," that is, "little Stepan."
24. **boyars:** noblemen.

Chapter 13

Peasant Violence:

Rebellion and

Riot in Early

Modern Europe,

1500–1789

In the meantime four regiments of *streltsy*[25] were dispatched from Moscow to subdue these brigands. They arrived with their big boats and as they were not used to the water, were easily beaten. Here Stenka Razin gained possession of a large amount of ammunition and artillery-pieces and everything else he required. While the above-mentioned *streltsy* were sent from Moscow, about 5,000 men were ordered up from Astrakhan by water and by land to capture Stenka Razin. As soon as he had finished with the former, he took up a good position, and, being in possession of reliable information regarding our forces, he left Tsaritsyn and came to meet us half way at Chernyy Yar, confronting us before we had suspected his presence or received any information about him. . . .

. . . We got out of our boats and took up battle positions. General Knyaz Semen Ivanovich Lvov went through the ranks and reminded all the men to do their duty and to remember the oath they had taken to His Majesty the Tsar, to fight like honest soldiers against these irresponsible rebels, whereupon they all unanimously shouted: 'Yes, we will give our lives for His Majesty the Tsar, and will fight to the last drop of our blood.'

In the meantime, Stenka prepared for battle and deployed on a wide front; to all those who had no rifle he gave a long pole, burnt a little at one end, and with a rag or small hook attached. They presented a strange sight on the plain from afar, and the common soldiers imagined that, since there were so many flags and standards, there must be a host of people. They [the common soldiers] held a consultation and at once decided that this was the chance for which they had been waiting so long, and with all their flags and drums they ran over to the enemy. They began kissing and embracing one another and swore with life and limb to stand together and to exterminate the treacherous boyars, to throw off the yoke of slavery, and to become free men.

The general looked at the officers and the officers at the general, and no one knew what to do; one said this, and another that, until finally it was decided that they and the general should get into the boats and withdraw to Astrakhan. But the rascally *streltsy* of Chernyy Yar stood on the walls and towers, turning their weapons on us and opened fire; some of them ran out of the fortress and cut us off from the boats, so that we had no means of escape. In the meantime those curs of ours who had gone over to the Cossacks came up from behind. We numbered about eighty men, officers, noblemen, and clerks. Murder at once began. Then, however, Stenka Razin ordered that no more officers were to be killed, saying that there must be a few good men among them who should be pardoned, whilst those others who had not lived in

25. **streltsy:** literally "sharpshooters." These military units, organized by Ivan the Terrible in 1550, were the first Russian troops to carry firearms. Recruited from all classes of commoners, these soldiers lived in their own settlements until Peter the Great disbanded their units in 1698 after a series of mutinies.

amity with their men should be condemned to well-deserving punishment by the Ataman and his *Krug*. A *Krug* is a meeting convened by the order of the Ataman, at which the Cossacks stand in a circle with the standard in the centre; the Ataman then takes his place beside his best officers, to whom he divulges his wishes, ordering them to make these known to the common brothers and to hear their opinion on the matter; if the proposals of the Ataman please the commoners, they all shout together, 'Lyubo, lyubo'.

A *Krug* was accordingly called and Stenka asked through his chiefs how the general and his officers had treated the soldiers under their command. Thereupon the unscrupulous curs, *streltsy* as well as soldiers, unanimously called out that there was not one of them who deserved to remain alive, and they all asked that their father Stepan Timofeyevich Razin should order them to be cut down. . . .

. . . When all the bloodthirsty curs had lined up, each was eager to deal his former superior the first blow, one with the sword, another with the lance, another with the scimitar, and others again with martels, so that as soon as an officer was pushed into the ring, the curs immediately killed him with their many wounds; indeed, some were cut to pieces and straightaway thrown into the Volga. My stepfather, Paul Rudolf Beem, and Lt. Col. Wundrum and many other officers, senior and junior, were cut down before my eyes.

My own time had not yet come: this I could tell by the wonderful way in which God rescued me, for as I—half-dead—now awaited the final blow, my [former] orderly, a young soldier, came and took me by my bound arms and tried to take me down the hill. As I was already half-dead, I did not move and did not know what to do, but he came back and took me by the arms and led me, bound as I was, through the throng of curs, down the hill into the boat and immediately cut my arms free, saying that I should rest in peace here and that he would be responsible for me and do his best to save my life. . . . Then my guardian angel told me not to leave the boat, and left me. He returned in the evening and brought me a piece of bread which I enjoyed since I had had nothing to eat for two days.

The following day all our possessions were looted and gathered together under the main flag, so that both our bloodthirsty curs and the Cossacks got their share.

Chapter 13

Peasant Violence:

Rebellion and

Riot in Early

Modern Europe,

1500–1789

Source 6 from C. A. Macartney, editor, The Habsburg and Hohenzollern Dynasties in the Seventeenth and Eighteenth Centuries *(New York: Harper and Row, Publishers, 1970), pp. 173–174. Copyright © 1970 by C. A. Macartney. Reprinted by permission of HarperCollins Publisher, Inc.*

6. Report of the Commission of Enquiry into the Conditions of the Peasants of Bohemia, presented to the Council of State in Vienna, June 1769

The *robot* gives rise to continual vexations. Even those nobles who have the best intentions are unable to protect their peasants, because their agents are rough, evil, violent and grasping. These burdens are terrifyingly heavy, and it is not surprising that the peasants try to evade them by every means. In consequence of the arbitrary allocation of the *robot,* the peasants live in a condition of real slavery; they become savage and brutalized, and cultivate the lands in their charge badly. They are rachitic,[26] thin and ragged; they are forced to do *robot* from their infancy. In their ruinous huts, the parents sleep on straw, the children naked on the wide shelves of earthenware stoves; they never wash, which promotes the spread of epidemics; there are no doctors to look after them. . . . Even their personal effects are not safe from the greed of the great lords. If they own a good horse, the lord forces them to sell it him, or if their good horse succumbs to the severity of the *robot,* they are compensated with a blind, old screw. In many places the serfs are forced to buy sick sheep from their lord at an arbitrarily fixed price. Implements of torture are set up in every village market square, or in front of the castle; recalcitrant peasants are thrown into irons, they are forced to sit astride a sharp wooden horse, which cuts deeply into their flesh; stones are hung on their legs; for the most trifling offense they are given fifty strokes of the rod; the serf who arrives late for his *robot,* be it only half an hour, is beaten half-dead. Many flee into Prussia to escape this reign of terror; there are hundreds of huts which their occupants have abandoned because they threatened to collapse and they had not the means to repair them. In other places the thatches have been taken off to feed the horses for lack of fodder, because these wretched creatures are forbidden to gather leaves in the forest for fear of their disturbing the game. Even when the harvest has been good they are obliged to ask for seed from their lord, and he sells it them at an extortionate price. The big landlords drive away the Jews, who make loans on better terms. . . . The Kingdom of Bohemia is like a statue which is collapsing because its pedestal has been taken away, because

26. **rachitic:** afflicted by rickets, a bone disorder resulting from vitamin D deficiency that generally afflicts children.

all the charges of the Kingdom are born by the peasants, who are the sole tax-payers.

Source 7 from Xavier Roux, Mémoire détaillé et par ordre de la marche des brigandages qui se sont commis en Dauphiné en 1789 *(Grenoble, 1891); reprinted in Yves-Marie Bercé,* Croquants et Nu-Pieds les soulèvements paysans en France du XVIe au XIXe siècle *(Paris: Gallimard/Julliard, 1974), pp. 125–128. Translated by Julius R. Ruff.*

7. Note on What Occurred Before and During the Devastation of the Château of Cuirieu During the Great Fear of July–August 1789

On Monday, July 27, 1789, about four in the afternoon, the tocsin in the market town of La Tour-du-Pin was heard to ring; a little later it was heard ringing in all the neighboring parishes.

On every side were heard only laments and cries of alarm, repeated on everyone's lips, that ten to twenty thousand men . . . were coming from the direction of Savoy[27] who were indiscriminately burning and killing. No sooner had they been said to have entered Dauphiné than it was said that they had entered La Tour-du-Pin. . . .

Upon hearing this alarm, a peasant host from different places, armed with guns, pitchforks, scythes, etc. came to La Tour-du-Pin, claiming to bring it assistance.

Couriers were dispatched in the direction that it was said the brigands were coming from . . . and they brought word that everything was calm and that this false alarm was caused by merchants hoarding food who were [seeking to profit from the false emergency by] offering wheat at 10 *sous* per measure above the current price in the Pont-de-Beauvoisin market; others subsequently arrived who gave other causes for this alarm. Thus one cannot rely on any version.

The next day, Tuesday, a band of about 150 persons, armed as above and claiming to be from Biol, Torchefelon, Châteauvilain Saint-Victor, and neighboring places, arrived at four in the morning at the Château of Cuirieu. They presented themselves at the gate . . . demanding entry for shelter from the rain, and, without waiting for the estate agent to return with the key to open the door for them . . . , they pushed on the door so hard that they forced it open. . . . They renewed an earlier assurance to the agent that they would not

27. **Savoy:** in the eighteenth century, Savoy was part of the territory of the Kingdom of Piedmont-Sardinia in northern Italy. Thus, what the peasants feared was probably a foreign attack.

Chapter 13

Peasant Violence:

Rebellion and

Riot in Early

Modern Europe,

1500–1789

harm him and said that they only wanted to warm themselves and drink a draught since they all were soaked. They also said that they had come from the Château du Pin where they had smashed in the doors of the wine cellar; several of them had bottles full of wine and appeared drunk. . . .

The next day, Wednesday, they learned at the Château of Cuirieu that a second band was at Vallin and that it was coming from there to Cuirieu. At five in the evening this crowd arrived with the objective of burning the *terriers*.[28] . . . The agent recognized a young man armed with a drawn sword at the head of a crowd of about one-hundred and fifty persons armed with guns, scythes, and other weapons; they were led by a drummer and marched in two columns. A few steps in front of them was the unarmed Sieur Domenjon, and the agent approached him. Upon entering the poultry yard at Cuirieu, the band shouted: "Long live the King!" and "Long live the Third Estate!" Sieur Domenjon said to the agent: "These people want your *terriers*; they have come from Vallin where they burned all the papers; if you have any old scrap paper, give it to them to satisfy them. . . ."

As soon as the band entered, it demanded to drink and eat; at the same time it began to make a racket. Sieur Domenjon reprimanded them and said to them: "No more noise. You know that you forced me to come and that you promised me that you would only do what I told you; thus, if you make a din, I will go no further with you." With the whole band shouting "We want papers!", Sieur Domenjon, assisted by four others drawn from the crowd, went up to the archives. The agent asked the priest of Saint-Blondine to please go up with him as he sought to satisfy the crowd. When he got there he turned over several bundles of papers and one or two very old manuscript books. On the books were maps upon which was written: "Inspected on such and such a year, month and day; useless or reported useless. . . ." These were thrown from the window to the band awaiting them in the courtyard. The band seized them, heaped them up, and set fire to them, saying that these were not the best records but that they would return.

Thursday, July 30, about five in the morning, a third band of about thirty men arrived led by a notary who they called "the Commandant." The notary told the estate agent that these men wanted all the *terriers* of Cessieu to make a fire of joy with them. . . .

A fourth band arrived on August 7 at six in the morning composed at first of thirty to forty persons but which grew all the time. . . . In the space of three hours, the château was laid waste and pillaged, all the furniture smashed or stolen, the linens stolen, the doors of the apartments pulverized so to speak, all the locks carried off, and the windows and stained glass windows

---

28. *terriers:* surveys that showed the ownership of land and, thereby, indicated to whom seigniorial dues were owed. By the eighteenth century, specialists in seigniorial rights drafted these documents to achieve maximum profits for the lord. Almost every château library had its collections of local *terriers*.

smashed. In the end, only that which the people of the château and the domestic servant aided by farmers and neighbors were able to secure was saved.

It was rumored that there was a man armed with a double-barreled gun, in a gray suit with a stylish waistcoat, who walked in the courtyard during the disaster without eating or drinking anything but who had the air of laughing at what was going on. He shortly left.

Source 8 from Bavarian State Archives, Munich, K1 641 ad 18, fol. 418–420 (first petition) and fol. 425–426 (second petition). Transcripts courtesy of Renate Blickle. Translated by Merry E. Wiesner.

8. The Petitions of Christina Vend to Duke Maximilian I, Elector of Bavaria, in February and March 1629

First Petition, February 1629

Most illustrious Elector[29] and gracious Lord:

I, a poor afflicted woman, in need so pressing that I would not otherwise bother your Electoral Grace with this insignificant letter, through the will of God, his beloved Virgin Mary, the Mother of God, and the Last Judgment, do call upon the mercy of your Electoral Grace to graciously listen to and look at my misery and pain.

On our manor and in our law court there has been a long dispute between the authorities of the abbey Rottenbuch and all of its subjects, but now—God be praised—it has come to a peaceful resolution. My husband has been treated in these events as if he were one of the instigators or leaders, but events show that even though I was forbidden from going home, [we] must conclude, he could not have been one of the instigators.

Gracious Prince and Lord, he was imprisoned not only in Munich and also in Landsberg, but no grounds for suspicion were discovered or accusations made, nor could they ever be made. Despite this he was banished from the

29. **elector:** one of the seven German rulers who, under the decree known as the Golden Bull of 1356, voted to select Germany's monarch, the Holy Roman Emperor of the German Nation. These rulers were the archbishops of Mainz, Trier, and Cologne; the king of Bohemia; the duke of Saxony; the margrave of Brandenburg; and the count palatine of the Rhine. In 1623, Emperor Ferdinand II deprived the count palatine of the electoral dignity because of his defiance of imperial authority in leading a revolt in Bohemia that began the Thirty Years' War, awarding it to the duke of Bavaria. In 1648, the Treaty of Westphalia created an eighth elector by restoring the vote of the count palatine. A ninth elector was added in 1692 when the rulers of Hanover received the electoral dignity.

Chapter 13

Peasant Violence:

Rebellion and

Riot in Early

Modern Europe,

1500–1789

country [Bavaria], his ear was cut off, and he was driven out with sticks. All this he bore patiently.

What is even more, the judge in Rottenbuch not only banished me and my poor innocent children from the manor, but on the Sunday just past he announced in front of the church, and forbade the whole community, that whoever helped or housed me or my children or let us stay overnight would be punished with a 10 Thaler fine for the first instance and 20 Thaler for the second. This must be lamented to God the Almighty in Heaven, that we come into this situation and into poverty innocently, and my husband bore everything that happened to him obediently and with patience.

So, gracious Electro and Lord, if it is necessary, I will get a letter and petition from the whole community and manor of Rottenbuch, that he was not an instigator or agitator, no matter what else is said. . . . If he had been an instigator or agitator, he said himself that he would not only have withstood his punishment obediently, but would have even given his life. . . . So [he] and I as his afflicted wife and his innocent children do not have to suffer and be driven from our homeland, [we] shall not leave off calling to Your Electoral Illustriousness in our deepest need in God's name . . . to let us maintain our property and to open the country again to my husband and let him come home. . . .

Your Electoral Illustriousness's poor distressed abandoned wife with two innocent children, Your obedient,

Christina Vend, the wife of George Vend, who has been exiled from the country.

Second Petition, March 1629

Illustrious Duke, Gracious Elector and Lord. I have had read to me the answer of my Lord Prior of Rottenbuch to my humble supplication, about whether I must continue to stay away from my piece of property at Rottenbuch. With the most sorrowful heart I understood that my request was heard, but that the situation was still to remain the same. Through this I gathered and understood that I and my two young orphans,[30] because of our husband's and father's insubordination, must unfortunately leave and go to him in bitter misery, and must be dispossessed.

Now I must certainly acknowledge, that my aforementioned husband definitely did wrong and earned his punishment, because he so strongly resisted the many warnings given him in a fatherly way. However, I have learned, that

---

30. **orphans:** in law, the banishment of George Vend represented "civil death," that is, the termination of his civil and property rights. Thus, his children were legally fatherless in Bavaria, even if Vend lived on in banishment elsewhere. Children without a living father were considered orphans, even if their mother survived.

others who were just as active as my husband or even more so in stirring up the Rottenbuchers to rebellion have, by calling on the grace of the Lord Prior or on that of Your Electoral Illustriousness, been allowed to return to their lands. Therefore I ask Your Electoral Illustriousness most humbly, and make the same request of the graciousness of the Lord Prior in Rottenbuch, that you don't let it continue that my young innocent orphans have to stay in misery, paying and making good on the debt that their father created through his insubordination. I ask this even more as my aforementioned husband, accepting your electoral penance, says that if he were allowed back in the country and again in your good graces, he would swear, that just as previously he was a bad example to his neighbors through his obstinacy, he would become from then on an example of the most indebted obedience. The Lord Prior will not be sorry that he let me and my young children back into his grace, and in return for the purchase of a privilege, and the payment of all other changes, tolerated us again on the property. I beg for Your Electoral grace, and together with my small children beg Your Electoral Illustriousness daily for your intercession, for which I will serve you every day and night of my life in the lowliest obedience.

Your Electoral Illustriousness's most humble Christina Vend

Source 9 from Jean Nicolas, La Savoie au 18ᵉ siècle: Noblesse et bourgeoisie, *Tome I:* Situations au temps de Victor-Amédée II *(Paris: Maloine s.a., Editeur, 1978), p. 528. Translated by Julius R. Ruff.*

9. Riot in Savoy: Le Sieur[31] Vuy at Gets, March 14, 1717

All the people, from the first to the last, threw themselves furiously onto me, except for five or six who sympathized with me without daring to assist me out of fear of being beaten to death by those who assaulted me. The crowd set upon me with calumnies, pushed and struck me with punch blows to the chin and blows of arms and legs from the rear, threatened me, and spat on me, shouting loudly that they must slaughter the Barnabites and all those acting on their behalf.

---

31. **le sieur:** a French legal term meaning, literally, "Mister."

Chapter 13

Peasant Violence:

Rebellion and

Riot in Early

Modern Europe,

1500–1789

Source 10 from Vladimir S. Ljublinski, La Guerre des farines: Contribution à l'histoire de la lutte des classes en France à la veille de la Révolution, *translated into French by Françoise Adiba and Jacques Radiguet (Grenoble: Presses universitaires de Grenoble, 1979), pp. 367–369. Translated into English by Julius R. Ruff.*

10. Interrogation of Louis Marais, May 6, 1775

Extract from the minutes of the scribe of the Generality of Paris[32] Maréchaussée quartered at Senlis drafted on May 6, 1775 in the Criminal Court of Senlis. Presiding were we, Charles Gabriel de la Balme, gentleman captain of cavalry and lieutenant of the Generality of Paris Maréchaussée quartered at Senlis, assisted by Jacques-Augustin De Bray, assistant Maréchaussée judge, and by our customary scribe.

We had an individual brought from his prison cell who had been arrested by the Louvres brigade on the third of the present month on charges of having led a riot. He had been transferred to the prisons of this town on the fourth, and was confined under the name Louis Marais. He is 5 *pieds* 3 *pouces*[33] tall, black haired and balding, with a high forehead, dark eyes, a big nose, and dressed in a short blue jacket, a blue and red printed cotton waistcoat, common pants, and black stockings. We made known to him our rank and that we would hear his case prevotally[34] and without appeal and then, having had him swear to tell the truth, we interrogated him as follows.

Interrogated about his name, surname, age, status, residence, and place of birth he said that his name was Louis de Marais, aged 42 years, a quarryman, living at Luzarches, native of Luzarches.

Interrogated if on the third of the present month he had not been at the head of a crowd of peasants and had not traveled to different farms in the village of Louvres for the purpose of forcing the farmers to sell wheat at 12 *livres* per *setier*[35] to this rabble, most notably at the farms of Brandin of the above-named place and Regnard. He answered that it is true that he went from Luzarches to Louvres that day with a number of peasants, without being at their head, for the purpose of getting wheat. It was said that wheat costing only 12 *livres* was available there. He went with a crowd first to the farm of

---

32. **Generality of Paris:** prior to the Revolution of 1789, France was divided into administrative units known as generalities, administered by officials called intendants.

33. **5 *pieds* 3 *pouces*:** measures of length used in eighteenth-century France. There were 12 *pouces* to a *pied,* and a *pied* was about 13 inches. Thus, the prisoner was about 5 feet 9 inches tall.

34. **Prevotally:** the Maréchaussée Courts were called *prévôts.* Thus, the prisoner was to be judged by a police court that dealt out summary justice to criminals who threatened the public order. These courts judged without appeal and had a very high conviction rate.

35. *setier:* a measure used for grains and other goods in eighteenth-century France. There were four *minots* in a *setier,* and the *setier* of the Paris region equaled 4.43 bushels.

Brandin where, for his part, he took 3 *minots* of wheat for which he paid 3 *livres,* that is to say at a price of 12 *livres* per *setier.* Next he was at the farm of Renard in the hope getting another 3 *minots* there. Seeing the majority of the women coming out carrying wheat for which they had not paid, he stationed himself at the door with Renard's sister to make the departing peasants pay 12 *livres* per *setier.*

Interrogated if he had not claimed to bear an order requiring the sale of wheat at 12 *livres* per *setier,* he replied that he had never said that he was carrying any order. But when the peasants demanded to know under what order he distributed wheat at a price of 12 *livres,* he replied that he had no more need of an order than those who had pillaged the lands of My Lord the Prince of Conti[36] and that, in addition, necessity dictates many things.

Interrogated about whether he had ever been a prisoner or whether he was a repeat offender, he replied no, and we found nothing to prove it [past offense].[37]

After the present interrogation was read, he replied that his statements contained the truth, and he repeated this and declared that he did not know how to sign this interrogation. . . .

Signed: De la Balme
De Bray

36. **Prince of Conti:** the head of a branch of the French royal family; the prince was a major landowner.

37. The judges apparently examined the defendant for the mark of the branding iron that was normally applied to the shoulders of those convicted of many crimes in eighteenth-century France to serve as a record of conviction.

QUESTIONS TO CONSIDER

The sources that you read allow you to examine closely six peasant rebellions and three examples of rioting drawn from the histories of six countries (England, France, Germany, the Habsburg monarchy, Piedmont-Sardinia, and Russia) over a period of three centuries. Your task in analyzing these events is to draw together their common features and thereby evolve explanations for and descriptions of rural collective violence. Use

the chapter's central questions to guide you in this endeavor.

First, what were the cause of these acts of collective violence by European peasants? Remember that we have already noted that peasants rebelled against either the demands of their seigniors or the taxes imposed by their monarchs. To assess adequately the roots of rebellions, analyze the societies that produced them and how these basic issues prompted people to take up arms. Consider each society's landholding system and the condition of its peasantry.

Chapter 13

Peasant Violence:

Rebellion and

Riot in Early

Modern Europe,

1500–1789

Were peasants facing new exactions from their seigniors? Was the fiscal or governmental authority of the state encroaching on the lives of peasants in new ways? In the case of riots, what material ills affected peasants? What sort of rumors may have triggered their actions?

Second, were the collective actions of peasants revolutionary in that they sought a new social, political, or economic order? In each case, ask yourself what the goals of the peasant rebels or rioters were. How do you find many of them searching for the restoration of an earlier social, economic, or political order? How do peasants justify their revolts? Do they use modern revolutionary terms, or do they refer to traditions and scripture in their justifications? Even in riots by mobs, what sort of traditional moral justification for violence do you find?

Third, what do these events tell you about traditional rural society in Europe? Consider this question on several levels. First, what are the basic features of traditional peasant existence? How do peasant rebellions and riots illustrate the society and world-view of these peasants, people whose failure to produce many written records led historians, until recently, largely to ignore them? How

might peasant demands for release from seigniorial restrictions and dues perhaps unintentionally have paved the way for a very different society? Why might you conclude that during the three centuries looked at in this chapter, society was in transition? Next, consider the role of the state in the unrest you have examined. Why might you again conclude that, governmentally, Europe was in a period of transition? What aspects of the modern state can you discern in the issues raised by peasants?

Finally, who participated in such violence, and who led it? Why might you conclude that peasant rebellions had the support of a broad segment of rural society, not just of its poorest elements? Who did peasants turn to for leadership in addition to local community leaders? What evidence do you find of clerical, noble, or artisan leadership?

Your consideration of all these issues should permit you to answer this chapter's central questions. What were the causes of these acts of collective violence? Were these actions revolutionary in that they sought a new social, political, or economic order? What do these events tell you about traditional, rural society in Europe? Who participated in such violence, and who led it?

EPILOGUE

By the late eighteenth century, the conditions that had produced the rebellions and riots that we have examined began to disappear.

An agricultural revolution, gathering force in the eighteenth century, created a much more productive agriculture that freed western Europe from most of the material problems that had produced violence in an earlier age. Those riots and rebellions had been made possible, in part, by the military weakness of early modern monarchs. Beginning in the second half of the seventeenth century, however, the dramatic expansion of state military resources made localized, collective violence much less possible. In this, France led the way. Under Louis XIV (r. 1643–1715), the royal army mustered some 500,000 men, and the number of rebellions dropped dramatically. Indeed, from 1675 to 1789, the only widespread French peasant violence was the millenarian revolt of the Protestant Camisards of the south in the first decade of the eighteenth century and the riots we have seen in the Flour War and the Great Fear. Since other monarchs aspired to the military might of the French king, rebellions disappeared elsewhere, too, as armies grew.

Seigniorial dominance of the peasantry also collapsed in the course of the eighteenth century. In France, the Great Fear prompted the revolutionary government after 1789 to legislatively end the rural old order. Elsewhere, the growing power of kings worked against the seigniorial powers that had earlier generated so much peasant unrest. Eighteenth-century monarchs needed taxpayers who were free of competing demands on their resources in order to meet the growing revenue needs of the state. Thus, monarchs took the lead in emancipating peasants from their obligations to seigniors; between 1771 and 1864, state action in thirty-eight European countries freed peasants of obligations to their lords.

These developments made rural nineteenth- and twentieth-century Europe, on the whole, a much more secure place than it had been a few centuries earlier.

[345]

CHAPTER FOURTEEN

STAGING ABSOLUTISM

The "Age of Absolutism" is the label historians often apply to the history of Europe in the seventeenth and eighteenth centuries. In many ways it is an appropriate description because, with the exception of England, where the Civil War (1642–1648) and the Glorious Revolution (1688) severely limited royal power and created parliamentary government, most European states in this era had monarchs who aspired to absolute authority in their realms.

The royal absolutism that evolved in seventeenth-century Europe represents an important step in governmental development. In constructing absolutist states, monarchs and their ministers both created new organs of administration and built on existing institutions of government to supplant the regional authorities of the medieval state with more centralized state power. In principle, this centralized authority was subject to the absolute authority of the monarch; in practice, royal authority was nowhere as encompassing as that of a modern dictator. Poor communication systems, the persistence of traditional privileges that exempted whole regions or social groups from full royal authority, and other factors all set limits on royal power. Nevertheless, monarchs of the era strove for the ideal of absolute royal power, and France was the model in their work of state building.

French monarchs of the seventeenth and early eighteenth centuries more fully developed the system of absolute monarchy. In these rulers' efforts to overcome impediments to royal authority, we can learn much about the creation of absolutism in Europe. Rulers in Prussia, Austria, Russia, and many smaller states sought not only the real power of the French kings, but also the elaborate court ceremony and dazzling palaces that symbolized that power.

Absolutism in France was the work of Henry IV (r. 1589–1610), Louis XIII (r. 1610–1643) and his minister Cardinal Richelieu, and Louis XIV (r. 1643–1715). These rulers established a system of centralized royal political authority that destroyed many remnants of the feudal monarchy. The reward for their endeavors was great: With Europe's largest population and immense wealth, France was potentially the mightiest country on the continent in 1600 and its natural leader, if only these national strengths could be unified and directed by a strong government. Creation of such a government around an absolute monarch was the aim of French rulers, but they confronted formidable problems, common to many early modern states, in achieving their goal. Nobles everywhere still held considerable power, in part a legacy of the system of feudal monarchy. In France they possessed military power, which they used in the religious civil wars of the sixteenth century and in their Fronde revolt against growing royal power in the mid-seventeenth century. Nobles also exercised considerable political power through such representative bodies as the Estates General and provincial assemblies, which gave form to their claims for a voice in government. Moreover, nobles served as the judges of the great law courts, the *parlements*, which had to register all royal edicts before they could take effect.

A second obstacle to national unity and royal authority in many states, in an age that equated national unity with religious uniformity, was the presence of a large and influential religious minority. In France the Protestant minority was known as the Huguenots. Not only did they forswear the Catholic religion of the king and the majority of his subjects, but they possessed military power through their rights, under the Edict of Nantes,[1] to fortify their cities.

A third and major impediment to unifying a country under absolute royal authority was regional differences. The medieval monarchy of France had been built province by province over several centuries, and the kingdom was not well integrated. Some provinces, like Brittany in the north, retained local estates or assemblies with which the monarch actually had to bargain for taxes. Many provinces had their own cultural heritage that separated them from the king's government centered in Paris. These differences might be as simple as matters of local custom, but they might also be as complex as unique systems of civil law. A particular problem was the persistence of local dialects, which made the French of royal officials a foreign and incomprehensible tongue in large portions of the kingdom.

The only unifying principle that could overcome all these centrifugal forces was royal authority. The task in the seventeenth century was to build a theoretical basis for a truly powerful monarch, to endow the king with tangible power that gave substance to theory, and to place the sovereign in a setting that would never permit the country to forget his new power.

To establish an abstract basis for absolutism, royal authority had to be strengthened and reinforced by a veritable cult of kingship. Seventeenth-

1. **Edict of Nantes:** In this 1598 decree, King Henry IV sought to end the civil warfare between French Catholics and Huguenots. He granted the Protestants basic protection, in the event of renewed fighting, by allowing them to fortify some 200 of their cities. The edict also accorded the Protestants freedom of belief with some restrictions, and civil rights equal to those of Catholic Frenchmen.

century French statesmen built on medieval foundations in this task. Medieval kings had possessed limited tangible authority but substantial religious prestige; their vassals had rendered them religious oaths of loyalty. French monarchs since Pepin the Short had been anointed in a biblically inspired coronation ceremony in which they received not only the communion bread that the Catholic church administered to all believers, but also the wine, which was normally reserved for clerics; once crowned, they claimed to possess mystical religious powers to heal with the royal touch. All these trappings served to endow the monarch with almost divine powers, separating him from and raising him above his subjects. Many seventeenth-century thinkers emphasized this traditional divine dimension of royal power. Others, as you will see, found more practical grounds for great royal power.

To achieve greater royal power, Henry IV reestablished peace after the religious civil warfare of the late sixteenth century, and Cardinal Richelieu curbed the military power of the nobility. With the creation of loyal provincial administrators, the *intendants,* and a system of political patronage that he directed, the cardinal also established firmer central control in the name of Louis XIII. Richelieu, moreover, ended Huguenot political power by crushing their revolt in 1628, and he intervened in the Thirty Years' War to establish France as a chief European power.

The reign of Louis XIV completed the process of consolidating royal authority in France. Louis XIV created much of the administrative apparatus necessary to centralize the state. The king brought the nobility under even greater control, building in Europe's largest army a force that could defeat any aristocratic revolt and creating in Versailles a court life that drew nobles away from provincial plotting and near to the king, where their actions could be observed. The king also sought to extend royal authority by expanding France's borders through a series of wars and to eliminate the Huguenot minority completely by revoking the religious freedoms embodied in the Edict of Nantes.

The king supplemented his military and political work of state building with other projects to integrate France more completely as one nation. With royal patronage, authors and scholars flourished and, by the example of their often excellent works, extended the French dialect in the country at the expense of provincial tongues. In the king's name, his finance minister, Jean-Baptiste Colbert (1619–1683), sought to realize a vision of a unified French economy. He designed mercantilist policies to favor French trade and build French industry, and he improved transportation to bind the country together as one unit. The result of Louis's policies, therefore, was not only a stronger king and a more powerful France but a more unified country as well.

Far more than previous French monarchs, Louis XIV addressed the third task in establishing absolutism. In modern terms, it consisted of effective public relations, which required visible evidence of the new royal authority. The stage setting for the royal display of the symbols of absolute authority was Versailles, the site of a new royal palace. Built between 1661 and 1682, the palace itself was massive, with a façade one-quarter mile long pierced by 2,143 windows. It was set in a park of 37,000 acres, of which 6,000 acres were embellished with formal gardens. These gardens contained 1,400 fountains that required massive hydraulic works to supply them with water, an artificial lake one mile long for royal boating parties, and 200 statues. The palace grounds contained various smaller palaces as well, including Marly, where the king could entertain small, select groups away from the main palace, which was the center of a court life embracing almost 20,000 persons (9,000 soldiers billeted in the town; and 5,000 royal servants, 1,000 nobles and their 4,000 servants, plus the royal family, all housed in the main palace). Because the royal ministers and their secretaries also were in residence, Versailles was much more than a palace: It was the capital of France.

Royal architects deliberately designed the palace to impart a message to all who entered. As a guidebook of 1681 by Laurent Morellet noted regarding the palace's art:

> The subjects of painting which complete the decorations of the ceilings are of heroes and illustrious men, taken from history and fable, who have deserved the titles of Magnanimous, of Great, of Fathers of the People, of Liberal, of Just, of August and Victorious, and who have possessed all the Virtues which we have seen appear in the Per-

son of our Great Monarch during the fortunate course of his reign; so that everything remarkable which one sees in the Château and in the garden always has some relationship with the great actions of His Majesty.[2]

The court ritual and etiquette enacted in this setting departed markedly from the simpler court life of Louis XIII and were designed to complement the physical presence of the palace itself in teaching the lesson of a new royal power.

In this chapter we will analyze royal absolutism in France. What was the theoretical basis for absolute royal authority? What was traditional and what was new in the justification of royal power as expressed in late sixteenth- and seventeenth-century France? How did such early modern kings as Louis XIV communicate their absolute power in the various ceremonies and symbols of royal authority presented in the evidence that follows?

SOURCES AND METHOD

This chapter assembles several kinds of sources, each demanding a different kind of historical analysis. Two works of political theory that were influential in the formation of abso-

2. Laurent Morellet, *Explication historique de ce qu'il y a de plus remarquable dans la maison royale de Versailles et en celle de Monsieur à Saint-Cloud* (Paris, 1681), quoted in Robert W. Hartle, "Louis XIV and the Mirror of Antiquity" in Steven G. Reinhardt and Vaughn L. Glasgow, eds., *The Sun King: Louis XIV and the New World* (New Orleans: Louisiana State Museum Foundation, 1984), p. 111.

lutism open the evidence. To analyze these works effectively, you will need some brief background information on their authors and on the problems these thinkers discussed.

Jean Bodin (1530–1596) was a law professor, an attorney, and a legal official. His interests transcended his legal education, however. He brought a wide reading in Hebrew, Greek, Italian, and German to the central problem addressed in his major work, *The Six Books of the Republic* (1576), that of establishing the well-ordered state. Writing during the religious wars of the sixteenth century, when government in France all but broke down, Bodin offered answers to this crisis. Especially novel for the sixteenth century was his call for religious toleration. Although he was at least formally a Catholic[3] and recognized unity in religion as a strong unifying factor for a country, Bodin was unwilling to advocate the use of force in eliminating Protestantism from France. He believed that acceptance was by far the better policy.

Bodin's political thought was also significant, and his *Republic* immediately was recognized as an important work. Published in several editions and translated into Latin, Italian, Spanish, and German, the *Republic* influenced a circle of men, the *Politiques*,

who advised Henry IV. Through the process of seeking to explain how to establish the well-ordered state, Bodin contributed much to Western political theory. Perhaps his most important idea was that there was nothing divine about governing power. Men created governments solely to ensure their physical and material security; to meet those needs, the ruling power had to exercise a sovereignty on which Bodin placed few limits.[4] Indeed, Bodin's concept of the ruler's power is his most important contribution to political thought. In the brief selection from Jean Bodin's complex work, examine his conception of the sovereign power required to establish a well-ordered state in France, and contrast this conception with the feudal state that still partially existed in his time.

The second work of political theory was written by Jacques Bénigne Bossuet (1627–1704), Bishop of Meaux. A great orator who preached at the court of Louis XIV, Bossuet was entrusted with the education of the king's son and heir, the Dauphin. He wrote three works for that prince's instruction, including the one excerpted in this chapter, *Politics Drawn from the Very Words of the Holy Scripture* (1678).

As tutor to the Dauphin and royal preacher, Bossuet expressed what has been called the *divine right* theory of kingship: that is, the king was God's deputy on earth, and to oppose him was to oppose divine law. Here, of

3. Bodin's religious thought evolved in the course of his life. Although he was brought up a Catholic and was briefly a Carmelite friar, his knowledge of Hebrew and early regard for the Old Testament led some to suspect that he was a Jew. The writings of his middle years indicate some Calvinist leanings. Later in life, his thought seems to have moved beyond traditional Catholic and Protestant Christianity. He was nevertheless deeply religious.

4. Bodin saw the sovereign power as limited by natural law and the need to respect property (which meant that the ruler could not tax without his subjects' consent) and the family.

course, the bishop was drawing on those medieval beliefs and practices imputing certain divine powers to the king. Because Bossuet was an influential member of the court of Louis XIV, his ideas on royal authority carried considerable weight. Trained as a theologian, he buttressed his political theories with scriptural authority. In this selection, determine the extent of the royal link to God. Why might such a theory be particularly useful to Louis XIV?

Source 3 is a selection from the *Memoirs* of Louis de Rouvroy, Duke of Saint-Simon (1675–1755). Saint-Simon's memoirs of court life are extensive, comprising forty-one volumes in the main French edition. They constitute both a remarkable record of life at Versailles and, because of their style, an important example of French literature. As useful and important as the *Memoirs* are, however, they must be read with care. All of us, consciously or unconsciously, have biases and opinions, and memoirists are no exception. In fact, memoir literature illustrates problems of which students of history should be aware in everything they read. The way in which authors present events, even what they choose to include or omit from their accounts, reflects their opinions. Because memoir writers often recount events in which they participated, they may have especially strong views about what they relate. Thus, to use Saint-Simon's work profitably, it is essential to understand his point of view. We must also ask if the memoir writer was in a position to know firsthand what he or she is relating or

is simply recounting less reliable rumors.

Saint-Simon came from an old noble family that had recently risen to prominence when his father became a royal favorite. Ironically, no one was more deeply opposed to the policies of Louis XIV, which aimed to destroy the traditional feudal power of the nobility in the name of royal authority, than this man whose position rested on that very authority. Saint-Simon was, quite simply, a defender of the older style of kingship, in which sovereignty was limited by the monarch's need to consult with his vassals. His memoirs reflect this view and are often critical of the king. But even with his critical view of the king and his court, that Saint-Simon was an important figure there, an individual privy to state business and court gossip, who gives us a remarkable picture of life at Versailles. Analyze the court etiquette and ritual that Saint-Simon describes as a nonverbal message from the king to his most powerful subjects. For example, what message did the royal waking and dressing ceremony convey to the most powerful and privileged persons in France, who crowded the royal bedroom and vied for the privilege of helping the king dress? What message did their very presence convey in turn to Louis XIV? Recall Bossuet's ideas of kingship. Why might public religious ritual such as that attending the royal rising be part of the agenda of a king who was not particularly noted for his piety during the first half of his life?

Studied closely, the three different kinds of written evidence presented— the work of a sixteenth-century

[351]

political theorist, the writings of a contemporary supporter, and the memoirs of one of the king's opponents—reveal much about the growing power of the French monarchy. What common themes do you find in these works? What were the sources of the king's political authority?

From these written sources, we move on to pictorial evidence of the symbols of royal authority. Symbols are concrete objects possessing a meaning beyond what is immediately apparent. We are all aware of the power of symbols, particularly in our age of electronic media, and we all, perhaps unconsciously, analyze them to some extent. Take a simple example drawn from modern advertising: The lion appears frequently as an image in advertisements for banks and other financial institutions. The lion's presence is intended to convey to us the strength of the financial institution, to inspire our faith in the latter's ability to protect our funds. Using this kind of analysis, you can determine the total meaning of the symbols associated with Louis XIV.

Consider the painting presented as the fourth piece of evidence, *Louis XIV Taking Up Personal Government in 1661*. Louis XIV had been king in name since the age of five after his father's death in 1643, but only in 1661, as an adult, did he assume full power. Remember that such art was generally commissioned by the king and often had an instructional purpose. What do the following elements symbolize: the portrayal of Louis XIV as a Roman emperor; the positioning of a figure representing France on his right; the crowning of

the king with a wreath of flowers; the figure of Time (note the hourglass and scythe) holding a tapestry over the royal head; and the presence of herald angels hovering above?

Now go on to the other pictures and perform the same kind of analysis, always trying to identify the symbolic message that the painter or architect wished to convey. For Source 5, study the royal pose and such seemingly superficial elements in the picture as the king's dress and the background details. Ask yourself what ideas these were intended to convey. Source 6 presents the insignia Louis XIV chose as his personal symbol, which decorated much of Versailles. Reflect on Louis's reasons for this choice in reading his explanation:

The symbol that I have adopted and that you see all around you represents the duties of a Prince and inspires me always to fulfill them. I chose for an emblem the Sun which, according to the rules of this art [heraldry], is the noblest of all, and which, by the brightness that surrounds it, by the light it lends to the other stars that constitute, after a fashion, its court, by the universal good it does, endlessly promoting life, joy, and growth, by its perpetual and regular movement, by its constant and invariable course, is assuredly the most dazzling and most beautiful image of the monarch.[5]

With Sources 8 through 13, we turn to analysis of architecture, which of course also served to symbolize royal power. You must ask yourself how great that concept of royal power was

5. Quoted in Reinhardt and Glasgow, *The Sun King*, p. 181.

as you look at the pictures of Versailles. The palace, after all, was not only the royal residence but also the setting for the conduct of government, including the king's reception of foreign ambassadors. At the most basic level, notice the scale of the palace. What impression might its size have been intended to convey? At a second level, examine decorative details of the palace. Why might the balustrade at the palace entry have been decorated with statuary symbolizing Magnificence, Justice, Wisdom, Prudence, Diligence, Peace, Europe, Asia, Renown, Abundance, Force, Generosity, Wealth, Authority, Fame, America, Africa, and Victory?

Observe the views of the palace's interior, considering the functions of the rooms and their details. Source 10 offers a view of the royal chapel at Versailles. Richly decorated in marble and complemented with ceiling paintings such as that depicting the Trinity, the chapel was the site of daily masses as well as of royal marriages and celebrations of victories. Note that the king attended mass in the royal gallery, joining the rest of the court on the main floor only when the mass celebrant was a bishop. Why might such a magnificent setting be part of the palace? More important, what significance do you place on the position the king chose for himself in this grand setting?

Sources 11 and 12 present the sites of the royal rising ceremony described by Saint-Simon. The royal bedroom, Source 11, was richly decorated in gilt, red, and white, and was complemented by paintings of biblical scenes. Notice the rich decoration of the Bull's Eye Window Antechamber, just outside the bedroom, where the courtiers daily awaited the king's arising. Why were the rooms decorated in such a fashion?

Source 13 offers an artist's view of Marly. Again, notice the scale of this palace, reflecting that it was, according to Saint-Simon, a weekend getaway spot for Louis XIV and selected favorites. How might the king have used invitations to this château, with the closeness to the royal person they entailed? Examine details of the palace. The central château had twelve apartments, four of which were reserved for the royal family, the others for its guests. The twelve pavilions around the lake in the center of the château's grounds each housed two guest apartments and represented the twelve signs of the zodiac. What symbolic importance might you attach to this?

Finally, return to Source 7, which recreates the pageant known as the Carousel of 1662, one of many such entertainments at court. The scale of such festivals could be huge. In 1662, 12,197 costumed people took part in a celebration that included a parade through the streets of Paris and games. Costumed as ancient Romans, Persians, and others, the participants must have made quite an impression on their audience. What kind of impression do you think it was?

What common message runs through the art and architecture you have analyzed? As you unravel the message woven into this visual evidence, combine it with the evidence you derived from Saint-Simon's portrayal of court life and the political theory of absolutism. Remember, too,

[353]

the unstated message: that the monarchy of Louis XIV possessed in Europe's largest army the ultimate means for persuading its subjects to accept the divine powers of the king.

You should be able to determine from all this material what was new in this conception of royal authority and the ways in which the new authority was expressed.

THE EVIDENCE

Source 1 from Francis William Coker, editor, Readings in Political Philosophy *(New York: Macmillan, 1926), pp. 235–236.*

1. From Jean Bodin, *The Six Books of the Republic,* Book I, 1576

The first and principal function of sovereignty is to give laws to the citizens generally and individually, and, it must be added, not necessarily with the consent of superiors, equals, or inferiors. If the consent of superiors is required, then the prince is clearly a subject; if he must have the consent of equals, then others share his authority; if the consent of inferiors—the people or the senate—is necessary, then he lacks supreme authority. . . .

It may be objected that custom does not get its power from the judgment or command of the prince, and yet has almost the force of law, so that it would seem that the prince is master of law, the people of custom. Custom, insensibly, yet with the full compliance of all, passes gradually into the character of men, and acquires force with the lapse of time. Law, on the other hand, comes forth in one moment at the order of him who has the power to command, and often in opposition to the desire and approval of those whom it governs. Wherefore, Chrysostom[6] likens law to a tyrant and custom to a king. Moreover, the power of law is far greater than that of custom, for customs may be superseded by laws, but laws are not supplanted by customs; it is within the power and function of magistrates to restore the operation of laws which by custom are obsolescent. Custom proposes neither rewards nor penalties; laws carry one or the other, unless it be a permissive law which nullifies the penalty of some other law. In short, a custom has compelling force only as long as the prince, by adding his endorsement and sanction to the custom, makes it a law.

It is thus clear that laws and customs depend for their force upon the will of those who hold supreme power in the state. This first and chief mark of sover-

6. **Chrysostom:** Saint John Chrysostom (ca 347–407), an early Father of the Greek church and a brilliant preacher whose religion led him to condemn the vices of the court of the Eastern Roman emperor.

eignty is, therefore, of such sort that it cannot be transferred to subjects, though the prince or people sometimes confer upon one of the citizens the power to frame laws (*legum condendarum*), which then have the same force as if they had been framed by the prince himself. The Lacedæmonians bestowed such power upon Lycurgus, the Athenians upon Solon;[7] each stood as deputy for his state, and the fulfillment of his function depended upon the pleasure not of himself but of the people; his legislation had no force save as the people confirmed it by their assent. The former composed and wrote the laws, the people enacted and commanded them.

Under this supreme power of ordaining and abrogating laws, it is clear that all other functions of sovereignty are included; that it may be truly said that supreme authority in the state is comprised in this one thing—namely, to give laws to all and each of the citizens, and to receive none from them. For to declare war or make peace, though seeming to involve what is alien to the term law, is yet accomplished by law, that is by decree of the supreme power. It is also the prerogative of sovereignty to receive appeals from the highest magistrates, to confer authority upon the greater magistrates and to withdraw it from them, to allow exemption from taxes, to bestow other immunities, to grant dispensations from the laws, to exercise power of life and death, to fix the value, name and form of money, to compel all citizens to observe their oaths: all of these attributes are derived from the supreme power of commanding and forbidding—that is, from the authority to give law to the citizens collectively and individually, and to receive law from no one save immortal God. A duke, therefore, who gives laws to all his subjects, but receives law from the emperor, Pope, or king, or has a co-partner in authority, lacks sovereignty.

Source 2 from Richard H. Powers, editor and translator, Readings in European Civilization Since 1500 *(Boston: Houghton Mifflin, 1961), pp. 129–130.*

2. From Jacques Bénigne Bossuet, *Politics Drawn from the Very Words of the Holy Scriptures*, 1678

TO MONSEIGNEUR LE DAUPHIN

God is the King of kings. It is for Him to instruct and direct kings as His ministers. Heed then, Monseigneur, the lessons which He gives them in His Scriptures, and learn . . . the rules and examples on which they ought to base their conduct. . . .

7. **Lacedæmonians:** the Spartans of ancient Greece. **Lycurgus:** traditional author of the Spartan constitution. **Solon:** sixth-century B.C. Athenian lawgiver.

BOOK II: OR AUTHORITY . . .

CONCLUSION: Accordingly we have established by means of Scriptures that monarchical government comes from God. . . . That when government was established among men He chose hereditary monarchy as the most natural and most durable form. That excluding the sex born to obey[8] from the sovereign power was only natural. . . .

BOOK III: THE NATURE OF ROYAL AUTHORITY . . .

FIRST ARTICLE: Its essential characteristics. . . . First, royal authority is sacred; Second, it is paternal; Third, it is absolute; Fourth, it is subject to reason. . . .

SECOND ARTICLE: Royal authority is sacred.

FIRST PROPOSITION: God establishes kings as his ministers and reigns over people through them.—We have already seen that all power comes from God. . . .

Therefore princes act as ministers of God and as His lieutenants on earth. It is through them that he exercises His empire. . . .

Thus we have seen that the royal throne is not the throne of a man, but the throne of God himself. So in Scriptures we find "God has chosen my son Solomon to sit upon the throne of the kingdom of Jehovah over Israel." And further, "Solomon sat on the throne of Jehovah as king."

And in order that we should not think that to have kings established by God is peculiar to the Israelites, here is what Ecclesiastes says: "God gives each people its governor; and Israel is manifestly reserved to Him.". . .

SECOND PROPOSITION: The person of the king is sacred.—It follows from all the above that the person of kings is sacred. . . . God has had them anointed by His prophets with a sacred ointment, as He has had His pontiffs and His altars anointed.

But even before actually being anointed, they are sacred by virtue of their charge, as representatives of His divine majesty, delegated by His providence to execute His design. . . .

The title of *christ* is given to kings, one sees them called *christs* or the Lord's *anointed* everywhere.

Bearing this venerable name, even the prophets revered them, and looked upon them as associated with the sovereign empire of God, whose authority they exercise on earth. . . .

THIRD PROPOSITION: Religion and conscience demand that we obey the prince.—After having said that the prince is the minister of God Saint Paul concluded: "Accordingly it is necessary that you subject yourself to him out of fear of his anger, but also because of the obligation of your conscience. . . ."

And furthermore: "Servants, obey your temporal masters in all things. . . ." Saint Peter said: "Therefore submit yourselves to the order established among

---

8. **sex born to obey:** women. The Salic Law, mistakenly attributed to the medieval Salian Franks, precluded women from inheriting the crown of France.

men for the love of God; be subjected to the king as to God . . . be subjected to those to whom He gives His authority and who are sent by Him to reward good deeds and to punish evil ones."

Even if kings fail in this duty, their charge and their ministry must be respected. For Scriptures tell us: "Obey your masters, not only those who are mild and good, but also those who are peevish and unjust."

Thus there is something religious in the respect which one renders the prince. Service to God and respect for kings are one thing. . . .

Thus it is in the spirit of Christianity for kings to be paid a kind of religious respect. . . .

BOOK IV: CONTINUATION OF THE CHARACTERISTICS OF ROYALTY

FIRST ARTICLE: Royal authority is absolute.

FIRST PROPOSITION: The prince need render account to no one for what he orders. . . .

SECOND PROPOSITION: When the prince has judged there is no other judgment. . . . Princes are gods.

Source 3 from Bayle St. John, translator, The Memoirs of the Duke of Saint-Simon on the Reign of Louis XIV and the Regency, *8th ed. (London: George Allen, 1913), vol. 2, pp. 363–365, vol. 3, pp. 221–227.*

3. The Duke of Saint-Simon on the Reign of Louis XIV

[*On the creation of Versailles and the nature of its court life*]

He [Louis XIV] early showed a disinclination for Paris. The troubles that had taken place there during the minority made him regard the place as dangerous;[9] he wished, too, to render himself venerable by hiding himself from the eyes of the multitude; all these considerations fixed him at St. Germains[10] soon after the death of the Queen, his mother. It was to that place he began to attract the world by fêtes and gallantries, and by making it felt that he wished to be often seen.

---

9. During the Fronde revolt of 1648–1653, the royal government lost control of Paris to the crowds and the royal family was forced to flee the city. Because Louis XIV was a minor (only ten years of age) when the revolt erupted, the government was administered by his mother, Anne of Austria, and her chief minister, Cardinal Mazarin.

10. **St. Germain-en-Laye:** site of a royal château, overlooking the Seine and dating from the twelfth century, where Louis XIV was born. The court fled there in 1649 during the Fronde.

His love for Madame de la Vallière,[11] which was at first kept secret, occasioned frequent excursions to Versailles, then a little card castle, which had been built by Louis XIII—annoyed, and his suite still more so, at being frequently obliged to sleep in a wretched inn there, after he had been out hunting in the forest of Saint Leger. That monarch rarely slept at Versailles more than one night, and then from necessity; the King, his son, slept there, so that he might be more in private with his mistress; pleasures unknown to the hero and just man, worthy son of Saint Louis, who built the little château.[12]

These excursions of Louis XIV by degrees gave birth to those immense buildings he erected at Versailles; and their convenience for a numerous court, so different from the apartments at St. Germains, led him to take up his abode there entirely shortly after the death of the Queen.[13] He built an infinite number of apartments, which were asked for by those who wished to pay their court to him; whereas at St. Germains nearly everybody was obliged to lodge in the town, and the few who found accommodation at the château were strangely inconvenienced.

The frequent fêtes, the private promenades at Versailles, the journeys, were means on which the King seized in order to distinguish or mortify the courtiers, and thus render them more assiduous in pleasing him. He felt that of real favours he had not enough to bestow; in order to keep up the spirit of devotion, he therefore unceasingly invented all sorts of ideal ones, little preferences and petty distinctions, which answered his purpose as well.

He was exceedingly jealous of the attention paid him. Not only did he notice the presence of the most distinguished courtiers, but those of inferior degree also. He looked to the right and to the left, not only upon rising but upon going to bed, at his meals, in passing through his apartments, or his gardens of Versailles, where alone the courtiers were allowed to follow him; he saw and noticed everybody; not one escaped him, not even those who hoped to remain unnoticed. He marked well all absentees from the court, found out the reason of their absence, and never lost an opportunity of acting towards them as the occasion might seem to justify. With some of the courtiers (the most distinguished), it was a demerit not to make the court their ordinary abode; with others 'twas a fault to come but rarely; for those who never or scarcely ever came it was certain disgrace. When their names were in any way mentioned, "I do not know them," the King would reply haughtily. Those who presented themselves but seldom were thus characterized: "They are people I never see;" these decrees were irrevocable. . . .

11. **Madame de la Vallière:** Louise de la Baume le Blanc, Duchesse de la Vallière (1644–1710), the king's first mistress.

12. Saint-Simon greatly admired Louis XIII, whom he had never met, and for over half a century attended annual memorial services for the king at the royal tombs in the basilica of St. Denis.

13. Anne of Austria (1601–1666), the mother of Louis XIV.

Louis XIV took great pains to be well informed of all that passed everywhere; in the public places, in the private houses, in society and familiar intercourse. His spies and tell-tales were infinite. He had them of all species; many who were ignorant that their information reached him; others who knew it; others who wrote to him direct, sending their letters through channels he indicated; and all these letters were seen by him alone, and always before everything else; others who sometimes spoke to him secretly in his cabinet, entering by the back stairs. These unknown means ruined an infinite number of people of all classes, who never could discover the cause; often ruined them very unjustly; for the King, once prejudiced, never altered his opinion or so rarely, that nothing was more rare.

[*On the royal day and court etiquette*]

[*The royal day begins*]

At eight o'clock the chief valet de chambre on duty, who alone had slept in the royal chamber, and who had dressed himself, awoke the King. The chief physician, the chief surgeon, and the nurse (as long as she lived), entered at the same time. The latter kissed the King; the others rubbed and often changed his shirt, because he was in the habit of sweating a great deal. At the quarter, the grand chamberlain was called (or, in his absence, the first gentleman of the chamber), and those who had, what was called the *grandes entrées.* The chamberlain (or chief gentleman) drew back the curtains which had been closed again, and presented the holy water from the vase, at the head of the bed. These gentlemen stayed but a moment, and that was the time to speak to the King, if any one had anything to ask of him; in which case the rest stood aside. When, contrary to custom, nobody had aught to say, they were there but for a few moments. He who had opened the curtains and presented the holy water, presented also a prayer-book. Then all passed into the cabinet of the council. A very short religious service being over, the King called, they re-entered. The same officer gave him his dressing-gown; immediately after, other privileged courtiers entered, and then everybody, in time to find the King putting on his shoes and stockings, for he did almost everything himself and with address and grace. Every other day we saw him shave himself; and he had a little short wig in which he always appeared, even in bed, and on medicine days. He often spoke of the chase, and sometimes said a word to somebody. No toilette table was near him; he had simply a mirror held before him.

As soon as he was dressed, he prayed to God, at the side of his bed, where all the clergy present knelt, the cardinals without cushions, all the laity remaining standing; and the captain of the guards came to the balustrade during the prayer, after which the King passed into his cabinet.

He found there, or was followed by all who had the entrée, a very numerous company, for it included everybody in any office. He gave orders to each for the day; thus within a half a quarter of an hour it was known what he meant to do; and then all this crowd left directly. The bastards, a few favourites, and the valets alone were left. It was then a good opportunity for talking with the King; for example, about plans of gardens and buildings; and conversation lasted more or less according to the person engaged in it.

All the Court meantime waited for the King in the gallery, the captain of the guard being alone in the chamber seated at the door of the cabinet.

[*The business of government*]

On Sunday, and often on Monday, there was a council of state; on Tuesday a finance council; on Wednesday council of state; on Saturday finance council. Rarely were two held in one day or any on Thursday or Friday. Once or twice a month there was a council of despatches[14] on Monday morning; but the order that the Secretaries of State took every morning between the King's rising and his mass, much abridged this kind of business. All the ministers were seated according to rank, except at the council of despatches, where all stood except the sons of France, the Chancellor, and the Duc de Beauvilliers.[15]

[*The royal luncheon*]

The dinner was always *au petit couvert*,[16] that is, the King ate by himself in his chamber upon a square table in front of the middle window. It was more or less abundant, for he ordered in the morning whether it was to be "a little," or "very little" service. But even at this last, there were always many dishes, and three courses without counting the fruit. The dinner being ready, the principal courtiers entered; then all who were known; and the first gentlemen of the chamber on duty, informed the King.

I have seen, but very rarely, Monseigneur[17] and his sons standing at their dinners, the King not offering them a seat. I have continually seen there the Princes of the blood and the cardinals. I have often seen there also Monsieur,[18] either on arriving from St. Cloud to see the King, or arriving from the council of despatches (the only one he entered), give the King his napkin and remain

---

14. **Council of Despatches:** the royal council in which ministers discussed the letters from the provincial administrators of France, the *intendants*.

15. **Sons of France:** The royal family was distinguished from the rest of the nobility as "children of France." The "sons of France" in the last decade of the seventeenth century thus were the king's son, his grandsons, and his brother. **Duc de Beauvilliers:** Paul de Beauvilliers, Duc de St. Aignan (1648–1714), was a friend of Saint-Simon and tutor of Louis XIV's grandsons, the dukes of Burgundy, Anjou, and Berry.

16. **Au petit couvert:** a simple table setting with a light meal.

17. **Monseigneur:** Louis, Dauphin de France (1661–1711), son of Louis XIV and heir to the throne.

18. **Monsieur:** Philippe, Duc d'Orléans (1640–1701), Louis XIV's only sibling. His permanent residence was at the Château of St. Cloud near Paris.

standing. A little while afterwards, the King, seeing that he did not go away, asked him if he would not sit down; he bowed, and the King ordered a seat to be brought for him. A stool was put behind him. Some moments after the King said, "Nay then, sit down, my brother." Monsieur bowed and seated himself until the end of the dinner, when he presented the napkin.

[*The day ends*]

At ten o'clock his supper was served. The captain of the guard announced this to him. A quarter of an hour after the King came to supper, and from the ante-chamber of Madame de Maintenon[19] to the table again, any one spoke to him who wished. This supper was always on a grand scale, the royal household (that is, the sons and daughters of France), at table, and a large number of courtiers and ladies present, sitting or standing, and on the evening before the journey to Marly all those ladies who wished to take part in it. That was called presenting yourself for Marly. Men asked in the morning, simply saying to the King, "Sire, Marly." In later years the King grew tired of this, and a valet wrote up in the gallery the names of those who asked. The ladies continued to present themselves.

After supper the King stood some moments, his back to the balustrade of the foot of his bed, encircled by all his Court; then, with bows to the ladies, passed into his cabinet, where on arriving, he gave his orders. He passed a little less than an hour there, seated in an arm-chair, with his legitimate children and bastards, his grandchildren, legitimate and otherwise, and their husbands or wives. Monsieur in another arm-chair; the princesses upon stools, Monseigneur and all the other princes standing.

The King, wishing to retire, went and fed his dogs; then said good night, passed into his chamber to the *ruelle*[20] of his bed, where he said his prayers, as in the morning, then undressed. He said good night with an inclination of the head, and whilst everybody was leaving the room stood at the corner of the mantelpiece, where he gave the order to the colonel of the guards alone. Then commenced what was called the *petit coucher*, at which only the specially privileged remained. That was short. They did not leave until he got into bed. It was a moment to speak to him. Then all left if they saw any one buckle to the King. For ten or twelve years before he died the *petit coucher* ceased, in consequence of a long attack of gout he had had; so that the Court was finished at the rising from supper.

---

19. **Madame de Maintenon:** Françoise d'Aubigné, Marquise de Maintenon (1635–1719), married Louis XIV after the death of his first wife, Marie Thérèse of Spain.

20. **ruelle:** the area in the bedchamber in which the bed was located and in which the king received persons of high rank.

Sources 4 and 5 from Château de Versailles/Cliché des Musées Nationaux-Paris.

4. Charles Le Brun, *Louis XIV Taking Up Personal Government*, ca 1680, from the Ceiling of the Hall of Mirrors at Versailles

5. Hyacinthe-François-Honoré-Pierre-André Rigaud, *Louis XIV,*
King of France and Navarre, 1701

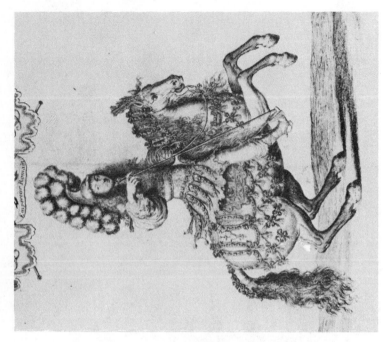

Source 7 from Charles Perrault, Festiva ad captia, 1670. British Library, London.

7. Rousselet, Louis XIV as "Roman Emperor" in an engraving from the Carousel of 1662

Source 6 from Musée de la Marine, Photographic Service.

6. Mask of Apollo, God of Light, 17th century

Sources 8 and 9 from French Government Tourist Office.

8. Garden Façade of Versailles

9. Aerial View of Versailles

Sources 10 through 13 from Château de Versailles/Cliché des Musées Nationaux—Paris.

10. The Royal Chapel at Versailles

11. Reconstruction of the King's Chamber at Versailles, after 1701

12. Antechamber of the Bull's Eye Window at Versailles

13. **Pierre Denis Martin,** *Château of Marly,* **1724**

QUESTIONS TO CONSIDER

Louis XIV is reputed to have said, "I am the state." Whether the king actually uttered those words is immaterial for our purpose; they neatly summarize the unifying theme in all this chapter's evidence, which demonstrates how royal power was defined as absolute and how that authority was expressed in deeds, art, and architecture.

Consider first the theories of royal authority, comparing the political ideas of Bodin and Bossuet. What are the origins of sovereignty for Bodin and Bossuet? How do they differ? Why can Bodin be said to have justified absolutism on the basis of expediency, that is, that absolute royal power was the only way to ensure order? Do the two thinkers ultimately arrive at the same conclusions? What is the difference between Bodin's conclusion that the royal power permitted the king to hand down laws to his subjects and receive them from no one and Bossuet's definition of the king as virtually a god on earth?

Royal ceremony and etiquette enforced this view of the king. Consider Saint-Simon's *Memoirs* again. The selection describes only limited aspects of court etiquette, but it conveys to us a vivid image of court life. Who was the center of this court made up of the country's most prominent nobles? Analyze individual elements of court ceremony. How does each contribute to a consistent message? Consider the royal dining ritual. To reinforce the lesson of royal power, who was kept standing during the king's luncheon? Who had the task, for most commoners performed by an ordinary waiter, of handing the king his napkin? A message of royal power is being expressed here in a way that is almost theatrical.

Indeed, the image of theater can be useful in further structuring your analysis. The stage setting for this royal display, the palace of Versailles, shows the work of a skilled director in creating a remarkably uniform message in landscape and architecture alike. Who do you suppose that director was? Examine his statement at Versailles. Look first at the exterior views of both Versailles (Sources 8 and 9) and Marly (Source 13). How do the grounds add to the expression of royal power? What view of nature might they suggest to a visitor? How did the stage set enhance the play described by Saint-Simon? How did it encourage the French to accept the authority of Louis XIV?

Look next at the interior of the palace. It was, of course, a royal residence. But do you find much evidence of its function as a place to live in? Examine the royal bedroom and its outer room (Sources 11 and 12). Modern bedrooms are generally intimate in size and decoration; how does the king's differ? Why? Notice, too, the art and use of symbols in the palace. Why might the king's artists and architects have decorated the palace so richly with biblical and classical heroes and themes (Sources 8, 9, 10, 11, 12)?

Finally, consider the principal actor, Louis XIV. Notice how his self-presentation is consistent with the trappings of the stage set. We find him consciously acting a role in Source 7, portraying an emperor in the Carousel of 1662. That engraving embodies a great deal of indirect information. What details reinforce the aura of royal power? Why should the king be mounted and in Roman costume? What strikes you about the king's attitude atop the prancing horse? Compare this picture with the Le Brun (Source 4) and Rigaud (Source 5) paintings. What elements do you find these pictures to have in common? How does the royal emblem of the sun (Source 6) contribute to the common message?

With these considerations in mind, return now to the central questions of this chapter. What was the theoretical basis for absolute royal authority? What was traditional and what was new in the justification of royal power expressed in late sixteenth- and seventeenth-century France? How did such early modern kings as Louis XIV communicate their absolute power in the various ceremonies, displays, and symbols of royal authority presented in the evidence?

EPILOGUE

We all know that any successful act produces imitators. In the seventeenth century, the monarchy of Louis XIV looked for a long time like the most successful regime in Europe. Royal absolutism had seemingly unified France. Out of that unity came a military power that threatened to overwhelm Europe; an economic strength, based on mercantilism, that increased French wealth; and an intellectual life that gave the culture of seventeenth- and eighteenth-century Europe a distinctly French accent. Imitators of Louis XIV's work were therefore numerous. At the very least, kings sought physically to express the unifying and centralizing monarchical principle of government in palaces recreating Versailles.[21]

But the work of such monarchs as Louis XIV involved far more than the construction of elaborate palaces in which to stage the theater of their court lives. The act of focusing the state on the figure of the monarch began the transition to the centralized modern style of government and marked the beginning of the end of the decentralized medieval state that bound subjects in an almost contractual relationship to their ruler. The king now emerged as theoretically all-powerful and also as a symbol of national unity.

The monarchs of the age did their work of state building so effectively that the unity and centralization they created often survived the monarchy itself. The French monarchy, for example, succumbed to a revolution in 1789 that in large part stemmed from the bankruptcy of the royal gover

21. Palaces consciously modeled on Ve- multiplied in the late seventeenth ar eighteenth centuries. They included f brunn Palace in Vienna (1694), Palace in Berlin (begun in 1698), Palace in Württemberg, Germar the Würzburg Residenz in ' many (1719–1744), and the (1729–1733) near Turin, Ital·

ment after too many years of over-spending on wars and court life in the name of royal glory. But the unified state endured, strong enough to retain its sense of unity despite challenges in war and changes of government that introduced a new politics of mass participation.

The methods employed by Louis XIV and other monarchs also transcended their age. Modern governments understand the importance of ritual, symbolism, and display in creating the sense of national unity that was part of the absolute monarch's goal. Ritual may now be centered on important national observances. The parades on such days as July 4 in the United States, July 14 in France (commemorating one of the earliest victories of the Revolution of 1789), and the anniversary of the October 1917 Revolution as it was celebrated until 1990 in the former Soviet Union all differ in form from the rituals of Louis XIV. They are designed for a new political age, one of mass participation in politics, in which the loyalty of the whole people, not just that of an elite group, must be won. But their purpose remains the same: to win loyalty to the existing political order.

Modern states also use symbolism to build political loyalty. Artwork on public buildings in Washington, D.C., and the capital cities of other republics, for example, often employs classical themes. The purpose of such artwork is to suggest to citizens that their government perpetuates the republican rectitude of Athens and Rome. Display also is part of the political agenda of modern governments, even governments of new arrivals in the community of nations. This is why newly independent, developing nations of the twentieth (and twenty-first) century expend large portions of their meager resources on such things as grand new capital cities, the most sophisticated military weaponry, and the latest aircraft for the national airline. These are symbols of their governments' successes and thus the basis for these regimes' claims on their peoples' loyalty. These modern rituals, symbols, and displays perform the same function for modern rulers as Versailles did for the Sun King.